Secondary School Teaching Methods

Secondary School Teaching Methods

SECOND EDITION

Leonard H. Clark

JERSEY CITY STATE COLLEGE

Irving S. Starr

UNIVERSITY OF HARTFORD

The Macmillan Company
Collier-Macmillan Limited · LONDON

Education, then, is a question.
XENOPHON

PREFACE

ALMOST a decade has passed since the publication of the first edition of this book. During that time many pedagogical innovations and experiments have been launched. The authors have attempted to incorporate the important changes into this revision. Otherwise the purpose and treatment, except for a minor reorganization to make the book more cohesive, remain the same in this edition as in the first, for despite innovations and experiments, the basic pedagogical principles have not changed.

This book was written to help prospective teachers learn how to teach. It is designed as a college textbook for a single semester course in general methods of teaching in the secondary school, although it might serve well as a reference work for student teachers and teachers in service. The authors have attempted to make the book as practical and useful as possible. To achieve this end, they have tried to write from a middle-of-the-road point of view, and to describe methods suitable for use in the type of school in which the student is likely to teach when he goes to his first position. For this same reason, they have attempted to write simply and clearly, to use numerous examples, to point up important understandings by means of questions at appropriate places within the text itself, and to keep quotations and references to scholarly works to a minimum. Detailed discussions of the nature of learning, the aims and objectives of education, the American system of education, and the secondary school curriculum have been omitted because the authors feel that such topics have little place in a general methods course. In fact, all discussion of educational theory has been omitted except when it seemed necessary to explain the why of the methods advocated. Nevertheless, the emphasis is, of necessity, on principles rather than recipes. There are no sure-fire recipes in teaching.

The authors wish to acknowledge their indebtedness to the many persons—students, teachers, and friends—who have helped them write this book. Grateful thanks are expressed to the students, teachers, superintendents, principals, and publishing houses who allowed the authors to reproduce their materials. A particular debt of gratitude is owed to Roy O. Billett, formerly professor of education at Boston University, in whose classes the authors formed many of their ideas concerning education; to

Professor William T. Gruhn of The University of Connecticut, who went considerably beyond the call of duty in reading and criticizing the manuscript of the first edition; to Idella M. Clark, whose help in the collection of the necessary data has been immeasurable; and to Maria A. Clark, who not only typed the manuscript innumerable times, but also read the copy and made suggestions for improving the wording, and without whose help the book could never have been finished.

L. H. C.
I. S. S.

Jersey City, New Jersey
Hartford, Connecticut

CONTENTS

ix

ASSIGN 1
Give : 12-4
Due · 11-18
205-250

PART *I*
Foundations of Method

CHAPTER *1*

What Is Teaching?

*T*EACHING is exciting, rewarding work. It has always been so, but today new knowledge about the psychology of learning and teaching, innovations in teaching technology, the increased professionalization of school staffs, and new curricular patterns are making teaching more satisfying than ever before.

However, like all other professions, it is demanding. The teacher must base his practice on firm knowledge of the nature of the learner, the nature of the teaching process, and the nature of subject matter. To be really proficient the professional teacher must have a vast reservoir of skills and knowledge from which to draw the right approach for each particular situation. Take the case of Joe, a tenth grader.

Joe is slightly under middle height. In class he is very quiet. He never causes disciplinary disturbances. Neither does he do any work. In fact, one would hardly know he was in the class at all. He just sits there. When the teacher cajoles him, he says that he "is dumb and can't do it, so there's no use trying." But this is not true. Test scores show him to be well within the normal range. His other activities do not indicate excessive dullness. He cannot read well (he is reading at a sixth-grade level), but he is one of the best soccer and basketball players in the school. On the field his playing is marked by its aggressiveness. As a matter of fact, his aggressiveness largely makes up for his lack of height in basketball. The coach says that he is one of the "smartest" forwards he has seen on the soccer field in the last few years.

Joe has never been known to pick up a book voluntarily. It has been a long time since he has turned in an acceptable paper. He knows that his failures will make him ineligible for varsity athletics, but he sees no reason for working because he believes that he will fail anyway. If he should pass, he will say that it is only because the teacher is "giving him a break." Seemingly, he has no interest other than athletics.

Difficult cases like Joe's challenge the ingenuity, the resources, and the skill of the teacher. The unskilled teacher might be overwhelmed by Joe's lack of enthusiasm and decide to give up. Not so the professional teacher. He knows that he must teach Joe—whether Joe wants to learn or not—and he has the knowledge and the resources with which to undertake this task.

Joe poses a difficult problem, but even cases like that of Billy need skillful teaching. Billy is an average eighth-grader with average intelligence. Usually a happy person, he gets along well with his teachers and his peers. Billy's mother is a homemaker and his father is a mechanic. There are two other children at home, one younger and one older than Billy. Home is the focal point of life in the family. Billy seems to have no great problems. Yet he does have trouble with some of his school work. All normal pupils do, and Billy is normal, not brilliant. Although he is a willing worker and as cooperative as he can be, he finds many of his assignments too much for him. It will take plenty of skillful teaching if Billy is to get the most out of his mathematics, for instance.

Cases like these are commonplace for the professional teacher. When one is a master of teaching techniques, helping pupils like these is a challenge which never allows the work to become humdrum. And when one's efforts are finally crowned with success, nothing could be more gratifying.

TEACHING, A DEFINITION. In the final analysis teaching is an attempt to help someone acquire, or change, some skill, attitude, knowledge, ideal, or appreciation. In other words, the teacher's task is to create or influence desirable changes in behavior, or in tendencies toward behavior, in his pupils. Some authorities say that as far as school classes are concerned, if the pupils have not learned anything, the teacher has not taught anything. This statement is probably too harsh, but it does introduce an important point: The goal of teaching is to bring about the desired learning in the pupils. Therefore, the only valid criterion of success in teaching is the degree to which the teacher has been able to achieve the desired learning in his pupils. Thus the teacher must know (1) what learning is desirable for his pupils, and (2) how to bring about this learning. The basic problem to be solved, then, in any teaching situation concerns the selection of content and method.

✻

Discuss the phrase: "There is no teaching unless there is learning." Is it true or partially true? What implications does it have for the teacher?

Do you agree that it is the teacher's job to teach Joe whether Joe wishes to learn or not?

✻

Role of Method

Content Versus Method

Throughout the past decade educators have indulged themselves in debates between "content" and "methods"—one group holding out for the primacy of teaching method and the other insisting that course content is all important. These positions are exemplified by two commonly held half-truths: (1) "Anyone who really knows how to teach can teach anything," and (2) "All that anyone needs to be able to teach a subject is to really know it."

A FALSE DICHOTOMY. Content and methods of teaching are not really dichotomous. Whenever one teaches one must teach someone something. That something is *content*, or subject matter. Without it no teacher can teach anything. But also, in order to teach anything to his pupils, the teacher must use some sort of technique or approach. This technique or approach is *method*, and it is to a large extent the method that determines what a pupil learns, how he learns it, and how viable this learning is to him. In fact, because selecting content for lessons, units, and courses is part of teaching method, method determines the content actually taught as well as the content actually learned by the pupil. It is time that we drop this method versus content dispute and realize that they both are legs on which the teaching process stands. Without either one of them the teaching process will collapse.

THE IMPORTANCE OF CONTENT. Because this is a book on teaching methods, we wish to state early and emphatically that teachers must know their subject matter. Modern secondary-school teaching techniques are dependent on the teacher's having great knowledge of the materials and resources available in the field and mastery of its content. To give a satisfactory lecture or to hear lessons based on a textbook does not require much scholarship, but to conduct unit assignments, laboratory classes, differentiated lessons, research activities, the solving of real problems, or true discussion groups require that the teacher have the flexibility that only the command of a large fund of immediately usable knowledge can give. Moreover, the teacher must be familiar enough with the material available in the field to put each pupil in touch with sources of information pertinent to the pupil's topic and suitable for his reading and interest levels on short notice. As a rule, the teacher who is not knowledgeable and comfortable in the content he teaches is doomed to dullness. Two of the keys of good teaching—and good teaching has many keys—are flexibility and the encouragement of inquiry. They both require of the teacher knowledge of content—much knowledge constantly re-newed.

At the secondary-school level, of course, one is not expected to be a research scholar. Rather, teachers are the mediators who present and interpret the work of scholars to others. Therefore, teaching requires more of the teacher than knowledge of the subject alone; he must assimilate it well enough to mediate it to his pupils.

Strategies and Tactics

Method in teaching concerns the way the teacher organizes and uses techniques of teaching, subject matter, teaching tools, and teaching materials to reach teaching objectives.

Evidently there is no one best method of teaching or any one method that will suit all occasions. Different objectives, different subject matter, and different pupils require different strategies and tactics.

By teaching strategy we mean the general approach to a relatively large goal. A strategy, then, includes the selection of suitable subject matter, and the general organization of the subject matter for instruction as well as the modes of instruction. Tactics, on the other hand, concern the handling of the individual episodes that combine to determine the success of the strategy, i.e. whether or not we succeed in reaching our teaching goal. Tactics are more likely to be spontaneous than pre-planned, but must, of course, be harmonious with the strategy. They are often called operations. These are the procedures used to achieve the goals of our strategy. In addition to strategy and tactics, there are also grand strategies which concern the overall approach to entire courses or cur-ricula.

The Problem of Method

In any teaching situation the first and most important consideration is the aims or objectives. What exactly are our purposes in teaching these young people? What changes do we want to bring about in them? These considerations are all important, because in planning lessons and units, the teacher should select approaches and teaching activities, that is, strategies and tactics, that seem best suited to the type of objective he is after and then aim these approaches and activities directly at the objective. Only in this way can we obtain effective instruction that will bring about the goals desired.

It follows, then, that the basic problem of method is selection. The teacher must first of all select the goals and set his direction. Next he must select the strategy by which to reach those goals. As part of the strategy he must select the content and the general approach. Then he must select the materials and teaching tools to use and, as he goes along, select the tactics to meet specific contingencies so as to carry out and implement the strategy. Finally he must select the proper instruments and techniques to evaluate and follow up what he has done.

❉

To what extent and in what ways does method determine content? And content method?

The basic problem of method is said to be selection. Do you agree? Explain.

❉

Verbalism, an Ever-Present Danger

NECESSITY FOR CLEAR CONCEPTS. The inordinate amount of verbalism in some of our secondary-school classes is an example of what may happen when the teacher does not select the appropriate strategy and tactics.

To understand something one must have clear concepts. Many times we think we know when actually we have only vague notions. If we do not know clearly enough to use the knowledge, we do not really know at all. How often we try to explain a word and find that we cannot do it. We say, "I know what it means, but I just can't explain it." More often than not, the truth is that we really have only a fuzzy idea.

There are several types of knowing: we can know *about;* we can know *that;* and we can know *how.* Learning about something is not the same as learning it, nor learning how to do it. Neither does one learning product guarantee another. The boy who only reads about how to swim may sink like a rock when he gets into the water. Similarly, the girl who learns the rules of grammar and can do all the exercises in her grammar work book perfectly may not be able to write a clear, idiomatic sentence. Or again, a graduate student may find that studying technical French has not helped him a bit when ordering a dinner in Paris. Neither does studying American history necessarily produce good citizens. To learn something we must study *it*—not about it or something like it. To learn to do something we must study and practice how to do it.

An example of this confusion is the common error of mistaking memorizing for understanding. We confuse the word with the deed, the name with the object. Children are often asked to learn words and phrases which mean nothing to them. It is quite possible to repeat that in a right triangle the square of the hypotenuse is equal to the sum of the squares of the opposite sides and yet not have the slightest idea of the meaning of square, hypotenuse, opposite sides, or right triangle. Thousands of persons can glibly recite that a noun is the name of a person, place, or thing, and yet not be able to pick a single noun out of a sentence. The cartoon of Miss Peach's class illustrates how well some elementary-school children understand the pledge of allegiance to the flag. This parroting is called verbalism. It is one of the banes of both the elementary and secondary school. Really to know something we must know it well enough to use the knowledge.

FIGURE 1

Miss Peach's pupils recite the Pledge of Allegiance to the Flag.

Copyright, 1957, New York Herald Tribune, Inc. Reproduced with permission.

NEED FOR BOTH VICARIOUS AND DIRECT LEARNING.   In some instances verbalism, parroting without understanding, is the result of an overuse of vicarious learning. Much of our best learning comes through direct experience like that of the burned child who learned to fear the fire. Fortunately, it is not necessary to get burned. We can learn vicariously—through the experiences of others. Not everyone can go to see the pyramids, but anyone can learn about them from descriptions and pictures. The direct experience usually results in more vivid learning, but it is not always efficient. Sometimes it is quite inefficient, time-consuming, and costly, as in the case of the burned child. "Learning the hard way," we call it. For this reason we must rely on vicarious experience for much of our schoolwork. To do so is quite proper. It saves time, money, and effort. Used properly it can be quite effective. In many instances it is the only type of experience possible. However, many high-school teachers rely too much on vicarious learning. This may lead to verbalism. A balance between vicarious and direct learning is imperative. In general, learning situations should be as realistic as possible.

NEED FOR REALISTIC LEARNING.   Realistic learning situations help make the learning meaningful to the pupil and thus help to avoid verbalism. Only meaningful material can be learned efficiently. To require boys and girls to learn things that they do not understand is absurd. In the first place, if the learning is meaningless to the learner it is useless. In the second place, meaningless material is much more difficult to learn than

Explaining is one of the clarifying operations by which the teachers build up clear concepts in pupils. Use of audio-visual materials helps reduce verbalism.

meaningful material. Yet many youngsters are required to learn things meaningless to them every day. How many youngsters have strived to learn:

> Once upon a midnight dreary, as I pondered, weak and weary,
> Over many a quaint and curious volume of forgotten lore,
> As I nodded, nearly napping, suddenly there came a tapping
> As of someone gently rapping, rapping at my chamber door.

even though they had not the slightest idea of what it was all about and could not translate "midnight dreary," "quaint and curious volume," "forgotten lore," or even "chamber door."

In order to avoid mere verbalism and inefficient learning among his pupils, the teacher should see to it that all learning situations in his classes are meaningful. To do so, he must eliminate meaningless material either by omitting it altogether or preparing the pupils for it so that it will be meaningful when they study it. In the foregoing example one might substitute a less difficult poem for *The Raven,* or one might prepare the pupils by studying the poem, its message, and its vocabulary before attempting to learn it. In any case, in guiding the pupils' activities the teacher should make every effort to ensure that the experience is meaningful to the pupils.

LEARNING BY BUILDING CONCEPTS.   One reason for the prevalence of verbalism in pupils is that it has become a general practice for teachers to teach (1) generalizations, or (2) a series of isolated facts or bits of information, or (3) a combination of (1) and (2) taught as though they were information. Such teaching has little meaning. Teaching should be aimed at building concepts, skills, attitudes, ideals, or appreciations. To build concepts efficiently one must give pupils opportunities to learn specifics and then encourage the pupils to build the desired concepts or generalizations themselves by inference from the data. In this fashion the concepts will become real to the pupil because they are his own.

LEARNING BY DOING.   Skills must be learned directly by actually performing the skill. Of course, one can, and probably must, learn a lot about the skill in other ways, but the only way to master a skill is to practice it. As Comenius pointed out in 1657,

What is to be done must be learned by practice. Artisans do not detain their apprentices with theories, but set them to do practical work at an early stage; thus they learn to forge by forging, to carve by carving, to paint by painting, and to dance by dancing. In schools, therefore, let the students learn to write by writing, to talk by talking, to sing by singing, and to reason by reasoning.

All too often teachers forget this obvious, long known fact. And so they make the mistake of trying to teach pupils how to write by teaching them grammar, and how to reason by memorizing rules and facts.

ATTITUDES, APPRECIATIONS, AND IDEALS.   One must develop attitudes, appreciations, and ideals by suitable, purposeful approaches. If a teacher wishes to develop an attitude in his pupils, he must provide opportunities that will foster that attitude. Critical attitudes suitable for scholarly work are not engendered by swallowing lectures whole. Appreciation of literature is not learned by studying literature as though it were content to be learned rather than to be savored and judged. To avoid making the teaching of attitudes become sheer mockery, teachers must attempt to provide an atmosphere conducive to the attitudes sought and to give pupils plenty of opportunities to practice the desired attitude or behavior.

*

Can you give examples of different types of knowing? What implications do these different ways of knowing have for the teacher?

Can you cite examples of verbalism from your own school experience?

What differences in strategy and tactics would be called for in teaching situations in which the main objective was (a) an appreciation; (b) a skill; (c) an attitude; (d) information?

*

Pattern of Teaching Strategy

In general, the procedure in most good teaching follows the same pattern:

1. Diagnosing the learning situation.
2. Preparing the setting for learning.
3. Guiding learning activities.
4. Evaluating the pupils' learning.
5. Following up.

To be competent a teacher should be a master of the techniques necessary to carry out each of these steps for they are, or should be, the basis of all teaching strategies.

DIAGNOSING THE LEARNING SITUATION. The first procedure in good teaching is to diagnose the teaching-learning situation. Somehow the teacher must find out what the needs of the pupils are so that he can plan experiences that will help them satisfy their needs. This entails knowing every youth as well as possible. Any physician will tell you it is impossible to know too much about a patient. In a sense the pupils are the teacher's "patients." When the pupil is in good academic health the teacher tries to keep him so. When he is not, the teacher's job is to bring him back to health as soon as possible.

A case in point: Learning is usually developmental. That is to say, *new learning builds upon previous learning.* A child needs to understand simple multiplication before he can succeed with long division. A pupil who does not know the principles of solving simple equations will probably have a difficult time with quadratics. Since this is so often so, learning should follow an orderly sequence with the new learning building upon past learning.

Moreover, learning is not merely the accumulation of new concepts, skills, ideals, attitudes, and appreciations. Rather it is the integration of these new learnings and the concepts, skills, ideals, attitudes, and appreciations already present. The new learning becomes interwoven into one's personality. The result is really a personality change of some sort or another. This takes time. Although many pupils learn many things rapidly, thorough learning is apt to be a relatively slow process.

Since learning is developmental, it follows that one learns better when one is ready to learn. The principle of readiness has confused both teachers and lay people. Psychologically it can have many ramifications, but for our classroom purposes it can be defined quite simply. Readiness is a combination of maturity, ability, prior instruction, and motivation. A person is ready to learn something when he has matured enough to learn it efficiently, when he has acquired the skills, knowledge, and strengths prerequisite to learning it, and when he is sufficiently motivated. When a pupil has reached such a state of readiness, the teacher's job is relatively easy; when he has not, the teacher's job is more difficult and sometimes absolutely impossible. No one would attempt to teach a toddler the classic ballet: one must learn to walk before he can learn to run. Therefore, an essential part of diagnosis is to determine what kinds of learning the pupils are ready for.

PREPARING THE SETTING FOR LEARNING. The job of a theatrical producer is to provide a setting in which the action of the play can take place. So it is with the teacher. He must provide a setting for learning. This setting for learning includes many things. It includes creating a pleasant physical environment that will invite the pupils to learn. It includes providing the materials of learning so that they will be in the right place at the right time. But more than that, it includes providing an intellectual setting that will cause boys and girls to want to learn. This subject will be discussed in more detail in Chapter 3.

GUIDING LEARNING ACTIVITIES. Once the stage has been set and the pupil is ready to work, the teacher must guide his learning. This can be done in many ways. The first job of the teacher is to help select the activities that are most appropriate for the pupil's goals and needs. As the pupil proceeds on the path selected, the teacher must help him toward the goal. The teacher can do this by showing the pupil how to do things, by presenting new facts and concepts, and by explaining and expanding old ones through such techniques as asking questions, giving vivid examples, and using audio-visual aids. The teacher can also guide the pupil by pointing out his errors. As the teacher watches the pupil's progress, he shows the pupil that here he has taken the wrong approach, here he has gone off on a tangent, here his thinking is illogical, here his premises are false, or here he is inconsistent. Praising good work and encouraging successful and profitable lines of endeavor are also among the effective techniques in guiding learning.

EVALUATING PUPIL LEARNING.   Guiding pupils' learning is also a continuous process of evaluation and re-evaluation. In order to ensure that learning proceeds on its proper course, the teacher must examine the progress of the learning. On the basis of this evaluation the teacher can determine what the next steps should be. From it he can learn what has been missed and what must be retaught, and where the emphasis should be placed in succeeding classes. Evaluation also tells the pupil where he has hit or missed the mark. It is essential to diagnosis and necessary to good instruction.

FOLLOWING THROUGH.   Much teaching is not truly effective because teachers often forget the final step of the pattern—the follow-through or follow-up. Without it teaching all too often becomes a case of "so near and yet so far," for it is the follow-through which drives home and clinches the learning. The follow-through can take any of many forms. At times a simple summary will do. Other times the teacher must repeat a point week after week. Often it consists of applying the learning in new practice situations. Then again it may be a simple matter of occasional review or a reminder. But in every case the teacher takes the learning just a little farther than the original presentation and by making an extra effort tries to drive the learning home.

In many instances this extra effort must consist of reteaching those things that the evaluation tells us the pupils have not learned, for the follow-through is not only an opportunity to clinch pupils' learning, it is also a chance for correcting mistakes and filling in gaps. Whatever is worth teaching is worth teaching well, and, if pupils miss it the first time around, the follow-up gives them a chance to make up the loss. A little additional effort can make the difference between half-baked learning and real understanding.

✳

Is the fact that a pupil has successfully passed the prerequisites to a course any guarantee that he is ready for it? How might one tell if the pupil is ready?

Without continuous evaluation teaching is seldom efficient. Why?

Can you think of any teaching-learning situation in which any of the five steps just described should be omitted?

Evaluation usually shows that not all pupils have reached the same point. What implications does this have for the guiding of learning activities?

✳

Teaching Tactics

Teachers have a multitude of teaching tactics or operations available. Hence the problem of selecting the best tactic for the immediate situation and using it in the way most likely to bring about teaching success in that particular situation requires considerable skill. This problem is complicated by the fact that no situation is identical with any other and so the teacher must adapt or create a new tactic for each situation he encounters. It is for this reason that no textbook in methodology can prescribe exactly what a teacher should do in the classroom at a particular moment. Anyone who claims to give definitive prescriptions to specific problems that may arise should be viewed skeptically. Certainly any claim that any single method or approach to the teaching of any subject is the best way to teach that subject has the elements of quackery latent in it—no matter who makes the claim or who supports it. However, the teacher who has a sound grasp of educational principles and mastery over a large store of teaching techniques will find himself ready to provide the tactics necessary for almost any situation that could arise in any of his classes.

FLANDERS' CATEGORIES. Most teaching operations are largely verbal. Amidon and Flanders[1] have divided the verbal teaching operations into ten categories. These categories are shown as Table I. Seven of these categories describe operations in which the teacher does the talking or initiates the talking. Of these seven, four categories describe operations in which the teacher influences the pupil indirectly by accepting his feelings, praising or encouraging him, accepting his ideas or asking questions. The remaining three teacher-talk categories include operations by which the teacher influences the pupils directly. In these categories we find such operations as lecturing, telling, giving facts or opinions, asking rhetorical questions, giving directions, criticizing, scolding, and justifying class procedures.

On the basis of a two-year study of junior-high-school teachers and pupils findings indicate that "all types of students learned more from working with the more indirect teachers than with the direct teachers"[2] and that in "both social studies and mathematics classes the students of the more indirect teachers scored higher on achievement tests than did the students of the more direct teachers."[3] However, the most successful teachers were the ones who could "shift their behavior as necessary. That

[1] Edmund J. Amidon and Ned A. Flanders, *The Role of the Teacher in the Classroom* (Minneapolis, Minn.: Paul S. Amidon and Associates, 1963), p. 12.
[2] *Ibid.*, p. 56.
[3] *Ibid.*, p. 57.

TABLE I

Summary of Categories for Interaction Analysis

Teacher Talk	Indirect Influence	1. ACCEPTS FEELING: accepts and clarifies the feeling tone of the students in a nonthreatening manner. Feelings may be positive or negative. Predicting and recalling feelings are included. 2. PRAISES OR ENCOURAGES: praises or encourages student action or behavior. Jokes that release tension, not at the expense of another individual, nodding head or saying "uhhuh?" or "go on" are included. 3. ACCEPTS OR USES IDEAS OF STUDENT: clarifying, building, or developing ideas or suggestions by a student. As teacher brings more of his own ideas into play, shift to category five. 4. ASKS QUESTIONS: asking a question about content or procedure with the intent that a student answer.
	Direct Influence	5. LECTURES: giving facts or opinions about content or procedure; expressing his own idea; asking rhetorical questions. 6. GIVES DIRECTIONS: directions, commands, or orders with which a student is expected to comply. 7. CRITICIZES OR JUSTIFIES AUTHORITY: statements intended to change student behavior from nonacceptable to acceptable pattern; bawling someone out; stating why the teacher is doing what he is doing, extreme self-reference.
Student Talk		8. STUDENT TALK-RESPONSE: talk by students in response to teacher. Teacher initiates the contact or solicits student statement. 9. STUDENT TALK-INITIATION: talk by students, which they initiate. If "calling on" student is only to indicate who may talk next, observer must decide whether student wanted to talk. If he did, use this category.
		10. SILENCE OR CONFUSION: pauses, short periods of silence, and periods of confusion in which communication cannot be understood by the observer.

15

is, they could be just as direct as any teacher in certain situations, but they could be far more indirect in other situations." In other words *the teachers who could best adapt their behavior to the situation were the most successful.* As a rule, however, the teachers who had this flexibility were the indirect teachers. The "direct" teachers were seldom able to adapt themselves to the situation requiring an indirect operation.[4]

IMPLICATIONS OF INTERACTION ANALYSIS. This research seems to have several implications for teaching. One is "that where the learner's goals are not clear to him an indirect approach which allows the pupil to set up his own goals is more effective than an approach in which the teacher tells the pupil what to do." Another is that recent tendencies to base courses upon classroom lectures are probably less efficient than courses in which the pupil is largely self directing. A third is that the teacher who has developed the social skills of accepting, clarifying, and using pupils' ideas is probably potentially more effective than a teacher who does not possess those skills even though he may be a skilful director and lecturer. A fourth is that the most capable youth probably develop intellectually more and more rapidly with teachers who use indirect tactics than with teachers who use direct tactics. It is therefore somewhat alarming to find Flanders' statement that

Two-thirds of the time spent in a classroom, someone is talking. Two-thirds of the time someone is talking, it is the teacher—for the teacher talks more than all the students combined. Two-thirds of the time that the teacher is talking, he is lecturing, giving directions, or criticizing the behavior of students. One-third of the time he is asking questions, reacting to student ideas, or giving praise.[5]

TYPES OF TEACHING OPERATIONS. Obviously each teacher must use a large number of teaching tactics of various kinds. Among them are

Operations designed to make pupils' ideas clear.
Operations designed to present new or different materials.
Operations designed to show pupils how to do things.
Operations designed to affect or change attitudes, ideals, appreciations.
Operations designed to give security.
Operations designed to motivate.
Operations designed to evaluate, or to measure.
Operations designed to guide or direct pupils' work.
Operations designed to arouse, to direct, or assuage emotions.

4 *Ibid.,* p. 57.
5 *Ibid.*

The important thing is to select the proper operation for the result one desires. Presumably in the Flanders and Amidon studies it was the indirect teachers' ability to select their tactics more skilfully than the direct teachers that make them more successful.

THE CLARIFYING OPERATIONS. The clarifying operations are operations by which the teacher helps the pupil make his ideas clear. For one must remember that no one can clarify understandings for anyone else. Neither can he have insights for anyone else, nor do any one else's thinking. Each person must do these things for himself. But it is possible for a teacher to help and guide a pupil to clearer understandings and insights. The clarifying operations are the tactics the teacher can use to accomplish this purpose. Some of them are described below. Note that almost all the operations described are based on questions and are examples of what Flanders calls indirect teaching.[6]

A typical clarifying operation is to ask the pupil to define what he means in his own terms. Another is to ask him to illustrate or demonstrate his meanings. Yet another is to ask him where he got his idea—what is its basis and is this basis a tenable one? Still another would be to throw back the pupil's idea to him, perhaps rephrased, to ask him whether that is what he means. If it is what he means, then another tactic would be to ask him to forecast the implications or logical consequences of this idea. In other words, if so, then what? Still another tactic is to ask the pupil to summarize what he means or to organize his meaning into a logical outline. Another is to question his basis for belief. Is he dealing with fact or opinion, fact or feeling, fact or emotion? Questioning the pupil about what causes his difficulty in order to help him solve it is still another example of a clarifying operation.

SHOW-HOW OPERATIONS. The show-how operations are mostly concerned with skills. They include such operations as demonstrations using visual and audio-visual aids, and helping pupils to perform the task, perhaps by showing them alternate or better methods to use, or by analyzing the pupils' present techniques to see where they are at fault. Telling a pupil how to do something and taking him through the task step by step can also be included as show-how operations even though they are often not so much "show-how" as "tell-how." So can correcting of faults in techniques or form during practice, as when the golf instructor tells the pupil to hold the club like this and not like that. (In this case practice is a teaching strategy.)

[6] The descriptions are largely derived from Louis Raths' *What Is Teaching?*, undated, mimeographed.

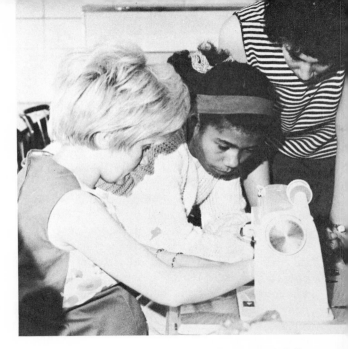

Show-how operations are necessary in the development of skills.

THE SECURITY-GIVING OPERATIONS. The security-giving operations are the operations that make it possible for pupils to feel free to learn. For many pupils school is a challenging and frightening experience full of many strong pressures. Teachers need to help pupils gain the confidence they need to meet the pressures and to cope with the challenges. The operations that provide these qualities are the ones by which the teacher lets the pupil know that he is welcome in the class and that the teacher respects his individuality, and will support the pupil in his efforts to learn, even when he makes mistakes. One of the most important aids to security giving is for the teacher to be consistent in his behavior and in the types of operations that he uses in his teaching.

OTHER KINDS OF OPERATIONS. Teachers may use many other kinds of operations. Among the operations are directing, requesting, explaining, suggesting, praising, pointing out possibilities and alternatives, creating problem situations, showing materials and methods; operations by which teachers try to motivate pupils; operations in which teachers compare, judge correctness and accuracy, observe pupil behavior, encourage pupils' self judgment, and do other things in order to evaluate properly their teaching and their pupils' learning. Especially worthy of mention, lest they be overlooked, are the operations by which teachers attempt to change or build attitudes, ideals, and appreciations. These include operations in which the teacher praises or condemns pupil behavior; operations in which he presents an attitude or behavior in a favorable light, or reinforces it with emotion or emotionally toned behavior; dramatic or musical presentations; and the pointing out of suitable models for pupils to follow. These operations are especially significant because the operations that bring about the learning of knowledge and skills will not suffice if teachers wish to change their pupils' attitudes, ideals, and appreciations.

✿

> Perhaps you would like to arrange the various operations in a set of categories of your own.
> List all the operations you can think of according to their categories.
> How can a teacher determine which operation to use in any specific situation?

✿

The New Technology

In the middle years of the twentieth century educational technology has grown with astonishing rapidity. The period since World War II has seen the development of new teaching tools, educational machines, instructional materials, new curricular and administrative organizations, and new kinds of school buildings and classrooms. These innovations have had and are having considerable impact on secondary education.

THE AIM FOR EFFICIENCY.   One of the by-products of the new technology has been a cry for more efficient use of teachers' time and more efficient teaching procedures. Proponents of innovations claim that at present one third of an average teacher's time is used up in clerical and other nonprofessional tasks that less qualified persons could do as well as he, and another one third of his time is spent doing tasks that might better be turned over to machines or other automated devices. They therefore demand that schools should be organized in such a way as to allow teachers to use their energies much more efficiently.

FREEDOM FOR TEACHING HIGHER MENTAL PROCESSES.   The evidence indicates that the innovators are at least partially correct. One seemingly obvious implication of the new technology is that teachers should not waste their time doing jobs that can be better done by machine. Ordinarily, classroom teachers cannot hope to prepare lectures that will be as effective as those prepared by an expert television teacher with many hours of preparation time at his disposal. Certainly a language laboratory properly constructed and used should be able to take on the onerous foreign language pattern drills period after period without the fatigue that can overwhelm a teacher. Furthermore, the language laboratory tape console can speak several sentences at once, even, if need be, in different languages, so that it can help several pupils practice different exercises at the same time, thus providing for differences in individual ability in a way no teacher could possibly do without assistance. Teaching machines, if their promise comes true, will be able to teach pupils facts and information with a thoroughness that has been quite rare usually, and thus free teachers to concentrate on learnings of higher and more important order. In sum, if the new teaching machines and devices prove to be as effective as their proponents hope, the teacher of the future cannot be merely a lecturer or an imparter of facts. His teaching will have a higher function.[7]

THE SYSTEMS APPROACH.   One result of the new technology has been the concept of the systems approach to school organization and teaching. The notion behind the systems approach is that men and material should be combined into the most efficient unit possible to get the job done. According to the theory, if certain instructional jobs can best be done by machines, then we should turn them over to the machines. If certain jobs can best be done by clerks, we should turn them over to clerks. If some teachers are showmen and lecturers, then they should be the teachers who lecture. On the other hand, if some teachers are excellent at leading discussions or at helping individuals, they should be the discussion leaders and the directors of pupils' individual study. In addition if some teachers have superior guidance skills then they should be homeroom teachers. In other words each teacher's work should be arranged according to his ability. For good or evil, the age of educational specialists has begun. The principle of the need for selecting the right tool or approach to do the job required applies more than ever.

*

In what ways is the new technology affecting teaching method?
What types of teaching jobs are best done by teachers? What, if any, can be safely turned over to machines?
Investigate team teaching as one aspect of the movement towards a systems approach.

*

[7] Not everyone has accepted these devices willingly and not all of the devices have been completely successful. Some people find instruction by teaching machines boring, for instance. There is little doubt, however, that eventually technology will be able to overcome most of its present faults.

The Role of Subject Matter

Three Positions

The professional teacher also selects his strategies and tactics on the basis of the subject matter to be taught and his notion of the role of subject matter. There seem to be three ways to think of subject matter. One is to consider it something valuable in and of itself. According to this position, one should learn the subject matter, whatever it is, because to know it is "good" and not for any contingent values that may come from knowing it. The second position is to think of subject matter as something valuable for its use. According to this position one should learn the content, whatever it is, because one can use that particular knowledge for some practical purposes, for example, to earn a living, or to get into college. The third position is to think of subject matter as a means of teaching process, methods, or structure. According to this way of thinking it is not so much the content as the skills, attitudes, and generalizations we learn by means of learning the content that has value. Thus if the real object of learning history is to learn historical method or to think historically, then it does not matter particularly what history we learn as long as we learn it in such a way that we learn the method. In this view content is only a vehicle to use to teach process.

Even though many teachers have never considered their own views about subject matter, their views tend to influence the content they select for their courses and the ways in which they teach. The philosophical orientation of the teacher, then, is whether he is aware of it or not, a determiner of educational method.

From this discussion perhaps we can draw the inference that *content is not necessarily information or fact, but it is also processes, skills, and attitudes.* Knowing how is as much part of curriculum content as knowing what.

The Structure of the Disciplines

Another determiner of teaching method is the structure of subject matter. By structure we mean the interrelationships or organization of parts. Thus the structure of subject matter includes the scope and sequence and vertical and horizontal organization of its content which in turn must be based upon the organization of the disciplines or selections from which the subject matter is obtained.

DIFFERENT STRUCTURES FOR DIFFERENT DISCIPLINES. An important point that has been lost sight of for many years by many teachers and administrators as well as parents and pupils is that the structures of the different disciplines vary from each other. Not only that, but the disciplines themselves have subdivisions whose structures vary from each other. That this important fact has not figured more prominently in educational thinking is strange, because persons who have stopped to consider have been well aware of it since the time of Aristotle.

ARISTOTLE'S THREE CATEGORIES. Aristotle divided the disciplines into three categories: the theoretical, the practical, and the productive. By the theoretical he meant those studies which consist of knowledge that we know absolutely; by the practical he meant those studies that require choice and decision like political science or logic; by productive he meant the disciplines like the fine arts, practical arts, or engineering that bring forth some tangible result or product. Schwab explains these three categories more explicitly.

The theoretical disciplines, devoted to knowing, concern themselves with those aspects of things which are fixed, stable, enduring. Hence, the theoretical disciplines are concerned with precisely these aspects of things which we cannot alter by making or make use of by doing. The productive disciplines are concerned with what is malleable, capable of being changed. The practical disciplines are concerned with another sort of malleability of human character, its ability to deliberate on its future and (within limits) to do as it sees fit.[8]

THE NEED TO DIFFERENTIATE. The Aristotelian analysis of the disciplines is only one of many. The interesting and alarming thing about this analysis of the disciplines, as Schwab points out[9], is that teachers have tended to teach all disciplines in the school curriculum as though they were theoretical. For example some teachers teach literature, composition, and even music and art as though they were history or science, and so, instead of reacting to poetry, treat it as fact to be learned. Such malpractice is tragic. The structures of the disciplines and their subdivisions require different teaching strategies for different studies. The disciplines differ according to purpose, substance, organization, and method of inquiry by which knowledge in the field is discovered and verified.

THE REVISIONIST NATURE OF KNOWLEDGE. The common tendency of teachers to treat all knowledge as though it were indubitable permanent truth is particularly regrettable because of the revisionist nature of all disciplines in modern times. The middle-aged teacher of

[8] Joseph J. Schwab, "Structure of the Disciplines: Meanings and Significances," in G. W. Ford and Lawrence Pugno, *The Structure of Knowledge and the Curriculum* (Chicago: Rand McNally and Company, 1964), p. 17.
[9] *Ibid.*

history today finds in modern historical research interpretations of the Colonial Era, the American Revolution, and the Civil War and the Reconstruction quite different from those he learned in the works of Beard and Muzzey he read in his student days. Similarly, a great number of the facts about the 92 immutable elements so earnestly taught to high-school pupils thirty years ago have turned out to be not so. In literature, too, styles of criticism have changed, and even the mighty rules of grammar are losing face.

Every day knowledge changes faster and faster. Consequently to attempt to teach pupils facts alone is to lead pupils to dissatisfaction when they learn that new discoveries have proved that the "facts" they learned are facts no longer. Instead of facts and information the pupil of the future needs to know how to cope with new knowledge. For this purpose he needs familiarity with the structures of the disciplines and knowledge of the mechanisms by which knowledge in the disciplines is created. Above all, he needs to master the intellectual skills and attitudes that allow him to keep himself well informed and well educated no matter what new knowledge appears. To meet these needs the teacher must adopt teaching strategies that will teach pupils to seek out rather than to accept knowledge.

The Futility of Subject Covering

He must also find strategies that give depth rather than superficiality. In the modern world to attempt to "cover the subject" is obsolete. No longer can anyone hope to cover the entirety of any subject. We can only attempt to select that material that seems the most desirable in view of our goals. Again, as with the revisionist nature of knowledge, the situation calls for an emphasis on the teaching of process and structure. What our criterion will be for the selection of subject matter depends somewhat on our philosophy. But no matter what that may be, we have come to the point where it is more important to eliminate well than to include. The watchword that must guide every teacher of every subject is: *Teach more effectively and thoroughly by attempting to cover less.*

✿

Aristotle says that disciplines differ. What are the implications of these differences for teaching?

How can we teach so that what the pupils learn will not be soon out of date?

According to one educationist any high-school teacher who believes that he must cover the subject is incompetent. What then should the teacher be doing?

✿

Summary

The criterion for success in teaching is the extent to which the teacher is able to bring about changes in pupils' behavior or tendency toward behavior. To meet his responsibilities the teacher needs much skill. As a rule, in spite of pupils who are recalcitrant, ill, or badly endowed, most failures in teaching result from poor teaching or poor curricula. One result of poor teaching is meaningless parroting which can be avoided if one teaches realistically and aims his instruction at the knowledge, skill, or attitude to be learned rather than at empty skills.

The role of method is to bring about learning. It includes both content and techniques, strategies and tactics. The key to method is to bring about the desired learning in pupils by selecting the proper strategies and tactics and consequently the proper content and techniques. To achieve this conclusion one must diagnose the situation, prepare for the learning, guide the activities, evaluate the learning, and follow up. Teaching tactics are the techniques and content by which one carries out a strategy. There are many different tactics or operations. The objective is to select the one best suited to carry out the goal of the moment. Unfortunately the operations most frequently used do not seem to be the most promising for most teaching-learning situations. The discovery of new technology has made it more important than ever that teachers choose and use the instructional tool or technique most appropriate for the kind of learning at hand so that the teaching can be most effective and efficient.

Subject matter is not all the same and so all subjects should not be taught in the same way. Rather, the teaching approach should vary according to the structure and methods of the disciplines concerned. No longer can teachers be content to teach pupils information and to cover the subject. The modern world contains too much information to cover and the facts are changing too swiftly. Modern teaching must concentrate on organization, method, process, and structure so that young people can cope with the new and different knowledge that will be discovered before they get the old knowledge well digested. It is for these reasons that the teacher must teach more by teaching less.

FOR FURTHER STUDY

AMIDON, EDMUND J., and NED A. FLANDERS, *The Role of the Teacher in the Classroom* (Minneapolis, Minn.: Paul S. Amidon and Associates, 1963).

BARZUN, JACQUES, *Teacher in America* (New York: Doubleday Anchor Books, Doubleday and Company, 1954).

BELLACK, ARNO A., *Theory and Research in Teaching* (New York: Bureau of Publications, Teachers College, Columbia University, 1963).

BIDDLE, BRUCE J., and WILLIAM J. ELLENA (editors), *Contemporary Research on Teacher Effectiveness* (New York: Holt, Rinehart and Winston, Inc., 1964).

BRAUNER, CHARLES J., *American Educational Theory* (Englewood Cliffs, N.J.: Prentice-Hall, Inc., 1964).

BRUNER, JEROME S., *The Process of Education* (Cambridge, Mass.: Harvard University Press, 1960).

HIGHET, GILBERT, *The Art of Teaching* (New York: Vintage Books, 1955).

HULLFISH, H. GORDON, and PHILIP D. SMITH, *Reflective Thinking* (New York: Dodd Mead and Company, 1961).

MALLERY, DAVID, *High School Students Speak Out* (New York: Harper and Row Publishers, 1962).

MELVIN, A. GORDON, *General Methods of Teaching* (New York: McGraw-Hill Book Company, Inc., 1952).

NATIONAL SOCIETY FOR THE STUDY OF EDUCATION, *Theories of Learning and Instruction*, Sixty-third Yearbook, Part I (Chicago: University of Chicago Press, 1964).

RYLE, GILBERT, *The Concept of Mind* (New York: Barnes and Noble, Inc., 1949).

SMITH, B. OTHANEL, *Language and Concepts in Education* (Chicago: Rand McNally and Company, 1961).

STINNETT, T. M., and ALBERT J. HUGGETT, *Professional Problems of Teachers*, Second Edition (New York: The Macmillan Company, 1963).

WILSON, CHARLES H., *A Teacher Is a Person* (New York: Holt, Rinehart and Winston, Inc., 1956).

CHAPTER 2

Knowing the Pupil

*I*N ADDITION to a knowledge of boys and girls and how they learn, teaching also requires a particular knowledge of each boy and girl in the class. The teen-ager who is our secondary-school pupil is an individual of complexities and enigmas. The business of growing up is a complicated one. The adolescent is torn by many conflicts and many moments of indecision. At one moment, he may struggle for complete independence; at the next moment he may need the reassurance and protection he required when he was younger. As he enters early adolescence, he brings with him personal, social, educational, and vocational problems which he is incapable of analyzing and for which he is incapable of setting up any logical solution. For example, let us examine the following case of Judy.

Judy, a pleasant girl of fifteen in the tenth grade, is a typical example of a teen-ager beset by the many problems of the adolescent. She is more concerned with the telephone than with homework; more concerned with her personal appearance than with that of her room or her locker; more interested in going on dates than in studying at home. Judy's school work is suffering, and feelings of antagonism have developed between her and her teacher. It seems as if Miss C. is usually punishing Judy for one thing or another. At home antagonism between mother and daughter also prevails, although Judy is doted on by her father. In fact, the parents often argue over Judy.

This picture of Judy is not at all unusual. The lives of many adolescents are quite stormy. Of course, most youngsters, especially those who come from healthy home and school environments, overcome these difficulties relatively unscathed. Still, the teacher who understands the reasons for an adolescent behavior can do much toward helping the pupil during this trying period. By getting to know and to understand the pupil the teacher is in a position to help the pupil solve these problems and to adapt his program to make the most of the situation.

It is here that the teacher must be aware of factors that contribute to many of the changes in behavior taking place. The early adolescent, beset with the mysteries of physiological changes, and concerned over the development of secondary sex characteristics, needs strong support, not only from home, but from school as well. The rebellion of the middle adolescent is understandable, too, if the teacher is cognizant of the conditions of life that help create the uncertainty, confusion, concern, and rebellion within this youngster.

Dr. William C. Kvaraceus has said that "in today's complex and mobile society, youth continues to be the most vulnerable segment of any group."[1] He goes on to say that he considers being a youth or teen-ager the most dangerous occupation in every society today. The rapid changes now going on are steadily increasing the hazards to youth.

Learning About the Pupil

Because pupils are so different, if the teacher is to provide the sort of teaching best suited for each pupil, he must be well acquainted with their abilities, potentialities, goals, backgrounds, problems, and needs. Without this knowledge the problems of motivation, provision for individual differences, adjusting curriculum and methods to meet pupils' needs, and of selecting the proper goals and instructional strategies and tactics becomes very difficult. Fortunately, teachers have many tools available to help them learn about pupils. These tools make it possible for a teacher to become fairly well acquainted with his pupils even though he may have five sections of thirty pupils each.

The Problem-Inventory Approach

One effective means of finding out what worries, problems, or concerns a pupil may have is the problem-inventory. Effective instruments of this type are the "Billett-Starr Youth Problems Inventory, Junior Level" and the "Billett-Starr Youth Problems Inventory, Senior Level."[2] These inventories are intended to provide the means of identifying the personal problems of individual pupils. They attempt to get at the intensity of a student's problems by allowing him to differentiate between those which bother him "some" and those which bother him "very much."

The Billett-Starr Youth Problems Inventory may be administered to an individual alone or to a group of students. The results of the inventory

[1] William C. Kvaraceus, Director of Youth Studies, Lincoln Filene Center for Citizenship and Public Affairs, in a speech at the University of Hartford, October 28, 1964.

[2] Roy O. Billett and Irving S. Starr, *Billett-Starr Youth Problems Inventory, Junior Level*, and *Billett-Starr Youth Problems Inventory, Senior Level* (New York: Harcourt, Brace & World, Inc., 1958).

A class consists of individuals. These pupils are much alike in many ways, but each is different.

may be classified as individual or group. The first use refers to the picture of each individual student in that it provides a record of the problems which he seems to have—their nature, their number, and their intensity. Such information provides the basis for individual counseling interviews. Group results may provide a school with information on the number of problems its students have and which problems are most prevalent. In either case, the teacher can find out much about his class, or about an individual in the class from the results of the inventory.

No inventory of this nature, nor any other personality test, should ever be administered by the teacher without the complete knowledge and involvement of the guidance department. The beginning teacher, especially, is warned never to use this sort of device without professional assistance. The guidance department is the source from which this assistance should come.

Observation As a Source of Information

Observation is one of the best means of getting to know a pupil. Through its use an alert teacher, properly trained, can often find clues to the causes for a pupil's behavior. However, one should not limit his observation to the pupil. Many times the teacher can understand a pupil's problems better after observing and talking with the parent. Therefore the teacher should meet the parent early in the school year—especially if the pupil shows signs of having difficulty in the classroom or elsewhere in school. By utilizing the information gleaned through observing and talking with his pupils and their parents, the teacher can often help the young people in his charge solve their problems. Techniques to help one in observing, such as checklists and rating scales, will be presented more fully in later discussions of evaluation and diagnosis. Here we shall limit ourselves to considering only the behavior log and the anecdotal record or report.

USING THE BEHAVIOR LOG. Observation of the everyday behavior of the pupils can tell the teacher much. By keeping a behavior log for each pupil the teacher can amass useful information about the attitudes, behavior, and abilities of pupils. A behavior log need not be very complicated. Usually it consists merely of a notebook with a page for each pupil. On this page the teacher notes any occurrences that seem to be significant. The entries should be brief and to the point, as follows:

Matthew McGuire

DATE	ENTRY
9/27	Matthew requested permission to build a model of the solar system.
9/30	M. was involved in an argument with John at the end of the laboratory period. Cause of the argument not determined. M. said J. was picking on him.
10/5	Conference with M. concerning his project. So far he has done nothing constructive. He says he would like to do something else.
10/6	M. was elected class treasurer at the sophomore class meeting.
10/7	M. has decided to go ahead with his project after all. He has finished his plans with working drawings. They were quite acceptable.

PREPARING ANECDOTAL REPORTS. Another common method of recording observations about individual pupils is the anecdotal report. This report should record significant or unusual behavior. It should describe for a given pupil briefly and matter-of-factly what happened, when, where, and under what conditions. Sometimes if the teacher thinks it desirable, he may attempt to interpret the happening. However, he should be sure to distinguish the interpretation from the description of the incident. It is usually better to report the incident without attempting to interpret it. A form for an anecdotal report follows:

Anecdotal Report Form

NAME OF PUPIL: DATE:
Description of incident:

Interpretation:

                                             Reported by:
                                             Position:

Such reports may be forwarded to the guidance office or be retained by the teacher for use in his own study of the pupil. In either case they can be very helpful.

Information from Other Teachers

The teacher who wishes to learn about his students should confer with other teachers also. Objective discussions with one's colleagues can reveal much. The discussions, however, ought to be planned; even if sometimes greatly illuminating, chance conversations are liable to be unproductive. On the other hand, planned conferences of all the teachers and guidance counselors concerned are often extremely helpful in bringing about an understanding of the personality and problems of a particular boy or girl.

The opinions and observations of faculty members can also be gathered from anecdotal reports, behavior logs, and cumulative records. The cumulative record may include much significant information because it is the repository of such records as

1. Pupils' personal goals.
2. Records of significant experiences.
3. Records of conferences.
4. Test data.
5. Health records.
6. Family history.
7. Course records.
8. Activity records.
9. Personality ratings and descriptions.
10. Questionnaires.
11. Administrative records.
12. Anecdotal reports.

Most cumulative records are made up of a folder or envelope on which one can record pertinent data and in which one can place other records and reports. An example of a cumulative record folder appears as Figures 2 and 3.

*

An example of a cumulative record form is shown in Figures 2 and 3. What information of value might you find in it? In what ways might the information in this cumulative record help the teacher in his teaching? What physical and health data would be helpful? Is there any information omitted from the printed form?

How might each of the records suggested in the list above be used by a teacher?

＊

Sociograms, Social Distance Scales, and Guess Who Tests

Reports from other teachers are helpful, but they can seldom give one all the information he seeks. Fortunately, many devices by which one may find information are available. Particularly useful are the devices that show the social aspects of the class and the natural grouping and friendships of the pupils. Both the social distance scale and sociogram are useful for this purpose.

CONSTRUCTING THE SOCIOGRAM. In every class, pupils tend to form natural groups and follow natural leaders. By observing the class and by using devices such as those described in this chapter, the alert teacher can find out who the natural leaders and group members are. He should do so because, as a rule, it is advantageous to make use of these natural groups and natural leaders, particularly when forming committees.

A device particularly useful for this purpose is the sociogram. This is nothing more than a diagrammatic representation of what seems to be the structure of the group in a class. Any teacher can make a sociogram easily by using the following procedure:

1. Ask the pupils to answer in secret such questions as: Which two pupils would you like to work with on a topic for an oral report? If we should change the seating plan, whom would you like to sit beside? Or, with whom would you most like to work on a class committee in planning? Sometimes one might also ask questions such as: With whom would you rather not work?
2. Tabulate the choices of each pupil. Keep the boys and girls in separate columns.
3. Construct the sociogram.
   a. Select a symbol for boy and another for girl.
   b. Place the symbols representing the most popular pupils near the center of the page, those of the less popular farther out, and those of the least popular on the fringes. It may be helpful to place the boys on one side of the page and the girls on the other.
   c. Draw lines to represent the choices. Show the direction of the choice by an arrow. Show mutual choices by a double arrow. Dislike may be shown by using dotted or colored lines.

FIGURE 2

A Sample Cumulative Personnel Record.

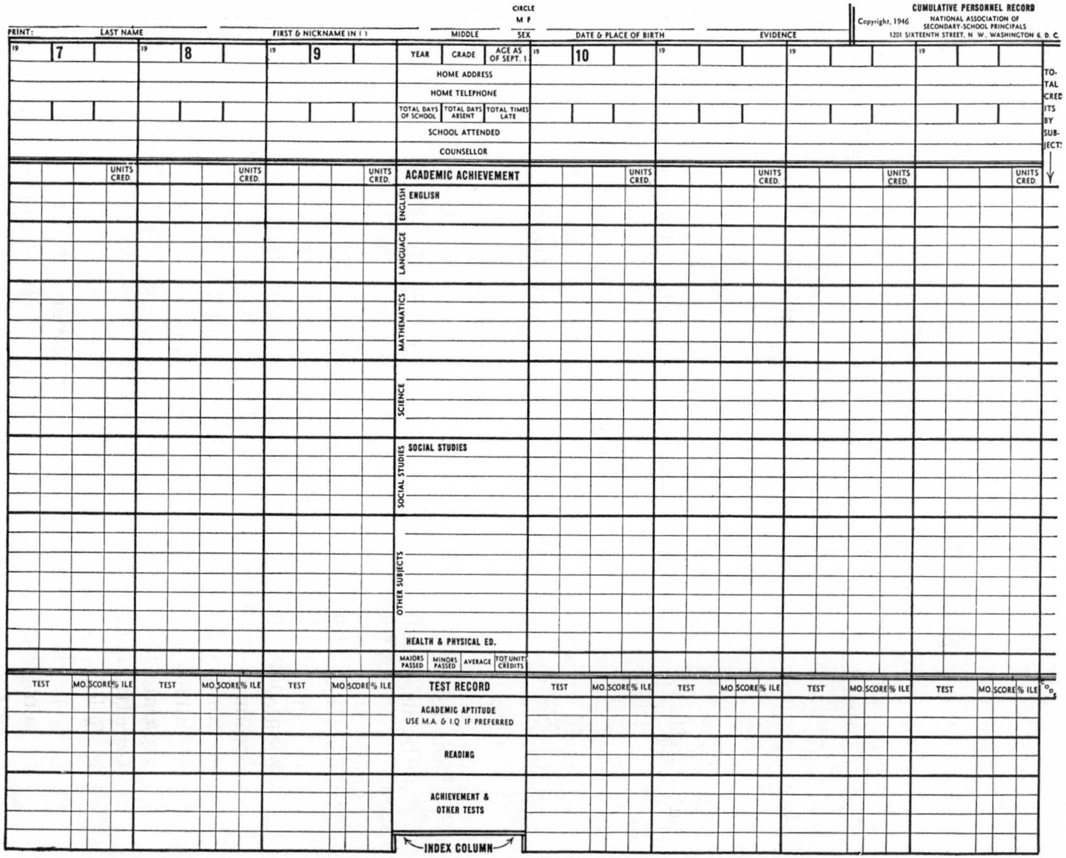

32

Reproduced by permission of National Association of Secondary-School Principals, copyright, 1946, Washington, D.C.

Figure 3

Reverse Side of Sample Cumulative Personnel Record.

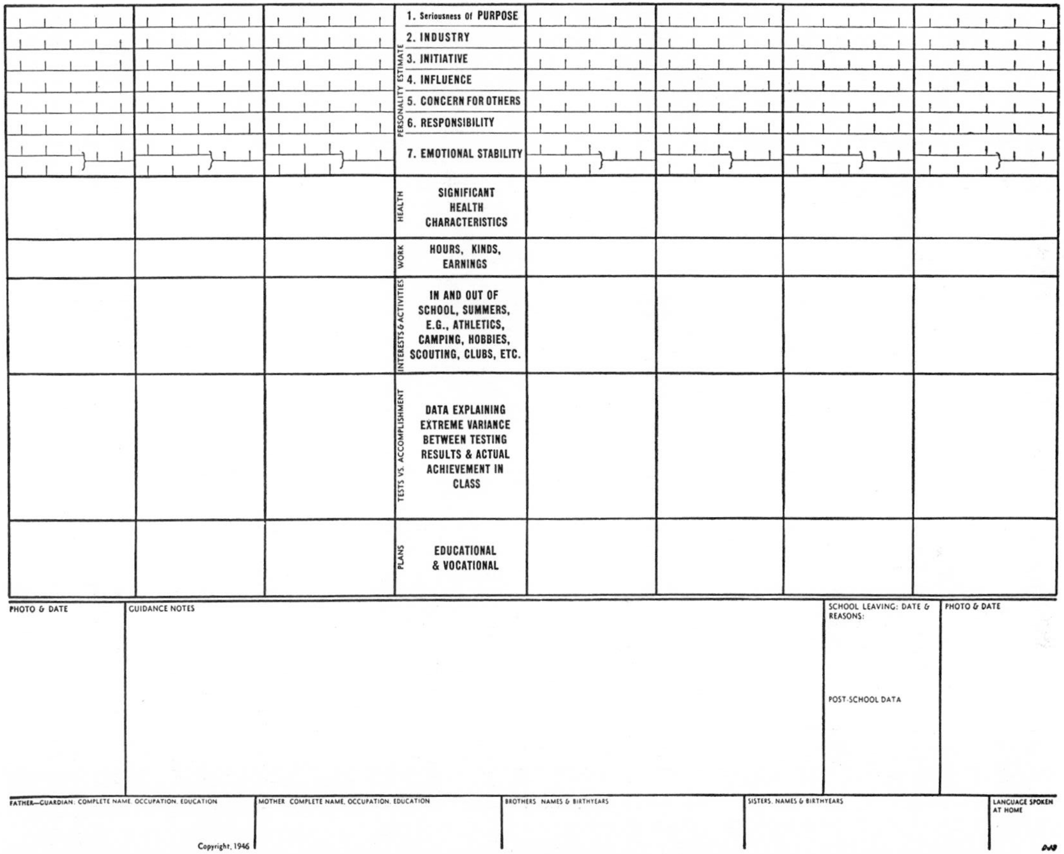

PERSONALITY ESTIMATE	1. Seriousness or PURPOSE
	2. INDUSTRY
	3. INITIATIVE
	4. INFLUENCE
	5. CONCERN FOR OTHERS
	6. RESPONSIBILITY
	7. EMOTIONAL STABILITY
HEALTH	SIGNIFICANT HEALTH CHARACTERISTICS
WORK	HOURS, KINDS, EARNINGS
INTERESTS & ACTIVITIES	IN AND OUT OF SCHOOL, SUMMERS, E.G., ATHLETICS, CAMPING, HOBBIES, SCOUTING, CLUBS, ETC.
TESTS VS. ACCOMPLISHMENT	DATA EXPLAINING EXTREME VARIANCE BETWEEN TESTING RESULTS & ACTUAL ACHIEVEMENT IN CLASS
PLANS	EDUCATIONAL & VOCATIONAL

GUIDANCE NOTES

PHOTO & DATE

SCHOOL LEAVING, DATE & REASONS:

PHOTO & DATE

POST-SCHOOL DATA

FATHER—GUARDIAN: COMPLETE NAME OCCUPATION EDUCATION

MOTHER: COMPLETE NAME OCCUPATION EDUCATION

BROTHERS: NAMES & BIRTHYEARS

SISTERS: NAMES & BIRTHYEARS

LANGUAGE SPOKEN AT HOME

Copyright: 1946

Reproduced by permission of National Association of Secondary-School Principals, copyright, 1946, Washington, D.C.

Figure 4 is a sociogram depicting the composition of an eighth-grade mathematics class.

✻

In the sample sociogram what natural groups do you find? Do you see any indications of group leaders? If you were to form four committees, would this particular sociogram be of any help?

What other information might a sociogram give? What evidence does the sociogram give of mutual choices, rejections, mutual rejections, cliques, friendships, isolates, chains?

How might one use the data to create new patterns in the class? How might one use natural relationships to encourage learning?

✻

THE SOCIAL DISTANCE SCALE. Another useful device for obtaining information about pupils is the social distance scale. This, too, is a very simple device. One merely asks each pupil to indicate his opinion of each of the other pupils on a scale such as the following.

	JIM	JACK	NANCY	WANDA	RITA	SAM
1. I'd like him for one of my best friends.	____	____	____	____	____	____
2. I'd like to have him for a friend and to work with him, but not as a best friend.	____	____	____	____	____	____
3. I don't mind working with him, but I don't want him for a friend.	____	____	____	____	____	____
4. I don't like him much. Prefer not to work with him, if possible.	____	____	____	____	____	____
5. I don't want anything to do with him.	____	____	____	____	____	____ ✻

✻ This Social Distance Scale and the Guess Who Test following are adapted from ones presented in Ruth Cunningham and Associates, *Understanding Group Behavior of Boys and Girls* (New York: Teachers College Bureau of Publications, Columbia University, 1951). *See also* Helen Jennings, *Sociometry in Group Relations* (Washington, D.C.: American Council on Education, 1948).

The social distance scale can give the teacher valuable information concerning the natural grouping of the pupils in his class. It can point out fairly clearly which pupils are likely to work together congenially.

THE GUESS WHO TEST. Another device helpful in determining some of the social characteristics of the class is the *Guess Who Test*. Actually,

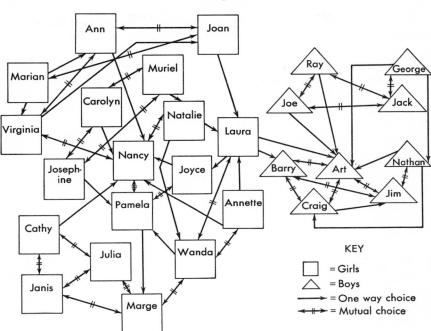

FIGURE 4

A Sociogram.

this test may be used to find out many things about your pupils—interests, friendships, hobbies, habits, problems, even emotional problems at times. To buy such a test is not necessary. A teacher or a group of teachers can construct one quite easily by making up a series of statements like the following and asking the pupils to identify which of their classmates the statements best describe.

This person is always daydreaming.
This person likes to read.
This person seems to be always worrying about something.
This person is always putting things off.

Information from Pupil Autobiography

Pupil autobiographies are another excellent source of information about pupils. From a pupil autobiography one may learn the pupil's likes and dislikes, his background, family history, and other pertinent facts. The beginning of the school year is perhaps the best time for the pupil to write his autobiography. A subject teacher may make the assignment as part of one of the pupils' regular classes, or it may be assigned by a homeroom or guidance teacher. In any case, the teachers should be careful to coordinate their assignments so that the pupil will not need to write more than one autobiography during a given period. The teachers should also cooperate in sharing and using the information from the autobiographies. Too often such information is allowed to stagnate in some teacher's file and never gets to the persons who could use it.

A SAMPLE OUTLINE. The following is a suggested outline for an autobiography used in the Manchester (Connecticut) High School. Notice that the list is only suggestive. The pupils are not required to include all the items.[3]

Freshman Autobiography Outline

Birth—place and date
Family—mother, father, brothers, sisters, etc.
    Place of birth
    Age of brothers and sisters
    Health
    Education
    Present occupations
    Special experiences
    Others who live in house—relationship, etc.
Home
    Present location and description
    Other remembered homes—location and general description
Home life
    Relationship among family—likes, etc.
    Own relationship with family members
    Social life at home
        Parties
        Friends to house
Personal history
    Education—schools attended
        Special honors or difficulties
        Attitude toward school
        Attitude toward teachers
        Studies particularly liked
        Studies particularly disliked
        School activities in which active
        Nonschool activities
            Organizations other than school—church, clubs, scouts, etc.
            Friends—few, many, older, younger, neighborhood, school

[3] Manchester High School, Manchester, Connecticut. Reproduced by permission.

Hobbies, past and present—reading, stamps, etc.
Recreation
Travel, past and present
Sports—active part
Work at home
Work experience outside of home, past and present
Things like most to do
Things like least to do
Health
Illnesses—date, kind, length
Physical defects—poor eyesight, etc.
Personal characteristics—shy, like people, friendly, lazy, etc.
Future
Purpose in coming to school
Finish high school
Continue beyond high school
Kind of school
Occupations in which interested
Occupations would most like
Occupations would least like
Conclusions—any other things to add

❊

Criticize the Manchester Freshman Autobiography outline. Are there any items omitted that should be included? Might some be deleted?
How might you use a Guess Who Test? What limitations does it have? Do you see any dangers in using it with high-school pupils? With junior-high-school pupils? Make a Guess Who Test of your own.

❊

Questionnaires As a Source of Information

The information sought by the Manchester autobiography might also be gathered by the use of a pupil questionnaire. The Interest Finder described in Chapter 3, the Social Distance Scale, and the Guess Who Test described earlier in this chapter are all specialized examples of the questionnaire. To prepare a questionnaire is quite simple even though it requires care. The author of a questionnaire merely determines what he wishes to know and then designs questions that will get that information. Whenever possible, the questionnaire should call for short answers only. In fact, when feasible a checklist will probably be most satisfactory. However, the teacher should always allow the pupil a chance to comment freely on any item.

Another way to get pupils to give information about themselves is to ask the pupils to examine themselves and to report *Things About Myself to Improve*. This device can be made more effective by using a questionnaire as a framework on which to base the report. Open-ended questions, which allow pupils to elaborate their answers as they please, may give a teacher considerable insight into his pupils' attitudes and values.

Information from Individual Conferences

To know one's pupils and to provide for their needs the teacher should have individual conferences with them. These conferences may vary from brief comments on some work or a question about one's health to long conversations about the youth's life objectives, adjustment problems, or difficulties with his school work. Conferences will take place for many reasons: to settle matters of discipline, to help pupils plan their learning activities, to help with difficult assignments, to diagnose pupil difficulties, to discuss pupils' academic or vocational goals, and many others. At times the conference can be the most important tool in the teacher's workchest.

Teacher-pupil conferences take time. Teachers may have difficulty in finding time for conferences with all their pupils. Considering that a teacher who has five classes of thirty pupils each teaches 150 pupils a day, finding time for individual conferences can be a real problem. Fortunately, the situation is not as formidable as it may seem. Many of the conferences need not be long. In fact, many of them will be very short and almost recreational in nature. Moreover, the teacher has many opportunities to confer with pupils if he will only take advantage of them.[4] Class time devoted to working with pupils individually can be well worth the effort. Therefore, the competent teacher tries to arrange his class periods so as to allow for such individual work.

Opportunities for becoming acquainted with the pupil are always present. The teacher is constantly learning about the pupil from observation, other teachers, other pupils, parents, and from the many devices open to him.

Three Basic Questions

Knowing the pupil boils down to three basic questions.

1. What should a secondary-school teacher know about each pupil?
2. Where can he find this information?
3. How can he use this information once he has found it?

---

[4] Among them are before school, after school, between classes, during free periods, during supervised study periods, during laboratory sessions, and while other pupils are working individually or in groups.

The following outline is a summary of the answers to these three questions as given by five graduate-class discussion groups.

What Should a Secondary-School Teacher Know About Each Pupil?

a. Vital Statistics
   (1) Name, grade, course, Intelligence Quotient rating (scholastic ability), etc.
   (2) Health record—mental and physical (defects?)
   (3) Any standard test results (reading grade level, aptitude and ability, etc.).
   (4) Attendance record
b. Home Situation
   (1) Family background
   (2) Intrafamily relationships
   (3) Social contacts with community (club membership, etc.)
   (4) Religious attitudes and affiliations
   (5) Economic status
c. Social Outlook
   (1) Friends
   (2) Social activities
       Spare time
       School extracurricular
   (3) Group acceptance
d. Personal Qualities
   (1) Ethical standards and attitudes
   (2) Talents and capabilities
   (3) Goals and ambitions (immediate and future)
   (4) Interests and hobbies (in or out of school)
   (5) Antisocial traits causing discipline problems

Where Can He Find This Information?

a. Records
   (1) Cumulative record folder (Permanent Record Card)
   (2) Test results (vocational, interest, aptitude, ability, intelligence, achievement, etc.)
   (3) Anecdotal records
   (4) Physical examinations (dental, visual, auditory, etc.)
b. Indirect Contacts
   (1) Home visitations
   (2) Reliable members of community (Boy Scout leaders, priests or ministers, police, etc.)
   (3) PTA contacts with parents

   (4) Guidance nurse or guidance counselor
   (5) Other dependable teachers
 c. Direct Contacts
   (1) Personal observations during
         informal discussions
         conferences
         special help periods
         nonschool activities
   (2) Conclusions drawn from
         autobiographies
         questionnaires
         sociograms

How Can He Use This Information Once He Has Found It?

Employing the preceding data and experience the teacher can

a. Judge more accurately what to expect intellectually from the student
   and in so doing perform the following functions:
   (1) Select and plan the subject matter of his course at such a level
       and in such a manner that it challenges the student if he learns
       rapidly, or encourage him if he learns slowly.
   (2) Transfer a student to classes or courses that are at the level of
       his ability before a critical situation arises where disciplinary
       action is needed as a result of the pupil's maladjustment.
b. Plan a seating arrangement and class grouping that will promote
   the greatest social, physical, and intellectual adjustment or progress
   for the student.
c. Encourage and use leadership qualities more effectively
   (1) to further individual development and
   (2) to secure greater class interest and cooperation.
d. Refer to the proper authority any problems arising from health difficulties.
e. Prevent many discipline problems and deal more intelligently with
   those that do arise.
f. Encourage the student to use any special abilities through recognizing his efforts, achievements, etc.
g. Aid more effectively in helping to guide the student's program.
h. Assist in home and group adjustments.
i. Integrate class as a group by preventing the formation of cliques.
j. Stimulate interest in hobbies and outside activities.

✲

   What do you think of the answers given by these students? Would
your answers to these three questions agree with theirs?

Turn back to the description of Judy. What information about Judy would help you understand her problems better? In what ways would a better understanding of Judy's problems help Miss C. in her teaching?

✽

Diagnosis

The Need for Diagnosis

In treating an ill patient, a physician must first find out what the patient's illness is and, if possible, what is causing it. Then, and then only, can he treat the disease successfully, for, if he cannot determine what the disease is, he can treat only the symptoms. Even if the patient is free from disease, the physician finds diagnosis a necessary part of his campaign to keep him in good health.

So it is with a teacher. Much of our work has to do with boys and girls who are in poor academic health. In order to improve their health the teacher must

1. Find that a difficulty exists.
2. Find exactly what the difficulty is.
3. Find the cause of the difficulty.

This is diagnosis. Without it, teaching flounders. To be sure, these steps must be followed up by teaching directed toward correcting whatever seems to be wrong or lacking. But without diagnosis, teaching can have little direction. It is as necessary when pupils are in good academic health as when they are ailing, for if a teacher is to teach his pupils well, he must know their academic strengths and weaknesses. Diagnosis is also essential as a basis for motivation, the selection of educational objectives and determining the most suitable methods and content.

The Levels of Diagnosis

For purposes of discussion we can divide diagnosis into two general categories. The first type is used in the ordinary classroom for the diagnosing of relatively normal pupils; the second is the diagnosis of particular individuals who are having difficulty. There is little difference in principle between the two types; the difference is mainly one of the extent and purpose of the diagnosis. Ordinarily, we should be more careful in analyzing a pupil for whom we are setting up a special remedial program than in analyzing a pupil who has no great problems, although, on occasion, examination and diagnosis of the supposedly normal pupil will show the need for more detailed analysis.

Burton[5] says there are three levels of diagnosis: (1) general diagnosis, (2) analytical diagnosis, and (3) psychological diagnosis. These levels are similar to the three steps mentioned earlier in the chapter: finding out if a difficulty exists, finding out exactly what the difficulty is, and finding out the cause of the difficulty.

GENERAL DIAGNOSIS. The first level of diagnosis seems similar to a physical examination. It gives us a picture of the status of the learning of the individual and of the class. In order to do this, we administer standardized tests and use other evaluative devices available to us. These devices show us whether our pupil is strong or weak, and just what his strengths and weaknesses are. If the pupil has something wrong with him, they show us, in general, where the trouble lies and, perhaps in general, what its cause may be.

Standardized tests are not the only source of such information. Teacher-built tests are also effective in giving the teacher the type of information he desires. Other good sources of information are cumulative records and reports and the results of observation, checklists, and conferences.

✢

Suppose that after studying the lever in a physics class, you gave a test and found that all of the pupils did not measure up to your expectations in their understanding of the fulcrum. What would your diagnosis of the situation be? Would it be different if most of the pupils did understand and only a few did not? Would it be different if only one or two did not understand? What could have caused these pupils to fail to learn as well as you expected?

✢

ANALYTICAL DIAGNOSIS. The second level of diagnosis is used when the teacher discovers that something needs to be done to help individual pupils with their learning problems. Suppose, for instance, that one of the pupils in your science class does not seem to be up to standard. What information would you need to help him? At this second level of diagnosis the teacher attempts to find out by a detailed analysis exactly what the pupil's difficulty is. Such analysis often requires the use of diagnostic tests and other devices. These devices are finer measures than those used at level 1. They enable the teacher to examine more analytically a smaller area of learning.

PSYCHOLOGICAL DIAGNOSIS. The third level, namely psychological analysis, attempts to find the causes underlying the pupil's learning diffi-

[5] William H. Burton, *The Guidance of Learning Activities, Second Edition* (New York: Appleton-Century-Crofts, Inc., 1952), p. 164.

culties. Why did he not learn? Why does the error persist? What is the real cause? The reasons for not learning are often quite complex and not readily available. Diagnosis at this level is an attempt to get underneath the symptoms, and may require a careful case study utilizing all the resources of the guidance department—anecdotal reports, cumulative records, conferences, health status, and home visits.

Initial Diagnosis in the Classroom

Diagnosis should be going on every day in every classroom. For the most efficient teaching the teacher should make a general diagnosis of the status of each pupil's learning at the beginning of the year and continue with similar diagnoses as each unit of work is carried to completion. For an initial diagnosis one can give a standardized survey test to ascertain each pupil's initial position in relation to the goals of the course. Frequently teacher-made tests are as satisfactory for this purpose as standardized tests. In many courses an objective paper-and-pencil test would be a good device to show how each pupil stands, while in others another type of test would be desirable. Paper-and-pencil tests are usually not the best device for measuring skills, attitudes, appreciations, and ideals. To get at these learnings, the teacher might do better with checklists, observation, analysis of papers, rating of skills, rating of products, questionnaires, and reports of previous teachers. While the initial diagnosis cannot always be completed immediately, it should be developed during the first unit. The more information the teacher has at the beginning of the course, the better and sooner will he be able to make this diagnosis.

Continuing the Diagnosis

After the initial diagnosis the teacher should continue to diagnose, revising, if necessary, as he goes along. Certainly the teacher should attempt to take stock at the end of every unit. This can be done simply by testing the pupils to see where they stand in relation to the goals of the unit. For example, two of the sample specific objectives on page 147 are

1. Strong ties of friendship have developed between the United States and Great Britain during the twentieth century.
2. The American State Department, beginning with the days of John Hay and continuing to the present, has cooperated with the British Foreign Office in matters of international importance to both nations.

In an objective test the teacher might use items like the following to see how well the pupils had achieved these objectives.

1. During the first half of the twentieth century, relations between the United States and Great Britain have been
   a. friendly
   b. neutral
   c. unfriendly
   d. inimical
   (Designed to check the first objective: Strong ties of friendship have developed between the United States and Great Britain during the twentieth century.)
2. Give five examples of how the British Foreign Office has cooperated with the United States in matters of international importance to both nations.
   (Designed to check the second objective: The American State Department, beginning with the days of John Hay and continuing to the present, has cooperated with the British Foreign Office in matters of international importance to both nations.)

Essay test items can be used in the same way. In this unit one specific objective was the ties [of friendship] which draw the United States closer to the Commonwealth are based upon our common language, customs, and traditions.

To test this objective one might use the following essay item: What tends to draw the United States and Great Britain together?

TESTING ATTITUDES, IDEALS, AND APPRECIATIONS. To test attitudes, ideals, and appreciations by means of paper-and-pencil tests is more difficult. Pupils are likely to give the answer the teacher wants rather than what they really believe. For instance, one of the attitudes that might be a goal in this same unit is: In international affairs, as well as private affairs, one should deal justly with all. If, to test this attitude, one should ask, "Should the United States respect the rights of other nations?" the clever pupils would answer "Yes," because they know that is the answer the teacher expects. However, if the teacher poses for discussion a problem in which the United States can gain an advantage by violating the rights of a small nation, one may learn individuals' true attitudes by observing their reaction to the problem. The reaction of the pupils during a discussion of this topic might be quite revealing. Other methods of getting at attitudes are observation, rating scales, check lists, questionnaires, and analysis of papers.

*

Following are four other attitudes, ideals, and appreciations which might be goals for the unit "From Empire to Commonwealth." How might one get at these objectives?

1. No nation can depend entirely on itself.
2. The achievements of the British deserve our respect.
3. Cooperation is more desirable than warfare in international relations.
4. One should respect the rights and feelings of others.

*

USING THE ITEM ANALYSIS. After the test has been given and scored, what does it tell us? If the test items have been aimed at specific objectives, an item analysis can give us the information fairly easily. All the teacher needs to do is to see how well each pupil responded to the items designed to test the various objectives. The following table is an example of an item analysis.

	Item	A	B	C	D	E	F	G	H	I	J	K
Obj. I	1	✓	✓	✓		✓	✓	✓	✓	✓	✓	✓
	2	✓	✓	✓		✓				✓		
	3	✓		✓				✓				
	4	✓	✓	✓		✓	✓	✓		✓		
Obj. II	5											
	6	✓			✓							✓
	7											
	8					✓						
Obj. III	9	✓	✓	✓	✓		✓	✓		✓	✓	✓
	10	✓		✓	✓	✓		✓		✓	✓	✓
	11		✓	✓	✓			✓				
	12	✓	✓	✓	✓	✓	✓	✓		✓		✓

A quick look at this table shows us that none of the pupils seems to have attained the second objective very well. Also it seems that although pupils D and K have mastered the third objective quite well, neither of them has done very well with the first or second objective. Pupil H, on the other hand, does not seem to have done well on any three of the objectives. Obviously the teacher would do well to give additional instruction to the entire class on objective 2 and individual or small group instruction to certain people in the other areas.

A BASIS FOR REMEDIAL PROCEDURES. At times it will become evident that some pupils are falling behind. Their difficulties may be more serious than their inability to reach the goal of a unit—in some cases much more serious. For these persons other techniques are necessary.

Some pupils may need the specialized help of remedial classes and teachers, if available. Others can perhaps be helped by the classroom teacher.

The first thing to do, after ascertaining that a difficulty exists, is to determine exactly what the nature of the difficulty is. For example, John is doing very badly in algebra. A check of his papers shows that one cause of his trouble seems to be his arithmetic. Consequently, the next step would be to try to find what about his arithmetic is faulty and why it is so. Perhaps a diagnostic arithmetic test can find the answers to these questions. If no such test is available, perhaps one can find out the trouble in a conference, or by a more minute study of the pupil's papers, or by giving him specific work in arithmetic and checking to see just what type of errors he makes. In any case, a painstaking search for the exact trouble is imperative if the remedial teaching it to be of any value at all.

USING DIAGNOSTIC TESTS. To find the pupil's difficulty, the teacher today has access to a multitude of diagnostic tests. Listings of such tests may be found in such books as Blair and Powell's *Diagnostic and Remedial Teaching*,[6] and Buros' *Mental Measurement Yearbooks*. Before selecting a diagnostic test for any particular mission, the teacher should examine several and compare them carefully. Not all of the tests are equally good. In fact, some tests are downright bad. Moreover, not all of the good tests do each job equally well. The teacher in search of a diagnostic test should consult the references and apply the criteria for test selection noted in Chapter 16.

USING OTHER DIAGNOSTIC DEVICES. In addition to diagnostic tests, many other devices may be used for diagnosis. One example of a device that might be employed is the following scheme sometimes used to determine whether or not a book is beyond a certain pupil's reading ability. The technique is amazingly simple. One just gives to the pupil a portion of the book to read and then tests him on it. If he can answer the questions, the work is probably not too difficult for him; if he stumbles, the teacher can try him on increasingly less difficult material until a book he can read and understand is found. If the teacher takes the selections from a graded series, he can also ascertain the pupil's approximate reading level by this technique. However, before using the technique as an index of reading level, the teacher should note that all books reported to be at a given level are not equally difficult, and also that some pupils find it more difficult to read in some subject matter areas

---

[6] Glenn Myers Blair and William Powell, *Diagnostic and Remedial Teaching,* Third Edition (New York: The Macmillan Company, 1967).

O. K. Buros, *The Sixth Mental Measurement Yearbook* (Highland Park, N.J.: The Gryphon Press, 1965). See also earlier editions.

than in others. Another example also concerns reading. One of the most common of pupils' reading problems is an inability to grasp the point of a paragraph. A simple method for testing this ability is to have the pupil read a paragraph and then ask him what it said. This technique may also be used in mathematics to see whether or not the pupil can read and understand a problem.

The techniques described above are forms of controlled observation. Other useful techniques include analysis of written work, analysis of oral work, analysis of records, checklists, rating scales, and conferences. Thus questioning a pupil about his mathematics paper might disclose that he does not know how to marshal his facts in order to attack a problem. In mathematics again, and in other subjects as well, an analysis of the pupils' papers might show errors in their thinking, poor problem-solving techniques, or a lack of understanding of the fundamental processes. Questionnaires and conferences with the pupil or his parents can often be very useful in uncovering faulty study habits and procedures. Descriptions of specific techniques can be found in reference works on diagnostic and remedial teaching such as the Blair and Powell book mentioned earlier.

✳

A practice teacher suggests that one method of diagnosing pupil difficulty is to ask the pupil about his troubles. What do you think of this technique?

A pupil in one of your classes, although seemingly bright enough in class discussion, invariably does poorly on the tests. What could you do to find out why this is so?

✳

The Psychological Level of Diagnosis

The tests and other diagnostic devices just described are used to locate the specific difficulty in a remedial situation. They are useful at diagnosis level number 2. They tell the teacher what is wrong. Often a direct attack at the difficulty, once it is known, will be sufficient to correct the trouble.

Sometimes, however, to aid the pupil one must get beneath the trouble and find what is causing it. This is diagnosis at the third level—what Burton calls *the psychological level of diagnosis*. In this type of diagnosis one tries to determine which of the possible blocks to learning are responsible for the pupil's not learning. Typical causes, among others, might include physical defects, poor health, emotional problems, social influences, home and community influences, intellectual limitations, and insufficient academic background.

To track down these causes, the methods described earlier in the chapter may be helpful. In difficult cases one of the most reliable approaches is the case study. Also effective are such techniques as analysis of records, observation, physical examination, and psychological examination. Many things can be done by the classroom teacher himself. For instance, he can conduct simple tests to find defects in vision or hearing and search records for data which may throw light on the difficulty. If possible, however, the teacher should enlist the aid of a specialist—a remedial teacher, a school psychologist, a guidance person, or a physician. When available, the services of an educational clinic are usually worthwhile. Diagnosis at this level deserves expert handling. The competent teacher will not try to handle it himself if specialist help is available.

Summary

Pupils are all different. In order to be efficient and effective, teachers need to know as much as they can learn about their pupils' interests, abilities, goals, and backgrounds. With this knowledge they can cope more successfully with problems of motivation, providing for individual differences, and selecting the proper subject matter and teaching methods.

Although learning to know each pupil well is difficult, teachers have sources of information available that enable them to learn a great deal about each pupil. The most obvious source of information is, of course, the pupil's cumulative record folder. In addition, the teacher should be able to gather considerable data himself. To help him in his observation he has at his disposal such tools as problem inventories, anecdotal reports, behavior logs, sociometric devices, and autobiographies.

Diagnosis is extremely important in determining the status of pupils' academic abilities. Burton states that there are three levels of diagnosis: the general, the analytical, and the psychological. The first two may be carried out by the classroom teachers by means of observation and testing programs. Although diagnostic tests on the market are very useful, teachers can prepare many diagnostic devices themselves. Diagnostic tests, for instance, are simply tests carefully made for diagnostic purposes and so are suitable for analysis. Psychological diagnosis and testing, however, should be left to the experts of the guidance, psychological, and medical staff or to an educational clinic. Although it is helpful if the teacher can spot difficulties such as poor sight or hearing, almost always diagnosis at this level requires skills beyond the classroom teacher's competency.

The problem inventory, the behavior log, anecdotal reports, conferences with other teachers, using the sociogram, the autobiography, and having frequent individual conferences, are all ways of getting to know the pupil. Each teacher, then, must decide (1) what he should know about the pupil; (2) how he can get this information; (3) how he can use the information obtained. To avoid blocks of learning and to provide the sort of teaching best suited to the students, the teacher must be fully acquainted with the abilities, potentialities, goals, environmental influences, problems, and needs of each of them. For this reason he should make continuous use of diagnostic techniques. The devices and techniques listed above are examples of good ways of learning about the students, but the best way of all is to be sincerely interested in the pupils as people.

FOR FURTHER STUDY

BLAIR, GLENN MYERS, and WILLIAM POWELL, *Diagnostic and Remedial Teaching*, Third Edition (New York: The Macmillan Company, 1967).

BURTON, WILLIAM H., *The Guidance of Learning Activities*, Third Edition (New York: Appleton-Century-Crofts, Inc., 1962), Chs. 7–11, 21.

COLEMAN, J. S., *Adolescents and the Schools* (New York: Basic Books, 1965).

CUNNINGHAM, RUTH, *et al.*, *Understanding Group Behavior of Boys and Girls* (New York: Bureau of Publications, Teachers College, Columbia University, 1951).

GINZBERG, ELI, *Values and Ideals of American Youth* (New York: Columbia University Press, 1961).

JENNINGS, HELEN HALL, *Sociometry in Group Relations* (Washington, D.C.: American Council on Education, 1948).

JEWETT, ANN E., and CLYDE KNAPP, *The Growing Years*, 1962 Yearbook, American Association for Health, Physical Education and Recreation (Washington, D.C.: The National Education Association).

MacIVER, R. M. (editor), *Dilemmas of Youth* (New York: Harper and Row Publishers, 1961).

MALLERY, DAVID, *High School Students Speak Out* (New York: Harper and Row Publishers, 1962).

N.E.A. RESEARCH DIVISION, *Student Behavior in Secondary Schools 1964*, Research report 1965 R12 (Washington, D.C.: The National Education Association, 1965).

NATIONAL SOCIETY FOR THE STUDY OF EDUCATION, *Adapting the Secondary School Program to the Needs of Youth*, 1952 Yearbook, Part I (Chicago: University of Chicago Press, 1953).

NORDBERG, H. ORVILLE, JAMES M. BRADFIELD, and WILLIAM C. ODELL, *Secondary School Teaching* (New York: The Macmillan Company, 1962), Ch. 4.

ROOT, J. H., *et al.*, *Diagnostic Teaching, Methods and Materials* (Syracuse, N.Y.: Syracuse University Press, 1965).

ROTHNEY, JOHN W. M., *The High School Student* (New York: Holt, Rinehart and Winston, Inc., 1953).

ZAPF, ROSALIND M., *Democratic Processes in the Secondary Classroom* (Englewood Cliffs, N. J.: Prentice-Hall, Inc., 1959).

CHAPTER *3*

Motivation

The Need for Motivation

The human mind cannot absorb knowledge like a sponge. Neither is the mind a wax tablet upon which a teacher can write. Nor is it a lump of clay the teacher can mold into the shape desired. A person is not an inanimate object, but a very active one, and in order to learn, he must act. He may solve problems. He may read. He may listen to his teachers or to his fellow pupils. He may practice. He may do any of a hundred things. But if he is to learn, he must do *something*. No one can learn for him; he must learn himself.

In other words, he learns through his experiences. Each experience is an interaction with the environment. We learn from what the environment does to us and from what we do to the environment. The burned child learns from the effect of the environment on him, but the boy who solves a puzzle learns from his effect on the environment.

Not all experiences result in learning, however. After constant repetition, for example, an experience seldom produces much learning; neither do experiences which lack meaning or in which the learner is not paying attention. How many steps are there between the first and second floor of your home or your dormitory? How many chairs are there in a row in your classroom? The chances are that unless you have paid particular attention to these details, you do not know. Any experience may result in learning, but many do not.

Since this is so, somehow the teacher must get boys and girls to engage in activities that will result in the desired learnings. To do so he must arouse and enlist effective motives. This process is called motivation.

Blocks to Learning

EXCUSES FOR NOT LEARNING. Why is it that pupils so often fail to arrive at the state of learning we so earnestly desire for them? There are many reasons, of course. But all too often the reasons we blame are false ones, as the following examples point out.

"Eileen is the silliest girl you've ever seen. She never pays attention to a thing. She can't keep her mind on anything." (But watch her at the theater. Engrossed in dreamland she sits. Seemingly no commotion in the theater could draw her attention from the plot.)

"John is the stupidest boy I've ever seen." (Yet he was able to learn to read music and become the highly successful leader of his own orchestra.)

"Joe is the laziest boy in school. He just won't do a thing. I don't think he has finished one algebra assignment this year." (But think of the hours of hard physical and mental work he has spent putting together his hot-rod. His mother has a hard time getting him away from that car long enough to eat his dinner.)

Real Causes for Not Learning

These accusations, as we can see, do not explain pupils' not learning. They probably describe symptoms of the real causes. What are the real causes? Let us look at a few of them.

First and most important is poor teaching. Teaching is often ineffective, because it is inadequately planned or because it violates the laws of learning. Some courses are poorly organized and lack direction. Some classes are poorly motivated. In some courses the work is too hard or too easy. Some teachers attempt to cover the subject rapidly instead of giving it time to sink in. Some teachers ignore the fact that pupils are individuals with varying backgrounds, talents, and interests, and attempt to teach everyone the same material at the same rate in the same way.

The curriculum itself is often a major cause of nonlearning. Too much of what is taught in the secondary school has little bearing on the lives or needs of the pupils. At least one educational philosopher has come to the belief that probably half of the high-school curriculum could be dropped from the school program tomorrow without anyone's noticing its passing. Be that as it may, in truth, all too frequently high-school curricula do little to interest pupils or to prepare them for life today or in the future in any significant way. It is not surprising that for many pupils their studies seem too futile and dead-ended to be worth their exerting any real effort to learn them.

Poor teaching and poor courses probably cause most failures to learn, but they are not the only causes. Pupils are often handicapped by poor health, fatigue, physical or mental limitations, emotional difficulties, environmental factors, or family attitudes. If a pupil's parents and friends feel that studying a Shakespearean sonnet is a waste of time and money, it probably will not be easy to convince the youth that he should devote much time to it. Or again, a young person may believe, as did the poetess, in burning the candle at both ends. Although this practice may give "a lovely light," it is not helpful because fatigue hinders learning and too many interests distract pupils from the desired learnings.

These, then, are some of the blocks to learning. If the teacher is to do his job—helping pupils learn—the blocks must be overcome. Of course, the teacher is not always in a position in which he can do much to overcome them. But a good teacher will take each youngster and try, by using the best methods and materials he knows, to help the pupil learn what he should learn in spite of any obstacles. This is a key challenge of teaching. It is the heart of motivation.

WHAT MOTIVATION IS NOT. At this point, so as to allay any misapprehensions, it may be wise to point out what motivation is not. Motivation does not imply that pupils should do only those things that interest them or that teachers should always make classes enjoyable. Nothing could be farther from the truth. At times pupils must learn lessons and participate in activities that they dislike. It is not the teacher's job to get each pupil to like every subject or activity, although it would help if he could; it is rather to get the pupil to learn as well as he possibly can whether he likes it or not. In many a classroom the problem of how to motivate the pupils is by far the most pressing one to the teacher.

MOTIVATION AND ATTENTION SPAN. A common manifestation of the problem of motivation is the non-academically inclined youth who, the teachers say, has a short attention span. Such pupils are legion in our secondary schools. But the notion that they have short attention spans is a myth. Every normally healthy secondary-school youth within the normal range of intelligence has a long enough attention span when he is confronted by a situation interesting and challenging to him. Watch him at the movies or trying to learn the techniques of his favorite sport. The trouble is not that normal adolescent boys and girls have short attention spans, but that they have low tolerance to boredom. Naturally they find it hard to keep their minds on lessons they hate and to which they see no point.

When pupils find their classes interesting, exciting, and personally worthwhile, teachers have few problems because of short attention spans even among the least academically inclined pupils. That is why skillful speakers are able, by the use of striking illustrations and homely examples, to capture and hold the attention of listeners of all ages.

❋

What is motivation? What are its implications for teaching?

"Learning takes place only through activity." What does this mean? What are the implications for teaching?

What causes people to do things? List the reasons why you have done the more important things you have done today.

❋

How to Motivate Pupils

Pupils must be motivated if they are to learn, but how does one motivate them? Unfortunately, motivation is not always easy. No royal road to teaching exists; neither is there a sure-fire method of motivating young people. Techniques that work well in one situation may be useless in another. Incentives that enthuse some individuals in a class leave others completely indifferent. About all one can do is to point out that the teacher must try to create the desire to learn and to suggest principles and possible techniques for creating that desire. Therefore, in the next few pages we shall examine six principles of motivation.

1. Take advantage of the pupil's present motives.
2. Make the potential learnings seem worthwhile.
3. Help the pupil establish suitable tasks and objectives.
4. Keep up the pace.
5. Develop a receptive mood in the learner.
6. Cultivate in the learner ideals and attitudes conducive to learning.

Utilizing Present Motives

The Importance of Interest

Pupils undoubtedly learn more efficiently those things that interest them. Therefore, that teachers should try harnessing pupil interest as a means to effective teaching seems to be self evident. This doctrine of interest does not imply that the whims of pupils should determine the curriculum. It does imply that when possible the teacher should use pupil interests already established or, if suitable pupil interests are not established, the teacher should somehow create interest or the lesson will fail.

As we grow older most of us find it increasingly difficult to know and understand the interests of young people. The goals of youth are not the same as the goals of adults. Adults are sometimes shocked to find that what they feel ought to be of the utmost intrinsic value to all youth, seems to be quite worthless to young eyes. Even young adults find that what is intensely interesting and exciting to them at twenty-two may not find a single response in a group of fifteen-year-olds. For this reason the beginning teacher should make a point to find out the interests, attitudes, ideals, and goals of his pupils. Once he knows what his pupils think is important, he can adapt his motivational techniques accordingly. This information can be gathered by using the devices and techniques discussed in the previous chapter. In addition, the teacher may use

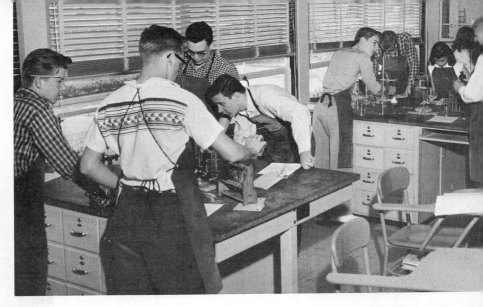

Activity and problem solving create interest. These pupils are anxious to see the results of their experiments.

devices designed specifically for the gathering of information about pupils' interests.

An example of such a device is the interest inventory. Through the use of such inventories, the alert teacher may gain insights into the reading interests and hobbies of his pupils. Such instruments may be devised by teachers quite easily. For example, one can build an "interest finder" by simply preparing a questionnaire of items designed to find out what the pupils' interests are, such as:

What is your favorite way of killing time?

If you could do anything you wanted to do, what would you want to do most?

What kind of movies or television programs do you like most?

Using Pupils' Attitudes and Ideals

Among the motives pupils bring to school are their ideals and attitudes. Insofar as he can, the teacher should attempt to harness such attitudes as cooperativeness, neatness, industry, fairness, courtesy, patriotism, and honesty, and utilize them in his teaching. A young person assigned to a group project role he does not particularly like might do his job well because the teacher has appealed to his cooperative attitude. Undoubtedly you can think of examples in your own school life in which you have performed downright distasteful tasks simply because an attitude or ideal told you that this was the thing to do under the circumstances.

Harnessing the Natural Motives

Every boy and girl comes to school with certain basic drives. These natural motives are often more powerful than any incentive the teacher can invent. The competent teacher is alert to these drives and uses them in his teaching, if he can. If he cannot utilize them, he at least strives to adapt his classwork so that it seldom conflicts directly with them.

One winter day an English teacher suddenly found the attention of his class leaving him. Something outside the window had stolen it away. A little irked, he looked out to see what the matter was. No wonder the class was diverted. A big gray cat was stalking a rabbit in the heavy snow. Stealthily, the cat sneaked up on the rabbit and just as he seemed to be within range and ready to pounce on his prey, the rabbit hopped out of reach. Undaunted, the stubborn cat tried again and again, but the deep snow prevented him from closing in. Few English literature classes can compete with such real life melodrama. In this instance, the teacher allowed the class to watch the struggle for a while and then dispatched someone to chase the animals away—ostensibly to save the life of the rabbit, although after a few minutes of watching it was obvious that the rabbit was in no danger. By doing this, the teacher avoided competing with the pupils' natural curiosity. Perhaps he could have harnessed this curiosity and interest by diverting the class to a discussion of the incident and tying it up with literature—plot, incident, suspense, conflict, characterization—or possibly he could have encouraged pupils to turn the incident into a bit of creative writing. Certainly he was wise not to attempt to continue with his original plan in the face of this strong natural motive.

Incidents like the above are not commonplace, but still it is typical of the kinds of incidents that bring into play strong natural motives. Let us look at a much more prosaic example. In a social studies class one morning the juniors were all upset because they had had a most interesting and exciting speaker on Russia at assembly. However, because some faculty members dominated the discussion, the students had not had a chance to ask the speaker their questions. So, rather than go on with his prepared lesson, the teacher took time to discuss their questions, in this way easing their frustration and taking advantage of their interest.

＊

The English teacher's predicament, although an actual incident, was very unusual. The second example is quite commonplace. Perhaps you can think of more commonplace examples of natural motives interrupting the normal course of learning. Have there been any instances in your college classes when the teaching has been hampered by the natural motivation of the students? What, if anything, did the instructor do? What might he have done?

✻

CAPITALIZING ON PUPIL CURIOSITY. People are naturally curious. Watch a little child examine things. Listen to him asking questions: Why? Why? Why? This curiosity abides in adults also and it is probably just as strong. Witness the crowds that gather whenever there is an accident. If teachers can capitalize on the curiosity of youth, the youngsters will do their schoolwork more eagerly because they want to find out. This is an important type of motivation.

The use of suspense gives us an example of a technique by which the teacher takes advantage of this innate drive—curiosity. Suspense catches and holds the pupils because they want to find out the ending. Everyone has sat through poor movies and bad television shows because he wanted to see how they came out. In such circumstances, because the author has kept us in suspense, we stay on to the end in spite of our better judgment. In the same manner, teachers who can create a feeling of suspense in the classroom can arouse the pupils' curiosity and hold their interest.

A student teacher in a general science class performed an experiment in which he attempted to demonstrate the power of air pressure by creating a vacuum in a large can. He first talked to the pupils telling them what he intended to do, and asked them what they thought would happen when he created the vacuum. Several theories were proposed, of course; among them the theory that the pressure of the atmosphere would "smash the can." "All right," he said, "let's see if the atmosphere can crush the can." He then heated some water in the can filling it full of steam. Capping the steam-filled can he said, "O.K., now let us see what happens." An air of intense expectancy hung over the classroom as the eighth-graders stared at the can. Suddenly one yelled, "There it goes," as the can slowly started to crumble. In a few minutes the class was off on a lively discussion of what had "smashed the can." By harnessing the natural appeal of curiosity, through the medium of suspense, the teacher had aroused the class to productive activity.

SOCIAL APPROVAL, SELF-ESTEEM, AND THE DESIRE FOR SUCCESS. Quite often praise and rewards spur us on to heights when we might otherwise rest on our laurels. Everyone wants to feel that he is important and respected by his friends and associates. This is particularly true of adolescents who sometimes will do almost anything to win approval. All of us want to be proud of ourselves. We desire and need success in order to build up our self-esteem and the approval of the group. No one wants to be a failure. For this reason the competent teacher gives his pupils plenty of opportunity to preen their feathers. He does his best to find something to praise in even the least successful of them. Recognition of one's success by others is most enjoyable. When this recognition takes a tangible form, it is usually even more enjoyable.

NEED FOR SECURITY.   Any threat to a young person's security makes learning a more difficult problem. For this reason one should probably avoid the use of fear as a classroom motivational device even though fear is one of the most powerful of motives.

The frightened person cannot think well. When intensely afraid he may become completely disorganized. Constant worry, a milder form of fear, may lead to mental and emotional idiosyncrasies if not to actual illness. Youths have fears and worries enough without our creating more. Fear should be saved for such important things as life and death situations, for example, preventing young people from driving too fast, or little children from crossing the highway alone.

It is for these reasons that the overuse and overemphasis on tests and marks should be discouraged. Also to be avoided are class recitations in which pupils are shamed if they answer incorrectly. Ignorance is not a crime to be punished. Overharsh attitudes keep pupils from trying their best and tend to make pupils who do try rigid so that they cannot think their best.

*

What does psychology tell us about the effect of praise, reproof, rewards, and punishment upon learning? What are the implications for teaching?

Should emulation, competition, and rivalry be used to motivate classroom learning? What are the advantages and disadvantages of each?

Evaluate the following as motivating techniques: sarcasm, ridicule, fear.

*

DESIRE FOR ADVENTURE AND ACTION.   Paradoxically, the need for security is accompanied by a desire for action, adventure, and excitement. This often causes youngsters to take chances that seem to belie their desire for security. Often the adventurer finds his security by seeking his adventure in groups and by soliciting the approval and admiration of his peers for his adventuresomeness. The teacher would do well to feature activities and materials that have plenty of excitement and action at least part of the time. In the junior-high-school grades teachers sometimes use competitive games to give excitement to practice and drill lessons. Alert history and English teachers can utilize stories of adventure to stimulate their classes. History is full of heroic adventures by heroic men. Teachers would do well to harness the exploits of such men as George Washington, Zebulon Pike, Lewis and Clark, Coronado, and Daniel Boone to furnish their history courses with excitement and high adventure.

DESIRE TO PLAY AND HAVE FUN. Enjoying oneself is a prominent goal in every person's life. We all need to play and amuse ourselves— even the hypochondriac who enjoys poor health. This motive is closely akin to the need for action, adventure, and excitement. The ordinary class abounds with opportunities to use games—an example is the use of pseudo-baseball games in drill activities. Another example of making a dull activity fun was that used in a mid-term test in a college course in German. The test was given just prior to the annual fall dance weekend. The test consisted largely of translating a hilarious account of the *Tanzwochende* to come and all the fun the *Mädchen* and *Knaben* were to have. The test was fun and many of the students found it enjoyable— if a mid-term test can ever be described as enjoyable.

THE NEED FOR FRIENDSHIPS. Youths are gregarious. One of the most powerful natural drives is the desire for friendship. Any attempt to keep boys and girls quietly working by themselves in a crowded classroom for long periods of time is against the laws of nature. Capable teachers will usually refrain from making such periods overly long and will not be too harsh on boys and girls who feel the need for conversing with their friends. Youth's gregariousness and friendships can be of considerable help to the able teacher—especially in grouping and in conducting group activities. Means of determining and profiting from natural groups and friendships in one's teaching are explored further in Chapters 2 and 11.

To have friends is exceedingly important for adolescents but most important of all perhaps are the heterosexual friendships which begin to form at this stage of life. Sex and the desire for one's own home are basic drives. Their power and importance should not be underestimated. It is too much, for instance, to expect a pretty girl to concentrate on Ohm's Law when she has a complexion problem the day before the junior prom.

Heterosexual interests also have some bearing on the type of subject matter and activities selected for a class. This drive does not play the same role in the lives of seventh-graders that it does in the lives of twelfth-graders. Romantic literature may have little meaning to a seventh-grade boy, but it may be of major importance to his older sister. The teacher should bear in mind the sex and age of his pupils in selecting the activities and materials of instruction.

Making Learning Worthwhile

Teacher Attitudes and Motivation

If a teacher wants his pupils to feel that the learnings of his course are valuable, he must feel so himself. The teacher who is sincerely enthusiastic about his subject is a much better salesman than the teacher bored by his own course. Some teachers' enthusiasm is hard to resist. Before the pupils realize it they begin to catch the teacher's spirit—sometimes in spite of themselves. Of course, enthusiasm alone will not fire up every member of the class, but it helps. No one should teach a subject he does not like.

One of the most successful teachers of English the authors ever knew was a literature enthusiast. One had only to sit in his class a minute to know that literature was important to him. His enthusiasm was infectious. It was hard to leave his classroom without feeling the fascination of literature. Moreover, he had the habit of selecting things to read and handing them to a pupil with such comment as, "You know, here's a story I bet you'll enjoy. It is about . . . . . Why don't you read it and tell me how you liked it?" Even his supervisor was not immune from his blandishments; frequently he left the classroom with an assignment. This teacher's eagerness and enthusiasm trapped pupils into wanting to read literature.

This same teacher also used effectively a technique which combined his enthusiasm for literature with an appeal to curiosity. With all the proper histrionic effects he would start to read a story to the class. Then, at a crucial point, he would stop to ask questions which could be answered only by completing the story. Often the pupils could hardly wait to turn to their books to find the answers.

The Importance of Pupil Values

Once a pupil is convinced that learning is vital he is usually willing to work to acquire it. It is well known that some pupils see little value in much of their school work and find it difficult to arouse much enthusiasm for their tasks. The teacher should try to make his classes seem worthwhile to all of his pupils. Unless the pupils think their lessons are worthwhile, their participation will be only grudging, no matter how valuable the lessons really are.

IMMEDIATE VALUES AND DEFERRED VALUES. If a pupil really wants to learn something, he will usually attempt to learn it at once. If he thinks that he would like to know something about the matter when he grows up, he is apt to turn to other problems which seem more immediate to him. Whenever possible, the teacher should make the pupils aware of the immediate values of his lessons if he hopes to raise their motivation to a high pitch. This can often be done by centering the classwork around everyday concerns of pupils, by including current issues in the school and community, by pointing out how the classroom learning may be used in other classes and activities, and by consciously attempting to tie the lessons to the present attitudes and interests of pupils. For example, in a mathematics class one might use graphs to illustrate problems being studied in the social studies class, or the study of percentages might be related to the standings of the major-league baseball teams. Such techniques are much more likely to succeed in setting pupils to work than exhortations to "study because you will need to know it in college."

SOMETHING SUITABLE FOR EVERYONE. What we know about individual differences tells us that boys and girls are not all interested in the same things. This variety may give spice to life, but it also complicates the motivating of a class of adolescents. We want our classes to seem worthwhile to the pupils in order that the pupils will work at high levels. But what one pupil finds worthwhile another may find a waste of time. What is the answer? Obviously the way out is to provide sufficient types of activities and materials so that everyone finds something interesting and worthwhile.

Pupils' notions of what is worthwhile are, of course, constantly subject to change. Consequently, teachers can frequently convince pupils that their assignments are truly worthwhile by simply presenting convincing arguments. But merely stating that so and so is important, or will be important, is not enough; the teacher should be prepared to show why. For example, one day a young beginning teacher asked his supervisor what he should do when his seventh-graders asked him why they should learn the names of the different climatic zones in their geography. "Why, tell them, of course," was the answer. "Yes," he said, "but I can't think of any reason for their learning them myself." If the teacher does not know why a certain learning is worthwhile, how can he expect a boy or girl to make the effort necessary to learn it?

＊

How would you have answered the seventh-grade geographers?
Can you justify teaching your major fields?
Go through a textbook you might use in your teaching. How can you make this material seem worthwhile to a group of teen-agers? Why is it worthwhile?

＊

INTRINSIC AND EXTRINSIC VALUES.   Any particular learning seems worthwhile to a pupil if it has either intrinsic or extrinsic value for him. If the learning is valuable enough to cause the pupil to act, he is acting because of its intrinsic value. This is intrinsic motivation. An example of intrinsic motivation is learning to drive a car. Most young people learn to drive because knowing how to drive has intrinsic value to them.

Some learnings seem to have no intrinsic value to the pupil although they have an extrinsic one, i.e., the learner sees relatively little value in the learning itself but does see value in what the learning may get him. An example of this may be the case of the youth who learns geometric theorems because he wishes to earn an A in the course or because his father has promised him a prize if he learns them. Here the goal is not the learning itself but something that can be obtained through the learning. Such goals are called incentives. They are really ulterior motives for undertaking activities otherwise not worth doing. Ordinarily, we should prefer that boys and girls do their schoolwork because of its intrinsic value to them. When this proves impossible or impractical, the teacher should use incentives that will create the desired response.

MARKS AS INCENTIVES.   The incentive most frequently used in our schools is the school mark. That it should have become so important is most unfortunate because in many classes the only thing that matters is the mark. When this happens, too much stress on the incentive has defeated the purpose of education.

The mark has equally failed as a motivating force for the nonacademic, noncollege bound pupils. Because they know they won't do well and because they suspect that their marks will never really have much influence on their lives, many of these young people could not possibly care less about school marks. To them good marks are unattainable and not very desirable. Even to the average pupil they are not a very sharp goad. Their only effect seems to be to arouse spasmodic bursts of effort to cram in as much knowledge as possible during certain periods of stress.

Teacher-Pupil Planning and Motivation

What a person elects to do himself usually interests him more than something imposed by someone else. At least, he is likely to think it is more interesting and is, therefore, more willing to start it. Consequently, boys and girls who plan their own activities may begin them more willingly than the pupils who do not. This gives the teacher a considerable advantage. If he can capitalize on this start, quite often the enthusiasm will carry on throughout the study of the topic or activity. The capable teacher will encourage pupil participation in the selection of topics and activities in order to capitalize on their motivational value.

Establishing Suitable Objectives

The Need for an Objective

If lessons are to seem worthwhile, the teacher should have a definite goal. Furthermore, the pupils should know approximately what this goal is and why it is important. *To become enthusiastic about a lesson when you don't know what you are about to learn or why you should learn it is most difficult.*

As a matter of fact, the pupil always participates in the selection of his own objectives. Everything he does is instigated by the occasion, by self-instruction, or by instruction from another. As a result of one of these influences, or a combination of them, the pupil elects to do something. That is to say, he establishes a task. This task is his objective. It may be considerably different from what the teacher had in mind. However, the teacher's role is to provide situations in which the pupil will select, or accept, tasks that will help him toward the learning desired. The teacher can do so through the use of directions and assignments.

The Assignment As a Motivating Device

A famous professor of education used to remark that boys and girls usually would be glad to do their schoolwork if they could only figure out what the teacher wanted them to do. There is more than a germ of truth in this statement. Most of us have been in classes in which we did not know what to do. This fault is all too common. When the teacher finds his pupils are not doing their assignments but instead are crying, "I did not know, I had no book," and the like, he should check his directions. As often as not the fault lies in the assignment. If teachers hope to keep pupils working, they must be sure their assignments are definite, the directions clear, and the materials available.

In the past the assignment has been almost synonymous with homework. In many classrooms, even today, the assignment consists of a hurried shout at the end of the period—often drowned out by the clamor of the bell and the scuffling of feet eager to be on their way. Today one should think of a good assignment in a different way. An assignment is a job to be done, whether at home or in class. It may be assigned by the teacher or arrived at through the cooperative effort of both teacher and pupils. No matter who prepares the assignment it should serve the following purposes.

1. Set the direction of study and outline the scope of the task.
2. Motivate the pupil and prepare him for the task.
3. Help the learner to the means for accomplishing his task, i.e., establish possible methods and materials.
4. Adapt the tasks to the needs of the various pupils.

Thus the assignment is an essential factor in motivation and a basic part of any lesson. Let us look at these functions briefly.

THE FUNCTIONS OF THE ASSIGNMENT. The first purpose of the assignment is *to set the direction and the scope of the task*. It is almost impossible to do anything unless one knows what to do. The purpose of the assignment is to make each pupil's task clear and definite to him. Some teachers tell the pupils just what is to be done. Others develop the task cooperatively with the group. In either case, however, the teacher should try to make sure that each and every pupil knows exactly what his task is. In case of a problem, for instance, the teacher must be sure that the pupils understand the problem, that the problem is well enough defined to be manageable, and that the pupils know how to go about solving it.

An example: Let us suppose that the class had just completed studying the Civil War period and is ready to go on to study the Reconstruction period. Let us further assume that as a result of class discussion the class had decided that they wanted to know the answer to some of the following questions:

After the war was over, how did the Confederate states get back into the Union?
How did the Southerners feel about the North? And vice versa?
If much of the South was destroyed, as by Sherman in his march to the sea, how did the people live in the South after the war?
What happened to the slaves?
What happened to the Confederate soldiers?

These questions could lead a group of students into all sorts of problems. These are not easy problems. Books have been devoted to them. On the other hand, impatient, subject-centered, ground-covering teachers often have tried to answer each of them summarily in a few sentences. If these questions are to serve as a basis for future study they must be delimited.

In any case, the assignment must be clear and definite before it is finally made. Probably it is best to reduce it to writing. Short assignments may be placed on the chalkboard. Longer assignments should be duplicated. Written assignments minimize pupils' forgetting what it is they were going to do. Also, setting the assignment down helps lessen chances for misunderstandings—both on the part of the pupil and the teacher—of what the task is.

The second function of the assignment is *to prepare the pupils for the job to be done.* This preparation includes supplying the background material the pupils need before starting the new task and providing for adequate motivation. Since the assignment determines what is to be done, it is particularly important in motivation. It is during the assigning that the teacher makes sure that the pupil knows why he should do this job and that the reasons for doing it are worthwhile.

Not only should the assignment make clear what is to be done, and motivate the pupil to attempt the task, but *it also must point out to him how to do it.* This is the third function of the assignment. Although teachers should avoid spoon-feeding the pupils, they should also be sure that each pupil knows how to go about his task. If it is a job of studying through reading, the key words should be pointed out, and suggestions concerning what to look for should be made. In other words, the teacher should try to be sure that the pupils know how to use the methods and materials available to them.

Thus, if in a history class the teacher wants the pupils to prepare a map exercise in which they map the boundaries of the grants made to the London and Plymouth Companies by King James in the charter of 1606, he needs to make sure that the pupils understand what they have to do, that they know how to plot latitude and longitude on a map, and that they can read the charter provisions. To prepare for their assignment he might well have to devote a half period to a review of map reading and another to the close reading of the charter as preparation for the assignment.

The fourth function of the good assignment is *to provide every pupil with a task appropriate for him.* It is hard to prove any subject matter is truly essential except as it meets the needs of youngsters. If this is true, any assignment which places subject matter above the individual differences of the youngsters is of doubtful validity.

THE MARKS OF A GOOD ASSIGNMENT.   What, then, are the marks of a good assignment? The following list will suggest some criteria for evaluating an assignment.

1. Is it worthwhile?
2. Does it seem worthwhile to the pupil? In other words, does it capitalize on pupil interest or create pupil interest?
3. Is it clear?
4. Is it definite?
5. Does it provide for the differences in pupils—i.e., their different aptitudes, abilities, and interests?

6. Is it reasonable as far as length and difficulty are concerned?
7. Does it show the pupil how to go about it? Does it suggest methods and materials which may be used profitably?
8. Does it provide the pupil with the background necessary for completing the assignment satisfactorily, e.g., vocabulary?

＊

Use these criteria to judge assignments given in your college courses.

Do your college assignments perform the functions assignments should perform? If they fail, in what ways do they fail?

A student teacher's assignment to his United States history class was, "Read pages 184–297 for tomorrow." In what way is this assignment deficient?

＊

MAKING THE ASSIGNMENT. In order to make an effective assignment, the teacher must take time to develop it sufficiently. Even for a short assignment the teacher will ordinarily need to allow at least ten minutes for his presentation. The use of one or more entire periods is not unusual. In fact, to develop properly a long-term assignment or a unit assignment in less than a period is virtually impossible, particularly if the assignment is developed by the teacher and class cooperatively.

It matters little whether the assignment is developed at the beginning, middle, or end of a period as long as the teacher allows time enough to do the job properly and makes sure that the assignment fits into that spot naturally. To be most effective, the presenting of the assignment should probably immediately precede the task to be done. Homework assignments should be presented at the propitious moment in the lesson when the content of the lesson is most suitable as a background for making the assignment.

Motivating by Means of Problems

Pupils are seldom interested in work that is too easy and that they already know. The teacher should try to challenge every pupil to do his best. Problem solving is particularly useful in challenging the interests of boys and girls. From time immemorial people have loved to try to solve problems. Challenging problems appeal to the natural drives of activity, success, and curiosity. They are effective motivating devices.

＊

It has been stated that marks, prizes, and punishment are poor motivating devices for school use. Why do some authorities take this position? Do you agree? Defend your position.

What techniques might a teacher use to induce pupils to adopt goals that will lead to the learnings desired by the teacher? Consider such things as

teacher talks and lectures	demonstrations
field trips	suspense
moving pictures	problem raising
stories	quizzes and tests
dramatizations	

Criticize some of the assignments given to you in your college work. How could they have been improved?

✽

Keeping up the Pace

Necessity for Lively Learning

Once a class is interested, the teacher must be constantly alert to keep the class free from dead spots. A dragging class can kill all the enthusiasm of the most eager group of pupils. Dull classes lead to wool-gathering and switching of attention and interests to other less desirable activities and goals. In every meeting of every class the pupils should feel that the class is going somewhere important. They should also feel a certain amount of pressure, however light, to exert themselves to go along too.

PARTICIPATING IN ONE'S OWN LEARNING. Learning may be its own reward. Learning is always emotionally tinged and usually quite gratifying to the learner. The opening up of new vistas and the excitement of new ideas and skills and the sheer involvement in the learning process can catch the young person up in the excitement of intellectual attainment. For many of us the intellectual experience alone is enough to keep us working diligently all the rest of our lives. It is important that we teachers give the pupils opportunities to really participate in true learning experiences. When we do, we give the pupils a chance to share the emotional experience that Keats had "On First Looking Into Chapman's Homer."

> Then felt I like some watcher of the skies
>   When a new planet swims into his ken;
> Or like stout Cortez when with eagle eyes
>   He stared at the Pacific—and all his men
> Look'd at each other with a wild surmise—
>   Silent, upon a peak in Darien.

Such experiences make learning worthwhile; for the person who has a real chance "to participate in his own learning" these experiences are rather frequent occurrences. Many scholars derive their greatest motivation from their involvement in the learning. Fresh ideas and fresh insights really make life exciting.

A VARIETY OF LEARNING ACTIVITIES. Although it is probably true that too much variety in method and activities may sometimes confuse the learner, it is just as true that the same activity or same kind of activity repeated endlessly usually bores him. In order to keep interest at a high level, the teacher should change his methods from time to time. Especially helpful are such interest-catching devices as vivid illustrations, audiovisual aids, field trips, demonstrations, dramas, and television programs.

Humdrum recitations with their continual repetition of boring answers to boring questions day after day after day should be avoided.

LIVELY ACTIVITIES RATHER THAN PASSIVE ACTIVITIES. Pupils are naturally active. They do not relish sitting still all day. Because they enjoy doing things, activities in which they can actively participate interest them. Moreover, once they are actively participating, their interest is much more easily kept at a high level. Witness the difference between the lecture and a workshop or laboratory. Quite often, the very persons who anxiously wait for the bell in lecture classes do not know when to stop in a workshop or laboratory situation. To keep motivation high, teachers should use such activities to the optimum.

Challenging but Not Discouraging Work

One way to keep up the pace is to see that the work is challenging but not discouraging. Some boys and girls do not do their schoolwork well because it does not challenge them. This is particularly true of the bright pupils. Youth wants to test itself. It wants to fly high. Boys and girls do not want baby work. An industrial arts teacher, for instance, was having trouble with discipline. This was not surprising because the class consisted largely of troublemakers, who were impatiently awaiting their sixteenth birthdays. Yet the problem was largely teacher caused. In an attempt to make the instruction fit the needs of these boys, the teacher had devised a course in home mechanics. The activities of this course consisted of such things as puttying windows, changing fuses, and the like. These activities were not interesting and provided no challenge. When the teacher switched to assigning more challenging activities, his discipline problems abated considerably.

Knowledge of One's Own Progress

Knowing how one is getting along also tends to keep one on his toes. Pupils like to know how they are progressing. Knowledge of one's progress makes it possible to reform one's goals and take further strides ahead. Nothing succeeds like success. The knowledge that one has accomplished a certain amount is often sufficient cause to go further—with renewed vigor. To make the most of this phenomenon teachers should try to see that pupils understand and appreciate their own achievement.

❊

Why is it that youngsters in laboratory-type classes seem to be more interested in their studies than pupils in other classes?

What activities might you use to keep a class in a subject in your field moving rapidly?

Some authors say that the lecture should not be used in secondary schools. What is your opinion? Why?

❊

Creating a Receptive Mood

A Principle of Salesmanship

Quintilian, the Roman teacher of rhetoric, once remarked that harsh discipline raises resentment which is transferred to the subject matter. He was right. Therefore, for the sake of good motivation, harsh, restrictive, disciplinary measures, unpleasant teaching methods, and anything else that may cause dislike and antagonism should be avoided. Remember that you are trying to sell a valuable commodity. People who dislike you, your product, and your store will not buy from you. Of course, punishment can also motivate, but it should seldom be used for classroom motivation because it tends to create an atmosphere of surly, sullen repression. In such an atmosphere pupils' work is usually half-hearted. Since the object of teaching is learning, we need to find a more efficient motivating device than punishment. Still, boys and girls must learn that if they misbehave or neglect their work they must suffer the consequences. Occasionally, the teacher will have to use negative measures to make these points clear. Poor papers should be redone. Neglected responsibilities should lead to loss of privileges. Undone work should be made up —perhaps in after school hours or detention periods, or even, on occasion, next term as a repeater. Such treatment should always be fair, just, reasonable, and preceded by fair warning.

That a customer must be put in a receptive mood is almost axiomatic among salesmen. As Risk has suggested, it is not often that we find salesmen who try to sell their products by insulting the customers.[1] So it is

[1] Thomas M. Risk, *Principles and Practices of Teaching in Secondary Schools,* Third Edition (New York: American Book Company, 1958), pp. 324–327.

A friendly, permissive class atmosphere aids in motivation.

with teaching. What we are after is to get learning across to the pupils. To make the learning or the learner disagreeable is unrealistic. Perhaps making your subject pleasant may seem to be "sugarcoating" it. If so, remember that it is the learning that counts. *Any method or device, within reason, that you can use to expedite learning is legitimate.* If to expedite learning one must "sugarcoat" the subject, then do not spare the sugar.

"The Pleasant House"

One method of placing your customers in a receptive mood is to provide a pleasant environment. It is axiomatic that boys and girls (and for that matter men and women) work better in pleasant surroundings. A dark, dirty, repressive atmosphere seems to hold back the average person. In a bright, cheerful atmosphere pupils are more likely to become interested in their school work and perform it conscientiously. A bright atmosphere tends to remove the tensions which so often hold back the learning process. Therefore, the teacher should strive for a pleasant classroom. It may be that he can do little about the classroom's decor, although he can usually help that considerably, but he can do much for the spirit of the pupils by eliminating overseriousness in the classroom. Learning is not necessarily solemn. People learn better in a happy frame of mind. Laughter, fun, humor, cooperation, pleasantness, and politeness all go to make the classroom a happy place. Vittorino da Feltre, the great Renaissance schoolmaster, called his school "The Pleasant House." As part of our motivational technique we should strive to make our schools "Pleasant Houses."

Cultivating Desirable Attitudes and Ideals

Earlier in the chapter an attempt was made to show how one might harness the pupils' attitudes and ideals. Fortunately for the teacher, attitudes and ideals are acquired, or learned, characteristics. Since this is so, it is possible to teach pupils new attitudes and ideals and change old ones. Teachers have frequently been able to convince pupils that what seemed to be a complete bore is really fascinating. Therefore, the teacher should do his best to create and cultivate attitudes and ideals that foster learning.

✽

What pupil attitudes and ideals would be desirable aids to classroom motivation? How might you use them? How might you develop them?

A certain teacher says that it is impossible to teach her pupils anything because of the no-failure policy of the school. The supervisor says that the teacher is merely excusing her ability to make her teaching interesting. React to these statements.

Prepare a list of motivational devices for possible use in a class you expect to teach.

✽

Summary

Motivation is too important in the teaching-learning process to be left to chance. Only pupils who are well motivated learn well. Fortunately all normal youth are potentially motivatable. The legend about their having short attention spans is a myth. Once their interest is aroused, their attention spans are long enough.

Since each teacher has a valuable commodity to sell to sometimes unwilling clients, it is important that he find a way to motivate them. If he can do so by positive means, the chances of successfully teaching his students will be greatly enhanced. Unfortunately, such positive motivation does not always come naturally. More frequently than not, the teacher must convince reluctant pupils of the value of his wares and create in them an inclination to buy. For this purpose the teacher has many tools and techniques at his command. One of them is to harness as far as possible the pupil's natural motives, such as his curiosity, his attitudes and ideals, his desire for success, self esteem, and security, his love of fun, adventure and action, and his need for friendship. Another method is to try to make the subject matter seem valuable to the pupil.

Perhaps the best way to do this is to really believe in the material's importance yourself. In this connection one should remember that pupils are more likely to be moved by immediate rather than deferred, and intrinsic rather than extrinsic values. Because people respond differently to things, individual motivation may be forwarded by making adequate provisions for individual differences. Marks have not proved to be adequate motivating devices for most boys and girls; teacher-pupil planning has been somewhat more successful.

Perhaps the best motivating device is a clear, definite, reasonable assignment. A good assignment serves the following functions.

1. It sets the direction of study and outlines the scope of the task.
2. It motivates the pupil and prepares him for the task.
3. It helps the learner to the means for accomplishing his task; that is, it establishes possible methods and materials.
4. It adapts the tasks to the needs of the various pupils.

If the assignments are good and the class proceeds at a lively pace in a friendly atmosphere, a teacher can expect relatively little "customer resistance," especially if the assignments let the pupils feel the thrill of "participating in their own learning," and "creating their own knowledge." If, in addition, a teacher engenders and cultivates in his pupils attitudes and ideals favorable to learning, his efforts should be well rewarded.

FOR FURTHER STUDY

ASCHNER, MARY JANE, and CHARLES E. BISH, *Productive Thinking in Education* (Washington, D.C.: The National Education Association, 1965), Part Two.

Association for Supervision and Curriculum Development, *Perceiving, Behaving, Becoming*, 1962 Yearbook (Washington, D.C.: The Association, 1962).

BURTON, WILLIAM H., *The Guidance of Learning Activities*, Third Edition (New York: Appleton-Century-Crofts, Inc., 1962), pp. 54–69.

FRYMIER, JACK R., "A Study of Students' Motivation to do Good Work in School," *The Journal of Educational Research* (January, 1964), 57: 239–244.

MOULY, GEORGE J., *Psychology for Effective Teaching* (New York: Holt, Rinehart and Winston, Inc., 1960), Ch. 10.

National Society for the Study of Education, *Learning and Instruction*, Forty-ninth Yearbook, Part I (Chicago: The University of Chicago Press, 1950), Ch. 2.

————, *Theories of Learning and Instruction*, The Sixty-third Yearbook, Part I (Chicago: The University of Chicago Press, 1964), Chs. 8–9.

PASSOW, A. HARRY, editor, *Nurturing Individual Potential* (Washington, D.C.: Association for Supervision and Curriculum Development, 1964).

RIVLIN, HARRY N., *Teaching Adolescents in Secondary Schools,* Second Edition (New York: Appleton-Century-Crofts, Inc., 1961), Ch. 3.

TOWNSEND, EDWARD ARTHUR, and PAUL J. BURKE, *Learning for Teachers* (New York: The Macmillan Company, 1962), Chs. 2–7.

TRAVERS, ROBERT M. W., *Essentials of Learning* (New York: The Macmillan Company, 1963), Ch. 5.

WELLINGTON, C. BURLEIGH, and JEAN WELLINGTON, *Teaching for Critical Thinking* (New York: McGraw-Hill Book Company, 1960), Ch. 5.

CHAPTER *4*

Discipline

The Perennial Problem

Discipline has always been a problem for teachers. In the last century many schoolmasters controlled their classes by might. So long as a teacher could lick any boy in the class, he could maintain discipline. If he was not up to a fight, as often as not the "scholars" would run him out of town. Certainly such was the case with the Hoosier Schoolmaster in nineteenth-century Indiana.[1] Discipline was also a problem in eighteenth-century England. In those days when caning was king and when Headmaster Keate of Eton obtained control by assembling the entire school to see the sixth form flogged, many of the famed public schools were rocked by student rebellions. In fact, on at least one occasion, the master had to call in the troops to rescue the school from the boys.

As a rule, of course, teachers of the twentieth century do not rely on fisticuffs or call in the militia in order to establish classroom control, but many teachers still find good discipline difficult to maintain. Most new teachers find it their major problem. Many experienced teachers are no less concerned with it. It is one of the most frequent causes for teachers' failing and leaving the profession.

Good Discipline

Nowadays our concept of the well-disciplined class has changed. Not many years ago the basic criterion was quietness. One could literally hear a pin drop. Some teachers and principals still believe silence to be a *sine qua non,* but, on the whole, modern thinking has adopted a more reasonable point of view. In the modern classroom the atmosphere is likely to be less repressed than in the classes of our ancestors. The amount of freedom varies with the type of instruction of course. Lectures and demonstrations require a high degree of quiet attentiveness; work sessions

[1] Edward Eggleston, *The Hoosier Schoolmaster,* a famous novel first printed in 1871 and well worth reading today to get the flavor of our profession a century ago.

and laboratory classes are likely to be buzzing with free activity. Accordingly, in the modern classes one may find some boys and girls talking quietly to each other about their work while others are moving about the classroom on one errand or another and still others are working alone at their desks. The scene is like that in a large office or business enterprise in which it seems as though everything was happening at once. At first glance it may seem confusing; yet all the activities are purposive—all aimed at getting a job done. So it is with the modern class. In comparison with classes of an earlier age the modern classroom may seem noisy and confused. But the seeming confusion is purposive—the many activities are all directed at the same goal. The noise is the whirring of the classroom machinery at work.

This changing concept of classroom discipline has led some neophytes to believe that order is not necessary. Nothing could be further from the truth. The classroom is a place for learning. Any disturbance which prevents or hinders learning is unpardonable. Orderliness is a "must." The difference between the classroom of today and that of yesterday is in the type of order. The teacher in today's ideal classroom tries to emphasize courtesy, cooperation, and self-control. Instead of the complete totalitarianism of some traditional teachers, who were in every sense dictators, the ideal modern class stresses the freedoms of democracy. The class is free from fear. The pupils are citizens of the class, not subjects of the teacher. Their job is to cooperate for the common good, to obey the laws of their classroom democracy, and to respect and obey proper authority. Their role in class is similar to our own as citizens of our country. Perhaps, on the whole, today's adolescents take their roles more seriously and are more law-abiding than adults.

✿

What is good discipline? How can you tell a well-ordered classroom? How much freedom should there be in a classroom?

✿

Causes of Misbehavior

Many Causes for Each Incident

Each individual case of misbehavior ordinarily has many causes. Seldom is any one motive the sole cause of any particular action, good or bad. What is it that makes a normally pleasant youth rebel toward the end of the last period on a sunny June day? Let us look at the possibilities.

A certain young man has been sitting in a hot classroom for almost an entire class period. For much of that time the sun has been shining into his eyes because of a broken window shade. This is the last period and he has had no food for several hours. He is tired, hot, and hungry. His head is beginning to ache. The class is deadly dull. All period long the class has been reviewing subject matter detail by answering questions. Around and around the class go the questions. What are the properties of chlorine? What is the formula for sulfuric acid? What is oxidation? The pupils do not seem to know the answers very well, and this exasperates the teacher. As each pupil fails to get an answer, the teacher berates him and threatens him with dire results on the examination for which they are reviewing. The glumness of the class increases. Our young man's mind wanders. He watches the freight train going down the track toward New York and counts the cars. Then he falls to dreaming about the new phonograph records he plans to add to his collection. Suddenly he hears his name.

"I am sorry Mr. ——, I did not understand the question."

"You would have understood it all right if you had been listening. How do you ever expect me to get you thick-headed nincompoops ready for this examination if you don't pay attention? I asked you, who was Lavoisier?"

At the moment our young man hasn't the slightest idea and mutters something to that effect in an undertone.

"What did you say? What are you muttering?"

Goaded beyond repair our young man blurts out, "I said I don't know and I don't care."

And then the sky falls. Who can say what caused the pupil to blow up? The heat, the sun, the headache, the hunger, the poor teaching, the boredom, the woolgathering, the teacher's exasperation, the nagging, the abuse? All these things contributed, with perhaps many others we do not know of. Almost every incident of misbehavior is the result of a multitude of causes.

The Community

One source of misbehavior is the environment in which the youth lives. In an area where crime, sex irregularities, drunkenness, drug addiction, barroom fights, and knifings are common, it would be naive to expect pupils to rise overnight to the prim middle-class mores of the ordinary school and school teacher. For youths from such areas achieving acceptable standards of behavior can be a long, hard process. Fortunately, these youths after their fashion want to be respected and be respectable. The idealism of youth may be warped in some of them, but it is there.

A school administrator never tired of relating an incident which occurred many years ago. Two girls were fighting on the street after the age-old manner of fishwives. The coming of the superintendent of schools brought the fight to a quick halt, but one of the girls thought that she should apologize and explain. She hurried up to him and blurted, "I know I shouldn't swear, Mr. C. but, honest to God, she made me so damned mad . . ." This young lady had not as yet achieved the standard of speech and conduct one would hope for, but, after her fashion, she was trying.

Home situations cause much school misbehavior. Boys and girls carry sibling rivalries, jealousies, and attendant high feelings to school with them. Pupils are often under parental pressure of one sort or another. Resentment and rebellion against such pressures can carry over into the classroom. Both neglected and overprotected pupils have not established desirable behavior patterns in many instances, and continue their misbehavior in school. Homes in which values differ from those of the school make the work of the teacher more difficult—particularly homes in which the parents have little interest in secondary education.

Emotional Difficulties

Teen-agers seem to have more than their share of emotional troubles. These disturbances are seldom serious, but they are frequently upsetting. The cause of the upset may have nothing whatsoever to do with the class or the school. Let us suppose, for instance, that a boy has been late for breakfast and has missed his bus. His father, who has had to drive him to school, has let him feel the sharp side of his tongue. Before school starts, the boy is already emotionally upset. A trifle may set him off.

Any threat to a pupil's security may lead to undesirable behavior. To prevent the loss of security, or to regain it once it is lost, the pupil may resort to subterfuge, escape, or something else equally undesirable. Many common classroom conditions are serious threats to the security of pupils. Threats of failure, rejection, ridicule, and inconsistency on the part of teachers are some of them. The misuse of tests is one of the most common. Overly difficult tests and unnecessarily high and rigid standards of achievement may cause fear, jealousy, and antagonism. The natural result is cheating. Similarly, ill-conceived practices such as sarcasm and criticism of individuals in front of the class cause embarrassment, resentment, and class tension. In such an atmosphere many pupils resort to misbehavior as a defense.

At times, misbehavior is symptomatic of social maladjustment. Boys and girls who are not accepted by the group often make nuisances of themselves in order to gain status. Indeed, some of them want attention and recognition so much that they welcome being punished to get it.

School-Caused Misbehavior

Proper handling of problem cases is, of course, a difficult and time-consuming business. Fortunately, most classroom offenses stem from causes within the teacher's control. Some of these causes are poor teaching, poor curriculum, poor classroom management, poor techniques of discipline, and personality defects in the teacher. *Curricula which do not provide for the needs and interests of youth sow the seeds of misconduct.* The further the curriculum gets from the life of the youth, the less likely he is to see its worth, and the more liable he is to seek entertainment during school hours. Similarly, poor teaching produces dead, pointless classes which breed misconduct. Like poor teaching, poor methods of discipline engender misbehavior by causing dissatisfaction, discontent, and tension. The succeeding section will discuss these causes more fully and attempt to show how to avoid them.

Adolescent Vigor

A certain amount of school misbehavior is simply the result of what our forefathers called an "excess of animal spirits." By nature adolescents are a restless lot whose basic needs and drives do not always run in complete harmony with even the best curriculum. In ordinary situations adolescents very quickly get tired of just sitting. Much pupil restlessness in class may be laid to a simple need to work off energy.

At this time of life, also, boys and girls are in the midst of carrying out some of their most critical and difficult developmental tasks, in particular learning to achieve a role in adult heterosexual society. An adolescent's classroom misbehavior may be an attempt to establish himself and his personality in the society of his peers. It may also be just a carry-over from his life away from school. After all, to most boys and girls social advancement and love affairs seem to be fully as important as algebra and geography. Life does not stop just because class is in session.

✻

Think back over the classes you have attended in which there have been disciplinary incidents. What seemed to be the cause? What were the causes of disciplinary incidents involving you or your friends when you were in secondary school?

Why do pupils misbehave? List all the possible causes for misbehavior that you can name. How might knowledge of the causes of misbehavior influence the teacher's action?

Many (some say most) behavior problems are teacher-created. Can you think of some examples? How can the teacher avoid creating such situations?

✻

Creating Self-Discipline

Since modern schools advocate self-discipline rather than imposed authoritarian rule, teachers must consciously try to develop self-discipline. Self-discipline does not come naturally; it must be learned. Becoming self-disciplined is a time-consuming process; the result of much practice. Teachers who are attempting to teach self-discipline should expect to proceed slowly.

Developing a Code of Conduct

The first step in achieving self-discipline is for boys and girls to find out what good behavior is. Seriously and carefully working out a class code of conduct can make a vital contribution to developing excellent personal behavior standards in the pupils.

One teacher had great success with the following technique. For many years at the beginning of the term he addressed his class in the following manner: "We are going to have to spend the rest of the year here together. In order to keep out of each other's hair we need some rules. Let's talk the situation over and see if we can figure out what rules we want to have in this class." Then the class set to work to discuss why they needed rules and what kind of rules they needed. Finally, they drew up a set of rules which a committee put in final form for class adoption. During the discussion the teacher presided and made suggestions. Most of his comments were questions such as, "What about chewing gum? Is that what you really want to do? Do you need that? Aren't you being a little strict?" The resulting rules were usually a workable code that the pupils could follow quite well. The teacher's greatest difficulty was to keep the rules from becoming too strict and too detailed. Sometimes, after a few weeks, the teacher had to suggest that the rules be reviewed and revised.

The technique just described worked for this social studies teacher for more than twenty years, but it may be unsuitable for other teachers in different situations. Each teacher must suit his methods to his class and his own personality. Some classes of teen-agers are not ready for democratic procedures and could not satisfactorily work out their own code of conduct. The important thing is to develop for each class standards of conduct the pupils will accept as reasonable and worthwhile.

Helping Pupils Improve Their Own Standards

Frequently youths' standards are not quite what we would like them to be. Sometimes they live in homes and neighborhoods that see no value in the standards set by the school. When this is so, their teachers should help them arrive at suitable standards. This they cannot do by legislating standards; neither can they do it by criticizing the standards of the youths' families and friends. Doing so may serve only to arouse hostilities. The teachers must depend on the reasonableness and workability of the standards rather than on authority alone. They can show youths how many people make their lives more enjoyable by living by good codes. They can also let their pupils know how teachers and other people feel about proper conduct. In this way teachers can often convince pupils that these standards will make life better for them and induce them to adopt more suitable patterns of behavior voluntarily.

Enforcing Rules as a Way to Self-Discipline

Enforcing rules may itself be an opportunity to teach the fundamentals of self-discipline. Whenever a youth commits an offense of any magnitude, the usual procedure is for the teacher and pupil to have a private conference. In this conference the teacher can analyze the incident with the pupil. Together they can determine exactly what the misconduct has been, why it is unacceptable, and what the pupil should do for reparation. Used skilfully, this type of conference can produce real learning in self-discipline.

In some schools, teachers encourage the pupils to carry out the enforcement of class rules. Properly guided, this technique can help pupils to achieve self-discipline, but it should be reserved only for classes that are ready for it. Throwing too much responsibility on a class newly introduced to democratic procedures may cause the program to break down. Like other democratic organizations, the group is much more adept at determining policy than at carrying it out. Enforcing the rules must be left up to the executive. Therefore, the enforcement of classroom rules should be the job of the teacher himself.

Achieving Classroom Control

Teacher Personality and Classroom Atmosphere

The personality of the teacher does much to create the atmosphere of the class. Teachers who rub pupils the wrong way, who don't like adolescents, who are more interested in the subject than in their pupils, who are inconsiderate, unhappy, and lack a sense of humor are likely to have disturbances in their classes. The teacher who can create a feeling of rapport with his pupils, like the skipper running a happy ship, usually has little difficulty.

For this reason as soon as possible the teacher needs to get to know his pupils as individuals and treat them so. Most particularly, from the very first he should learn each pupil's name and use it in class. This practice is not only good for the pupil's ego but also serves to notify the pupil that any misbehavior on his part will not be anonymous. In addition, if the teacher knows something of the pupil's background and interests, he can use this knowledge to cement friendly relations and to direct pupil interests in desirable directions.

Teachers' attitudes tend to spread to the class. If the teacher dislikes schoolwork, the class will probably dislike it too. Tense teachers usually convey their tensions to their pupils, and teachers who expect misbehavior usually get it. Perhaps, the first rule to follow is not to look for trouble, for "he who looks for trouble shall surely find it." In the classroom his approach should always be positive; the emphasis should be on the *do's*, never on the *don'ts*. By acting on the assumption that everything is going to be all right, and by concentrating all his efforts on the main job, i.e., teaching, the teacher will eliminate a good share of the potential disturbances. In securing and maintaining good classroom relationships a businesslike, matter-of-fact bearing can be very persuasive.

Nevertheless, even in the best-regulated classes and schools, youngsters do misbehave. In some neighborhoods they seem to do little else. The teacher must try to take misbehavior in his stride. This calls for keeping a tight rein on his own emotions—not always an easy thing to do.

Achieving the Proper Perspective

Perhaps the best technique for keeping on an even keel is not to take one's self too seriously. Teachers are human, too. They do not know everything, and they do make mistakes. What is more, the pupils know it. No amount of dissembling can keep the truth from them. The sooner the teacher realizes this and relaxes, the better off he will be.

Many young teachers seem to think that every incident of pupil misbehavior is a personal insult. This is not so. Actually—although this may prick the pedagogic pride—most teachers are not important enough in the pupils' scheme of things to be acted against personally. The effect of misbehavior on the teacher rarely enters the miscreants' minds; but if they find that their misbehavior annoys the teacher, watch out, for what is more fun to a group of teen-agers than to plague a resentful victim? Teachers should not be upset by pupils' misconduct any more than they should be upset by pupils' lack of knowledge. This is the way youngsters are; the teacher's job is to help them achieve the highest goals they can. If a teacher views pupil misdemeanors as personal insults, he may soon find that they have become just that.

In other words, a teacher needs a sense of humor and a sense of proportion. When the teacher gets to the point where he can laugh at his own failings, he is well on the way to developing a pleasant classroom atmos-

Busy pupils seldom cause discipline problems.

phere and good classroom control. Clowning in the classroom should not be encouraged, but when something is funny, laugh at it and then turn the good feeling toward the work of the day. Laughing with pupils clears the atmosphere. It is always easier to learn in a pleasant class than in a repressive one, and after all, pupil learning is what you are after. The teacher needs a sense of perspective, too. He needs to put first things first. He is not a policeman. He is a teacher. His primary job is not to enforce rules, but to draw out learning. He should not let little things upset him.

Creating a Friendly Atmosphere

The teacher should also try to make the classroom a friendly place. By his actions, rather than by his words, the teacher should let the pupils know that he would like to be a friend. This does not mean that he should attempt to be a "buddy." In such cases familiarity may breed contempt.

No one can be a boon companion of everyone, and teachers must avoid creating favorites. Besides, adolescents prefer that adults act their age.

Perhaps the best summary of what we have tried to say is that the teacher should set a good example. If his behavior in the classroom is truly considerate, courteous, patient, pleasant, and sympathetic, then that of the class will probably be so, too.

✻

What can you do about the pupil whose behavior problems arise from the home? From emotional difficulties? From social problems?

Think back to your high school days. Try to picture the teacher who had the most trouble and the teacher who had the least difficulty. What was it about those teachers that made the difference in their relations with pupils?

✻

An Ounce of Prevention

Proper planning is indispensable for establishing and maintaining good classroom discipline. As a general rule, boys and girls wish to behave properly, and, what is more, they usually want to learn if the subject matter seems to be worth learning. Many, if not most, disturbances result from poorly organized classes—classes that lack purpose, classes that start late, classes in which pupils have nothing to do. Careful planning can usually eliminate faults of this sort.

Many teachers bring troubles on themselves by neglecting individual differences. Picture the discipline problem of the tenth-grade teacher who planned to spend four weeks on *The Tale of Two Cities*. Four or five of her brightest boys read the story over the weekend and so had time on their hands. To find something to do, they organized a ball game, using a soap eraser and a ruler. Providing for individual differences might have eliminated this problem.

"Our teacher is funny," a small boy reported to his mother during his first school experience. "She wants you to keep at work all the time whether you have anything to do or not."[2] This anecdote is no less true today than it was in 1892. The devil makes work for idle hands. Pupils who have nothing to do will find things to do. Planning that leaves dead spots in the class encourages trouble. To avoid these empty spots, the teacher must be sure that everyone has plenty of worthwhile activities to do. Classes in which the teacher does all the work and the pupils just sit and vegetate should be avoided. This is why the teacher should be wary of the beginner's tendency to overuse the lecture.

He should also make a point to get the lesson rolling the moment the

2 Sarah L. Arnold, "Waymarks," *Journal of Education*, February 4, 1892.

period begins. Neophytes, a little unsure of themselves perhaps, are sometimes tempted to give themselves a little respite by stalling a minute or two at the opening of the class. Doing so is dangerous; the class that has time to fool around before the lesson starts may never find time to get down to business before the period ends. It is wise, however, for the teacher to wait until the group is quiet before he begins to talk to them. The teacher who allows pupils to be noisy while he is talking, is wasting his time and at the same time encouraging discourtesy.

An essential of good planning is to provide plenty of good materials for pupils to work with. Failure to provide enough of the right materials can cause the worst dead spots of all. In order to eliminate mischief-breeding periods of waiting, the teacher's lesson planning should ensure that the materials needed for the lesson are on hand and include procedures for rapid delivery and collection of materials.

Much misbehavior is caused by teachers' ignoring pupils' predispositions. Any class procedure that violates the natural inclinations of boys and girls creates a situation that can lead to misconduct. Adolescents are naturally gregarious social creatures. It is unreasonable to insist on an absolutely quiet classroom in which "you can hear a pin drop." A class that is all keyed up—having just come from an exciting assembly, perhaps —cannot easily settle down to a placid routine. By adjusting the material and tempo of the instruction to the predispositions and mood of the class and of individual members of it, the predispositions of pupils may be made an aid to learning rather than a threat to peace. In his planning, the teacher must allow for these predispositions; he must also be flexible enough to be able to change his plans, when necessary, to fit the mood of the class. Switching from lecture or recitation to a snap quiz or written assignment is a most effective example of this principle.

Above all, the teacher must make the class interesting. He will have little need to worry about discipline if his planning keeps the pupils busy with something that appeals to them. To keep the class moving smoothly and to avoid dead spots, the teacher should carefully routinize all organizational and administrative details such as passing out and collecting papers. The work necessary to provide plenty of good materials and a proper plan is usually rewarded by easier discipline. It lessens both the opportunity and the need for mischief. One might call this approach preventive discipline.

A Few Definite Rules

Unfortunately, a teacher can seldom plan a class so well that all his problems are completely solved. The best laid plans "gang aft agley"; consequently, each class must have rules. One of the maxims of our country's forefathers was that the government which governs least governs best.

This maxim seems to apply, to some extent, to the modern classroom. Well-disciplined classes are classes with few rules. Every class needs some rules; no class needs many. Too many rules are confusing to pupils, and may become unenforceable. A few definite rules which make sense to pupils and teachers alike will prove to be the most successful.

It goes without saying that every class rule should seem reasonable to the pupils. Any attempt to enforce what pupils find unreasonable is bound to lead to a struggle. Rules that are too strict create tensions. Rebellion, misdemeanors, and an occasional blow-up may be the result. On the other hand, teachers who let pupils do whatever they please create equally severe difficulties for themselves. Such classes are bound to become noisy and disorderly. Teachers—and there are some—who believe that by removing all controls they are creating a permissive atmosphere are mistaken. A permissive atmosphere is a friendly atmosphere in which the pupil is not afraid. Freedom from controls is not permissiveness; it is *laissez-faire*. Generally speaking, little worthwhile learning comes from *laissez-faire* teaching. Clear, definite rules which specify the expected norms and limits of behavior help clear the air and avoid clashes caused by pupils' attempting to go too far. It is unusual to have good teaching without good rules. Perhaps the best way to develop acceptable rules is to have the pupils define their own standards of behavior. Pupils usually abide by their own rules willingly.

✿

What rules or standards for behavior are appropriate for a high-school class?

Should a set of rules for classroom behavior be provided? (Some texts say, yes; some say, no.) If so, who should make it and how should it be enforced? Be prepared to defend your position.

Do you agree with the practice of having the pupils develop their own rules for behavior? How would you go about developing such rules?

✿

Enforcing the Rules

Once rules are made, they must be enforced. The pupils should have no doubt that these rules are operative and that breaking them will not be countenanced. Laxity in the enforcement of rules makes them worthless. The pupils lose respect for them and resent subsequent attempts to enforce them. The American Revolution was caused, at least in part, by a British attempt to enforce laws, some of which were quite reasonable, after a long period of laxity.

Although it is possible to be too rigid, one characteristic of the teacher with good control is consistent enforcement of the class rules. Boys and girls like to know where they stand. The teacher whose rules are sacrosanct today and of no importance tomorrow is anathema to them. Also, since getting away with mischief may be possible, the pupils will be tempted to try their luck.

Along with consistency goes fairness. The teacher must treat all pupils alike. The teacher who has favorites or who treats some pupils preferentially may be creating behavior problems. Playing favorites loses the teacher the respect of his pupils and engenders active dislike in the pupils not so favored.

The teacher, then, should try to be consistent and fair. This, of course, does not mean that one should never make an exception to a rule. As long as pupils have different personalities, they must be treated differently from one another. The punishment that one pupil might take as a lark could be devastating to another. To this extent the punishment must suit the offender. Nevertheless, the enforcement of the rules must remain consistent even if the means of enforcement may vary. Exceptions to this rule should be truly exceptional and made only for extraordinarily good reasons. It helps considerably if the reasons and their merits are evident to the class as a whole. Otherwise, the teacher may be accused of favoritism and unfairness in the minds of his pupils.

Avoiding Poor Enforcement Techniques

The teacher should guard against nagging for it disturbs the lesson and may cause additional pupil misbehavior. At times, he will do better to disregard minor infractions than to attempt ceaselessly to correct the pupils. Nagging often results from insistence on unnecessarily high standards of pupil behavior and from poor organization of classes. If a teacher finds it necessary to keep admonishing a pupil, he should check to see whether the pupil has something worthwhile and appropriate to do. Sometimes a good remedy is to direct a question to the youth whose mind seems to be wandering or to start the restless pupil off on a new activity. Often just moving in the direction of an incipient behavior problem will bring the potential culprit back in line before anything really untoward has had a chance to happen. Such techniques distract youths from mischief. The teacher who keeps alert can often head off cases of misbehavior before they start.

Besides nagging, other poor methods of enforcing rules also cause misconduct. Harsh punishment, for example, often brings about resentment and revolt. In the old English public schools it sometimes resulted in open rebellion and the thrashing of the teachers by the pupils. In spite of the number of people who believe in force as the supreme disciplinary agent, harshness has never been really successful. Quintilian, the great Roman teacher, shows why. Corporal punishment will make the pupils hate their studies and often causes them to rebel or to stop trying. Besides, it may lead to more trouble since harshness often merely hardens pupils in their misbehavior. A good teacher, he said, can do better without it. These warnings are still valid after 1,900 years. Harsh punishment is likely to create more discipline problems than it cures.

In enforcing his rules, the teacher should avoid making big scenes out of insignificant acts. To do so is utter folly. Most little things can be brushed off lightly. Often a look or a pleasant word will suffice. The teacher who makes major issues of minor transgressions soon finds that they do not remain minor. He would do better to save his fire for something important. Such a policy will not only help the teacher avoid unpleasant scenes, but will also prevent nagging and a repressive, punitive atmosphere in the classroom. The latter should be avoided at all costs because it is a deterrent to learning.

In this connection, the teacher should also shun threats and ultimatums. These create scenes and, if a pupil misbehaves, fetter the teacher's course of action, since he must carry out his threats if he is to keep the pupils' respect.

The Role of Punishment

Sooner or later, no matter how sensible the rules and how careful the planning, some pupil will commit an offense for which he must be punished. The Mikado probably meant well when he sang

> My object all sublime
> I shall achieve in time—
> To let the punishment fit the crime—
> The punishment fit the crime;
> And make each prisoner pent
> Unwillingly represent
> A source of innocent merriment,
> Of innocent merriment![3]

But his scheme would not have worked well. Punishment should never be used as a source of "innocent merriment." But it should be appropriate and, whenever possible, constructive. If a pupil smashes a window wilfully or carelessly, let him clean up the mess and make proper restitution for it. In general, if his punishment is the logical result of his misconduct, the pupil is likely to accept it without resentment and may learn not to offend in the same way again. For that matter, any punishment is more likely to be effective if the pupil sees its reasonableness. The teacher

---

[3] W. S. Gilbert and Arthur Sullivan, *The Mikado*, Act II.

should always try to help the pupil see the appropriateness of his punishment before initiating it.

Punishment should be used sparingly because overuse of it creates the repressive atmosphere teachers wish to avoid. Furthermore, overusing punishment takes the force out of it. Punishment should be held back as a reserve for important offenses. The teacher who commits his reserve too soon or too often finds he has little to fall back on in real crises.

When punishment is used, it should be swift, sure, and impressive. The teacher should never punish on impulse; he should think twice before he acts; but he should act at once. Should he himself become emotional, however, he would do well to calm down before prescribing the punishment, for punishing pupils in anger can be disastrous. It requires a cool head to ascertain without the shadow of a doubt that one has correctly identified the guilty one and to select a punishment appropriate for both the offense and the offender.

Harsh punishment should be avoided. Sarcasm, ridicule, humiliation, corporal punishment, and unnatural punishment often do more harm than good. Verbal punishment should be delivered in private. Although punishment should not be harsh, it should be severe enough to impress the pupil. Demerits and detention quite often do not have much meaning to the pupil. For instance, a certain teacher kept a boy after school every afternoon for a month, apparently without effect. One afternoon he found out why: the boy had to wait for his father every afternoon anyway and was sometimes hard put to find ways to kill time. Detention to him was no hardship at all and so was quite ineffective.

A Word About Corporal Punishment

Some teachers, clergymen, and newspaper editors blame all the ills of modern civilization on the schools which no longer beat out the tune with a hickory stick. That anyone should have so much faith in corporal punishment is astonishing in view of its centuries-long history of little success. Although it may be true, as some writers claim, that certain types of youngsters, particularly those from disadvantaged areas, may understand and accept physical punishment better than any other kind, it is almost always wiser to use some other method in punishing secondary-school pupils. Pupils of this age are too nearly grown up for this type of punishment. High-school girls are young ladies and fall under the taboo against striking women. High-school boys are young men who may not accept such punishment graciously.

The wise teacher never touches a secondary-school pupil except in a formal situation with suitable witnesses according to the laws of his state and school district. Otherwise, he may lay himself open to accusations and legal difficulties. All in all, if corporal punishment must ever be used, discretion tells us to send the pupil to the principal and let him take over.

Other Punishments

One reason that teacher punishments are not always very effective is that the teacher really has very few punishments available to him. Apart from the corporal punishments, he is limited to the use of detention, verbal punishments, isolation, extra work, deprivation of privileges, and not much else.

DETENTION. Detention, or staying after school, is one of the most frequently used punishments. In general, there are two types of detention periods. One is the sort common in large schools in which the pupils must report to a detention hall. The other is a do-it-yourself arrangement whereby each teacher looks after his own detainees. In spite of its widespread use, detention is not very effective except when the pupil has something else vitally important to do after school—a condition that, surprisingly, does not obtain so very often. Also, detention is all too often a source of difficulty in other areas of a student's life. It can, and often does, cut into other activities that the pupil needs more than disciplining. In at least one school, detention sessions assigned by one teacher kept a potential dropout from attending remedial tutorial sessions scheduled by another teacher. Likewise, pupils' part-time jobs may conflict with detention. For a pupil to lose his job for a simple infraction of school rules can be a severe and unjust punishment. Still another difficulty in some schools comes from the bus schedule. Further, detention periods are a waste of time unless they are used constructively. Their force as a deterrent is not strong enough to warrant keeping the pupil sitting doing nothing. If a school must use detention periods, they should be combined with a conference or some educationally valuable activity.

VERBAL PUNISHMENT. An occasional scolding never really hurt anyone who really needed it and knew he needed it. Yet like many other measures its effect soon dissipates when it is overused. Then it becomes mere nagging, the futility of which we have already discussed. Although minor reprimands are common and acceptable in most classrooms if they are made in a nice way, a scolding should generally be delivered in private so that no one other than the culprit can hear it. From time to time, however, a whole class may need to be told the hard facts of life. Whenever such explanations are in order they should be businesslike and matter-of-fact. It is not a time for emotionalism.

Sarcasm and ridicule are two other common types of verbal punishments. Educational methods textbooks customarily point out that neither of these punishments should be used, although in faculty lounges one is likely to be regaled with stories of the Mr. Chips type who ruled his classes with a tongue of acid and so endeared himself to the hearts of generations of his pupils. Of course, the effectiveness of such weapons depends upon the pupil, the teacher, and the teacher-pupil relationship. Where some youngsters might relish a teacher's sarcasm as a big joke, others might wither in spirit; where some could brush off ridicule without a qualm, others may be blighted. Because the teacher can never be sure just what the effect will be, he would be wise to avoid such punishments.

ISOLATION. Changing seats to break up seating arrangements that permit cliques and friends too much opportunity for social visiting is a common practice. This procedure has much to recommend it as long as the teacher does not create a situation in which the pupils who formerly whispered to each other now shout and pass notes. Another similar plan is to change the seat of a chronic offender so that he is isolated from the rest of the class all alone somewhere in the back of the room. Other teachers like to put their behavior problems up front in the first row next to the teacher's desk or podium. Placing the pupil up front may be objectionable for two reasons: (1) it places the pupil where he is assured of an audience if he wants to show off, and (2) it seems to assume that the teacher will work entirely from his desk at the front of the room, a practice not generally recommended.

ASSIGNING EXTRA WORK. At one time the most common method of punishing secondary-school pupils was to assign them a number of lines of Latin verse to translate. Today the assignment of extra work continues to be a common punishment in spite of the fact that experts advise against it. Their objection is that associating school work with punishment creates a prejudice against the subjects in the minds of the pupils. This objection is probably well founded. However, there should be no objection to making pupils redo sloppy work again and again— in fact, the teacher who accepts papers that have been carelessly prepared encourages poor work habits. Likewise, there should be no objection to keeping pupils busy at class assignments during detention periods.

DEPRIVATION OF PRIVILEGES. One of the few punishments that seems to be both effective and acceptable to experts in pedagogy is to take away privileges from pupils who misbehave. In general, this practice is a good one. Unfortunately all too many pupils do not have any privileges the loss of which would greatly concern them. In poor schools and for chronic offenders it may carry no weight at all.

DEDUCTING FROM ACADEMIC MARK.   Punishing pupils by lowering their marks in the course is a tempting technique which should be avoided. Academic marks, if they are to have any validity at all, must be based upon pupils' achievement. To lower a pupil's course mark because he misbehaves is unfair to him, his parents, and prospective employers or college admissions officers. Under no circumstances can such punishments be tolerated.

After reading such a devastating description of the punishments at his disposal, the prospective teacher may be somewhat discouraged. Is there nothing that can be done? Yes, of course, there is. The answer to the problem lies almost entirely in positive measures many of which have been described early in the chapter.

✻

Why should the teacher avoid use of the following?
   sarcasm
   threats
   nagging
   yelling
   constant vocal correction
   arguments with pupils
   corporal punishment.
Are any of the above ever permissible? If so, when? Justify your reply.

✻

Some Other Techniques

SENDING PUPILS TO THE OFFICE.   Sometimes behavior is of the sort which makes it necessary for the teacher to send the miscreant to the office. As a general rule, principals and vice-principals are not overjoyed by the visits of these young people. A certain vice-principal was discussing an important matter with a visitor when a surly-faced girl of fifteen arrived in his office with a note from her teacher. He looked at it and then sent her into another office to wait. As soon as she had left he exclaimed to his guest, "Now what am I supposed to do with her? I don't mind having them come up here once in a while, but you'd think that woman could handle some of her own discipline!" Evidently an eager, new teacher would be wise to determine as well as he can the feelings of his principal before he sends too many problems to the office.

Each teacher is responsible for his own discipline. Sending the pupil to the office should be reserved for really serious offenses. The principal or his assistant is not in a good position to deal with routine cases. He is handicapped by not knowing exactly what has happened, and his special disciplinary powers are best suited to dealing with major offenses. Sometimes his sympathies lie with the pupil. Furthermore, sending the pupil to the office may be taken as a sign of weakness in the teacher and lower his prestige among the pupils. Doubtless there are crises in which the teacher must cast pupils into outer darkness, but these occasions should be kept to a minimum. If he handles his own discipline problems, the teacher will usually rise in the esteem of his pupils and of his principal as well.

In spite of the warning contained in previous paragraphs, the teacher should not hesitate to send bad actors to the office for correction when it is necessary—for example, when dealing with the pupil would disrupt or interfere with the progress of the class lesson, or when the offense is beyond the scope of the teacher's power and authority. In no case should the misbehavior of one pupil be allowed to break up a class. When sending a pupil out of class the teacher should be sure to inform the pupil just where he is to go and what he is supposed to do, and also to inform the official to whom the pupil is to report just exactly why the pupil is coming to him, either by a note or by the intercommunications system.

Although most principals and other superiors expect teachers to handle their own discipline problems, they welcome the opportunity to be of help. The beginning teacher should certainly go to his superior for assistance. The latter will gladly give the teacher sound advice and practical help, if he can.

Helping the Problem Child

Every school has problem pupils who for some reason or other do not seem able to adapt to the school program. This inability to adjust to a school situation may be caused by problems at home, the social environment in the community, or personality defects. Frequently such pupils seek release from their problems in undesirable ways. These pupils need to be helped. They should be treated with sympathy and understanding. In most cases, they should be referred to guidance counselors for help. In the meantime the teacher should try to find out as much as possible about these pupils and treat them accordingly.

Some youths deviate far from the normal. Although the teacher should attempt to help each boy and girl if he can, the time necessary for attending to difficult cases may cause him to neglect the rest of the class. Besides, the teacher probably does not know what to do anyway. The teacher's job is to get problem pupils specialized help as soon as possible. For him to try to provide the help himself might well be unethical.

Teachers are usually well aware of the obstreperous pupil. However, a behavior problem which is fully as dangerous is presented by the quiet, withdrawn pupil. Such pupils often develop severe emotional problems.

Any person who seems to be too quiet and withdrawn should also be referred to the guidance counselor.

✻

Criticize the following "rules" for discipline:
1. Watch carefully for the first small signs of trouble and squelch them at once *with no exceptions.*
2. Hold your group to very high standards at first. You can relax later if the situation warrants it.
3. Be a real friend to the children.
4. Employ self-government only if you are sure the class is ready for it.
5. Be fair.
6. Be consistent.

Criticize the following practice reported by a national wire service: "The Boston School Committee recently directed that the following commandments be read biweekly to pupils in grades 7 through 12.
1. Don't let your parents down; they've brought you up.
2. Be smart, obey. You'll give orders yourself some day.
3. Stop and think before you drink.
4. Ditch dirty thoughts fast or they'll ditch you.
5. Show-off driving is juvenile. Don't act your age.
6. Pick the right friends to be picked for a friend.
7. Choose a date fit for a mate.
8. Don't go steady unless you're ready.
9. Love God and neighbor.
10. Live carefully. The soul you save may be your own."

✻

Summary

Modern discipline emphasizes cooperation and self-discipline rather than authority. Incidents of misbehavior can have many causes. Among these causes are faulty personalities, poor home and neighborhood conditions, emotional difficulties, social maladjustments, fatigue, bad physical conditions, poor teaching, poor curricula, and poor classroom management. The fault lies with the teacher and the school as often as it does with the pupils.

The following rules should help the teacher achieve classroom control. *Set a good example:*

Don't take yourself too seriously.
Develop a sense of humor.
Do as you would be done by.
Be friendly, but not too friendly.

Control your own temper.

Let sleeping dogs lie: expect good conduct; do not go looking for trouble.

Plan classes well:

Eliminate lags and dead spots.

Provide for individual differences.

Vary classroom activities.

Make classes interesting.

Make classes seem worthwhile.

Help pupils feel important.

Have a few definite rules and enforce them:

Let pupils help make the rules.

Be fair and consistent.

Don't make mountains out of molehills.

Avoid scenes.

Avoid ultimatums.

Avoid threats.

Do not nag.

Take it easy.

Punishment should be rare but, when necessary, swift and certain:

Never use sarcasm, ridicule, harsh or humiliating punishments.

Never embarrass pupils.

Avoid corporal punishment. If it must be used, let one of your superiors do it.

Don't punish the entire class for the faults of a few.

Try to develop self-discipline.

Refer problem cases to the guidance staff.

Stand on your own feet; assume the responsibility for your own classroom control.

FOR FURTHER STUDY

BARUCH, DOROTHY, *New Ways in Discipline* (New York: McGraw-Hill Book Company, 1949).

BOWMAN, H. J., "Review of Discipline," *Bulletin of the National Association of Secondary School Principals* (September, 1959), 43: 147–156.

CUTTS, NORMA E., and NICHOLAS MOSELY, *Teaching the Disorderly Child* (New York: David McKay Company, Inc., 1957).

DRAYER, ADAM M., *Problems and Methods in High School Teaching* (Boston: D. C. Heath and Company, 1963), Ch. 1.

GNAGEY, WILLIAM J., *Controlling Classroom Misbehavior* (Washington, D.C.: National Education Association, 1965).

HYMES, JAMES L., JR., *Behavior and Misbehavior* (Englewood Cliffs, N.J.: Prentice-Hall, Inc., 1955).

————, *Discipline* (New York: Bureau of Publications, Teachers College, Columbia University, 1949).

INLOW, GAIL M., *Maturity in High School Teaching* (Englewood Cliffs, N.J.: Prentice-Hall, Inc., 1963).

LARSON, KNUTE, and MELVIN R. KARPAS, *Effective Secondary School Discipline* (Englewood Cliffs, N.J.: Prentice-Hall, Inc., 1963).

N.E.A. Research Division, *Student Behavior in Secondary Schools,* 1964, Research Report 1965 R-12 (Washington, D.C.: National Education Association, 1965).

OLIVA, PETER F., "High School Discipline in American Society," *Bulletin of the National Association of Secondary-School Principals* (January 1956), 40: 1–103.

SHEVIAKOV, GEORGE V., and FRITZ REDL, *Discipline for Today's Children and Youth,* Revised Edition (Washington, D.C.: Association for Supervision and Curriculum Development, 1956).

VREDEVOE, L. E., "School Discipline," *Bulletin of the National Association of Secondary-School Principals* (March 1965), 49: 215–26.

PART *II*

Planning

CHAPTER *5*

Planning for Teaching

=====================================

*T*HE KEY to successful teaching is good planning. There is no substitute for it. Good planning helps create correct discipline, pleasant class atmosphere, and purposeful activity free from dead spots and waste motion—in short, good planning is likely to result in worthwhile learning. No one can teach well for long without planning.

The Basic Ingredients

What are the basic ingredients of a good teaching plan? Probably in teaching they can be reduced to the following:

1. What we expect the pupils to learn.
2. How we hope to bring about this learning.

In addition, although we may not include it as part of every lesson plan itself, we should make some provision for evaluating the effectiveness of the plan.

The remainder of this chapter and the chapter following will be devoted to these ingredients as they concern the planning of courses, units, and lessons. Because of its importance and the difficulty of describing it, an entire chapter has been given to the planning of units. The present chapter will be concerned with the planning of courses, lesson planning and teacher-pupil planning. The reader should remember, however, that all of these are parts of the same process.

Planning the Course

The Teacher's Responsibilities

Every course should be planned carefully and imaginatively. The proceedings and facilities for the planning of courses differ greatly from school to school and school system to school system. Some school administrations furnish courses of study, syllabi, or curriculum guides. These provide suggestions concerning the goals that should be achieved, the content of the course, the methods that might be employed, and materials that might be used. Some schools provide source or resource units. These units give suggestions for topics, objectives, and activities for the units to be used in the courses. Some systems provide no course outlines or guide of any sort other than texts, workbooks, and teaching materials.

Still, no matter what the system has provided to aid the teacher in designing his courses, the responsibility for the content of the course rests squarely upon the teacher. If the school provides a course of study, syllabus, or curriculum guide for a course, the teacher should make use of it. Not to do so may introduce confusion into a carefully planned school program. Even so, courses of study are usually suggestive and allow for considerable variation. Even when courses are rigidly laid out, the good teacher must vary the course to suit the interests, needs, and abilities of his pupils. This he can do by changing the course sequence, modifying the time spent on various topics, determining which topics should receive most emphasis, and varying the methods of teaching. In the final analysis it is the teacher who decides precisely what is to be taught and how it is to be taught.

✲

One day a supervisor visited a beginning teacher who was having difficulty. This young person had taken on a job which was almost too much for him. He was teaching material difficult for him and was having considerable difficulty keeping up with the class. When the supervisor asked him for his plans, he replied, "I am so busy I have not been able to make any lesson plans yet." What would your answer be to this beginning teacher?

A well-known teacher once said that there are three things important in good teaching. They are: determining what the children are to learn, why they are to learn it, and how they best can learn it. Criticize this statement.

✲

Some Principles of Course Planning

Whatever one uses as a basis for his planning, the procedure for planning a course is relatively simple. The teacher may enlist the aid of his pupils in carrying out the procedure, or he may do it all himself. In either case, the responsibility for all the decisions made is his. The procedure consists of the following steps.

1. Decide what it is that the pupils are to learn from the course. These are the course objectives which should determine the nature of all later procedures.

2. Decide the course content that will bring about the desired objectives. This course content consists of two parts: (a) the subject matter of the course, i.e., the sequence of topics, and (b) the approach to be used in teaching the topics.
3. Decide the amount of time to be spent on the various topics in the sequence. This step is essential to ensure that the various portions of the course receive the attention they deserve. Neglect of this step is one cause of the all too common practice of proceeding slowly in the beginning of the course, and then rushing through the last weeks of the course because of lack of time.

These steps are quite simple, but they should be done carefully to provide a course of maximum benefit to the pupils. When executing them the teacher should keep the following principles in mind.

1. The teacher should determine the course objectives on the basis of their presumed ultimate value to the pupils. Once they are clearly established, he should constantly keep them in mind. The objectives should be the touchstones he uses in making decisions in later steps.
2. The subject matter and procedures which make up the content of the course should be such that they will contribute toward achieving the objectives of the course. Subject matter and procedures which are not consistent with the objectives should be discarded.
3. The course should be psychologically organized.
4. The course content should be so selected and so organized that it gives the maximum amount of transfer and retention.

SELECTING THE OBJECTIVES. The objectives of the course are extremely important. Ideally they should be the most important factor in determining both the subject matter and method of teaching in the course. Let us assume that the specific objectives for Level 1 French are

1. To develop facility and fluency with spoken French.
2. To develop the reading and writing skills to the point where the students can read and write anything they say.
3. To develop, through the language, an insight into and an appreciation of the French civilization and its influence on the United States.[1]

We know that in laying out the rest of our plan for Level I French we must (1) place our primary emphasis on the spoken word, (2) that we should limit instruction in reading and writing French to material the

[1] Philip D. Smith, Jr., *Course of Study for Foreign Languages*, Department of Education, State of Nevada, Carson City, Nevada, 1962.

pupils have already learned to speak, and (3) that for reading we should select French literature that not only does not exceed their spoken vocabulary, but that also will highlight French civilization and show French influences on our own culture. We also know that we should minimize the teaching of such things as grammatical laws because they are not directly pertinent to the objectives of the course. In this way the course objectives should determine the content of the course.

The major consideration in selecting the objectives is the potential value of the learning to the pupil and to society. To an extent this value is dependent upon the nature and structure of the subject matter or discipline concerned. Therefore in assessing what will be of the most worth, the teacher must make his decisions in relation to the discipline and subject matter. Thus the objectives of the course of study for Level I Latin in Nevada are different from those for Level I French, even though they are both beginning foreign language courses.

1. To develop the ability to pronounce and use Latin words.
2. To develop sufficient knowledge of syntax and inflection forms for comprehensive reading.
3. To develop the ability to recognize, define, and use English derivations encountered during Level I.
4. To develop an appreciation for Roman life and culture and its contributions to Western civilization.[2]

In general, knowledge of subject matter has very little value of itself alone. Rather, its value lies in its availability for use. Ordinarily, therefore, one should select as his course objectives concepts, skills, attitudes, ideals, and appreciations that the pupil can use now or later—not just a mere accumulation of knowledge. In other words, the course objectives should consist of things that are useful now and that appear most likely to be useful in the future in view of the goals, potentialities, and opportunities of the pupils and the needs and expectancies of the nation. This doctrine is sometimes called the *doctrine of contingent value.*

PLANNING THE OBJECTIVES. With these principles in mind, you are now ready to decide what you wish to achieve in the course. In theory, you should be able to determine the course objectives from your study of the subject and your knowledge of the pupils. In practice, many teachers find this task too demanding and too time-consuming. For this reason, many school departments have provided curriculum guides or courses of study that contain suggestions. These documents usually contain statements of objectives with which you may, or may not, agree.

[2] *Ibid.,* p. 45.

For instance, the language arts curriculum guide for the Santa Barbara Schools gives the following general objectives for the English program.[3]

General Objectives

1. To foster an appreciation of the English language.
2. To further a correct usage of language.
3. To acquire such knowledge of grammar as will furnish the student with standards for measuring his own construction.
4. To build an adequate and an enriched vocabulary.
5. To develop effective organization and expression of thought in writing, in conversation, and in public discussion.
6. To listen courteously and objectively.
7. To create a permanent interest in reading that the student may find in it both enjoyment and information.
8. To fit the individual student in his need as well as in his ability.
9. To promote good citizenship.
10. To instill a desire for truth and beauty.

These objectives are very general. At first glance they may seem to be so general as to give us no help at all. Yet, on closer examination, they do establish directions. We know that grammar should be a means rather than an end in itself, that the program should vary for different pupils, that considerable importance is attached to the spoken word, that attention should be given to correctness and clearness of usage and expression, and that the pupils should get some understanding of the language and its beauty. If we should go on now to examine the scope and sequence charts or content outlines of the various courses and various levels, we would have collected ideas enough to use as a basis for preparing our objectives.

If no curriculum guides are available, the teacher can determine what goals to pick for his course by studying the textbook or books commonly used in courses of this sort. The content of the texts will show him what others have thought the course should contain. After studying these books he can decide how much of their thinking to accept, how much to reject, what he wishes to add, and what he wishes to emphasize. Then, once his decisions have been made, he can write down his objectives as the concepts—probably generalizations—skills, and attitudes he hopes to achieve.

FITTING TOPICS TO GOALS.   Once the objectives have been selected, the teacher must select a sequence of topics and approaches for teaching those things that will bring out the objectives. Too often planners forget this necessity. To reduce the argument to absurdity, if in French I your

[3] "Program for the Low, the Average and the High Student for the 7th Through the 14th Grades," edited by Robert S. Shannon, Chairman, Language Arts, Santa Barbara Schools, Santa Barbara, Calif., 1956–57.

primary object is to teach pupils how to speak French, then the bulk of your coursework in Level I should consist of exercises in speaking French, not in translating written French, written English, or in learning rules of grammar. In some courses the subject matter and the manner of teaching it seem to have absolutely no relationship to the goals the teachers claim to have.

✻

Who should decide what the goals of a course should be?
How would you decide what a course should include?

✻

ORGANIZING THE COURSE PSYCHOLOGICALLY. A teacher can organize his courses in two ways: (1) according to the logical development of the subject matter, or (2) according to the psychological development of the pupils. At the secondary-school level, courses should be organized psychologically. That is to say, they should be organized around the pupils rather than subject matter. In other words each course should

1. Be adapted to the level of the pupils.
2. Allow for variation from pupil to pupil and for the same pupil from time to time.
3. Be selective, making important omissions in subject matter.
4. Encourage logical memory and problem solving and emphasize teaching through guidance of experience.
5. Use both vicarious and direct experience in a proportion suitable to the level and experience of the pupils.[4]

From the foregoing list one can see that the topics for any course must be selected with greatest care. The competent teacher selects topics suitable to the pupils' activities and interests. If possible, he picks topics of immediate intrinsic value to them, frequently with the help of the pupils. He sees to it that the course does not limit the pupils to book learning alone, but that it is a judicious mixture of vicarious and direct experience.

Furthermore, the competent teacher adapts the topics he has selected to the needs of his class. Since all pupils are individuals, a predetermined selection of topics will not be appropriate for all pupils. The teacher should provide opportunities for differentiation within the topics and, if necessary, addition to, deletion from, or substitution for the normal sequence for some individuals.

Some highly gifted pupils, for instance, go all the way through junior-

[4] Adapted from Roy O. Billett, *Fundamentals of Secondary School Teaching* (Boston: Houghton Mifflin Company, 1940), pp. 162–163.

high school without ever having a new topic introduced in many of their subjects because they have learned the ordinary course content years before. Such pupils should not have to walk lockstep with the other pupils. The teacher should find out what they can do, and then proceed to a point that is new and challenging to them.

PLANNING FOR RETENTION AND TRANSFER OF TRAINING. Using the outcome of one learning situation in another situation is called transfer of training. Thus, when a pupil uses in a history class skills he originally learned in English, transfer has taken place. If such transfer does not take place, the learning is of little value.

Transfer is not usually automatic. It is more likely to result when the application of the learning to other situations is pointed out. When that is not done, transfer may not take place because the learner does not see the relationship. Transfer also results from components common to the original learning situation and the situation in which the learning is to be used. In effect, this means that the more the "learning situation" is like the "using situation," the more likely it is that the learning will transfer.

Another aid to transfer is thorough learning. One can transfer what one knows and understands thoroughly much more readily than something less well known. Thorough knowledge also helps us retain our learning, but the best way to retain what we learn is to use it. What we do not use we tend to forget. Of course, we remember extremely vivid happenings well and we have learned some things so well that it seems we can never forget them. Still, in spite of exceptions, the rule holds. Even one's native tongue becomes rusty if one does not use it. The key to retention is renewal through frequent use.

Both transfer and retention are encouraged by the mastering and use of generalizations for, as a rule, generalizations can be remembered and used better than detail. The best remembered generalizations, and therefore the generalizations most available for use, are the ones the pupil derives for himself from specifics. Predigested generalizations worked out by the teacher and handed to the pupil are liable not to take at all, or to remain at the level of "mere verbalism." When a teacher does present generalizations to pupils, he should probably support them by much "forgettable detail," in order to make the generalizations stick. Ordinarily, however, it is more effective to give the pupils the details and encourage them to draw their own generalizations.

In preparing course plans, then, teachers should strive for a maximum amount of transfer and retention. To do so, they should provide for an optimum of usable learning and opportunities to use the learning in their classes and many occasions in which the pupils can both draw their own generalizations and also utilize these generalizations in new situations. Teachers will find the problem approach particularly useful for these purposes.

Planning the Sequence

With all these principles in mind, the teacher can set up the sequence of topics for the course. This sequence should consist of broad topics that can be expected to take two to four weeks of classtime to accomplish. At this time it is not advisable to map out the course in great detail day by day, because, at this stage, no one can forecast just how the course will develop. One should delay filling in the details until one sees how the pupils are progressing.

As he picks his topics and arranges them in order, the teacher should also estimate the amount of time to be spent on each topic. Again the decisions should be approximate—in weeks and fractions of weeks rather than days. The teacher should, however, base his course calendar on the days available in the school year. In making this estimate he should remember to allow for assemblies, examinations, storms, and other contingencies that cause class periods to be cancelled. Ten days is a reasonable allowance for missed periods. If at the end of the year the teacher finds that this allowance is too great, he can use the extra time for review or for a special topic at the end of the term.

At this time one should also consider the general approach for the various topics and any major assignments such as research papers and projects. These items need to be considered because they will to some extent affect the time allotments of the various topics, and also, of course, they need to be scheduled as to be integral parts of the course.

COURSES OF STUDIES AND CURRICULUM GUIDES. In deciding the sequence of topics, a course of study or curriculum guide can be a great help to the teacher. Many courses of study or curriculum guides outline in great detail suggested topics and sequences. The Teaneck, New Jersey, High School course outline for Physical Science, for instance, lists a sequence of sixteen units for the course with a suggested course calendar.[5]

1. Air. Introduction to Physical Science. The Scientific Method. (4 weeks)
2. Water (2 weeks)
3. Fuels (3 weeks)
4. Forces (3 weeks)
5. Chemicals (5 weeks)
6. Metals (2 weeks)
7. Plastics (2 weeks)

5 Physical Science, Teaneck High School, Teaneck, N.J., August 6, 1959, pp. 3–9.

   8. Textiles (2 weeks)
   9. Food and Drugs (2 weeks)
 10. Sound (1 week)
 11. Light (2 weeks)
 12. Electricity (2 weeks)
 13. Vacuum Tubes (1 week)
 14. Atomic Energy (1 week)
 15. Earth Science (8 days)
 16. Astronomy (8 weeks)
     Review (2 weeks)

Other courses of study and curriculum guides, although they do not suggest the topics to be studied, do suggest what content should be covered. The Santa Barbara Language Arts Curriculum Guide, previously cited, is an example of such a guide. In the area of Sentence Structure and Punctuation for low ninth-graders the Santa Barbara guide suggests among other things that teachers[6]

1. Insist upon legible handwriting.
     * * *
3. Improve the quality of the simple sentence.
4. Use simple dictation frequently.
     * * *
7. Reteach the distinction between the fragment and the sentence.

Frequently this sort of information can be found in the Scope and Sequence charts contained in courses of study and curriculum. However presented, it can be an invaluable boon to the teacher.

THE TEXTBOOK AND COURSE PLANNING. Obviously courses of study and curriculum guides can be of great help to the teacher planning a course. If they are not provided, the most common method of selecting the content of a course is to follow a basic textbook. The chief merit of this plan is that it gives the beginning teacher an organized outline of the subject content to follow. However, the teacher should recognize that all chapters are not of equal importance.

Furthermore, the text sequence is not always the best for every class. Slavishly following a textbook is poor practice. It may cut one off from many opportunities for creativeness, from new ideas, from flexibility of approach, and from variety of method. It often leads to merely "covering the subject" rather than significant learning.

COVERING THE SUBJECT. Probably the greatest danger to guard against in planning a course is the temptation to include too much. One of the worst diseases in American education is the belief of so many

[6] *Ibid.*, p. 33.

secondary-school teachers that they must cover the subject. Usually covering the subject results in the pupils' learning nothing about much, or at best a little about a lot. It would be much more satisfactory for them to gain clear concepts and skills in a less diffuse area. One cannot teach pupils everything on any subject. The modern teacher must limit his course to the most important topics. He does not have time for unnecessary and marginal topics. Better to teach more by attempting less than to attempt more and teach nothing.

✿

One author says that one should not follow a text in planning a course. Do you agree? Why, or why not?

Of what value are textbooks, curriculum guides, courses of study in the planning of a course? How should each of them be used? How rigidly should they be followed?

✿

Planning Lessons

Once the course has been planned, the teacher must plan for the actual instruction. Some teachers use the unit plan as the basis for their planning. Others develop their topics on the basis of daily lessons. Since the latter procedure is the older and more deeply entrenched of the two, let us consider it first. Unit planning will be the topic of the following chapter.

Preparing the Lesson Plan

A lesson is a short period of instruction devoted to a specific topic, skill, or idea. In preparing a lesson, the first thing to do is to decide what the pupil should learn from it. This is called the objective of the lesson. Deciding what these learning products should be is the responsibility of the teacher. That is true even though the lesson as a whole is developed cooperatively with the class.

In selecting the objectives, the teacher should keep certain criteria in mind.

1. The objective may be a concept, skill, attitude, ideal, or appreciation, any one of these, or a combination of them. But no matter what it is, it should be a specific learning product or terminal behavior so definite and specific that the teacher can aim directly at it, and by means of educational measuring devices tell whether he has been successful or not.

2. Each objective should be a worthwhile learning product pertinent

to the course. One should always have a valid answer for the pupil who asks, "Why do we have to study this?"

3. The teacher should have each learning product clearly and definitely defined in his own mind. In order to be sure that his objectives are clear, the teacher would do well to describe just what the desired learning products are in a few simple declarative sentences. He may be surprised to find out that he is not always so clear about them as he thought he was.

4. The objectives must be feasible. To try to teach something that is too difficult or something that cannot be completed in the time allotted is pointless. Do not try for too much. We reiterate: *It is better to do a little well than try to do a lot, and do it badly.* One or two major concepts are quite enough for one period.

5. The objectives should allow for differences in individuals. All pupils cannot learn the same things in any class. What is too easy for one may be too difficult for another. Therefore, one's objectives should allow pupils to achieve them in different amounts and in different ways.

✿

What would be a suitable objective for a lesson on Edgar Allan Poe's *The Raven* to be given in grade 10?

How can one's objectives allow pupils to achieve them in different amounts and different ways?

✿

SELECTING THE SUBJECT MATTER. At this point it might be wise to mention the subject matter of the lesson. No lesson can get very far if the teacher neglects subject matter. The subject matter selected should, of course, lead to the objective of the lesson, and can hardly be separated from the activities. It is often wise to outline the subject matter to be studied or discussed. This outline might be included in the lesson plan itself, or placed on a separate sheet of paper. In choosing subject matter, it is particularly important to be selective. One cannot learn everything. Therefore the teacher should avoid attempting to include too much, and rather should include only that subject matter which seems to him to hold the most promise.

PLANNING THE ACTIVITIES. Once the teacher has chosen his objectives for the lesson he must decide how to reach them. The means he uses are the activities both he and the pupils pursue during the lesson. This phase of the lesson plan is often called the procedure. Experience is not just the best teacher; experience is the only teacher. Consequently,

To be successful, laboratory as well as other experiences must be well planned.

the planning of suitable activities is crucial. They are the experiences through which pupils learn. Unless the activities are properly planned, one can hardly expect the pupils to reach the desired goal.

Activities may be called the teacher's tools, and should be used accordingly. Just as a carpenter uses a rip-saw for cutting with the grain and a cross-cut saw for cutting across it, so the teacher needs to select the proper activities for the job to be done. To this end, the teacher should learn to conduct many different kinds of activities. The more activities the teacher knows how to conduct, the more likely he will be able to find the activity most suitable for any given situation.

As in the planning of objectives, the teacher must be careful to choose suitable activities. If he wishes, he may enlist the help of pupils in deciding upon the activities. Still, the teacher is responsible for the quality and suitability of the activities chosen. Some criteria he may consider in selecting activities are

1. Will the activity lead to the goal desired? Is it suitable?
2. Is it efficient? Will it lead us to our goal directly and economically?
3. Is it suited to the pupils' abilities and interests?
4. Do we have time for it?
5. Do we have the material for it?
6. Does it allow for individual differences?
7. Is it suitable for the room in which it is scheduled to take place? If not, can we find a suitable place?

In addition to selecting the activities the teacher must also decide how to conduct the activities. He therefore tries to determine the sequence of the activities and the approximate time to be spent on each activity. He plans how to introduce the lesson and how to launch the various activities. He also provides for finishing each lesson with a culminating activity—a summary, for instance.

Four points need to be emphasized in detail here, because many new teachers never learn the truth about them until it is too late. The first is that every activity contained in every lesson should be aimed directly at an objective of that lesson. Anything less than that leads to soft pedagogy and drifting classes. If any activity does not contribute to your goal, leave it out.

The second point that needs reiterating is that the portion of the lesson plan that outlines the activities, i.e., the procedure, should be detailed step by step. These activities should be explicit, definite, and detailed. It is not enough to say "Lecture on the amoeba—15 minutes"; you should state what will be in the lecture. It is not enough to state that there will be a discussion on the civil rights law; state the direction the discussion will take, the main points it will bring out, and the questions you will use. It is not enough to state that we shall have some problems done at the board; state which problems and work out the answers.

The third point is that in setting up the plan for his activities, the teacher should consider the motivation of his pupils. Teachers should consider the activities to be sure that they have appeal and that the pupils are ready for them. If it appears that the activities do not have appeal, or that the pupils are not ready for them, the teacher should consider what steps he should take to be sure that the pupils put out their best effort. Sometimes he may need to withdraw the activities and substitute others; at other times he may wish to attach some extrinsic reward to them, or he may decide to postpone these activities until he has prepared the pupils for them. What the teacher does must depend upon his analysis of the situation.

The fourth point is that every objective needs to be driven home. Many teachers fail—when they fail—because they neglect to make the little extra effort that would clinch the learning that is their objective. Again, how to do this clinching depends upon the situation. In many lessons the clincher may be a summary at the end of the session. In others it may be a review or drill. In still others it may be a pupil summation to the question: "What was the main point that we were trying to get at in this discussion, John?" At times it might even be a short quiz. Even though sometimes lessons must carry over to the next class, one can take it as axiomatic that any lesson plan that does not make provision for the clincher is not a complete plan.

THE PROBLEM OF TIME. In listing the activities in the procedure of his lesson plan the teacher should estimate how much time the class will spend on each activity. Beginning teachers find this estimate so difficult to make that they often ask for ways of determining just how long to allow for each activity. Unfortunately no one can give them this help, because there is really no way to tell how people will react. An activity that can be done in five minutes in one class may take fifteen minutes in another. All this notwithstanding, we shall attempt to provide a few rules of thumb to use as guides.

1. The first of these is to make your procedure too long at first. By doing so you may prevent the embarrassment of running dry with the period half over. Beginning teachers tend to talk fast and move swiftly, because of the tenseness caused by the newness of the classroom situation. As a rule this tendency wears off with experience. The new teacher often is troubled because he does not have enough material; the experienced teacher's trouble is more likely to be that he never has enough time.

2. The second rule of thumb is to provide a few minutes at the beginning of the period for taking attendance and the making of announcements, and five or more minutes at the end of the period for clinching the lesson. One also needs to provide, at some point, time enough to make an adequate homework assignment. It is this need to provide for classroom and teaching chores that accounts for the astonishing fact that a forty-minute moving picture is too long for a fifty-minute period.

3. A third rule of thumb is to mark in your procedure by an asterisk or by underlining (some teachers use red ink) the activities that really must be covered during the period in case time starts to run out. This procedure can save one from such situations as never getting around to showing pupils how to do their homework assignments, and so on.

4. A fourth rule of thumb is to give pupils time to learn. Don't rush. Points have to be made and remade. The fact that one of your bright pupils grasps the answer in a flash is no sign that everyone else does. Take time to be sure by asking others about the same point in different ways. One makes concepts clear by turning them over and over in one's mind. Give the pupils a chance to do that. Introduce your points and follow them up. If one takes time to be sure about ideas, he makes haste slowly but surely.

5. Finally, if you do run out of material, don't panic. Use the time for a review of what has gone on before, or for a chance to let the pupils start their homework under supervision. For a while at least,

the new teacher would be wise to have some extra activities planned just for such a contingency.

PREPARING FOR THE ACTIVITIES. The teacher must also prepare for the activities. If he plans to use questions, he decides what questions to ask, and notes down the wording of the more important ones. If he plans to use demonstrations or films, he gathers the necessary materials and equipment beforehand and checks them carefully to be sure that everything is in working order.

Before attempting any experiment or demonstration one should try it first to make sure of one's apparatus and technique. Nothing is flatter than a demonstration that will not work. Similarly, before one assigns a problem or exercise, one should check to see that it is solvable and that he himself knows how to solve it. Picture the plight of the beginning teacher who, in a physics class, was stumped by one of the exercises he had assigned to be worked on the board. A brilliant pupil finally showed him how to do it. Mistakes of this kind can cause the pupils to lose respect for the teacher.

✿

What activities might a teacher use to teach the objectives he decided were suitable for a discussion of *The Raven?* Plan the activities for a lesson designed to achieve these objectives.

✿

OTHER ELEMENTS OF THE LESSON PLAN. In his plan the teacher should list the materials and equipment needed for the lesson. He should also note special things he plans to do, such as announcements to be made. Also, he should write down things he wishes to remember to do or say, such as speaking to John about trying to be a little tidier, or to give Joe a hand with setting up equations. Part of his planning will, of course, provide for any new assignments.

The Lesson Plan Format

The authors of this book do not insist on any particular format for the lesson plan. The format is up to the teacher. He should use whatever format is best for him. But he should use a format that is easy to follow, one that lists the activities in order of use, provides for the maximum amount of detail in the minimum space, and makes provisions for each of the following elements, although they all need not be present in every lesson plan.

1. The objective. A precise statement of what is to be learned in the lesson.

2. Subject matter. An outline of the subject matter to be covered is often very helpful. If it is to be used, it can be included here.

3. The activities (or class procedure). The activities through which objectives will be reached should be listed in order of occurrence with provisions for introducing them and for culminating activities. Evaluative activities should be included also.

4. The materials needed. Planning includes acquiring the materials needed for each activity and getting them ready for use. Preparing the classroom for the lesson should also be included.

5. Special notes. Reminders of anything that may be forgotten. This section usually includes matters that are out of the ordinary. Announcements and special work for individuals are examples of the type of thing often included.

6. The new assignment. This section will be devoted to the assignment.

An outline based on the six headings above seems to be as satisfactory as any other format. However, in selecting a format a teacher should remember that his lesson plans are for his use alone (except in emergencies), and so he should use the format he finds easiest and most comfortable to use when he is teaching.

SOME SAMPLE LESSON PLANS. On the following pages you will find examples of lesson plans prepared according to various formats. Most of these plans were prepared by college students. None of them is perfect. Feel free to criticize them.

Lesson Plan*

Chemistry

1. *Objectives*

   A molecule is the smallest possible division of a substance which can be made without destroying its properties.

   Energy is the ability of matter to move other matter, or to affect the motion of other matter.

   The two kinds of energy are: active or kinetic, and stored or potential.

   Matter and energy are related since matter cannot be moved without some force to cause the movement.

2. *Subject Content*

   Text reference: pages 34–9, covering topics: molecules, elements and compounds, matter and energy, and two kinds of energy.

3. *Class Procedure*

   a. Initiate lesson with brief review of matter, and introduce its composition;

   b. Read pages 34–9 orally and then go over the sections slowly, explaining the more difficult passages;

   c. Display a picture of an atom and list the elements;

   d. Have a discussion on energy and its kinds;

   e. Have each student write examples of some form of matter having a particular kind of energy;

   f. Have some of these examples contributed to the class.

4. *Instructional Materials*

   Text—*Our Environment;* general chemistry textbook.

5. *Assignments*

   Memorize the definition of energy and its two kinds: potential and kinetic.

---

* This is a lesson plan prepared by a college student. It is designed to be used in a twelfth-grade chemistry class. Evaluate this lesson plan. Can you suggest any ways in which it might be improved?

Lesson Plan*

English III

OBJECTIVE	ACTIVITIES
Proper punctuation, proper word choice, and proper construction help make sentences clear.	1. Return compositions. 2. Explain marking system (Two grades: one for comp., one for mechanics). 3. Review theme. Point out that the story must carry out the premise in order to be successful. 4. Go over the following sentences selected from the composition. *Note:* Exercise should be considered a help. First correct sentences on paper, then discuss them. Rewrite, if necessary.

What is wrong with each of these sentences?
   a. The body of the dead wolf loomed up before him. (*loomed up* is inappropriate, perhaps *lay, appeared*)
   b. Coming into the room Mother asked What is the matter? (dangling phrase, quotation marks)
   c. Now I've really tried it, he'll be on my back the rest of the week were Johnny's thoughts. (quotes, half sentences)
   (*Five other sentences have been omitted to conserve space. In actuality the teacher had listed these on a separate sheet of paper.*)
Summary questions: Why punctuate? Why good sentence structure? Why be careful of words?

Assignment: Read *The Spectre Bridegroom*. What do you think the premise to be in this story?

Note: Period cut to 10:14 because of grade reports.

Remember to show Allan how to develop premise. He missed original explanation. He should rewrite the composition.

* This plan was used by a senior student teacher in an 11th grade English class. You may wish to criticize it.

114

Lesson Plan*

Algebra I, Grade 9

1. Course: Algebra I
               9th grade
               average group

2. Topic: Factoring polynomials having common factors.

3. Vocabulary:
     Old: factor, product, polynomial, monomial.
     New: common factor, greatest common factor.

4. Concepts:
     Old: Distributive law.
     New: Factoring polynomials that have common factors is the inverse process of multiplying a polynomial by a monomial.

5. Skills:
     Old: using the distributive law.
               multiplying a polynomial by a monomial.
     New: finding the greatest common factor.

6. Method of presentation:
     teacher-pupil discussion

TIME SCHEDULE

     10 min.   —review homework
     15 min.   —present new material
     15 min.   —supervised study

ASSIGNMENT

Read pp. 244–245
p. 245, 1–29 all odd numbers

PROCEDURE

1. Review: a) What is a product?
              b) What is a factor?

2. Give the problem: $3a + 4b$ What are the factors?
                       $\times \quad 4a$ How do we find the products?
                                     What is the product?

---

* This plan follows a form for lesson plan advocated by the Mathematics Department of Jersey City State College. Note that items 3–5 of the outline are really objectives. Also note the great detail of the procedure.

By permission of John Reckzeh, Chairman, Dept. of Mathematics, Jersey City State College, Jersey City, New Jersey.

3. Can we write this problem another way?

    $4a(3a - 4b) = 12a^2 - 16ab$

    What gives us the right to do the problem this way? [Dist. Law]

    What is the Dist. Law?

4. Give examples: $[2a(m + 3n), 3x(2x - 1), a^2(a^2 + b^2)]$

5. $a(x + y + z) = ax + ay + az$

    What law is this?

    When multiplying a polynomial by a monomial what may be said about the product? [The monomial is seen in each term of the product.]

    We may say that a is ? to each term in the product? [common]

6. $2ax + 2ay =$ What is the common factor? $[2a]$

    Where do you think we would put the common factor?

    What do we do to each term in the product?

    [divide it by the common factor and put quotient in parenthesis]

    Just as division is the inverse of multiplication what can we say the relationship between factoring polynomials and the process of multiplying a polynomial by a monomial is? [the inverse]

7. $6m + 6n = 6(m + n)$ ⎰ What is the common factor?

    $mn_2 + m1 = m(n + 1)$ ⎱ Where do I put it?

    $3a_2 - 3a = 3a(a - 1)$ ⎰ What do I do to each term in the product?

8. $4a + 12a = 4a(a + 3)$

    Could I write $4a^2 + 12a = 4(a^2 + 3a)$? Why?

    What is $4a$ called? [greatest common factor]

    What is G.C.F. in the above problems?

9. $6xy - 3x^2 = 3x(2y - x)$ ⎰ What is G.C.F.?

    $2\pi r - 2\pi R = 2\pi(r - R)$ ⎱ Where do I put it?

    $2a + 4ab + 2ac = 2a(1 + 2b + c)$ ⎰ What do I do to each term in product?

10. Given the example: $6a^2b - 15ab^2 = ?$ $[3ab(2a - 5b)]$

    This check would still be valid if G.C.F. had not been chosen, ex. $3a$ instead of $3ab$. Therefore, what should we do to check for G.C.F.? [Inspect each term in the polynomial to make sure no single number or letter is seen in each term]

Lesson Plan*

Social Studies II: United States History and Problems
Unit: "Evolving A Foreign Policy"
Topic: The Changing Relationship of Puerto Rico to the United States in the Twentieth Century

OBJECTIVES: To assist pupils
1. Understand the evolution of the political and economic ties between Puerto Rico and the United States.
2. Listen and read for information, analytically.
3. Appreciate the unique role of Puerto Rico in current inter-American affairs.
4. Relate current problems to their historical antecedents.

PROCEDURES:
1. Conclude some unfinished business: an oral report comparing life in Maryland suburbia with life in the rural Dakotas.
2. Review by means of puzzle: see attached sheet.
3. Establish purposes for listening to oral reports by offering listening guide questions: see attached sheet.
   Present reports sequentially in order to trace the changing relationship of Puerto Rico to the United States.
   a. "The Island of Puerto Rico Before 1898."
   b. "Political and Economic Change, 1898–1940."
   c. "Luis Muñoz Marin and Operation Bootstrap."
   d. "Puerto Rico: The Cultural Bridge Between the Americas."
   e. "Teodoro Moscoso and the Alliance for Progress."
4. Summarize by means of a special assignment, which the pupils will copy from the chalkboard upon entering the classroom.

ASSIGNMENT: Read "Crisis in Latin America," a speech made by the Governor of Puerto Rico. Keep these questions in mind:
1. Why does the author caution us about the use of political "labels?"

* This plan is one used by an experienced teacher in 11th grade U.S. History. Note the teacher's explanation of the plan: "During recent discussion in literature class of the social protest writing that came out of the mid-west at the end of the last century, and in history class of the Populist crusade, a pupil whose grandparents have always lived in the Dakotas offered some interesting comments. The class was intrigued, and the pupil has promised some further observation. Her remarks will serve as appetizer before today's main course. Though obviously not a direct part of the lesson's topic, the theme of cultural difference is not totally foreign to the topic."

Also note that two guide sheets to be given to the pupils are part of the plan, but they have been omitted here to save space.

2. In what ways is the term "Latin America" really an unsuitable expression?
3. What are the particular problems which Latin America faces?
4. In the Alliance for Progress, what role does the author hope the United States will play?
5. Why is there stress on the phrase "Operation Seeing-Is-Believing?"
6. What unique function does the Governor feel his own island can play in the Alliance for Progress?

Lesson Plan*
(50 minute period)

Sophomore Biology Class—Advanced

The Microscope and Its Use

OBJECTIVE: To learn the parts and the proper use of the microscope.
PROCEDURE:

Assign one microscope to every two students and record the microscope numbers.

Inform the class of the proper manner in which to carry and hold a microscope, so as not to damage it.

Show the prepared diagrams of the microscope on the overhead projector, and point out the various parts and their functions.

Point out the parts on the prepared diagrams and have the class locate the same on their microscopes.

Pass out the mimeographed material on the proper use of microscopes. This information is as follows:

Skill in using the microscope can be developed only by following all steps correctly. Read and perform each step in the order given.

1. Place the microscope on the table with the arm toward you and with the back of the base about one inch from the edge of the table.
2. Adjust your position and tilt the microscope so that you can look into the eyepiece comfortably.
3. Wipe the top lens of the eyepiece, the lens of the objectives, and the mirror with lens paper.
4. Turn the disk to the largest opening so that the greatest amount of light is admitted.
5. Turn the low-power objective in line with the body tube.
6. Place your eye to the eyepiece and turn the mirror toward a source of light, but never directly toward the sun. Adjust the mirror until a uniform circle of light without shadows appears. This is a field. The microscope is now ready for use.
7. When you receive the prepared slide, place it on the stage, clip it into place, and move the slide until the object is in the center of the stage opening.
8. Watching the bottom lens, turn the low-power objective down as far as it will go, using care not to touch the slide.

* This is another plan by a college student. It has several faults.

9. Place your eye to the eyepiece, and as you watch the field, turn the course adjustment slowly toward you, raising the body tube. Watch for the material to appear in the field.

Go through each step with the class, making sure the students understand the procedure of using low magnification.

Ask for volunteers to describe the slides they are examining.

When they have grasped the procedure of using low-power magnification, instruct the class to turn the high-power objective in line with the body tube and use the fine adjustment slowly until the object comes into the field. Go around the room and help individuals who are having difficulty.

Ask for volunteers to compare the differences between low power and high power.

Instruct the students to replace the microscope in the cabinets and prepare for leaving.

MATERIALS: Microscopes, lens paper, overhead projector, prepared diagrams of the microscope and labeled parts, mimeographed information on the proper use of the microscope, and prepared slides on insects.

NOTES: Be sure to instruct the class as to the proper technique of handling slides. Caution them that they are responsible for damaged slides.

ASSIGNMENT: Know the parts of the microscope and their functions in preparation for a short quiz at the next meeting.

A Poor Lesson Plan

Here is a poor lesson plan used by an experienced teacher. Perhaps, if you follow along the plan as you read the criticism, it will help you to see what is needed in a good lesson plan.

Huckleberry Finn: A Picaresque Novel

PURPOSE

General: To discuss the development of *Huckleberry Finn* by Mark Twain as a picaresque novel.
Specific: 1. To define the picaresque novel.
2. To discuss the basic methods of revealing a character used by Mark Twain.
3. To analyze the development of the character, Huckleberry Finn, as a picaresque hero.

PROCEDURE

1. Introduce the term *picaresque* to the students.
2. Discuss the basic methods of revealing a character used by Mark Twain.
3. Trace Huckleberry's excursion along the Mississippi.
4. Discuss his beginning as a confused boy and his development as an independent individual.

ASSIGNMENT

Using specific references from the text, analyze the incident which proves to be the turning point in Huck's development.

Criticism of a Poor Lesson Plan

Neither the general nor specific objectives are objectives at all. They do not in any way set the goals of what the pupils are to learn during the lesson. Rather than being descriptions of specific terminal learnings or learning products to be achieved in the classroom, they are descriptions of general method—too vague and general to be of any real value.

The procedure is too loose and general. We do not know from the lesson plan (nor could the writer tell from the lesson as given) how the teacher had planned to introduce the term *picaresque*. Neither are any real clues given to just how the teacher plans to conduct the discussion of Mark Twain's techniques for character development; nor is there any indication of who is to trace Huck's excursion, in what detail is he to trace it, and which elements of the trip are essential and which not; furthermore, we are not told how the discussion of Huck's growth from a confused boy to an independent individual is to develop.

The assignment too is so scanty that the pupils were not sure about what they were supposed to do. Not everyone knew what the "turning point incident" was, or how to find out what it was, or what the teacher meant by "analyzing" by means of specific references.

In the hand of a skilled teacher who has taught *Huckleberry Finn* many times, such a plan might be successful—not because the plan is good enough, but because of planning and resources that the written plan does not show. But the inexperienced teacher should never trust himself to so skimpy a plan. He must know what the pupils are supposed to learn from his lesson and plan definitely his tactics as well as the strategy. The lesson plan is quoted because the objectives are not clear and, although there is a semblance of a strategy, there is no tactical plan for carrying it out.

Following the Plan

On the whole, the new teacher would do well to follow his plan fairly closely. Doing so is about the only way he can be sure to do what he has intended to do. Otherwise, in the hurly-burly of an active classroom situation a teacher can easily get sidetracked and loose sight of his objective. Nevertheless, a teacher should not let his plan handcuff him. There are at least two types of situations that require him to leave his plan: (1) When the lesson planned is going so badly that something must be done to save it, and (2) when something happens before or during the class to indicate that the pupils would benefit more from a different attack.

As a rule a teacher is foolish to stick by a lesson plan that is obviously not succeeding. Of course it should be only seldom that such a contretemps occurs, yet the new teacher would be wise always to have an alternate approach ready to use in case of emergency.

Often a change of pace is needed to cut off an incipient behavior problem. Pupils who are growing restless in a lecture or recitation may be ripe for a discussion or a problem-solving activity. Sometimes a written assignment can be quite effective for channeling energies that seem about to break the bonds of propriety. At other times a teacher can see by the looks on pupils' faces that what one is trying to teach is not getting through to them. In such cases a few well-directed questions may tell what the difficulty is so that the teacher can reorient himself and start off with a different approach or perhaps switch to a different, more elementary lesson.

At times pupils raise questions during the lesson that are sufficiently important to warrant immediate follow up. Sometimes the point or problem is worth pursuing in detail. In such circumstances perhaps the teacher should discard his lesson plan completely and devote the class's attention to this new point. More often, the pupils' questions warrant only a short diversion from the planned procedure.

Sometimes events of importance may occur within or outside the class to make your plan obsolete. In the case of an event of national importance or of great importance to the school or community, it may be desirable to interrupt the class to talk about the event even though it has no visible relationship to the course or subject concerned. On December 8, 1941, teachers of mathematics, science, and English classes quite rightly turned on radios in their classrooms in order to hear President Roosevelt's speech asking Congress to recognize the existence of a state of war with Japan, *and a quarter of a century later many who were in those classes remember the lesson learned that day more vividly than anything else they learned in their high-school programs.* In the case of an exciting school event, it may be wise to let pupils talk about it for a few minutes at the beginning of class so as to let them blow off steam a little before they settle down to work.

No one can tell any teacher when he should stick to his plan and when to depart from it. What a teacher does must be decided on the basis of what seems best at the time. The criteria on which to base one's decision are simple: (1) What will benefit the pupils most? (2) What will advance the cause of learning most? (3) How relevant and significant to the course is the change? The teacher should remember that, after all, his plan is only a means to an end. If something better comes along he should feel free to use it.

On the other hand, no teacher should change plans capriciously. Some teachers frequently change their plans, because inspiration has found something better on the spur of the moment. On the whole, if you are inspired by a better idea during a lesson it is wise to resist it and stick to your original plan. Good inspirations are hard to find. The chances are that your original plan will serve you better than any spur of the moment idea, although sometimes it pays to be daring and to discard your plans.

Sources of the Lesson Plan

Most teachers draw their lesson plans from their teaching experiences over the years. Teachers who have had little experience or narrow experience have relatively little to draw from other than their textbooks. The new teacher needs help in determining what goals to strive for, what activities to include, and what materials to use. Many school administrations provide such help through a variety of means. One way is through supervision. Almost always the supervisor will be willing to suggest techniques, approaches, and sources of materials if the teacher wants him to. Many supervisors make it a practice to go over teachers' lesson plans in order to point out ways of improving them. The new teacher should welcome such inspection. By following up his supervisor's suggestions he can usually learn much.

Other sources of help in building lesson plans are curriculum guides, curriculum bulletins, and resource units. Many of these list specific suggestions that can be particularly helpful for specific lessons in specific topics. Among the materials available for help in planning lessons, the resource unit is often the most valuable. The scope of the potential aid a good resource unit can give to teachers planning lessons is indicated by the content of the St. Paul resource unit *"Democracy vs. Communism"*[7] which includes

An overview
A list of desired outcomes divided according to
    Understandings
    Attitudes
    Skills
An outline of content
A list of activities divided according to
    Initiatory activities
    Developmental activities
    Culminating activities
An annotated bibliography
An annotated list of films
An annotated list of film strips.

[7] *Democracy vs. Communism, A Resource Unit for High School Social Studies Classes,* Curriculum Bulletin No. 86, St. Paul Public Schools, St. Paul, Minnesota, 1961.

Teachers who utilize sources such as this usually find it easier to prepare good lessons than when they go on unassisted.

Using Plan Books

School officials often provide teachers with plan books with which to plan their lessons. These are valuable for planning the long-term sequence for the school year. Unfortunately, some of the commercial plan books do not allow enough space for one to enter an entire plan. Since this is the case, the teacher may want to prepare his daily plan on a sheet of composition paper or in a notebook designed for that purpose.

Even though the teacher keeps more detailed plans elsewhere, he needs to keep in his plan book at least skeleton plans as he forecasts them for at least a week ahead. Here he should record the lessons to be studied, the assignments, and a word about the approach. Keeping these plans up-to-date is important because they may be used as the index for an estimate of the adequacy of the course by supervisors and as a basis for teaching the class if a substitute has to take over.

Teacher-Pupil Planning

During the twentieth century there has been an accent on pupil participation in the planning of their own classes that has never been found in the formal schooling of any earlier period, although it has always been present to some extent in informal learning situations. This sort of planning is commonly called teacher-pupil or cooperative planning.

To what extent pupils participate in the planning of their own learning activities varies greatly from school to school and class to class, the range being from almost no participation at all to pupils' making almost all the decisions for entire units and courses. In almost every course, however, the pupils do some of the planning, if only to select and carry out their own "projects," reports, outside readings, and similar activities.

How much pupils should be encouraged, or even permitted, to cooperate in the planning of class activities is open to debate. It seems obvious that pupils do not have enough knowledge about any of the secondary-school subjects to know either what can be learned from them or what potential values they may hold for secondary-school youth who learn them. It is also axiomatic that the teacher, having been appointed by the school authorities to guide the learning of pupils, cannot turn his responsibilities for the progress of his courses over to pupils. On the other hand, certain benefits do accrue from teacher-pupil cooperation in planning. Principally these benefits come as an increase in pupil motivation and the development of skills in planning and decision making.

MOTIVATING BY MEANS OF TEACHER-PUPIL PLANNING. Pupil participation in planning can be an aid to motivation. No one knows what the pupil finds interesting and important better than the pupil himself. Since teachers should select material that is important and interesting for boys and girls to study, what could be more natural than to ask them to help select the topics and activities?

Once an activity is planned by the group, it becomes a group activity. In other words, if the planning has been really successful, the responsibility for completing an assignment becomes a group concern. The young man who fails to do his part no longer faces the displeasure of his teacher alone; he must also face the displeasure of the group he has let down. And, for an adolescent, the displeasure of one's peers is much more powerful than that of an adult.

A LABORATORY OF DEMOCRATIC CITIZENSHIP. One of the aims for which many teachers and educational theorists claim schools should strive is the ability to think. Another aim frequently mentioned in the literature on education is the ability to choose wisely. One of the reasons for advocating public education is to develop good citizens. All of these educational aims imply the ability to plan one's own work, and the ability to work with others in planning group activities. What better experience can one gain in this sort of thing than by participating in the planning of class activities and lessons? *Teacher-pupil planning offers one a laboratory in thinking, in making choices, in planning—in short, in democratic citizenship.*

How to Conduct Teacher-Pupil Planning

In a social studies classroom a group of junior high school pupils were conducting a lesson. This lesson consisted of a series of committee reports on "research projects" just completed and a class discussion of the implications and significance of each of the reports under the quite capable direction of the young lady in charge.

This young lady was a ninth-grader. The lesson, the culmination of several weeks work, had been organized and conducted by the pupils under her chairmanship. Three or four weeks before, the pupils had selected their topic from a short list of alternatives suggested by the teacher as one naturally following from their previous unit. In a group discussion they had decided the various facets of the topic they thought ought to be the most important to investigate. Committees were formed to look into the various aspects of the topic to be investigated and to report to the group what they had learned. But before letting the committees start their work, the class as a whole had set up a set of standards to guide them in their research and to use in evaluating their success. Now they had come to the last step.

Almost every activity in this unit had been planned by the pupils themselves under the surveillance of the teacher. At no time had the teacher dictated to them just what they must or must not do. Neither had she ever left them without support or guidance. She was always there to remind them of the essentials, to suggest alternatives, to point out untapped resources, to correct errors, to question unwise decisions. This sort of teaching is teacher-pupil planning at its best. To do it well requires great skill, much forbearance, and the careful training of one's pupils.

It also requires careful preparation by the teacher. Since cooperative planning may take the group off in any one of several directions, the teacher-pupil planning situation often necessitates the teacher's having several possible plans ready to suggest so that he can provide the pupils with guidance no matter which direction they take.

TEACHER-PUPIL PLANNING FOR BEGINNERS. One good way to start on the road to teacher-pupil planning is for pupils to begin by helping plan their own individual activities. From this point they can move up to the planning of small group activities. In these activities the teacher must expect them to make some errors. He should be ready with help; in this respect the use of guide sheets can be quite helpful.

As they develop more maturity and skill in working as groups, they can proceed to the more difficult task of planning class activities. Later, when they have become more sophisticated, they can move on to such difficult tasks as planning what to include in a topic, and, finally, what topics to include in a course. With inexperienced pupils one should not expect great success initially. The secret of success is to give them small responsibilities at first and gradually to increase these responsibilities as the pupils show they are ready. This principle of moving from a small beginning shows up in other techniques recommended for introducing teacher-pupil planning. One of these is to present alternate plans and to allow the pupils to select the plans they prefer. Thus, in a general mathematics class which is studying how to prepare a budget, the teacher might ask the class whether they would prefer to make up a personal budget or to set up an organizational budget. In a music class the teacher might ask the group to choose between preparing "The Soldiers Chorus" or "When the Foeman Bares His Steel." In an English class the pupils might decide whether to study the short story or the drama next.

Another way to involve pupils in the teacher-pupil planning is for the teacher to propose a plan of action and then ask for their suggestions and approval. In business education, for example, the teacher might ask the pupils if they would like to go to a bank and see how a bank operates. If they agree that this idea has possibilities, then they might discuss ways and means of making the visit and things they might wish to see when they get there.

DISCUSSION TECHNIQUES IN TEACHER-PUPIL PLANNING. As groups become skilful in using teacher-pupil planning techniques, they can do much of their planning in group discussion. *Discussion techniques are especially useful in deciding what to include in a topic.* As a class is about to begin the study of insects, the teacher might ask, "What do you think we should learn about insects?" During the discussion the pupils might propose such things as:

What do insects eat?

How do they reproduce?

What are insects anyway?

How do you make an insect board? And so on.

The teacher will undoubtedly have some things to suggest. Somewhere in the discussion he might ask: "Don't you think we ought to know something about the insect's life cycle?" Perhaps the pupils will not know what a life cycle is. Probably when they do know, they will want to include it. If they do not, the teacher should indicate the importance of the life cycle and point out the necessity for including it in the study.

Discussion techniques can also be used to plan learning activities. For example, as the class decides what it wants to study, the teacher or leader can bring up the question, "How do we go about it?" Thus, through class discussion, committees can be formed, readings can be suggested, dramatic roles can be cast, and field trips can be projected. Sometimes the class may ask a pupil or group to investigate and report on the feasibility of a project. Included in these plans should also be plans for evaluating what has been learned.

The same group discussion techniques can be used by a relatively mature group to select a topic for study. A good way to launch such discussion is to ask the pupils to suggest possible plans for consideration. Perhaps one might ask the pupils to skim a chapter or a book to find topics in it they would like to learn about. Perhaps their curiosity may be piqued by a movie, a story, a teacher talk, or a discussion of some current event. Consider what happened in a certain general science class the day after the first artificial earth satellite was launched. After a short discussion of the new satellite, it was obvious to all that the boys and girls of that eighth grade were anxious to know more about astronomy and were ready to work on it.

If discussion techniques are used in teacher-pupil planning, someone should keep a record of the decisions as they are made. If this record is kept on the chalkboard where everyone can see it, it makes the planning easier. As soon as the group has finished its planning, the final plan should be reduced to writing and given to the pupils, or posted on the bulletin board or the blackboard, so that the pupils will have it for ready reference.[8]

Some Words of Caution

As you can see, cooperative planning is a difficult technique. It is an excellent method of involving pupils in the learning process. It is particularly effective in long-term planning such as weekly or unit planning, but it is hard work, for cooperative planning is not pupil planning but teacher-pupil planning. Under no circumstances can the teacher abdicate his responsibilities and role as mentor. The teacher must guide and limit; seldom, if ever, should he turn the pupils completely free. The amount of freedom the pupils should have depends upon many things, such as the pupils' maturity, their ability level, the subject, and their previous experience in cooperative planning. Pupils who have not learned how to plan will be overwhelmed if suddenly allowed to direct themselves.

Moreover, in order to plan, a teacher needs some information to use in his planning. The following anecdote, concerning a professor who found himself substituting for a sick colleague at a moment's notice, may be illustrative. The class he was to teach was the first one in a course in educational psychology. His only instructions from his stricken colleague were for the students to discuss what they would like to get out of the course. The discussion failed because the students did not know what they could get from such a course, and the instructor was not well enough prepared to help them out. Secondary-school pupils who do not know the possibilities open to them cannot be expected to do what college students cannot do. Either the teacher should explain to them potential directions they can take, or he should direct them to activities that will give them the knowledge they need, even if to do so he must assume the major role in the planning and make most or even all of the decisions.

---

[8] In making group decisions, straw votes are usually helpful. The technique seems to be to avoid putting the question to a formal vote, but frequently to seek an expression of opinion. This allows easy elimination of unpopular alternatives and avoids foundering on difficult decisions. When the straw vote shows a split decision, further discussion can often bring the pupils to agreement. If no agreement is reached, the pupils will usually be willing to compromise, e.g., "first your topic, then ours." If necessary, one can resort to a formal vote, but doing so may defeat the purpose of teacher-pupil planning and is liable to split the group.

Teacher-pupil planning is usually more satisfactory when the group has some criteria on which to base its decisions. These criteria can be made jointly or by the teacher with class approval. During the planning session the teacher may often have to remind the class of the criteria. "Is this the sort of thing you really wanted to do? Is this really pertinent to our problem?" By so doing he can usually improve the quality of group decisions without seeming to impose his own will on the pupils.

Teacher-pupil planning is probably not suited for every course and every teacher. To ask pupils to plan the topics in a course whose sequence is largely determined by the nature of the subject matter—as in mathematics—seems pointless. Pupil-teacher planning should not be used in the same way with all pupils, nor in all subjects.

Moreover, such planning may not be appropriate for all teachers. Conducting courses in this fashion requires considerable skill. It requires a teacher who is not afraid to subordinate himself to the group, who does not need to be the center of the picture, who is not afraid of making errors, who can command respect without demanding it, and who is relatively sure of his control of the pupils. The new teacher should go slowly in introducing teacher-pupil planning. Not to do so may result in chaos.

✻

What are the advantages of teacher-pupil planning? What are its dangers? When and where would you use it? How would you set about to use it?

Is teacher-pupil planning really better suited to certain subjects and courses than to others? Explain your answer.

✻

A WORD OF WARNING. Sometimes teachers are tempted to utilize teacher-pupil planning as a device for coercing pupils to do what they had already planned for their pupils to do. Such planning is not teacher-pupil planning. It is fakery. In all things the teacher should be honest with his pupils. If he plans for them to choose within limits, let him prescribe the limits in advance. If he does not, he should go along with the pupils' decision even though it be a poor one. To allow the pupils to plan and then to veto or revoke the plan is dishonest and it destroys the pupils' faith in their teacher. So do attempts to manipulate pupils' decisions.

Teacher-Pupil Planning for Individual Pupils

So far this discussion of teacher-pupil planning has been limited to group activities and group planning in which the entire class cooperates in the planning of a unit or topic. Teacher-pupil planning should also be used with individual pupils and small groups.

If their goals are firmly fixed and the pupils know what activities they may choose from, or what activities may help them learn what they want to learn, then individuals can do much of their own planning without the teacher's doing much more than approve their plans. Of course, the teacher will usually need to suggest a few changes of plan, recommend sources of materials and references, and guide the pupils as they work along. This procedure relieves the teacher of much of the detail, so that he has more time to work with individuals. In addition, the pupils learn through their own planning. It is unfortunate that many pupils have been deprived of this type of learning by overzealous teachers. *If people are ever to develop into scholars they need to learn the skills of planning and carrying out their own learning activities.* The sooner they learn these skills the better.

✿

To what extent and in what ways should the pupils participate in planning of the course?

How would you introduce pupil-teacher planning to a high-school class that had never had experience in planning?

How can you prepare for individual differences in the initial planning of a course?

What would you look for in selecting materials for your course?

✿

Team Planning

The developments in instructional technology bring with them increasing need for "team planning," in which various members of the staff cooperate to bring forth coordinated plans so that various aspects of the instructional program will fit together harmoniously. This type of planning may be part of formal teaching team arrangement or simply informal *ad hoc* arrangement between colleagues. An example of such a flexible arrangement is that in which a social studies teacher and an English teacher finding that they by chance shared the same group of ninth graders decided to collaborate on their assignments. Another more formal arrangement is that in which the social studies, science, and English teachers agreed to cooperate on the assigning and reading of major research papers. In this instance, the teachers of social studies and science suggested topics for the major research papers and read the papers for their content, while the English teachers taught the pupils how to prepare a research paper and evaluated the papers for excellence in style, usage, format, and other elements of English. Another type of more formal team planning arrangement in a junior high school involves multidisciplinary teams which share the same pupils in their classes. The members of a team meet regularly to coordinate the planning in the various courses. Still another type of team planning is that of the formal teaching team of the so-called Trump Plan in which different teachers play different roles, some conducting large groups, some small groups, and so on. Teams of this sort require careful planning. To allow sufficient time for such planning, team-planning sessions may be incorporated into the daily schedule.

Except for the fact that it is done cooperatively by the team, team planning is not so very different from other planning. The problems of what, how, when, and where bear the same importance in cooperative efforts as in individual planning. The real difference is that the planning is complicated by the need to unite the varying notions and inclinations of several teachers into one unified, workable whole. Bringing about such harmony requires team members who are well versed in group process and careful attention to details so that everyone knows what he is supposed to do and how and when he is supposed to do it. It also requires an infinite amount of following through and checking to ensure that the plans are properly executed.

Team planning does not necessarily imply teaching teams of any sort. In most schools teachers who teach the same or similar courses collaborate on the planning of course sequences and course content. Such planning can be instrumental in making a harmonious, well articulated curriculum.

Summary

Planning is a key to successful teaching. It is absolutely essential if the teacher is to make full use of his knowledge and skill. Poor planning has ruined many classes. In fact, it has been described as the most common cause of not learning.

The responsibility for planning is the teacher's. He must plan his courses, his units, and his daily lessons, although he may have curriculum guides, courses of studies, source units, textbooks, and other materials to draw from. In planning his courses, the teacher can find these devices greatly helpful, but he should guard against their restricting him too much. In selecting the topics and subject matter for the course, the teacher should try for psychological organization and for maximum retention and transfer.

Every lesson needs a plan. The essentials in a daily lesson plan are the objectives, the subject matter, the activities, the list of materials needed, the assignment, and any special notes. These essentials tell us what to do and how to do it. The format a teacher uses for his lesson plan is not so very important. Sometimes daily lesson plans used in conjunction with units need not be very detailed. The important thing is to know what it is we wish to teach in the lesson and to provide activities that lead to these goals. One test of a lesson plan is to ask how each activity in the procedure will help to bring about the desired goal. Once the teacher has decided on his plan of action he would be wise to keep to that plan unless there seems to be important reasons for changing course.

Although the responsibility always rests on the teacher's shoulders, the pupils can often cooperate with the teacher in planning. If such planning is to be successful, pupils must be taught to plan. Usually the teacher and the pupils should start by designing class activities together. For a class to decide what it hopes to learn from a topic and what the topics of a course should be requires considerably more sophistication. With inexperienced pupils one should not expect great success initially. The secret is to give them small responsibilities at first and then increase the responsibilities as the pupils show they are ready.

FOR FURTHER STUDY

ALCORN, MARVIN D., JAMES S. KINDER, and JIM R. SCHUNERT, *Better Teaching in Secondary Schools*, Revised Edition (New York: Holt, Rinehart and Winston, Inc., 1961), Part II.

ALDRICH, JULIAN C., *How to Construct and Use a Resource Unit* (New York: Joint Council on Economic Education, not dated).

BLOOM, BENJAMIN S., *Taxonomy of Educational Objectives, Handbook I, Cognitive Domain* (New York: David McKay Company, Inc., 1954).

CALLAHAN, STERLING G., *Successful Teaching in Secondary Schools* (Chicago: Scott, Foresman and Company, 1966).

HOCK, LOUISE, and THOMAS J. HILL, *The General Education Class in the Secondary School* (New York: Holt, Rinehart and Winston, Inc., 1960), Ch. 4.

INLOW, GAIL M., *Maturity in High School Teaching* (Englewood Cliffs, N.J.: Prentice-Hall, Inc., 1963).

KRATWOHL, DAVID R., et al., *Taxonomy of Educational Objectives, Handbook II, Affective Domain* (New York: David McKay Company, Inc., 1964).

LEE, JAMES MICHAEL, *Principles and Methods of Secondary Education* (New York: McGraw-Hill Book Company, Inc., 1963), Ch. 8.

MAGER, ROBERT F., *Preparing Instructional Objectives* (Palo Alto, California: Fearon Publishers, 1963).

PARRISH, LOUISE, and YVONNE WASKIN, *Teacher-Pupil Planning* (New York: Harper and Row, Publishers, 1958).

RIVLIN, HARRY N., *Teaching Adolescents in Secondary Schools*, Second Edition (New York: Appleton-Century-Crofts, Inc., 1961), Ch. 5.

ZAPF, ROSALIND M., *Democratic Processes in the Secondary Classroom* (Englewood Cliffs, N.J.: Prentice-Hall, Inc., 1959), Chs. 4–6.

CHAPTER 6

What Is the Unit Method?

In essence the unit method is a method of organizing subject matter, teaching techniques, and teaching devices in order to create effective teaching-learning situations. It is a comprehensive and systematic way of applying with proper emphasis the basic educational principles that should operate in good teaching and learning situations. Each unit may be said to have two parts: (1) the *learning products* the teacher hopes will result from the unit; and (2) the *activities and experiences* that are intended to produce these learnings.

The potential learning products are the teacher's goals. These goals are the skills and understandings and their attendant attitudes, appreciations, and ideals that the teacher is trying to instill in the pupils. Real learning products are changes in the pupil. Unless these changes occur, no lesson is successful. Of course, the same changes will not occur in every pupil. Some will learn more than others; some will learn more thoroughly; some may become enthusiastic about the learnings; others may be left apathetic. The teacher's goals, then, do not represent the real learning products of the pupils; they represent what the teacher hopes the learning products will be. If the unit is successful, the real learning products of the individual pupils will approximate the teacher's goals.

The second part of the unit consists of the experiences and activities in which the pupils engage in order to acquire the learning products. These activities we shall call the *unit assignment*. All of the activities and experiences are designed to help the pupils achieve the potential learning products that are the teacher's goals. Although all the activities and experiences should help produce the desired learnings, not all the pupils participate in each activity. There are, however, certain activities that may be required of all pupils. We shall call these activities the basic or core activities. Other activities may be purely optional. Pupils usually select the optional or related activities from a list given by the teacher or developed by the class. In carrying out a unit assignment, much of the direction and planning comes from the pupils themselves. Each pupil may be provided with a mimeographed study guide. With this guide and the teacher's help the pupils can plan their individual activities to a large extent. Thus they can begin new activities without waiting for the other members of the class, and the teacher is freed to work with pupils who need help, guidance, and counseling. As one can readily see, the unit assignment, usually lasting from two to six weeks, is a refined form of the differentiated assignment.

A UNIT IN ACTION. Mr. Jones teaches Problems of Democracy at Quinbost High School. In his course outline he has listed a unit on minority groups. Mr. Jones always tries to make his course interesting and challenging, stimulating and motivating his students. On the day he was to begin the unit, he came to the classroom seemingly in an angry mood, tossed his books on the desk and glared at the class. He then began a tirade on a particular minority group, telling the class of something a member of this group had done to him the day before, and concluded by saying that all members of that particular group were alike.

Immediately, his class began to challenge him, disagreeing, telling him he was unfair generalizing on one incident, and that he shouldn't talk like that. Seizing upon this reaction, Mr. Jones then asked the class whether or not they had ever expressed such feelings toward any group. As the animated discussion continued, the class members began to see what the teacher was doing. Almost as one body they said that they wanted to discuss minority groups as a class topic.

The stage had been set! The teacher had fired their interest; the desire to study the topic was evident. He, then, set the class to discussing what subject matter they felt should be discussed and what outcomes there should be. This led to general teacher-pupil planning. Soon pupils were choosing committees and projects on which to work. Then, with the aid of study guides and their committee and project assignments individual pupils completed tentative plans for their role in the unit.

The study guide they used consisted of three parts (*see* p. 155). The first part noted questions and problems everyone was to find answers for and suggested where the pupils might look to find these answers. The second part listed a number of readings and activities that the pupils might find interesting. All pupils were expected to do some of these, but no one had to do any particular one. These activities were quite optional. In none of these activities nor the required problems and questions was the pupil held to any prescribed reading or procedure. All he was asked to do was to carry out the activity, solve the problem, or find the information; he had free choice of ways and means. The third part of the study guide was a bibliography.

Once the teacher and pupils had finished the planning, they began to work. Except for two periods that Mr. Jones used for motion pictures, the next two weeks were devoted to laboratory work. The committees met; the researchers researched; the pupils carried out their plans.

Then the committees began to report. Some of the groups presented a panel. One did a play. Another conducted a question-and-answer game. In all of these activities pupils tried to bring out what they had learned. In between these reports, Mr. Jones and the pupils discussed the implication of the findings and other points they thought pertinent and important.

Finally the unit ended with everyone's setting down his ideas concerning the treatment of minority groups and with a short objective test based on the teacher's objectives as shown in the questions of the study guide.

Thus, after a little over three weeks, the unit was finished. Note that in the unit the pupils did a share of the planning and that much of the time was taken up in individual and group work laboratory fashion. Note also that the unit consisted of four phases: an introductory phase that included motivating and planning activities; a laboratory phase that included individual and group work; a sharing phase in which pupils pooled their experiences; and an evaluating phase in which the teacher and pupils estimated the learning accomplished during the unit.

TYPES OF UNIT. This unit is typical of many to be found in our schools lately. At present, many authors differentiate between units and classify them by types. For example, it has been a practice to speak of subject matter units and experience units. The beginning teacher should not let this terminology confuse him. A unit is a unit. As in our example, all units consist of both subject matter and experience. One cannot teach without subject matter because subject matter is what one teaches to the pupils. Since one learns only through one's experience, whatever is taught must be taught through experience. We usually think of experience units as those which emphasize the experiences or the learning process, while subject matter units are those in which subject content is emphasized. The difference is not a significant one—merely a difference in emphasis. Some writers also refer to appreciation units, process units, and other special-purpose units. These are merely units in which a certain type of learning product is emphasized. For our present purpose these differences may be disregarded.

THE UNIT PLAN. All units must be planned even though in some units many of the activities pursued by the pupils are developed by teacher-pupil planning while the unit of work is in progress. As with his other plans, when planning the unit, the teacher must concern himself with general and specific objectives, the learning activities, the materials needed for the unit, and the means for evaluating it. In general, his plan will necessarily follow a pattern like the one outlined below.

1. An overview which describes the nature and scope of the unit.
2. The teacher's specific objectives which are the understandings, skills, attitudes, ideals, and appreciations he hopes his pupils will get from the unit.
3. The unit assignment which includes activities the class will participate in during the teaching of the unit. The activities will be of two types: (1) the basic activities to be done by all pupils to some extent in some time and (2) the optional related activities.
4. The study and activity guide which will contain the instructions for carrying out the core activities to be done individually and in small groups.
5. Special study and activity guides which contain the instructions for carrying out the optional related activities.
6. A list of materials and readings for the boys and girls to use in their study.
7. A short bibliography and list of materials for the use of the teacher alone.
8. A test to be used in evaluating the success of the unit. This test should test adequately each of the learning products described in 1 and 2 above.

The Teaching-Learning Cycle

As we have seen, the teaching-learning cycle in unit teaching consists of four phases: the introductory phase, the laboratory phase, the sharing of experience phase, and the evaluating phase. In his lectures on the Unit Method, Roy O. Billett, Professor Emeritus, Boston University, stresses that the excellence of the teaching-learning cycle depends upon ten basic principles. Since the discussion of unit teaching presented in this chapter is based almost entirely on Dr. Billett's teaching, let us summarize these basic principles briefly before discussing the phases of the teaching-learning process in detail.

1. Education is guided and directed growth.
2. A pupil's activities are given direction by some goal which he seeks to attain.
3. Problem solving is the way of human learning.
4. Learning is most effective when optimally emotionalized.

5. Persistence in problem solving behavior varies with the explicitness of the directions which the pupils receive.
6. Knowledge of progress is a powerful incentive to effort.
7. All learning involves integration.
8. Application of the learning product is essential if transfer is to take place.
9. Independence in learning is encouraged if the pupil has some choice in what he is to do; how, and when.
10. Because of individual differences, pupils should not begin necessarily at the same place nor proceed at the same rate, in the same direction, and in the same way.

The Introductory Phase

"A good beginning is half the battle." Perhaps this adage is an exaggeration, but it certainly has a point as far as teaching is concerned. A great deal of the success of any unit depends upon the introductory phase or, as it is often called, the approach. This phase consists of activities designed to launch the unit. In it the teacher attempts to

1. Arouse the pupils' interest.
2. Inform the pupils of what the unit is about.
3. Learn more about his pupils—their interests, their abilities, their present knowledge of the topic.
4. Show the relationship with preceding units and other courses.
5. Plan the rest of the unit with the pupils.

Sometimes an introductory activity sets the mood for an entire course or unit. If it is pleasant, friendly, and lively, perhaps the impetus of the first day will keep the class atmosphere pleasant, friendly, and lively. For this reason the first activities should be purposeful and businesslike. When a class gets off to a fast start, the pupils are likely to get the impression that in this class there will be no nonsense because it is going somewhere. On the other hand, one can readily see what the pupils will expect of a class that starts late with much confusion and waste motion. Similarly, if the introductory activities are dull, to convince the pupils that later activities may be interesting will be more difficult. An introductory activity is a device to get things going, and a good one does just that. Every course, unit, or lesson should start off promptly with an activity which tells the pupil, "Hold on to your hat, we are on our way."

To get things moving quickly, one chemistry teacher makes a practice of starting his unit on oxidation with a "bang." As he starts his introductory talk, he casually mixes together the ingredients for a demonstration that he says is yet to come. Suddenly an explosion nearly rocks the pupils off their seats. The teacher and pupils quickly follow the explosion with questions and discussion. What happened? Why? And so on.

*

The following was suggested as a possible interest-catching introductory activity in a biology unit. What do you think of it?

1. Select five substances with characteristic odors, such as an onion, orange, fish, or peanut. Place them in small corked bottles. Blindfold your companion and be sure he holds his nose so he cannot smell. Let him taste each substance separately and describe it to you. Record each description carefully. Make two trials.

2. Keep him blindfolded, but do not hold his nose. This time let him smell each substance and describe it. Make two trials.

3. Compare the descriptions of the taste and smell of each substance as he gives them to you. How do they differ? Can you draw any conclusions about a person's relative ability to taste and smell? Do you think a cold in the nose makes any difference in the enjoyment of food? Why?

Could the above be used as an interest-catching introductory activity? Why, or why not? If not suitable as is, how might you adapt it for such an activity? Perhaps you will want to compare your answer now to your answer after you have completed reading this section.

*

MOTIVATIONAL VALUES OF INTRODUCTORY ACTIVITIES. A good introductory activity may not only catch the interest of the pupils, it may set the pupils' mental gears in motion; it may start young minds to thinking about the topic; it may arouse their curiosity; it may challenge them; or it may give them a taste which will make them crave more. In other words, a good introductory activity can and should motivate learning. Thus to motivate his pupils, a mathematics teacher may give the pupils a puzzle or problem of the "Mathematics for the Millions" variety to challenge the pupils' ingenuity. In a social studies class, the teacher might propose a troublesome problem facing the nation and challenge the pupils to seek possible solutions.

PUPIL PLANNING IN THE INTRODUCTORY PHASE. A main purpose in the introductory phase is to give the pupil direction. Although the pupil need not know the teacher's goals for the unit, he should have some ideas of where he is going and what he can get out of it so that he can set goals of his own. Thus part of the introductory phase must be spent in planning. Planning is particularly necessary at this point because the class will spend much of the time in succeeding class sessions in individual and small groups. A good method is to distribute the study and activity guides here and let the pupils, under guidance, prepare their own plans. A sample form for a plan follows. The pupils should not be held closely to their plans; they should be permitted to change and amplify them throughout later phases of the unit.

Work Plan

NAME ______________________ CLASS __________

UNIT ______________________ DATE __________

Activities I plan to do.

Committees I plan to work with.

Materials I plan to read.

Things I plan to make.

PROVIDING A BASIS FOR PLANNING. Not only can the introductory activity give the class an opportunity for planning, it can give the pupils the basis on which to plan. By means of a teacher talk, a motion picture, a dramatization, a reading, or some such activity, one can orient the pupils so that they have the information necessary for each to know where he is and where he is going.

A good introductory activity can help the teacher get to know his pupils better both as a group and as individuals. Such information is essential to good planning. Activities and devices useful in this respect have been discussed in Chapter 2.

✲

What specifically might you do to challenge and motivate youngsters to learn in a subject which you plan to teach?

What are the merits of using a pretest as an initiatory activity? Under what circumstances would you recommend using a pretest?

✲

TYPES OF ACTIVITIES IN INTRODUCTORY PHASE. Teachers can use introductory activities for many purposes. However, they should not expect any one introductory activity to do everything they might wish in initiating a course or unit. Almost always one needs to use two or more different introductory activities to perform the functions desired in the introductory phase of any unit. For instance, it may be desirable to use one activity to help teacher and pupils get acquainted, another activity to arouse pupil interest, and still another to help pupils plan, all in the same unit.

THE TEACHER'S ROLE IN THE INTRODUCTORY PHASE. The teacher's leadership is particularly important in introductory activities. Since the pupils are starting afresh, they have little or no framework in which to fit themselves, nor do they yet know in what direction they are going. Consequently the teacher must use better-than-average leadership or the class may flounder. This is particularly true in the introductory phase of the first unit of a course. For this reason introductory activities may well be teacher-centered.

One of the most popular introductory devices is to talk to the pupils. If a teacher is good at it, this is an excellent method, but the talk must be interesting, sprightly, and pointed. It should hold promise, but not false promise. Perhaps it may outline what is to come, but the outline should not be overly detailed.

Teacher talks are only one type of many introductory activities. Other types of activities high on the list are demonstrations, motion pictures, discussions, pretests, questions, and planning.

NECESSITY FOR AN EXCELLENT INTRODUCTION. The introductory phase often becomes vestigial as the natural carry-over from unit to unit eliminates the necessity of many of its functions and as the teachers learn to know their pupils better. But in every unit the teacher should use the most appropriate introductory activities he can employ. Because a good start is so important, introductory activities are worthy of one's best teaching. They can make or break a unit.

The Laboratory Phase

In the laboratory phase the pupils go to work on their activities. During this phase they are free to attempt, under guidance, whatever activities seem best to them. In this way they can capitalize on their own interests and abilities. Activities during this phase will consist largely of individual and small group work: committee projects, construction activities, individual research activities, extensive reading, and the like. From time to time the class may be called together by the teacher or the pupils to engage in common activities such as talks, discussions, moving pictures, and field trips. To a large extent the programming can be done by the pupils themselves. Many times the class selects a steering committee to coordinate the activities.

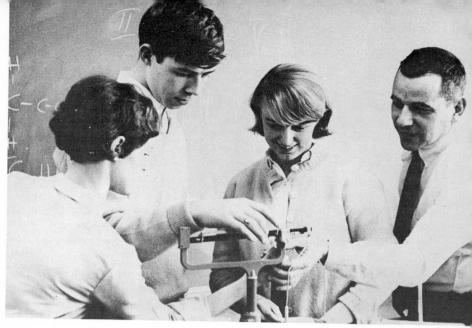

Problem solving is the heart of the laboratory phase of the teaching unit.

The Sharing of Experience Phase

Logically, the laboratory phase should be followed by the sharing of the interesting things learned during the laboratory phase. This part of the unit must be carefully planned. Nothing can be more boring, and less conducive to learning, than pupil reports repeated endlessly. Ordinarily, the pupils should do the programming themselves, but the teacher must guide them carefully to ensure variety and sparkle. Some devices which may be used are

1. Panels.
2. Oral talks.
3. Dramatizations.
4. Writing up the activities for publication.
5. Debates.
6. Group discussions.
7. Meetings of the class.
8. Exhibits.
9. Demonstrations.
10. Preparing an anthology of pupil work.
11. Presenting and defending a position.
12. Recordings and tapes.
13. Audio-visual materials.
14. Moving pictures.

The use of these techniques is described in Part IV.

The Evaluating Phase

Finally we come to the evaluating phase. Naturally, a good unit assignment will consist of many evaluations. The teacher evaluates the pupils' progress as they perform the activities, and so do the pupils. However, the end of the unit is a particularly good time for evaluation. Here the teacher stops to see how well pupils have progressed toward the goals, for he needs to know the pupils' present status in order to determine what to do next. Consequently the evaluative devices the teacher uses should be largely diagnostic. Chapters 2 and 15 discuss the preparation and use of such devices.

The Flexibility of the Teaching-Learning Cycle

Perhaps this description of the teaching-learning cycle makes it seem pretty rigid, but it is not so. It does not always roll forward relentlessly. Instead, it may vary from pupil to pupil. For some it speeds; for others it dawdles. For many pupils it starts, stops, turns back, and then starts again. If one group has finished the preparation of a dramatization and is ready to present it to the class early in the unit long before any other group is ready to share the experience, a good unit plan must be flexible enough to allow this group to present its dramatization then and there. Later the pupils may go to some other activities. Thus the unit has passed from the laboratory phase to the sharing of experience phase and back again.

❊

Explain the teaching-learning cycle. What happens in each part of it? What are the introductory phase, laboratory phase, pooling and sharing phase, evaluation phase? Give an example of each of the phases.

❊

Planning the Unit

Planning a unit and a unit assignment is a relatively simple matter. In general, the job can be reduced to the following steps.

1. Select the topic.
2. Select your goals or objectives, i.e., the skills, understandings, attitudes, ideals, and appreciations which you hope the pupils will learn from their study of the topic.[1]

[1] Some authorities advocate first selecting the objectives and then selecting the topic and activities to bring the objectives about. However, the beginning teacher will find the present order much easier even though theoretically perhaps not as desirable.

3. Prepare the unit assignment.
   a. Select the teacher-pupil activities and subject matter by which the pupils will learn the learning products.
   b. Select the activities and subject matter all pupils should do to some extent at least.
   c. Select the activities that are to be optional.
   d. Organize the activities into a plan. Prepare for pupil programming of their own work.
4. Plan and prepare the evaluation materials and exercises. Prepare tests. *Note:* Tests should be planned before the class starts the assignment.
5. Plan, prepare, and secure the materials necessary for the activities.
   a. Study and activity guides.
   b. Special study and activity guides.
   c. Teacher bibliography.
   d. Pupil bibliography.
   e. Audio-visual materials.
   f. Equipment and supplies.
   g. Reading materials.

The ensuing paragraphs will explain in more detail what each of these steps entails and how to carry them out.

Selecting the Topic

As in any other planning, the first step in unit planning is to select a topic. For practical purposes the topic is the name of whatever you are going to study. It may be an adolescent need or problem, or a bit of subject matter. In any case it should meet the criteria for topics suggested in the preceding chapter.

❊

How can a teacher determine whether a particular topic is worth the time and effort?

It has been stated that the basic criteria for judging a topic are (1) the nature of the pupil and (2) the society in which he lives. Is this a valid statement? Why, or why not?

Where might one turn to find suggestions for suitable topics?

❊

Planning the Objectives

Preparing the Objectives

After the topic has been selected the teacher must decide what learning the pupils should acquire from the study of the unit. This selection is the responsibility of the teacher alone. However, in carrying out his responsibilities and selecting the objectives, he can get tremendous help from supervisors, administrators, and faculty committees. Written materials which may be of help are courses of study, curriculum guides, source or resource units, and curriculum bulletins. If such are available the teacher should study them carefully. They are usually a fruitful source of ideas. Sometimes the objectives suggested in such materials can be used without any change. More often they must be adapted and revised. Sometimes they will not be suitable at all. The teacher should not let the objectives suggested in such material fetter him and stunt his creativity. He is the person who must decide what learning products he should strive for.

The pupils can help greatly by telling the teacher what they want to know. Knowing what the pupils wish to know allows the teacher to select learning products of value to them. They, of course, cannot themselves be responsible for selecting the learning products because they do not know enough about the subject.

The Overview

Once the teacher has decided what the objectives of the unit are, he should describe them in writing. It is usually helpful if the teacher writes a *general statement or overview* of what he is hoping to accomplish. This can be in the form of a paragraph or two describing what is to be learned in the unit as in the following example from a unit in international relations entitled "From Empire to Commonwealth."

During the twentieth century there has been developing between the United States and the British Empire, now called the Commonwealth, a real friendship based upon our common language, customs, and traditions. The great English-speaking nations, including all the British Dominions, linked by friendship, have come to be recognized by the nations of the world as a tremendous force for keeping the peace and for success in war. Britain and the United States have many problems in common in dealing with colonial possessions, particularly those that wish to have complete self-government. In the period from 1919–1956 Great Britain changed from a solidly united Empire, one of the great powers of the world, to a great Commonwealth of Nations where the various parts that make up the whole are held together by reasons of trade and commerce.

Sometimes the overview may be given as a sort of *table of contents* as in the following unit on the machinist's square.

The understandings and skills desired as an end result for each pupil are: (1) the ability to manufacture a machinist's square using the hand tools found in the machine shop: the milling machine, shaper, drill press, power hack saw, and the pedestal grinder; (2) an understanding of the source, characteristics, value and properties of cold rolled steel, from the viewpoint of consumer

ure fabricator; (3) an understanding and appreciation of the metal-
ndustry in present-day civilization in reference to materials and
employed, finished products, and the resulting effect of these mate-
esses and products on the worker and the consuming public; (4) an
ding and appreciation of the work performed by those employed in
the metalworking industries and closely allied shops, with emphasis on the
opportunities and requirements for employment in these industries; (5) to
develop an understanding of some of the problems involved in common types
of construction, and in repair and maintenance of machine and hand tools;
(6) to develop an interest and appreciation of the methods and problems of
industrial production; (7) to develop the ability to cooperate with fellow
workers to attain mutual satisfaction.

At times the overview may be presented as *a series of problems or
questions* presumably of importance to the pupil as in the following unit
on woodcuts:

Why do people use woodcuts? Who first invented woodcuts? How does one
make a woodcut? What tools do you need? What kind of wood do you need?
What kind of tools are necessary? How do you use them? How do you prepare
the block? How do you get the picture or design on paper?[2]

The Teacher's Specific Objectives

After the teacher has described the nature and scope of the unit in
the overview, he is ready to state the specific objectives of the unit. These
objectives, as we have noted earlier, are the understandings, skills, attitudes, ideals, and appreciations the teacher hopes the pupils will learn
from the unit. Sometimes they are called terminal behavior. Their selection is important. What to leave out is as important as what to include.

OBJECTIVES AS LEARNING PRODUCTS. Since these objectives are
the potential learning products of the unit, they should be stated as learning products; that is, each objective should be expressed as a clear,
declarative statement describing a specific understanding, skill, attitude,
ideal, or appreciation that the teacher hopes his pupils will have acquired
upon the completion of the unit. Some authorities recommend that objectives be presented in infinitive phrases. However, questions and
infinitive phrases are usually not satisfactory because they do not
describe understandings or skills that should be learned. Rather they
tell about the understandings or skills. For example, compare the following specific objectives prepared for a seventh-grade unit on graphs.

2 These overviews have been adapted from units written by Dorothy Quigley,
Errol Terrol, and Philip J. Agacinski, graduate students at the School of Education,
the University of Hartford.

1. To understand bar graphs.
2. Bar graphs are usually used to picture a situation as it is at a given time. They use wide bars to represent quantities.

The first example is vague and general. It really tells us nothing. The reader has no way of knowing what the learning product desired in this instance is. The second example is a rather clear statement of what the pupils should undertsand about bar graphs. There is little doubt concerning this specific goal of the teacher.

If one does use infinitive phrases one should make an especial effort to be sure that they are clear and specific. "To understand bar graphs" could be changed to read, "To understand that bar graphs are usually used to picture a situation as it is at a given time."

Writing down the learning products as statements has several uses.

1. It ensures that the teacher has acquired the learning himself. A teacher who cannot describe the learning probably has never learned it thoroughly himself.
2. It gives the teacher a definite goal for which to aim.
3. It gives the teacher a standard by which to evaluate pupil achievement.
4. It helps to eliminate fuzzy thinking about the learning and thus helps to avoid soft pedagogy—i.e., pedagogy that results in no learning or little learning.

LISTING THE SPECIFIC OBJECTIVES. In listing the specific objectives, any order that seems desirable to the teacher may be used. Probably to arrange the list in a logical order will help the teacher better to understand his goals and to organize his thinking. *In no circumstances should the list of specific objectives be an attempt to indicate the order in which the pupils will learn them.* That sequence is a matter for each individual pupil.

However, some teachers find it helpful to list the skills, understandings, appreciations, ideals, and attitudes separately under definite headings. Although it is not essential, doing so seems to make it easier for the teacher to visualize his goals. The following are a few specific goals selected from the international relations unit "From Empire to Commonwealth" quoted earlier in the chapter.

Understandings

1. Strong ties of friendship have developed between the United States and Great Britain during the twentieth century.
2. These ties which draw the United States close to the Commonwealth are based upon our common language, customs, and traditions.

3. The American State Department, beginning with the days of John Hay and continuing to the present, has cooperated with the British Foreign Office in matters of international importance to both nations.
4. The English-speaking nations have been a force for keeping the peace of the world as evidenced from the Hague Court, the World Court, International Conferences, and the United Nations.
5. The English-speaking peoples have banded together in wars of recent times, World Wars I and II and the Korean War, to carry on successful campaigns against aggressor nations who threatened the peace of the world.

Attitudes, Ideals, Appreciations

No nation can depend entirely on itself.

The British people have done many noteworthy deeds and are worthy of respect.

Cooperation is more desirable than warfare in international relations.

In international affairs as well as private affairs one should deal justly with all—powerful or weak.

One should respect the rights and feelings of others.

Criteria for Good Objectives

In selecting the objectives for a unit the teacher should ask himself several things. Among the most important are:

1. Is this objective pertinent to this course? If not, no matter how earthshaking it may be, it is obviously not valid.
2. Is it a specific understanding, skill, attitude, ideal, or appreciation? Except for certain physical skills that seem to defy description, the authors recommend that these be clearly stated in declarative sentences. If not, they are liable to be too nebulous to be adequate.
3. Can it be achieved in the time allotted? If not, it should be re-examined. Perhaps only a portion of the goal should be attempted.
4. Is it worthwhile and is it the most worthwhile of the possible objectives? If not, perhaps the teacher should change his objectives.
5. Is it suitable for the level of the pupils? If it is too hard or too easy, it can cause the unit to fail.
6. *Does it allow for individual differences? Unless the objectives allow some pupils to achieve more than others and in different ways from others, the unit cannot succeed.*

※

Do you agree with the authors that the teacher's objectives should be presented as learning products written in declarative sentences? Why, or why not? Give arguments both for and against.

Apply the criteria cited above to the following objectives in a biology unit on infectious disease, prepared by a student teacher.

✲

Infectious Disease

Overview

Infectious diseases are caused by parasitic bacteria which succeed in overcoming body defenses and enter the body of the host.

Certain hygienic and sanitary procedures are necessary for the prevention and control of disease.

Specific Objectives

UNDERSTANDINGS

1. Infectious disease is disease caused by parasitic microorganisms.
2. A parasite is a dependent organism which gets its food directly from another organism, the host.
3. Bacteria are very simple one-celled plants classified into three main categories, the cocci, bacilli, and spirilla, by virtue of their form.
4. Bacteria reproduce by simple cell division or by spore formation.
5. All disease-producing bacteria are called pathogenic.
6. Infection takes place when disease germs overcome body defenses.
7. There are many ways bacteria enter the body of the host. Among these are through the nose, mouth, breaks in skin, eyes, ears, and the digestive tract.
8. The incubation period is the period between time of exposure to infectious disease and its development.
9. A contagious disease is one that is readily transmitted by direct or indirect contact between a diseased individual and one who is healthy.
10. Transmission of bacteria from one individual to another takes place through the following means: spit, spray, dust, air, contact, handkerchiefs, towels, utensils, food, water, insects, and animals.
11. Favorable conditions for bacteria are presence of organic matter (food), moisture, and moderate temperature.
12. Unfavorable conditions are dryness, extreme cold (not fatal), high temperature, sunlight, and chemical poisons.
13. To protect himself, the individual should
    a. Avoid taking into the mouth water, food, etc. that may have been exposed to infection.
    b. Maintain personal cleanliness.

    c. Avoid use of common towel, cup, etc.

    d. Disinfect cuts, wounds, etc.

    e. Avoid contact with known or suspected cases of infectious illness.

14. To protect others we should

    a. Avoid spitting where germs may be carried away.

    b. Cover face when coughing or sneezing.

    c. Avoid touching food, dishes, etc. to be used by others.

    d. Protect food, water, etc. from dust.

    e. Cooperate with home and community in maintaining sanitary conditions.

ABILITIES

1. Ability to use compound microscope.
2. Ability to prepare slides for microscopic examinations of bacteria.
3. Ability to prepare materials for simple experiments with bacterial cultures.

ATTITUDES

1. A favorable attitude toward observing habits of personal cleanliness in order to prevent the spread of disease.
2. A favorable attitude toward desirable and healthful practices in the home in order to prevent spread of disease.
3. A favorable attitude toward maintaining and observing health rules and regulations in the community for the preservation of health and the prevention of the spread of disease.

Planning the Unit Assignment

After the objectives have been chosen and described, the teacher must plan the activities by which the class may achieve the objectives. These activities are the heart of the unit. If they are not carefully planned and organized, the chances of the unit's being successful are reduced to zero, since it is through the activities that the learning products are gained. The organization of the activities is the unit assignment.

Selecting the Activities

To develop a unit assignment one must first identify the activities one might use to achieve the desired learning. These activities will fall into two groups.

First, the activities that will help all pupils to reach the objectives and should be done to some extent sometime before the completion of the unit. These we shall call the basic activities.

Second, those activities that will help some youngsters reach the objectives but need not be attempted by all pupils. These we shall call the optional related activities.

The Earmarks of a Good Activity

What kind of activities should the teacher select? In the first place, *each activity should contribute directly to at least one of the teacher's objectives.* Time is too precious to waste on any activity not pertinent. Busy work wastes time; aimlessness discourages learning. The school can afford neither.

This brings us to the second criterion: *The activity should seem worthwhile to the pupil.* That the activity should be worthwhile is obvious, but that it must seem so to the pupil is perhaps not so obvious. Yet if the activity does not seem worthwhile, the pupil will not participate with maximum effort and no one can make him. The result is an inefficient teaching situation.

Maximum effort is often stimulated by challenging, thought-provoking situations. A third criterion, then, is: *The activity should be stimulating and thought-provoking.* To be maximally effective pupil activities should relate to the life of the pupil; for example, work in other courses, extracurricular activities, social functions, and home life. Thus a fourth criterion is: *The activities should relate to the pupils' aims and interests, and pertain to their lives both in school and out.*

❋

One authority on the unit says that the unit assignment should consist largely of a series of problems. Do you agree? What would the advantages be?

❋

Organizing the Unit Assignment

After the possible activities have been assembled the teacher must organize them into the best possible sequence for the teaching-learning situation. In organizing these activities, the teacher must allow for such things as the time available; the ability level of the pupils and their interests; the nature of the subject matter; the local school situation including rules, equipment, opportunities, and materials available. At this point the teacher may find that he should eliminate certain activities and add others. When doing this, he should always be careful to consider his objectives.

The organization arranged by the teacher before the class begins the

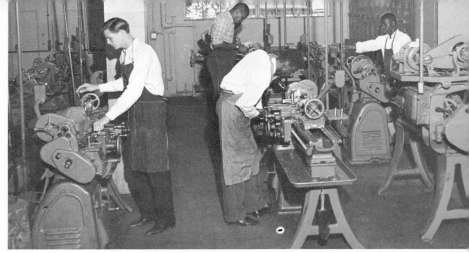

Lifelike, worthwhile, basic activities stimulate learning.

unit must be flexible. It must allow the boys and girls opportunity to follow their various bents and to give each of them a chance to participate in the planning of the sequence of activities most desirable for him. No teacher can tell just what is going to happen in any class, so the plan must allow for any contingency. As the pupils progress, both teacher and pupils may want to change the sequence of activities to fit the situation as it develops. Frequently, current happenings, school, local, state, or national, will make a change in plan desirable and profitable.

THE BASIC ACTIVITIES. The activities in which every boy and girl should participate may be called basic activities.[3] These should be prepared so that all the pupils may have experiences suitable to their own levels. At least some of the activities should be appealing to the non-academically minded youngsters. Many teachers reserve all the interesting project-like activities for optional related activities or extra-credit work after the required work has been finished. This is poor practice. The youngster who needs stimulation most never has a chance to do anything stimulating.

The pupil should be able to reach all of the teacher's specific objectives by way of the basic activities. To be sure that the activities really do contribute to all of these learnings, the teacher should note just what learning product or products each activity is supposed to produce. This practice will help ensure that each activity does contribute to some objective and that all the objectives are provided for.

THE OPTIONAL RELATED ACTIVITIES. Optional related activities are activities that pupils may do if they wish. They should be truly op-

[3] Another name for these is *core activities*. We are using the term *basic* in order to avoid confusion with the term *core curriculum*.

tional. No pupil should be required to do any of them, although an effort may be made to interest particular pupils in specific optional related activities that might be particularly beneficial to them. The pupil's mark should not depend upon his completing any of them. If a pupil starts an activity that proves to be distasteful, the teacher may allow him to drop it if it seems desirable.

In a sense the optional related activities are projects. The pupils should be encouraged to suggest other activities not yet included in the unit assignment. Often pupil-suggested activities are the best of all.

Optional related activities are not necessarily activities to be done after the basic activities have been completed. A pupil might well start with an optional related activity. This is particularly true when the pupil has been difficult to interest in that subject or has a special flair.

✲

How can a teacher provide for individual differences if he prepares a unit assignment in advance?

Should optional related activities be done only by the brilliant students who finish early?

✲

The Study and Activity Guide

In order that the pupils may know how to proceed throughout the unit, each should be given a mimeographed study and activity guide. This guide should include the instructions for each core activity, except perhaps such activities as listening to a teacher talk. Since the activities in the unit should be largely problem solving, the guide should consist mostly of questions, problems, and projects designed to stimulate thinking and investigating by the pupil. These should be presented in enough detail to allow the pupil to proceed on the activities without constantly resorting to the teacher for help. On the other hand, they should not be so detailed as to be recipes. Too detailed instructions of the recipe type can destroy initiative and prevent thinking. For instance, instead of saying:

Mix X and Y in a test tube. A precipitate should form. This is Z.

One could say:

Mix X and Y in a tube. What result do you observe? What should result? See references 10 and 13.

Or again, instead of saying:

Who said, "Give me liberty or give me death"?

A study guide might ask:

What was the importance of Patrick Henry's speech and what effect did it have on American history? Why did Patrick Henry say what he had to say? If you had been a member of the House of Burgesses how would you have reacted?

Some modern theorists decry the use of study guides on the basis that study guides may limit the creativity and originality of the pupil. To some extent this may be true, but a good study guide seems to have advantages that outweigh the disadvantages.

1. They give the pupil a *source* to which he can refer if he forgets his assignment.
2. They give the pupil a *picture* of what activities he might want to do so that he can pick his choice of activities and the order in which he wishes to do them.
3. They give the pupil a *definite assignment* so that he can go ahead to new activities on his own without waiting for a new assignment from the teacher.
4. They give *definite instructions* which should eliminate misunderstandings about assignments and many excuses for incomplete or unattempted assignments.

A SAMPLE STUDY AND ACTIVITY GUIDE. This guide was developed for a unit on race relations in a twelfth-grade class in Problems of Democracy.

General Study and Activity Guide

1. What are the various groups that make up the population of the United States? 2:42–45*
2. Make a classification of the different groups and give numbers. 14:521–527
3. What is the composition of our population in Middletown?
4. What are the various sects (religious) in the United States? 1:101
5. Give the names and numbers of the ten highest. 1:101
6. How many of these religions are represented in Middletown? In Middletown High School?
7. How have these various groups affected the growth and development of the United States? Name the contributions of these groups. 14:512–517, 521–524
8. What are some of the problems of harmonious relationships between different races and groups? 14:498–502
9. When is a group regarded as a minority? 6:582
10. How does prejudice destroy harmony between groups? 6:586–587
11. What is prejudice? 26:Ch. 1
12. How do we get our prejudices? 26:16; 22:29–33
13. What are the principal races in the world? 6:84–89

* These numbers refer to readings that the pupil may consult to find the answers to a particular problem.

14. What is the meaning of discrimination? 6:89
15. Give one example of political, social, and economic discrimination from your own experience.
16. How can we improve on the existing efforts to destroy prejudice and discrimination?
17. What is the work of the Commonwealth Fair Employment Practices Commission?
18. What can you do to prevent discrimination?
19. Name four types of groups often regarded as minorities. 6:582–606
20. What is the dominant group in America? 6:582–606
21. What constitutes the differences between groups? 6:606
22. Name the effects of prejudice on the person who practices it. 27
23. Discuss the relationship of prejudice to Democracy. 27
24. Is there such a thing as "racial superiority?" Explain your answer. 6:84–95
25. Make a full report in writing on social adjustment involving the immigrant.
26. Read the Roll of Honor in your neighborhood for World War II. Copy ten names at random and try to determine their ancestry. Conclusion.

LIST OF MATERIALS AND BIBLIOGRAPHY. As part of each study guide the teacher includes a list of any materials needed by the students, and a bibliography. The bibliography should consist largely of materials at the reading level of the pupils. However, there should be books difficult enough to challenge the brightest pupils, as well as others for the slow learners. References in the text may be keyed into this bibliography by a system similar to that illustrated on page 154.

Lists of materials required for specific activities should be part of the description of the activity. If including the list makes the description of the activity too long, the detailed description may be filed on 4×6 or 5×8 cards or placed on the bulletin board, thus keeping the size of the study guide reasonable.

✿

Should all pupils begin at the beginning of a unit assignment and proceed with the suggested activities in order? Why, or why not? If not, how should they proceed?

At what point and how much should the pupils plan the unit assignment or their part in it?

✿

Special Study and Activity Guides

Usually the optional related activities should be described by title and perhaps a brief notice in the study and activity guide or on a bulletin board. This serves to make the pupils aware of optional related activities which might interest them. Detailed instructions for such activities can be kept on 5×8 or 4×6 file cards. Should a pupil spot an optional activity that seems challenging to him, he can go to the file and examine the card. If the activity seems to be worthwhile, he can then elect to carry it out with the teacher's permission. This means, of course, that several cards must be available for each activity. If this seems impossible, the pupil can himself copy the instructions.

Another type of special study guide is that which is prepared to help the pupils get more out of such activities as field trips and moving pictures. Such special activity and study guides are used to point out the things that one should observe and the things one should investigate in such activities.

The following is an example of a special guide for an optional activity in the Problems of Democracy unit on Race Relations described earlier in the chapter.

Special Activity Guide

REPORT ON AMERICANIZATION WORK IN MIDDLETOWN
1. Interview Mr. Rand in Room 310. Mr. Rand is head of the evening school in Middletown. Ask him questions along this line and take notes on his answers.
   a. What is the work of the Americanization classes?
   b. Who teaches these classes? What are their qualifications?
   c. What people are eligible for these classes?
   d. Why are the classes necessary?
   e. What subjects are taught and why?
   f. When a person completes the course what happens?
   g. How long does this course last?
   h. Who pays for it?
   i. What is the attitude of the people in the class toward America?
   j. How many people in Middletown have completed the course in the last ten years?
   k. Where do these people come from?
2. Write up the answers in the form of a report and submit it to the teacher for approval. Indicate whether you would be willing to give the report to some other class if called upon to do so.

THE TEACHER'S LIST OF MATERIALS, EQUIPMENT,
AND READINGS

The teacher should also prepare for his own guidance, a list of materials, equipment, audio-visual aids and readings pertaining to the unit. It indicates the materials and equipment that are needed and references the teacher should read to ensure that he has been properly prepared.

THE DAILY LESSON PLAN IN THE UNIT

The unit plan does not eliminate daily planning. Before each class the teacher must think through what is to be done that day and jot down the agenda for the day. This plan will include such things as announcements, programs of activities, reminders to work with certain pupils or groups, notes for teacher talks, and the like. Since the major part of the planning has been taken care of by the unit assignment the daily plan may be quite sketchy and informal. At times it may be as simple and brief as "continue laboratory session"; at other times it may be simply a list of the committee and individual reports or activities to be presented that period. Sometimes, however, experienced teachers find it preferable to use detailed lesson plans as described in the preceding chapter.

❋

What part of the unit assignment should be placed on cards or on the bulletin board? Why?

What is the use of a study guide? Some authorities do not approve of using study guides. Do you?

What is the use of a special study guide?

❋

Summary

The following is an outline of the type of unit plan suggested in this chapter.

1. An overview that describes the nature and scope of the unit.
2. The teacher's specific objectives which are the understandings, skills, attitudes, ideals, and appreciations he hopes his pupils will get from the unit.
3. The unit assignment which includes activities in which the class will participate during the teaching of the unit. The activities will be of two types: (1) the basic activities to be done by all pupils to some extent in some time and (2) the optional related activities.
4. The study and activity guide which will contain the instructions for carrying out the core activities to be done individually and in small groups.
5. The special study and activity guides which contain the instructions for carrying out the optional related activities.
6. A list of materials and readings the boys and girls may use in their study.
7. A short bibliography and list of materials for the use of the teacher alone.

8. A test to be used in evaluating the success of the unit. This test should test adequately each of the learning products described in 1 and 2 above.

In carrying out such a unit plan the unit assignment should be introduced by introductory activities that will catch the pupils' interest and help the teacher know the pupils. Following the introductory phase comes individual and small group work interspersed by class activities. After this laboratory phase the pupils share their experiences and learnings. Finally the unit of work ends in some sort of evaluative exercise.

These four steps or phases make up the teaching-learning cycle. In practice the four phases do not always follow in regular order, but vary to suit the occasion. Arranging the classroom as a laboratory increases the effectiveness of the unit assignment and the teaching-learning cycle.

FOR FURTHER STUDY

ALBERTY, HAROLD B., and ELSIE J. ALBERTY, *Reorganizing the High-School Curriculum* (New York: The Macmillan Company, 1962).

ALDRICH, JULIAN C., *How to Construct and Use a Resource Unit* (New York: Joint Council on Economic Education, not dated).

BILLETT, ROY O., *Teaching in Junior and Senior High Schools* (Dubuque, Iowa: William C. Brown Company, Publishers, 1963), Chs. 5–8.

BURTON, WILLIAM H., *The Guidance of Learning Activities*, Third Edition (New York: Appleton-Century-Crofts, Inc., 1962), Ch. 13.

CALLAHAN, STERLING G., *Successful Teaching in Secondary Schools* (Chicago: Scott, Foresman and Company, 1966), Chs. 3–7.

GWYNN, J. MINOR, *Theory and Practice of Supervision* (New York: Dodd-Mead and Company, 1961), Chs. 4–5.

PARRISH, LOUISE, and YVONNE WASKIN, *Teacher-Pupil Planning* (New York: Harper and Row Publishers, Inc., 1958).

RIVLIN, HARRY N., *Teaching Adolescents in Secondary Schools*, Second Edition (New York: Appleton-Century-Crofts, Inc., 1961).

STEEVES, FRANK L., *Fundamentals of Teaching in Secondary Schools* (New York: The Odyssey Press, Inc., 1962).

ZAPF, ROSALIND M., *Democratic Processes in the Secondary Classroom* (Englewood Cliffs, N.J.: Prentice-Hall, Inc., 1959), Chs. 3–7.

PART *III*

Providing for Individual Differences

Provisions for Individual Differences

*I*NDIVIDUALS differ in a multitude of ways—in physical make-up, in interests, in ability, in aptitude, in home background, in experience, in prior training, in social skill, in ideals, in attitudes, in needs, in vocational goals, and so on *ad infinitum*. This is an inescapable fact of human nature—a fact fraught with profound implications for the teacher. Because of these differences, to treat individuals as though everyone were just alike simply will not work. Somehow, some way, teachers must adapt their teaching to individual differences.

Not only are pupils different, but each learns in his own way and at his own rate. No two persons ever learn exactly the same concepts from any learning situation. Nor do any two persons ever develop exactly the same method and degree of efficiency. Each individual's learning is shaped by his interests, his physical and psychic make-up, his past experiences, and his goals for the future and so differs from that of anyone else. Teachers should capitalize on these differences and make them a means of furthering learning.

❖

Observe the members of your own class. In what ways do they seem similar? In what different?

If possible, visit a junior-high-school class or senior-high-school class. What evidence of individual differences do you find?

❖

A Description of Two Boys

The following paragraphs describe two boys. Both are tenth-graders in the same English class. Each of them lives in the same neighborhood, has approximately the same socio-economic status, is of Italian parentage, and belongs to the same church. Yet they are completely different individuals.

Pete is a tall, thin boy. He looks as though he has not had a decent meal in a long time. His constant lack of energy seems to confirm this look. This may also explain his complete lack of interest in sports of any kind. He is exceptionally interested in music and plays the piano well. In fact, for the past few months he has been playing dinner music at a downtown restaurant as one of a trio. He is talented in other ways also. His I.Q. shows him to be well into the genius class. Yet his classwork is very poor; he does little or nothing in school. For several weeks he has not turned in a respectable paper. He has read few, if any, of the stories assigned in the study of the present topic—short stories. Still, he seems to have read recently many of the current best sellers and quite a number of biographical works and popularized histories. Works having to do with politics and politicians seem to have a special appeal to him. He takes part in no school activities of any sort other than those assigned in class. He has few friends and keeps pretty well to himself, perhaps because he is inclined to give himself airs and to poke fun at the efforts of the other "kids." In spite of an air of sophistication one gets the impression that this is an unhappy youngster whose many talents are going to waste.

Steve is about medium height and inclined to be a trifle stocky. His skin is dark and from time to time breaks out in a rash of pimples which annoys him somewhat. In the past he has been the victim of a serious speech defect. He still stammers badly at times, but his parents have been sending him to a local speech therapist who has helped him greatly. In spite of his disability Steve is one of the most popular boys in school and something of a ladies' man. He is president of his class and active in myriads of other activities. His real hobby is sports, although he is not especially good in them. Still, he is captain of his intramural basketball team. His lack of skill is made up for, at least in part, by his aggressiveness. He is about the scrappiest player in the league. He is one of the varsity team's most ardent supporters. Probably he will be the varsity manager in his senior year, since he is leading all present contenders for that position.

Steve's great virtue, from the teacher's point of view, is his dependability. Rarely does he miss an assignment. Although he is only slightly better than average intellectually, he consistently does better than average, if not outstanding, work. His regular reading consists of popular magazines and the newspaper. Sometimes you may find him engrossed in a book of science, *Popular Science,* or a work of science fiction. Science is his best subject and we hear that at home he spends considerable time "fooling around" with a science hobby kit.

These two boys are individuals. Their personalities differ in many ways. The competent teacher tries to adapt his teaching so as to turn these differences to his advantage whenever possible.

*

Would you think it wise to try to teach both these boys the same material in the same way?

A famous professor of education says, "We should not have a standard; we should have standards." What do you think he means? Is it possible to require one pupil to do more or better work than another? How would you go about implementing the professor's statement?

✻

Administrative Provisions for Differences in Pupils

For a long time secondary-school administrators have been trying, with rather indifferent success, to find answers for the instructional problems caused by individual differences. Most of the procedures that they have inaugurated to meet this problem have been based upon selecting or categorizing pupils. Recently, however, some schools have been moving toward attempting to provide for individual differences by making their curriculum organization more flexible.

Tracks, Streams, and Homogeneous Groups

To group pupils according to interest or ability is common practice in secondary and elementary schools both in the United States and abroad. American high schools usually offer several curricula based supposedly on the goals of the pupils. Thus we find a typical high school offering such varied curricula as college preparatory for those pupils planning to go to college, secretarial curricula for girls planning to become office workers, vocational agriculture for boys who plan to become farmers, home economics curricula for girls planning to become housewives, and general curricula for pupils having no particular plans for the future.

The track or stream is another administrative device for reducing the range of heterogeneity in classrooms. Usually tracks or streams are curricular sequences based upon pupils' ability in the area. Thus the mathematics program for a school might be divided into four tracks, the first for talented mathematics students, the second for ordinary college preparatory pupils, the third for noncollege preparatory pupils, and the fourth for slow learners.

HOMOGENEOUS GROUPING. Homogeneous groups are similar to tracks or streams except that they are not planned sequences, but merely groupings made up for the year or term only. Although some homogeneous groups are based on homogeneity of interest or educational objectives and many classes in such subjects as home economics, industrial arts, physical education, and biology are grouped according to sex,

most homogeneous groups are ability groups. By such grouping administrators hope to make it possible for teachers to teach more effectively
and to adapt the curriculum to the varying needs of all the pupils.

Administrative grouping of pupils is not a direct responsibility of
classroom teachers, but it does affect them and their teaching. The basic
implication for the teacher is that he should differentiate his material
and methods for the various groups so that he will be teaching the
content best suited for each class in the way best suited for that class.
Sometimes teachers find their attempts to teach academic subject matter
to "slow" groups frustrating. As a result they tend to blame their lack
of success on the poorness of the group. Such a narrow view defeats
the purpose of the ability grouping. Each teacher should try to adapt
his teaching so that each pupil can learn to the best of his ability. Some
comments on how to do this will follow in a later section.

Another danger which comes from homogeneous grouping, tracking,
and streaming is that the teacher may get the idea that the group is
really homogeneous. It is not; no group of people is. All that can be done
in grouping pupils is to reduce the range of one or another characteristic
or group of associated characteristics. In a high-ability group the pupils
may all be of relatively high ability, but they will differ in many other
ways—in interests, in ambitions, in motivation, in goals, in personality,
in aggressiveness, and so on. They even differ in intelligence and ability.
Look at the I.Q. range of the pupils of a good college preparatory class
in a New Jersey high school listed in Table II. There pupils have intelligence quotient scores ranging from slightly above normal to very bright.
Ergo teachers who teach ability grouped classes have problems of providing for individual differences just as other teachers do.

TABLE II

I.Q.'s of Homogeneous College Preparatory Tenth Grade Class

James	136	David	125
Craig	135	Gerald	124
Charlene	135	Peggy	124
Sally	134	Bruce	123
Michelle	133	Jim	123
Judy	133	Margaret	123
Susan	131	Richard	122
Steve	130	Betty	121
Prudence	130	Christine	120
Tim	128	Guy	119
Gail	128	George	118
Joan	126	Wayne	116
Joanna	126	Neil	109

Some teachers seriously object to homogeneous grouping because they believe it to be undemocratic. This objection probably stems from a misunderstanding of the principle that "everyone is created free and equal." These critics seem to believe that by placing pupils into homogeneous groups we are depriving them of their rights of equal treatment. However, the democratic concept is that everyone has an equal opportunity to make the most of his talents. The truly democratic teacher recognizes the differences in individuals and tries to make the most of them.

✿

How could one prevent a caste system from developing as a result of homogeneous grouping of class sections throughout the school?

Examine a high-school honors class. What range interests, abilities, life goals, and academic backgrounds do you find?

✿

Other Administrative Techniques

In addition to plans involving grouping, administrators utilize varying promotion schemes to provide for individual differences. In some school systems pupils can move through grades 7 to 12 in five years and spend the year saved at college or doing college work in the high school. Such acceleration is quite common although not all school administrators accept it as desirable. Also quite common is the old practice of making pupils who fail repeat a grade or course. In the past some administrators have tried to lessen the sting of failure by promoting every half year. Recently there has been a movement toward continuous promotion in ungraded schools. Basically the plans consist of dividing the course work of the curriculum into short steps or levels and allowing the pupil to advance from level to level as he becomes ready for the next step. Undoubtedly these plans have merit. They should make providing for the differences in individual pupils easier and more effective. But they will not relieve the teacher of his responsibility of providing for individual differences within his classes.

Providing for Differences in the Classroom

In the ensuing pages we shall attempt to indicate some ways in which teachers can take advantage of individual differences in the classroom and make the instruction more profitable. This discussion is predicated on the assumption that adequate provisions for individual differences must be based upon thorough knowledge of the abilities, interests, ambitions, problems, and other characteristics of the pupil outlined in foregoing chapters.

Differentiating the Assignment

The Differentiated Assignment

An assignment consists of activities laid out for the pupils to do. A differentiated assignment is a class assignment that allows different pupils to do different things during the time covered by the assignment. Many types of differentiated assignments can be made. Ordinarily, the differentiated assignment is a long assignment covering a period of several weeks. However, it can also be very short.

DIFFERENTIATING THE LENGTH OR DIFFICULTY OF THE ASSIGNMENT. Teachers often arrange their assignments so that slow learners will not have to do quite as much as their more able colleagues. In the sample assignment in the following section the teacher attempted to do this by assigning group 3, the fast group, considerably more work than group 1, the slow group. In a mathematics class he might have assigned five problems to the slow pupils, eight problems to the average pupils, and ten problems to the fast pupils. In the sample assignment the work assigned to the groups also varies in difficulty. Group 3 is reading in what the teacher considers a "hard" eighth-grade book; group 2, an "easy" eighth-grade book; and group 1, a sixth-grade book. All are studying about the same thing but at different levels of difficulty. In a mathematics class the teacher could have assigned more difficult problems to the better pupils. In actual practice many teachers vary both the amount and difficulty as in the sample assignment.

DIFFERENTIATING THE TYPE OF WORK. Not only the amount but the type of work should vary from pupil to pupil. The pupil who thinks best with his hands should be allowed to create with them. The bright pupil should be encouraged to undertake minor research problems. Thus, by varying the type as well as the amount of work, the teacher can provide tasks suited to the pupil's abilities and interests. In this way the skillful teacher, by capitalizing on the pupil's interest and ability, may be able to enlist his enthusiastic cooperation and encourage him to learning unheard of in dull humdrum classes. In order to do this, the teacher must accept different means of expression and different indices of growth.

Many youngsters have unique abilities which can make any class profitable and enjoyable. Every youth has some contribution to offer. Each should be encouraged to make his special contribution. It may be that the socially promoted boy who reads at an abysmally low level can and will, if encouraged, draw illustrations for the novel that is being read, or can build or help build a setting for a dramatization for part of the plot. Another youngster or group of youngsters more literarily inclined might write the script for the dramatization. Pupils who are neither artistic nor literary might be the actors. Everyone should contribute. If pupils are encouraged to participate after their own fashion, then the class will be fuller and more meaningful and learning will be more likely to go on apace.

For example, not everyone needs to express his understanding of the ante-bellum South by writing essays and answering questions about it. Many other media are available. Talented youngsters might produce illustrations of life in the South; a boy interested in mechanical drawing might draw a layout of a plantation; a girl interested in homemaking might investigate the menus of the era, or run up a costume appropriate to the period; a young engineer might construct a cotton gin; a young choreographer might score and dance a ballet in the *Gone with the Wind* motif; a poet might contribute some lyric poetry, perhaps an ode or two.

Also pupils with special interests might read and investigate in their fields of interest. In a science class the musically inclined might want to investigate why different tones result when varying lengths of catgut are scraped by horsehair, or why lightly scraping the strings of a violin can make a sound that can be heard all over the concert hall. In a mathematics class a pupil interested in design might solve problems having to do with the mathematics of design.

The teacher who would make the most of the potential of any class must permit boys and girls to learn through various media. The possibilities are limited only by the media available and the various talents of the pupils. However, the teacher must guard against the danger of encouraging boys and girls to participate in activities which in no way contribute to significant learning. If a boy or girl is to spend considerable time creating a dance in connection with the study of the ante-bellum South, that activity should result in real learning about the South. If it does not, that activity has no place in that classroom.

A SAMPLE SHORT DIFFERENTIATED ASSIGNMENT. The following short differentiated assignment was prepared and used by a beginning teacher while teaching "The Westward Movement" in an eighth-grade American history class. In this class the teacher divided the pupils into three groups on the basis of their presumed ability. Note that in this assignment group 1 is reading *Your Country and Mine* which the teacher considers to be at the sixth-grade reading level, group 2 is reading *Your Country's Story* which he considers easy reading for eighth-graders, and group 3 is reading *This Is America's Story* supposedly a difficult book for grade eight.

A Short Differentiated Assignment

GROUP 1

Reading Assignment *Your Country and Mine*, pages 36–41:

1. Form into assigned groups.
2. Select one member to serve on each committee:
   a. Bulletin Board
   b. *Who's Who in American History*
3. Choose one of the following assignments:
   a. Write a story about Daniel Boone.
   b. Draw a picture of Boonesborough in its early days.
   c. Draw a map showing how Daniel Boone got to Boonesborough (page 43).

GROUP 2

Reading Assignment *Your Country's Story*, pages 160–163:

1. Form into assigned groups.
2. Select one member for each of the following committees:
   a. Bulletin Board
   b. *Who's Who in American History*
3. Choose one of the following assignments:
   a. Make a report on the nature and characteristics of the Indians as seen by the early settlers in Kentucky and Tennessee.
   b. Make a map showing the different routes to the West.
   c. Write a report telling why the Ohio Valley was so attractive to early settlers.

GROUP 3

Reading Assignment *This Is America's Story*, pages 223–231:

1. Form into assigned groups.
2. Select one member for each committee:
   a. Bulletin Board
   b. *Who's Who in American History*
3. Choose one of the following assignments:
   a. Prepare a short report on the history of political parties in the United States.
   b. Make a report on Hamilton's policies in solving this country's financial problems.
   c. Write a short report explaining why Jefferson and Hamilton had different views on many things.

4. Answer completely Check-Up Questions 1–3 (page 227) and 1–4 (page 231).
5. Give a brief account of the Northwest Territory and of its importance in the development of the West.

✻

In what ways has this beginning teacher attempted to differentiate the assignment? How successful do you think this assignment would be?

How would you go about preparing a differentiated assignment for a course in your major field?

✻

Homogeneous Groups Within the Classroom

Teaching is usually easier when the range of differences among pupils in a group is kept relatively small. As we have seen, the range can be reduced by homogeneous groupings, that is, by putting pupils of similar abilities, interests, ambitions, or other attributes together. Just as school administrators use homogeneous grouping throughout entire schools, teachers can group their pupils homogeneously within their classes. This grouping can be accomplished in several ways, such as

1. Placing the slow achievers in one group, the average achievers in another, and the rapid achievers in a third.
2. Placing pupils into groups according to their interests.
3. Placing pupils with similar interests and similar goals together to solve a particular problem or to do some sort of research.
4. Placing pupils into groups according to special needs.

Certain critics have objected to the the use of homogeneous groups within the class for several reasons. Many experienced high-school teachers claim that to teach more than one group in the same room is impossible or too difficult. Yet anyone who has watched a skillful teacher conduct a one-room school or a primary room knows that this is not so. Teaching several groups at once is hard work, but then, all good teaching is hard work. Actually, using groups is often easier than attempting to teach the unready something they cannot learn or the uninterested something they will not learn. In the small rural high schools of the Catskills and other areas teachers experimenting with multigrade classes in which they teach pupils of two or more grade levels (e.g., Spanish I, II, & III) in the same classroom have found that they can teach multigrade classes fully as successfully as they can single classes.

Another serious objection is that homogeneous grouping labels some pupils as inferior. Although the danger does exist, homogeneous grouping within classes may not be as dangerous as one might expect. The pupils usually know which of their classmates are bright and which dull academically. As a rule in grouping we are merely recognizing what everyone already knows and accepts.

Nevertheless these dangers are real ones. We must not allow a caste system to develop in any classroom. The danger may be avoided by seeing to it that the membership of the groups changes from time to time, that many types of groups are used so that the pupil is not always in the same group, and that the pupil has ample opportunities to work as an individual and as a member of the entire class. To divide a class into three or four ability groups and to keep these groups together constantly for an entire term is malpractice.

❊

If you were to divide your class into groups, what basis for grouping would you use? How would you go about grouping the class? How long would you keep the same groups?

❊

Accelerating the Brilliant Pupil

One way to help the brilliant pupil make the most of his talent is to let him proceed through the course more rapidly than his classmates. In a certain Latin class the teacher arranged the classwork so that the brilliant pupils could do most of the work independently at their own speed without waiting for slower classmates to catch up. One brilliant girl completed one year's work early in April and was well into the next year's work by the end of June. The teacher had made this acceleration possible by preparing units for the entire year in advance. When the pupil had completed one unit, she went right on to the next one.

In such teaching, since the accelerated pupil will finish the regular course work before the end of the school year, the teacher needs to provide additional work for the pupil. In the example cited, the pupil went on to units in the next year's work. In other instances one might prefer that the pupil study more deeply certain aspects of the present course or aspects of the course ordinarily omitted because of lack of time.

Differentiating the Work Completely

At times it is desirable to assign to certain pupils work that is entirely different from that of the rest of the class. An example of this is the case of Pete, the brilliant youth described earlier in the chapter who had been doing such poor work in his English class. Upon examining the situation, the teacher realized that the boy was finding the assignments too easy. He was bored. To remedy this, the teacher excused the boy from the regular assignment and substituted one he had had in college. Rising to this bait, the boy accomplished this assignment in a fashion acceptable for any college introductory literature course. By substituting an entirely different assignment, the teacher was able to inspire this boy to do work well beyond the level of his grade. This is an excellent way to help a gifted youth. If a pupil is competent in grammar and knows to perfection the parts of speech the class is presently studying, he should be studying something else. Why not put him to work on a problem in literature, or something else worthwhile? It does not matter particularly what the pupil does as long as it results in valuable learning.

✽

What practical problems arise from allowing a pupil to go on to the next year's work? How might these problems be minimized?

In the example cited above, the accelerated pupils worked individually almost entirely. Is this a good practice? How might one accelerate pupils in a class without making the work entirely individual?

✽

Individualizing Instruction

If instruction is to meet the needs of individual pupils, ways must be found for individualizing assignments and instruction. At first glance this task seems to be insuperably difficult, but on closer analysis it is not nearly as overwhelming a task as one might fear.

Conducting the Class As a Laboratory

A profitable way to provide for individual differences is to conduct the class as a laboratory. It is this feature that makes the unit method such a good approach to solution of the problem of individual differences. Here the pupils can work on their various tasks individually or in small groups under the teacher's guidance. In such a laboratory a committee might be working in one corner of the room preparing a dramatization, in another corner another group might be preparing a report. At their desks individual pupils might be working on "research projects." Others might be reading required or optional readings. In the rear of the class a pupil might be putting the finishing touches on a model to be presented and explained to the class. Around the teacher's desk another group might be working with the teacher in planning a group project.

Laboratory classes allow pupils to work alone or in small groups at interesting assignments differentiated to individual academic and personal needs.

As the pupils work at their tasks, the teacher helps and guides them. Among the many things he can do to help them are

1. Observe pupils to diagnose poor study habits.
2. Show pupils where to find information.
3. Show pupils how to use the tools of learning.
4. Clarify assignments.
5. Show the pupils how to get the meat out of their studying.
6. Help pupils form goals for study.
7. Help pupils summarize.
8. Point out errors and incorrect procedures.
9. Suggest methods for attacking problems.

Laboratory classes of this sort allow the freedom necessary for different pupils to work at a variety of tasks at speeds suitable for them. To a lesser degree supervised study periods in which the pupils work on their assignments under the teacher's supervision and guidance can provide the same freedom.

Individualized Instruction

Whether he uses the laboratory approach or not, each teacher must somehow find time to work separately with each pupil. This does not usually take as much time as one might think. Many pupils need a minimum of guidance. If they are provided with clear instructions they can often work alone for considerable periods.

SPECIAL HELP. The most common type of individualized instruction is the special help given to certain pupils. Teachers have always helped boys and girls who were having trouble with their studies through extra help after school, during conference periods, in study halls, and in class. No matter what method of teaching is used, the teacher will need to provide special help for some pupils.

Not only do pupils having trouble with their studies need special help; pupils who are doing well need it also. Everyone at times needs encouragement, criticism, discipline, correction, and inspiration. Taking time to look over a pupil's paper and compliment him on his progress and to point out possible modes for improving it can be beneficial for both the most successful and the least successful of one's pupils.

Nevertheless, in spite of the value of special help, it alone cannot meet the demands of individual differences. Stronger measures are needed. Insofar as possible the teacher must provide individual instruction designed for the individuals to be instructed. Such provision can usually be made most easily within the framework of the classroom laboratory, the differentiated assignment, or the unit approach. In the following paragraphs we shall discuss some techniques that can be used for individual instruction within such plans.

SELF-INSTRUCTIONAL DEVICES. The availability of self-instructional devices and materials has made individualizing of instruction in ordinary sized classes much easier than in the past. The most spectacular of these devices are the many different sorts of machines now on the market. Pupils of foreign languages practice pronunciation, pattern drills, and other aspects of the spoken language by means of the language laboratory which is really little more than an elaborate tape recorder or combination of tape recorders. In some schools it is possible for pupils studying different languages, or different levels of the same language, to use the language laboratory at the same time. There is no reason why similar procedures cannot be used in language laboratories for oral English exercises.

Even without language laboratories such teaching is feasible. If each pupil has a tape of his own, he can use the tape recorder to record his voice and compare it to models. Using this recording as a basis of diagnosis, the teacher can then assign the pupils individual tape recorder exercises designed to help the pupils hear and correct their faults. Such exercises can be done during class laboratory sessions, free periods, or after school—in fact at any time that the pupil and a tape recorder are free. In some schools individual exercises of this type are the medium of much instruction in oral English.

Tape recorders can also present other types of lessons to individuals or small groups. Before a class the teacher might dictate to a machine a lesson with instructions for an individual. During the class the teacher can turn the pupil over to the tape recorder and its pre-taped lesson for a time. In one instance the teacher has prepared a tape recording of an account of the religious life of primitive man. This tape also includes a short introduction to tell what the tape is about and to direct the pupil's attention to important pertinent points and a short follow-up to reemphasize these points. An individual pupil can put on the tape recorder earphones and go to work on this lesson without bothering anyone else in the class. Whenever he finds a point difficult, if he wishes, he can turn the tape back and replay the bothersome section without disrupting anyone else's progress.

Similar lessons have been worked out for use on eight millimeter self-loading individual-viewing motion picture projectors. Ordinary filmstrip projectors can be used in the same way. Sometimes two-by-two slides can be arranged in lessons for individual use by teachers who do not have desired film strips available. Pupils can follow the slide sequence on dittoed commentary sheets. Preferably such slide sequences should be presented in trays for automatic or semi-automatic projection. If such are not available and one must use a single-shot machine, one should be sure the slides are numbered in proper order and that the top right hand corner is marked so that the pupil can tell which way to insert the slides into the machine.

Teaching machines that use automated teaching programs are the most exotic of all the auto-instructional devices, although the secondary-school teacher will probably find that in his school automated programs must be presented by means of programmed texts or similar devices rather than by machine. Because the programs are devised for individualized teaching, they should make it possible for teachers using them to cope with great ranges of ability within the class. The self-instructional features of the programs and machines make it possible for pupils to work through programs as rapidly or as slowly as seems most desirable and to pursue different programs at the same time.

If the teaching programs have an advantage over other materials, it is because they are usually carefully built and tested. However, they are not the only type of self-instructional or auto-instructional material available. Examples of other self-instructional materials one can purchase or make include the self-administering and self-correcting drill and practice materials described in Chapter 11. Usually self-correcting materials can be used only for teaching information and skills; the self-correcting format cannot be adapted easily for instruction in the higher mental processes. Even so, such materials can help free the teacher from much busy work so that he can give more time to helping individual pupils learn at higher levels.

STUDY AND ACTIVITY GUIDES. Dittoed or mimeographed study guides can be a great help to teachers in individualizing instruction. Study guides can be of several kinds. One may be a general study and activity guide to be used as a guide by all pupils throughout a unit. Another may be a special study guide for use with a certain book, movie, field trip, or other activity and which should help direct the study of any pupil engaged in this particular activity. Another type of special study and activity guide consists of directions for studying prepared for a particular pupil (or group of pupils) so that he can proceed at work different from those of other pupils without having to wait for special oral directions from the teacher who may be busy working with someone else. Similar study and activity guides can be recorded on tape for use by pupils whose reading level is not up to their understanding level.

INDIVIDUAL AND GROUP PROJECTS. Both individual and group projects as described in Chapter 11 are useful for individualizing instruction. Since the basis of the project is that it be selected, planned, and carried out by the pupil because of some intrinsic value to him, the individual project is one of the techniques best suited for developing and capitalizing on individual interests and abilties.

PROVIDING FOR DIFFERENCES BY MEANS OF FREE PERIODS. Occasionally, pupils may be given free periods in which they are permitted to follow their own interests as much as possible. The activities of such a free period should be limited to those which are suitable to the classroom and to the subject. Such periods are usually more appropriate for reading and literature than for other subjects, although this does not need to be so. They are often instrumental in forming new tastes in reading, art, music, and other areas, and often open new vistas of appreciation to the pupil. They also have the additional advantage of giving the teacher opportunities to help pupils who need individual attention.

✽

How can a teacher find material to suit the varying reading levels of his students on a limited school budget?

How can different types of work areas within a classroom help to provide for individual differences? How can they be used?

How can self-correcting material be used in providing for individual differences?

How can self-evaluation of a pupil's progress be used to motivate him?

✽

Finding Time for Individual Instruction

PUPIL PARTICIPATION IN PLANNING AND EVALUATION. To provide properly for individual instruction takes time. One of the keys to finding the necessary time is to allow the pupils to take a greater share in the responsibility for their own studies. *Adolescent boys and girls, particularly the brilliant ones, are quite capable of planning, directing, and evaluating their own work, particularly if they have study guides to help them.* When the teacher allows them to do so, he not only helps them to acquire skills in self-direction, but he also frees himself for individual and small group work. Moreover, the use of pupil planning and evaluation makes it possible for each pupil to map out an individual plan suitable to his own needs.

The Use of Pupil Help

Talented boys and girls can often help other pupils who are having difficulty. This technique can be quite beneficial if done carefully. It gives the teacher some assistance so that he can find time to do more individual teaching. It teaches the gifted youngster how to share his talents and to communicate his ideas to others. It helps foster the idea of service. Most important of all, it helps the talented youth to learn the subject more thoroughly. Moreover, youths frequently learn more readily from their peers.

This is an excellent method, but, if not used judiciously, it can be dangerous. First, the teacher may call on a brilliant pupil to do teaching that the teacher should do himself. This could result in the exploitation of the brilliant youth, while the dull pupil is deprived of the professional help he deserves. Then, too, one must avoid holding back the gifted youth. *It is not right for the bright pupil to mark time repeating the same material when he might be going on to more advanced study.* To help the brilliant youths make the most of their talents is one of the teacher's most important tasks. He must not sacrifice them to help the mediocre. Used with care, however, the practice of having bright pupils help the slow ones is an effective method of meeting individual differences.

❖

How can pupils help each other? How can such help be used to provide for individual differences?

How can a teacher of a large class find time to work and confer with individual pupils? List occasions when the teacher might consult with pupils informally.

How would you go about setting up a classroom laboratory in a course you might teach? How could you use a classroom laboratory?

❖

Accepting Different Evidences of Accomplishment

If pupils are encouraged to learn through many different media, the teacher must accept different types of growth as evidence of achievement in the course. Certainly the essential learning in any lesson should be common to all the pupils, but the teacher cannot let the matter rest there. He must also accept various kinds of evidence of growth. The youngster who has increased his stature through creative writing, the girl who has grown through art, and the boy who has increased his technical skill through building models have all grown in desirable ways. All pupils do not acquire identical learning in any unit. The teacher should recognize that various types of growth are desirable and therefore should accept them as evidence of progress in the course.

Need for Variety of Materials

Providing for individual differences requires a wealth of instructional materials. It goes without saying that one cannot expect every member of the class to be interested in the same thing. Therefore, we must provide instructional materials which will suit many interests. Material too easy for bright pupils may be so difficult that it may frustrate the slow pupils. Consequently, the teacher should no longer limit himself to just one textbook. He must provide readings suitable to the various levels and interests found in his class. In addition to the readings the teacher should provide ample materials for other types of activities. A later chapter will show in more detail how to obtain and use such materials.

Not only should we provide a wealth of materials, we should also make them available when the pupil needs them. One of the characteristics of the classroom laboratory is an abundance of attractive, appropriate materials immediately on hand, ready for use. Thus the pupil can get whatever he needs at the appropriate moment without disturbing anyone.

Summary

Every pupil is different from every other one, and so each one's education should be different if he is going to benefit from it optimally. These differences cause many pedagogical problems. On the other hand they also offer the teachers levers by which to make their teaching more effective.

Secondary-school administrators have attempted to provide for the individual differences by organizational devices. Among these devices have been such things as tracks and streams, homogeneous grouping, acceleration of the brilliant, and ungraded schools. None of these plans have been able to provide the complete answer to the problem. Even when the administrative devices are successful, they can cope with only part of the problem. As in all other instructional matters, the final solution must be worked out by individual teachers.

Luckily the teacher has at his disposal many techniques for coping with individual differences in pupils. He may differentiate his assignments by varying the difficulty, length, or type of work from pupil to pupil. He may find it desirable to group his pupils within the classes according to need, interest or abilities, or to partially differentiate the work through individual or group projects. Sometimes he may find it advantageous to allow pupils to move through the course more quickly, or more slowly, than the average pupil, or to encourage pupils to enrich their learning by going into topics more deeply than other pupils do.

Individualizing instruction is not as difficult as teachers fear, and it is necessary. One way to meet this need is by conducting the class as a laboratory. In laboratory periods many pupils can proceed with a minimum of guidance while the teacher helps pupils who need assistance. Particularly valuable as means of freeing teacher's time for those who need help are the many self-instructional devices which help pupils teach themselves. Among these devices are teaching machines and programs as well as older devices like self-administering and self-correcting practice material. Dittoed or tape recorded study and activity guides can be extremely helpful and should be used. Free periods in which pupils are allowed to follow their own bents are also useful.

Finding time for individual instruction is difficult, but when teachers give pupils more time to participate in the planning and evaluating of their own studying, they can free a lot of time without slighting any pupils. Also teachers can make time by encouraging pupils to help each other.

If one provides well for individual differences one must expect to have to evaluate pupils' learning on new bases for they will not learn the same things in the same way. As a corollary one must also expect to use a much greater variety of materials in traditional classes. Not only will he require many readings, but also materials for many other kinds of activities.

FOR FURTHER STUDY

Association for Supervision and Curriculum Development, *Individualizing Instruction*, 1964 Yearbook (Washington, D.C.: The Association, 1964).

BILLETT, ROY O., *Provisions for Individual Differences, Marking and Promotion*, Bulletin 1932, Number 17, National Survey of Education Monograph 13 (Washington, D.C.: U.S. Government Printing Office, 1933).

BROWN, B. FRANK, *The Non-Graded High School* (Englewood Cliffs, N.J.: Prentice-Hall, Inc., 1963).

DRAYER, ADAM M., *Problems and Methods in High School Teaching* (Boston: D. C. Heath and Company, 1963), Ch. 4.

ECKSTROM, RUTH B., *Experimental Studies of Homogeneous Grouping: A Review of the Literature* (Princeton, N.J.: Educational Testing Service, 1959).

JENKINS, JAMES J., and DONALD G. PATERSON, *Studies in Individual Differences* (New York: Appleton-Century-Crofts, Inc., 1961).

National Society for the Study of Education, *Individualizing Instruction*, Sixty-first Yearbook, Part I (Chicago: The University of Chicago Press, 1962).

————, *Adapting the Secondary-School Program to the Needs of Youth*, Fifty-Second Yearbook, Part I (Chicago: The University of Chicago Press, 1953).

Project on the Instructional Program of the Public Schools, *Planning and Organizing for Teaching* (Washington, D.C.: The National Education Association, 1963).

THOMAS, R. M., and S. M. THOMAS, *Individual Differences in the Classroom* (New York: David McKay Company, Inc., 1965).

TYLER, LEONA E., *The Psychology of Human Differences* (New York: Appleton-Century-Crofts, Inc., 1965).

VAN TIL, WILLIAM, GORDON F. VARS, and JOHN H. LOUNSBURY, *Modern Education for the Junior High School Years* (Indianapolis: The Bobbs-Merrill Company, Inc., 1961), Unit V.

CHAPTER *8*

Teaching Special Pupils

*P*ROVIDING for individual differences in pupils who deviate considerably from the norm requires special measures. All too often schooling is frustrating and deadening to them because teachers forget this elemental fact.

Poor Learners

Pupils who have difficulty learning academic material are an especially difficult problem for secondary-school teachers because, as subject specialists, the teachers wish to teach their subjects well and these pupils are not able to learn them well. Because they seldom have learned to learn by themselves, poor learners are more dependent on instruction than other pupils are. This fact tends to place considerable strain on the teacher. Nevertheless poor learners must be taught, and should be taught well. Although some teachers find teaching them burdensome, most good teachers look on teaching them as a challenge rather than a chore.

Characteristics of Poor Learners

More often than not, the poor learner is dull intellectually. He cannot think fast or learn academic things quickly. He needs time to learn. To rush him through an assignment may result in no learning at all. But when we give him enough time, he may be able to learn more than we expect of him.

Most intellectually dull pupils have little interest in abstract ideas. Indeed, they usually have great difficulty understanding the abstract, and more often than not find it particularly hard to generalize. This makes it difficult for them to cope with the normal academic curriculum and to transfer what they have learned in one situation to another. Solving-problem activities are likely to be too much for them because of their lack of intellectual ability. On the other hand, they may be able to memorize, albeit sometimes excruciatingly slowly, and to solve problems that are not too difficult.

Because of the lack of ability and lack of interest in ideas, intellectually dull pupils are easily discouraged by difficult academic material. Further, their lack of ability, poor vocabulary, and slowness often make it difficult for them to understand directions. When an intellectually dull pupil claims that he does not know what to do, he is probably telling the truth. Not understanding what to do and trying to cope with material that is too difficult can be particularly frustrating. One can readily understand why so many intellectually dull youths are bored and discouraged. As often as not, such pupils become behavior problems of one sort or another.

Still, although the intellectually dull pupil has little interest in the abstract, he is not devoid of interests. Rather, his interests are likely to concern things and concrete situations. Similarly his thinking is more likely to deal with specific situations than with generalizations.

Many dull boys and girls are much slower than they need to be. Sometimes they are only very poorly prepared. Because former teachers did not realize the problems and potentialities of these youngsters, they taught them much less than they should have. Such pupils can frequently be salvaged if their teachers only take the trouble.

BRIGHT BUT SLOW PUPILS. It has become customary to call pupils who have difficulty keeping up with the norm in learning academic material slow learners. All slow pupils are not dull pupils; neither are they necessarily poor learners or slow in all curriculum areas. Sometimes slowness is little more than a sign of the inability to read, or an indication that the pupil has never been taught how to learn by means of verbal academic material.

Quite possibly a child who has difficulty learning schoolwork based on textbooks may be quite adept at solving intricate problems involving mechanical ability, a high understanding of physical relationships, and high reasoning ability. Pupils have many different talents. The fact that a pupil lacks academic or literary talent does not preclude the possibility of his having talent, latent or active, in mechanics, arts, or social skills.

In addition, some pupils are slow because of other reasons not related to academic ability at all. Pupils from certain cultures may lack motivation to move quickly. Others, for a variety of reasons, are not motivated academically. Some pupils are slow and deliberate. Their "life style" is slow. Some use up their energies in other activities so that they have none left to use on school work. Some may be "late bloomers" who, for one reason or another, develop slowly for a while and then pull ahead to surpass their seemingly faster age mates. To lump these types of pupils together as dull or slow is a great injustice to them.

GENERAL CHARACTERISTICS. Pupils who are truly intellectually dull are likely to be dull in other ways. The folk belief that nature usually compensates for the dull youth's lack of intellectual ability by giving him manual talents is a myth. Although both intellectually bright and dull people may be skilfull with their hands, dull pupils are less likely to be so than bright ones. If classes that feature manual skills are more satisfactory for dull pupils than academic classes are, it is only because the manually oriented lesson is likely to be less abstract and therefore more meaningful to them than academic classes. In this respect, as in others, dull pupils vary greatly in their potential, just as other people do.

THE READING PROBLEM. The poor learner's most common handicap is poor reading ability. Teachers should be careful when selecting reading material for these pupils. They must also give much class time to making sure that the pupils understand what they read. One step in this process is to check to see that pupils understand the words. In a social studies class, for instance, a ninth-grade girl was insistent that people in New Jersey were not hostile to Puerto Rican immigrants because the old inhabitants did not like the Puerto Ricans and did not want them around, and besides they were afraid they would take their jobs. A little questioning brought out the fact that she thought *hostile* was synonymous with *hospitable*.

With classes of pupils who read badly, the teacher can often put greater emphasis on audio-visual teaching aids and the use of nonliterary techniques. In the social studies class just mentioned, the teacher found that the pupils had difficulty following the news for current events classes in the newspaper, but that they could and did follow her assignments on the television newscasts. With television as a source of information, this "slow" group's current events discussions sometimes rivaled those of the "faster" sections.

PHYSICAL HANDICAPS AND POOR LEARNING. Sometimes poor learners are handicapped by ill health or physical disability. They seem to be particularly prone to deficiencies of sight or hearing. If these handicaps and health problems are the cause of their poor learning, correcting the handicaps can be a step toward reducing academic deficiencies. More often, however, lack of physical fitness is another sign of their general inability, for physical and intellectual potential seem to go hand in hand. Being below par physically may be another manifestation of the fact that the poor learner is not well endowed.

Teaching Poor Learners

The teaching techniques that are most effective for poor learners are, for the most part, the same ones most useful for dealing with average pupils. (One must remember, however, that the best techniques for teaching average pupils are not always the ones most frequently used; sometimes the ones most frequently used are not the most effective for teaching anyone, especially not pupils of less-than-ordinary academic talent.) However, for poor learners one should ordinarily keep to a slower pace and to easier materials than in other classes.

THE CURRICULUM FOR POOR LEARNERS. Ordinarily the standard secondary-school curriculum holds little of value for poor learners. By and large the usual subject matter offerings are too abstract for them. Besides, the divisiveness of the departmentalized school program seems to confuse them. Many of the standard secondary-school courses have little relevance to their present or future lives. Even if they could profit from them academically, one wonders how much real benefit the courses could give them. Probably such pupils can be served best by block-of-time courses made up of broad units centering about preparation for citizenship and vocational adjustment.

The curriculum for poor learners should be developmental rather than remedial. Remedial work is necessary, of course, but as a rule the emphasis should be on the pupils' continuous development of skills and knowledges with only occasional reversions to short, intense doses of remedial instruction. Because these pupils' needs are more likely to be in the realm of personal development than of academic enrichment, their curriculum should contain strong guidance and homeroom programs. The content should concentrate on things important in their lives outside of school, such as home maintenance, family budgeting, consumer education, vocational and prevocational preparation, with special emphasis on things they can use in their out-of-school life now. Work-school programs have proved to be particularly good for them.

Among the skills most important for poor learners to learn are those pertaining to clear thinking. These pupils need to know how to reason just as much as other people do. Because they are apt to be easy marks for propaganda, false advertising, and shady deals, they need special help in learning how to analyze propaganda and false arguments so that they can protect their own interests. To learn these skills pupils need to practice them in practical, realistic situations.

In summary, then, *the curriculum of the poor learner should be simple, practical, realistic, and meaningful.* There is little place in it for the purely cultural or academic. However, it is a mistake to believe that the way to help poor learners is to enroll them in ordinary shop and homemaking courses. Poor learners are seldom more apt in these areas than in the academic ones. Although poor learners may profit more from such courses than from other courses because they are less abstract, the courses are not really suitable and so poor learners do not get as much from the ordinary courses in vocational arts as they would from courses designed for them specifically.

NEED FOR FREQUENT DIAGNOSIS. Diagnosis is important in all teaching, but it is doubly so in teaching poor learners. Their academic difficulties make them susceptible to misunderstanding and error. Therefore, the teacher needs to measure and evaluate their progress often. With such pupils one cannot expect success from shortcuts. To attempt to teach poor learners materials for which they are not ready is futile. Often one must repeat and reteach what has been done before. If the teacher does not constantly evaluate the progress of these pupils, they and he may become completely lost.

Constant evaluation is also necessary in teaching poor learners because of their tendency to do careless, slipshod work unless frequently reminded of the need to be careful. This tendency is, of course, present in all pupils, but in poor learners it may be more of a problem. Because academic learning does not come easily to them, poor learners may find schoolwork something of an ordeal and so are inclined to stop working somewhat short of perfection.

TO MAKE THINGS CLEAR. Because poor learners have difficulty understanding, teachers of poor learners need to make special efforts to be clear. They should keep their language as simple and direct as they can. It is especially important for teachers to refrain from speaking in generalities when they can speak in specifics. In giving instructions teachers of poor learners need to go into detail. Poor learners need plenty of instructions. Again one would be wise to avoid shortcuts, for with these pupils shortcuts will more than likely turn out to be short circuits. Because poor learners find it difficult to transfer their learning, teachers should be careful to point out the implications of each lesson in some detail.

TEACHING TECHNIQUES FOR POOR LEARNERS. Teaching poor learners requires great patience and understanding, but patience and understanding are not enough. The teacher must also be competent in the appropriate teaching technology. These techniques are approximately the same as those that good elementary-school teachers use with younger pupils. However, since poor learners in secondary schools are not children, but adolescents or young adults, they are liable to resent teaching tactics by which teachers seem to treat them as children. The secondary-school teacher should guard against talking down to his poor learners or giving them childish assignments. At the same time, he must also be sure that his language and his assignments are clear and simple. To walk this tightrope between the childish and the too difficult is often quite hazardous.

CONCRETE, SIMPLE ACTIVITIES. In general, the usual, principally verbal, teaching methods are not suitable for the academically dull. The teacher should keep his instruction concrete and tangible. Handwork is valuable because it makes the learnings real and concrete to the dull pupil. This type of work is important for he can frequently understand the concrete when the abstract would be too much for him. For this same reason the judicious use of *realia* and audio-visual aids will help slow pupils learn. Demonstrations, observing phenomena, motion pictures, making collections, building exhibits and models, and caring for a model home are all examples of concrete, tangible activities that can be used with slow learners.

Activities for poor learners should also be kept simple. Assignments should be kept short so as not to discourage and confuse the pupils. Lessons should be limited to a very few points. Field trips should contain only a few things for the pupils to do. If community problems or activities are used—and they can be used quite successfully—the poor learners' participation should deal only with aspects that are concrete, tangible, and not very complex. This need for simplicity is the reason for the common recommendation that when using pictures or other audio-visual aids one should use only a few at a time.

At times, of course, one must teach complex matters to poor learners. In some instances such teaching goals require large amounts of practice so as to bring about habituation. Usually, a teacher is most successful if he starts with the simple and gradually moves to the complex by an easy transition. The teacher in such a situation should make the continuity quite clear so that the pupils will be able to see the relationships as they move on. Thus it is that in teaching spelling, it is necessary to include a considerable amount of formal spelling. In doing so it would be advisable to introduce only a few words at a time and to use these words in sentences in order to make their meaning clear.

Realistic activities are good for use with poor learners because they help motivate them and make transfer of learning relatively easy. Sometimes these slow pupils may find it difficult to see the relevance of many mathematics problems, but when the problem has to do with the cost of purchasing, financing, and maintaining a particular car the pertinence of the mathematics involved may become both obvious and interesting to them. So also in English classes letter writing to real people can make composition more realistic. A class newspaper may help pupils see the

The judicious use of realia and other audio-visual materials helps pupils in slow classes to learn.

importance of their work. Similarly, the presentation of an assembly or the preparation of an exhibit can be used to make the learning process real. Creative activities are also useful. Pupils are usually interested in dramatizations and can learn much from them. The value of exhibits, collections, and class newspapers made by the pupils has already been discussed. These activities have the advantage of not only being realistic, but also of actively involving the pupil.

Obtaining Materials for Poor Learners

Teaching slow pupils requires an assortment of materials. Particularly desirable are reading materials suitable for high-school and junior-high-school pupils, yet written at elementary-school reading levels. Fortunately, publishers and suppliers have come to realize this necessity and suitable materials are appearing on the market. At times reading material designed for younger pupils in lower grades may be used successfully for slow pupils. However, pupils resent being asked to read from books they consider to be childish. Moreover, some slow pupils may be ashamed to be seen with books designed for younger pupils. Since attempts to disguise the grade level of textbooks have not been very successful, teachers should not insist on pupils' using material designed for younger pupils unless they are willing.

When no stigma is attached to such books they may be excellent for slow learners. One way to use them is to pull the book apart and bind its more useful sections separately into plain cardboard binders. When this is done, the pupil does not need to carry a "kid's" book with him for any length of time. Furthermore, the practice allows the teacher to vary his assignments more easily.

In similar fashion the teacher can procure much other reading material. Fortunately, many periodicals and newspapers contain relatively easy reading materials, often of high motivational value. In a fairly short time a teacher can collect from such sources quite a selection of easy but interesting materials suitable for slow adolescents.

In some instances the teacher may find it desirable to create some of the materials himself. This is not as difficult as it may seem. If the teacher remembers to limit his vocabulary and to keep his sentences and paragraphs short and simple, he can prepare reading material of seemingly adult level which the pupils can read satisfactorily.

Since dull pupils find it difficult to learn through symbols, teachers should attempt to find materials that do not depend on words. Actually, to see things and to act things out will more likely result in learning than to hear or read about them. To this end, pictures, models, *realia*, and other concrete materials are useful. Methods for obtaining such materials are explained in Part V. However, in dealing with slow pupils, the teacher should remember to keep the material simple, clear, and realistic. To keep from confusing slow pupils and to keep the material within their scope, teachers should avoid presenting too much material too fast. A few pictures carefully presented are likely to be more effective than a large number of pictures presented hurriedly.

❋

Is the fact that some pupils feel that there is a stigma attached to being assigned to a section of slow pupils a serious problem? What might one do to reduce this feeling in the pupils?

Is it possible to teach slow pupils adequately in normal classes? If so, how would you do it?

In what ways would the methods you would use in slow classes differ from those you would use in regular classes?

*

Marking and Promoting Poor Learners

Marking poor learners causes a serious problem that has never been solved. If a teacher marks them on their effort, he may run the danger of seeming to report achievement much greater than that they have actually attained. Similarly, to mark a poor learner on the basis of his achievement as compared to his expectations, again runs the risk of giving the recipient of the report a false impression. But, if one marks him solely on his achievements as compared to those of his peers, one dooms him to a school life of poor marks and failures.

Some schools have tried to solve this problem by reporting more than one mark, e.g., a mark based on effort, a mark based on performance as compared to his individual potential, and a mark based on performance as compared to that expected of other pupils of his age and grade. Others indicate the achievement with the usual marks plus a subscript to denote the level of the section. Unfortunately, none of these marking systems has proved to be really successful. *Perhaps the only solution is to free pupils from marks and grade levels by placing them in ungraded schools or classes and to report their progress by written or graphical descriptions of their accomplishments.*

Culturally Deprived Youth[1]

Culturally deprived youth are frequently lumped together with slow or poor learners in our thinking. Of course it is true that there is enough overlap between the two groups to make it seem that deprived children are poor learners, but appearances can be deceiving. The range of native intelligence is just as great among the culturally deprived as among the culturally affluent. Some culturally deprived youth are really gifted. Many culturally deprived youth have more basic academic potential than teachers give them credit for. Because of their unusual problems and their great hidden potential, deprived youth need and deserve special consideration.

[1] This section is based largely on the work of Riessman and others who have worked primarily with the urban disadvantaged. The experience of the present authors, however, leads them to believe that the generalizations stated here are also applicable to many other kinds of socially disadvantaged pupils.

Characteristics of Culturally Disadvantaged Youth

In reality, culturally disadvantaged pupils are more educationally deprived than culturally deprived for they all come from cultures rich in many ways and in certain aspects perhaps richer than the common middle-class American culture familiar to most of us. The difficulty seems to be that their cultures are different and therefore difficult for middle-class teachers and administrators to understand. Teachers of deprived youth need to develop an understanding of the culture so that they can capitalize on its strengths and avoid competing against its mores and ideals. They should not derogate it or attempt to reform it. The nation and country may benefit more from pluralism than from conformity. Teachers need not and should not try to force all pupils into the same mold.

THE LANGUAGE OF THE DISADVANTAGED. In spite of what many teachers seem to think, most deprived pupils are quite verbal. In their own vernacular they can speak precisely and colorfully. Their language difficulties come from the fact that their vernacular is often quite different from the standard English of other groups. Formal language, like that in books, is usually quite foreign to them. Consequently their creative abilities and flights of fancy are likely to be lost or hidden by a language barrier in the classroom.

PHYSICAL ORIENTATION. Although deprived pupils are facile verbally, it is also true that they are less likely to be word bound and word oriented than middle-class people. Instead, they tend to react positively to what they can see and do and to approach things physically rather than verbally. Therefore, many deprived pupils are apt to learn better from physical activity and visual presentation than from listening. In short, learning by doing seems to be especially effective for them.

The culturally deprived youth's tendency to be physically oriented also tends to give their culture a masculine orientation. In the urban slums and ghettos, at least, much of their life is rough and uncouth. They enjoy adventures, sports, and boisterousness. Sometimes this tendency leads to delinquency. In the classroom it may result in "horsing around." It also makes it possible to interest and motivate them by means of games and physical activities.

AUTHORITARIANISM AND TRADITIONALISM. The masculinity of the culture of the deprived—even when their families are matriarchal—may be responsible for, or a manifestation of, their authoritarianism and traditionalism. Pupils from such cultural backgrounds tend to like things to be definite. Often they are used to and expect rigid authoritarianism severely enforced by rough punishment. Parents, in their experience, seldom resort to reasoning, coaxing, or coddling. Rather, they enforce their desires with sharp words and blows quickly given and quickly forgotten. Because punishment is swift and hard, children seldom have doubts about why they are getting it; neither are they plagued by long drawn-out periods of nagging and threatening.

THE EXTENDED FAMILY. One reason for their punishment pattern may be the fact that culturally deprived people often live in extended families. When grandmothers, aunts, uncles, father, mother, and children all crowd together in a small house or a cramped tenement, the elders are not likely to put up with much nonsense from the young people. Such a background also explains deprived pupils' ready acceptance of authoritarianism.

It also explains their anti-intellectualism. Large poor families do not provide opportunity for amenities. Pupils raised in such situations are bound to be interested in the vocational and practical. On the whole, persons from deprived groups probably see the need for education just as clearly as other people. Parents from these groups would like to see their children educated so that they can get ahead and so that they will no longer be the dupes of sharp operators and bureaucrats. Many of them feel that only by means of education can their children ever get their rights.

The Disadvantaged Child in School

The culturally disadvantaged youth does not ordinarily like school. Even though he sees the value of the three R's, science, and information that will keep him from being cheated, he seldom takes kindly to academic studies. More often than is necessary, he does badly in them and so drops out of school after a history of frustration and failure.

FAILURE, FRUSTRATION, AND HUMILIATION. The culturally disadvantaged youth tends to blame his frustrations and failures on the school. He is often right. Teachers frequently treat him as a second-class citizen. They assume that he is not intelligent and so cannot learn. After a time the pupil may be convinced of his lack of ability and live down to the teachers' expectations.

And so the disadvantaged pupils learn not to expect much from school. Even if they did have good expectations, their lack of school knowledge and middle-class *savoir faire* would soon discourage them, for many disadvantaged pupils never have a chance to learn the qualities and skills that give one success in school.

WHY THEY FAIL. Since for many deprived children school is just one humiliating failure after another, it is not strange that they view school and teachers with hostility. Authorities have noted many reasons why the underprivileged do not learn well in school. Most commonly mentioned are

1. The lack of an "educational tradition" in the home, few books, etc.
2. Insufficient language and reading skills.
3. Inadequate motivation to pursue a long-range educational career, and poor estimate of self.
4. Antagonism toward the school, the teacher.
5. Poor health, improper diet, frequent moving, and noisy, TV-ridden homes.[2]

Although he realizes that these reasons are partially valid, Riessman is convinced that they do not represent the problem accurately because they fail to take into account the school environment and what the school could do to attack the problem. Therefore, he has tried to reformulate a more valid list of basic deterrents to school learning in underprivileged pupils.

1. The discrimination, frequently unintentional, seen in the classroom, Parent-Teacher Association, guidance office, psychological testing program, etc., which alienates Johnny and his family.
2. Johnny's *ambivalence* toward education—not simply rejection of it —his lack of school know-how, test-taking skills, information concerning college, and his anti-intellectualism.
3. The culture of the school which overlooks and underestimates his particular skills and mode of intellectual functioning that arise out of his culture and way of life.
4. The deficits in Johnny's background which necessitate special *transitional* techniques to bring him into the academic mainstream. These do not require a "soft" approach, a lowering of standards, a capitulation to his deficiencies.[3]

On the basis of these lists and other considerations Riessman has made specific recommendations for teaching culturally deprived youth. In the following paragraphs we shall consider briefly some of these recommendations.

Teaching the Educationally Deprived

Because the educationally deprived pupil comes to school with small expectations, to teach him successfully is liable to be rather difficult. It

[2] Frank Riessman, *The Culturally Deprived Child* (New York: Harper and Row, Publishers, 1962), pp. 4–15.
[3] *Ibid.,* pp. 5, 6.

is not, however, impossible. Culturally deprived youth frequently have much more potential than they appear to have on the surface.

THE FALSE I.Q. Teachers of educationally deprived pupils are sometimes convinced that they are dealing with poor learners when they are not. As we have pointed out earlier, slow learners are not necessarily poor learners. Some learners may be slow because they are thorough, or unsure, or cautious, or because they use poor study techniques, or have never learned to read or figure properly. Some pupils may even be slow and gifted.[4] Teachers should be alert to the fact that sometimes good intellectual potential may be hidden behind low I.Q. scores caused by poor reading ability or poorly designed intelligence tests.

Teachers should be especially aware that poor reading may be the handicap holding back the learning of the deprived youth and that adjustments in pupil reading level may make the difference between pupil learning and pupil frustration. They should try to find easy reading material suitable for the pupils' age and interest levels. (Certain metropolitan newspapers are written for adult readership at quite low reading levels, for instance.) In addition, the teachers should try to utilize nonreading activities that will lead to the desired learning.

Physical activities are very useful in classes of disadvantaged pupils. Acting out scenes or role playing can sometimes be very effective, particularly in teaching history or interpreting literature. The tendency of disadvantaged pupils to be physically oriented also makes it likely that they will take favorably to teaching machines and other gadgetry. Active games may also be useful to draw pupils' attention and interest. In some situations, however, such activities can lead to chaos. In any case teachers should give the pupils plenty of chances to learn by doing, for such activities will ordinarily be much more successful than lecturing and other primarily verbal techniques.

REALISTIC ASSIGNMENTS. The work the teacher of disadvantaged pupils lays out should be realistic. Disadvantaged pupils have had so much experience with failure that very challenging work may frighten them away rather than urge them forward. Still, they do not want to be insulted with childish pap below their dignity. To pick assignments that are just right requires teacher ingenuity and a thorough knowledge of one's pupils.

In giving assignments, directions should be clear and explicit. Teachers can often help pupils tremendously if they will only show them how to study. Because of the probable defects in disadvantaged pupils' home and school backgrounds teachers should be ready to teach them all sorts of

4 *Ibid.*, p. 63.

skills that are usually presumed to be part of a normal secondary-school pupil's equipment, for example, how to ask questions.

COMBATING ANTI-INTELLECTUALISM. A main task of the teacher of the disadvantaged is to fight anti-intellectualism. The strategy is to crack the anti-intellectual prejudices of the pupils by any means possible at first, and then to build increasingly favorable intellectual attitudes on these small beginnings. Try to capitalize on their interests and point out the practical value of what is to be learned. Take advantage of their belief in the usefulness of the fundamentals, the vocational, and the scientific. Utilize the boys' masculinity. Let them read the sports page, science fiction, or anything else that will get them started. This is no time for intellectual snobbery.

In doing all this, the teacher must respect the pupil and his culture. Accept the pupil as a person and let him know by your behavior that you are on his side. Undoubtedly, because of unfortunate past experiences, the pupils will need a great deal of convincing. Try to overcome the hostility by deeds not words. Don't talk down to the pupils. Don't be condescending. Don't demean yourself. Tend to your teaching and concentrate on getting the material across. Explain things to them carefully in good but simple English. Do not try to imitate their slang. You are an adult and a teacher, and they expect you to act like one. On the other hand, make it evident that you expect them to learn just like anyone else. If you convince the pupils that you respect them and are trying your best to teach them, you may find that their hostility will be replaced by loyalty and respect.

MAINTAINING CLASSROOM CONTROL. Discipline is often a problem with disadvantaged pupils. With school-caused frustrations and hostilities so common, it is unreasonable to expect it to be otherwise.

Probably the best way to prevent classes of disadvantaged pupils from getting out of control is by concentrating on teaching and letting the pupils know by your actions that you intend to do your best to teach them as well as you can. In this respect it is probably best to run a rather traditional class. Disadvantaged pupils seem to distrust new approaches and particularly loose progressive techniques.

In addition, the teacher should set up and enforce clear, definite rules. Culturally deprived youth believe in authority. Being authoritative will probably work to the teacher's advantage. If possible, the teacher should also determine the natural leaders in the class and solicit their support. This solicitation should be done slowly and indirectly, however.

As in any other class, consistency is a virtue. In this way you can make clear to the pupils where you and where they stand. Avoid favoritism.

Treat everyone fairly and evenly. Be especially careful about accepting the advances of pupils who come to you. The pupils who first seek the friendship and attention of the teacher may well be renegades who are not accepted by the group. By gaining them you may lose the rest of the class. If the teacher tries to treat each individual fairly, consistently, and respectfully, there is a good chance that his relations with the entire group will become easy and pleasant after a time.

✿

> Examine some of the textbooks for junior-high-school courses in your field. Are there any reasons why they would be unsatisfactory for educationally disadvantaged pupils?
>
> What could you do to help pupils from a non-English speaking background?
>
> Are there any things you could do to combat directly the deterrents to school learning that Riessman considers basic?

✿

Remedial Teaching

Teaching designed specifically for boys and girls who have not achieved desired goals is called remedial teaching. Many teachers seem to think there is something esoteric about remedial teaching. There is not. Remedial teaching is merely good teaching concentrated directly on the pupil and his needs. Usually it is more effective than ordinary teaching only because it is more thorough and more carefully designed to remedy a specific need.

Some teachers seem to feel that remedial teaching should be reserved for extraordinary pupils and for remedial classes. Nothing could be further from the truth. It is probably no exaggeration to say that every youth needs remedial teaching at one time or another. Remedial and diagnostic teaching should be a part of every unit. To provide such teaching in each unit is relatively easy to do if evaluation is continuous and the teacher centers his teaching on the youth rather than on the subject matter.

Diagnosing the Difficulty

If we know exactly what skills, concepts, attitudes, ideals, and appreciations we are striving for, it should be quite easy to construct devices that would tell us whether or not those concepts, skills, attitudes, ideals, and appreciations have been developed. An objective or essay-type test constructed by the teacher can be excellent for showing whether or not the pupil understands, if the teacher chooses the questions carefully. However, the teacher will frequently find it necessary to rely on evaluative devices other than tests to get at these learnings. Examples of these devices may be found in Chapters 2 and 15.

Reteaching Poorly Learned Material

In the regular class remedial teaching ordinarily consists of reteaching those things that boys and girls have not learned. For instance, if the boys and girls in a class that should already have studied the fulcrum do not seem to understand what it is, the lesson should probably be repeated for all. If only a few persons did not get it, they should probably be retaught in a special group. If it becomes evident that just one youngster missed it, he should be retaught individually. To reteach in this fashion may mean spending several days with the entire class on the missed learning, or revamping the next unit to include this learning again, or it may entail no more than just a few minutes of review and explanation, or a short conference with one pupil. Similarly, when it is found that boys and girls lack basic knowledge prerequisite to any unit, the teacher must take time to reteach this understanding. In cases of this sort the ordinary techniques of teaching suffice for remedial teaching, if they are carefully aimed at the trouble. Remedial teaching is aimed firing; barrage techniques will not do.[5] Actually, this type of remedial teaching is little more than providing for individual differences; the techniques explained in Chapter 7 and earlier in this chapter should be very helpful.

The following illustration will serve as an example of remedial teaching in the regular classroom. In going over the test papers of one of his mathematics classes, the teacher noted that one of the pupils was having considerable difficulty with the problems. An analysis of her papers showed that the pupil was neglecting to convert all the parts of the problem to the same terms. At the next class meeting the teacher pointed out to the pupil the error she was making. He then quizzed the girl to see that she understood how to convert from one unit to the other and assigned to her several special problems by which to practice the technique directly.

❋

Of what value can self-correcting exercises be in remedial teaching?
In what ways is remedial teaching different from regular teaching?
How can practice materials be utilized in remedial teaching?

❋

[5] Barrage firing is firing in which the artillery or missile unit covers an entire area with fire thereby hoping to deny the area to the enemy and to destroy any already there.

Teaching the Seriously Deficient

More serious cases of inadequate learning often turn up. These require more careful handling. Frequently these disabilities warrant remedial teaching by specialists outside of the regular classroom. When such help is available the teacher should use it. However, as long as some schools limit remedial classes to pupils who are retarded at least three years, and many other schools have no such services at all, the teacher must be ready to assume the burden himself. Moreover, many of the problems are not so serious that the regular classroom teacher cannot take care of them competently.

For instance, we find quite often that one reason a pupil is having trouble with higher mathematics is that he never mastered his arithmetic essentials. If this is the case, the teacher should test him to find out what the actual fault is, then teach him how to do the specific arithmetical process properly, and finally give him plenty of practice until he has mastered the difficulty.

Another example concerns a pupil who seemed to have a great deal of trouble with punctuation. Upon examination the teacher found that the pupil knew the rules for punctuation well enough, but that he did not know how to apply them. To correct this fault the instructor arranged a series of lessons in which the pupil learned to translate the rules into terms he understood, and then prescribed exercises designed to apply the rules to sentences.

As in any remedial situation, correcting severe disabilities depends upon careful diagnosis and careful reteaching. Techniques suitable for such special classes are beyond the scope of this text. Teachers would do well to take special courses in this area and read some of the excellent books on the subject.

✱

Can you give examples of the need for remedial teaching of brilliant youth from your own experience? How should this type of remedial teaching best be handled?

Supposing about one third of your class missed an essential part of the last unit. You estimate that it would take about two days to reteach it properly. What would you do?

✱

The Gifted Pupil

By "gifted youth" we mean those who have special abilities in some subject field. A person, no matter how dull he may be in other fields, is gifted if he has a special talent. Conversely, a pupil, gifted in one field, may be below average in others. In most school situations teachers are inclined to think only of the academically bright youth as the gifted youth. Certainly intellectually bright youths are gifted, but so are the people with special talents in art, music, and mechanical arts. The truly talented in these areas need to have plenty of opportunities to make the most of their special talents. At the same time, the school must see to it that in exploiting his talent, the pupil is not kept from the education best suited for his needs and abilities in other areas.

Characteristics of Talented Youth

In dealing with talented youth we should remember that their special abilities and characteristics make the teaching problem somewhat different from that of teaching normal pupils. Because of their ability, and the interest which usually accompanies ability, talented young people can accomplish more work in a shorter time than their classmates can. Not only can they do more work more quickly, they can do work of a higher order. Brilliant youths like to use their brains; they are intrigued by puzzles and problems; the abstract holds no fears for them; they can maintain interests in academic problems and assignments for long hours without flagging. Therefore, work that the ordinary pupil finds difficult may bore them because of its easiness. Often they have studied and read independently to the point that they are well above the level of the normal class and even sometimes above the level of their teachers.

Yet the talented youth is in many ways a normal youth. He has most of the normal youth's traits and problems. He is not a thing apart and should not be treated as if he were. The problem is to make it possible for him to make the most of his talent while keeping the rest of his personality healthy. This is no small order, for the talented youth has probably not learned to discriminate and take care of himself any better than his less talented brother.

Teaching Talented Pupils

In many school systems special programs, and sometimes even special schools, are provided for the talented pupils. These are excellent and should be encouraged, but of more concern to most teachers is how to help the brilliant pupil in the regular classroom. To meet this problem, each one of the techniques for meeting needs of individual pupils described earlier may be used. Because of their ability, brilliant pupils should stretch their horizons by attempting high-level assignments. Where the ordinary youth may be satisfied to read about the westward movement in a text, the brilliant pupil could be reading The Oregon Trail. When studying World War II, the brilliant pupil might try to reconcile the accounts given by Sir Winston Churchill, General Eisenhower, and others.

In metalworking the brilliant youth might, in addition to doing fine work, study such topics as metallurgy, the metal trades, the economics of metals, and the effect of metal on history. The importance of keeping standards high becomes extremely apparent when we realize that according to Kingsley,[6] superior pupils often work up to only 40 per cent of their capacity, although less capable pupils may work up to 80 per cent. Allowing superior youths to waste their talents creates poor work habits and slovenliness. Brilliant youths should be held to high standards that will challenge the best in them.

In addition to attempting assignments of a high order the brilliant pupil should meet high standards of workmanship. He can do choice work; the teacher must see to it that he does. The teacher must not accept careless, poorly written, or poorly executed work from talented pupils. To do so engrains in them slothfulness and mediocrity.

Furthermore, the bright pupil can accept considerable responsibility for his own direction. Brilliant youths should have experience in planning and evaluating their own work. Since they are potential leaders, they need the experience in planning, organizing, making decisions, and carrying out plans. Moreover, they should have many opportunities for leadership and service in their classes.

Sometimes attempting to hold brilliant pupils to standards higher than those of their classmates may backfire. Some bright pupils may resent having to do better work than other pupils. With bright pupils this pitfall usually can be avoided by appealing to their pride, by attempting to convince them that the assignments are really worthwhile, and by making the assignments exciting and challenging rather than drudgery. Some teachers provide opportunities for recognition of the brilliant pupils in their testing by adding additional difficult "extra" questions at the end of the test making it possible for a pupil to get more than 100 per cent of the questions on the test. This device has been somewhat successful. However, the threat of marks is usually of little value. Bright pupils can earn good marks without half trying. To get the most from these pupils the teacher must call upon more genuine motives. Usually this is not hard to do since the talented youth almost always enjoys challenging tasks.

＊

What can be done to provide brilliant pupils with work sufficiently challenging?

A teacher complained that her bright pupils were not working up to capacity because she could not make them do more work than

---

[6] Robert W. Frederick *et al.*, *Describing Learning* (New York: Appleton-Century-Crofts, Inc., 1938), pp. 132–134.

ordinary pupils. What would you suggest that the teacher do to help keep the bright pupils working up to capacity?

In some schools teachers use the services of brilliant pupils in teaching the less brilliant. What is your estimate of this practice?

How would you attempt to catch the interest of a brilliant pupil who was obviously bored in one of your classes?

How would you go about to tempt brilliant pupils into doing considerably more and harder work than other pupils?

*

READING FOR THE GIFTED. It should not be necessary to go into detail in describing specific teaching techniques for classes of gifted pupils because most of the techniques ordinarily used in our secondary schools were originally developed for use with talented pupils. Similarly, as we have already pointed out, many of the techniques described in the earlier chapter concerning individual differences in regular classes are the same techniques used to teach gifted pupils. The important thing is to provide them with opportunities to use their minds to the fullest. The content they encounter should be aimed at developing generalizations, realizations, and abstractions. Moreover, it should be new to them. *Some bright high-school pupils go to class month after month without ever encountering any subject matter that they have not already learned.* They really should have the chance to go into the topics more deeply or to skip them altogether.

Ordinary high-school textbooks seldom meet the needs of gifted pupils. This lack can be filled in many ways: pupils can read their assignments from college texts, primary sources, original writings, or other works. Much use can be made of individualized reading to supplement or substitute for the ordinary assignments. In many courses the pupil himself with only a little guidance can profitably choose his own readings. Often they will profit from reading several selections on a topic. A good technique is for the pupil to make a list of proposed readings and what he hopes to learn from them, and submit it to the teacher before he begins his work. Another method is to give the gifted pupils study guides with suggested problems for investigation and a list of suitable, pertinent readings.

RESEARCH AND DEPTH STUDY. Not only should the subject matter of brilliant pupils deal with generalizations and abstractions, but the pupils themselves should have a chance to develop their own generalizations. Memorizing facts and other information is not enough for pupils with good minds. They should find things out for themselves. In science their laboratory work could include real problems. In history their work could consist of digging out real history. In literature they could write some real criticism. In music they could perform and compose. Their school projects could be actual scholarly research projects, or, at least, the study of a topic in depth. By studying in this manner, the pupil would not only be able to fix basic facts and skills securely in his mind, but he could go beyond to create new concepts for himself and his peers by making logical inferences from the information available to him. The topics to be studied can be closely allied with the course syllabus or range far from it.

THE SEMINAR APPROACH. Small seminar classes of bright pupils are excellent devices for utilizing the impact of depth study. One type of seminar consists of a member's presenting a paper on a topic he has prepared for the group to discuss. Another type consists of general discussion on topics all have studied in some detail. In either case the pupils are encouraged to bring all their knowledge and skill to bear on the problem in a penetrating, logical analysis. In such discussions the interchange must be free and open. No rules, except those of logical analysis and courtesy, should bar the way. The purpose of the seminar is to encourage hard, incisive examination of carefully researched material.

ACCELERATION. A common practice in many schools is to accelerate the gifted pupils—that is, to encourage gifted boys and girls to proceed through the curriculum more rapidly than the other pupils. By acceleration, many gifted pupils are able to complete the equivalent of four years work in three. Where classes are homogeneously grouped, it is quite common practice for the "upper" section to move through courses more quickly than the lower sections. Similar methods can be adopted for individuals or small groups in heterogeneous classes. Thus the brilliant student may be allowed to work through the ordinary mathematics courses more quickly than the others and then proceed to more advanced topics toward the end of the semester. If the teacher provides the pupil with study guides or similar materials, the bright youth will be able to direct himself and to check out his own work much of the time. The teacher must, of course, keep the student under his eye, but the time involved in helping the brilliant need not be excessive. Furthermore, it is usually enjoyable—so enjoyable that teachers must guard against giving too much time to the gifted when the other pupils really need their help.

When working with gifted pupils, the teacher always has the problem of determining whether to go into things deeply or to move through them quickly; that is, to accelerate or to study in depth. With heterogeneously grouped classes, depth study for the gifted is sometimes easier to conduct than acceleration. However, it is a problem that each teacher must settle for himself in view of his own talents, the talents of his pupils, the materials available, and the subject matter concerned.

Summary

Pupils who deviate from the norm create special problems in teaching. Pupils who fall into this category include the poor learners, disadvantaged pupils, and the talented.

Teaching poor learners requires much skill and patience. Careful diagnosis of each pupil is necessary so that he can receive the kind of help he needs. This diagnostic activity is particularly important because poor learning is often the result of insufficiencies in his earlier education. In general, the curriculum for poor learners should be simple, practical, realistic, and meaningful. Teaching methods should emphasize concrete, simple activities with sufficient practice and review to make the learning stick. The materials of instruction used ordinarily should be less verbal than in other classes. Reading material should be short and easy, but not childish. Consequently, teachers may find it necessary to develop their own materials.

Disadvantaged youth often have many of the problems of poor learners because of gaps and differences in their cultural backgrounds. However, there has been a tendency to underestimate the potential of disadvantaged youth. Their academic failures are more often failures of the school and the community than pupil failures. In dealing with these youth one must treat them with the respect they deserve. As a rule, they tend to accept authoritarian classes whose orientation is physical, practical, and realistic.

Much of the teaching of slow and disadvantaged youth must be remedial. So should be a considerable amount of the teaching of average and gifted youth. Remedial teaching differs from other teaching only in that as a rule it is concentrated directly on the pupil and his needs after thorough diagnosis.

The key to teaching gifted youth is to urge them forward and not hold them back. Most of the academic techniques common in secondary schools were developed for teaching the most talented youth; therefore, special techniques for teaching them need not be discussed in detail. Since they enjoy the abstract and like to learn, the gifted pupils need plenty of opportunities to exercise their minds. In doing so they can accept a great amount of the responsibility for directing and evaluating their own learnings if the teacher gives them adequate guidance.

FOR FURTHER STUDY

BLAIR, GLENN MYERS, and WILLIAM POWELL, *Diagnostic and Remedial Teaching*, Second Edition (New York: The Macmillan Company, 1967).

DeHAAN, ROBERT F., and ROBERT J. HAVIGHURST, *Educating Gifted Children* (Chicago: The University of Chicago Press, 1961).

EVERETT, SAMUEL (editor), *Programs for the Gifted* (New York: Harper and Row Publishers, 1961).

FEATHERSTONE, W. B., *Teaching the Slow Learner*, Revised Edition (New York: Bureau of Publications, Teachers College, Columbia University, 1951).

FLIEGLER, LOUIS A. (editor), *Curriculum Planning for the Gifted* (Englewood Cliffs, N.J.: Prentice-Hall, Inc., 1961).

FREEHILL, MAURICE F., *Gifted Children: Their Psychology and Education* (New York: The Macmillan Company, 1961).

GETZELS, JACOB W., and PHILIP W. JACKSON, *Creativity and Intelligence: Explorations with Gifted Students* (New York: John Wiley and Sons, 1962).

National Society for the Study of Education, *Education for the Gifted*, The Fifty-seventh Yearbook, Part II (Chicago: The University of Chicago Press, 1958).

PASSOW, A. HARRY (editor), *Nurturing Individual Potential* (Washington, D.C.: Association for Supervision and Curriculum Development, 1964).

RIESSMAN, FRANK, *The Culturally Deprived Child* (New York: Harper and Row, Publishers, 1962).

School Programs for the Disadvantaged, Educational Research Circular No. 2 (Washington, D.C.: The National Education Association, February, 1963).

SCHREIBER, DANIEL (editor), *The School Drop Out* (Washington, D.C.: The National Education Association, 1964).

The Gifted Child in Portland (Portland, Oregon: Portland Public Schools).

U.S. Department of Health, Education, and Welfare, Office of Education, *The Gifted Student*, Cooperative Research Monograph No. 2 (Washington, D.C.: U.S. Government Printing Office, 1960).

————, *Programs for the Educationally Disadvantaged*, OE-35044, Bulletin 1963, No. 17, U.S. Office of Education (Washington, D.C.: U.S. Government Printing Office, 1963).

————, *Teaching Rapid and Slow Learners in High School*, Bulletin 1954, No. 5 (Washington, D.C.: U.S. Government Printing Office, 1954).

PART IV

Techniques of Teaching

CHAPTER 9

Some Specific Teaching Techniques

$\mathcal{T}$HE SKILLFUL teacher has many methods and techniques at his command. Although some of these are better than others, not one of them can be regarded as the best, for there is no best technique. In fact, techniques that are good for one subject or for one group of pupils may be quite unsatisfactory for another. The teacher should have many strings to his bow, so that he can select techniques and methods suitable to his own personality, to the pupils in his class, and to the subject he is teaching. For example, in a French class one should undoubtedly teach conversation by group techniques, but pupils can probably master irregular verbs more readily through individual study. This chapter and those following will attempt to show how some of these methods and techniques may be used to advantage.

Team Teaching

Advances in teaching technology are largely concerned with methodology and organization. Since the middle of the 1950's many school executives and teachers have been trying to develop methods and procedures that will combine the varying talents of individual teachers into teaching teams. The following paragraphs are an attempt to describe some ways of organizing and conducting team teaching. Later in this chapter and in other chapters the reader will find descriptions of many teaching techniques. As he reads about them, the reader should realize that all of these techniques may be used by team teachers as well as by individual teachers not working in teaching teams, for team teaching, like the unit method, is basically only a way of organizing instruction. Creative teachers can utilize almost any of these techniques in any type of instructional organization—team teaching, unit teaching, or day-by-day lessons.

GENERAL ASSUMPTIONS. Basically team teaching is "any plan whereby two or more teachers teach the same group of pupils cooperatively."[1] Although the plans in use differ in many respects, in general all of these plans are based on the same or similar assumptions and purposes. Lloyd Trump, the leading authority in the field, lists five assumptions.[2]

1. The quality of education depends largely on the quality of teaching.
2. The results of instruction depend largely on the ways in which teachers function in a school.
3. Methods of teaching should be related to the purposes of instruction.
4. Different levels of competence and training are needed for the various functions teachers now perform and which they are likely to do in the future.
5. Teachers differ in their interests and abilities to perform the various functions of teaching.

COMMON PURPOSES. From these assumptions educational innovators have developed a variety of team teaching schemes all having similar general purposes.

1. To improve the quality of teaching.
2. To relate the method of instruction to the purposes of instruction.
3. To allow for individual differences in teachers and to capitalize on individual teachers' varying capabilities, interests, and potentialities.
4. To add increased flexibility to the school curriculum and daily program.
5. To provide teachers with more time for planning, preparation, and follow-up.
6. To provide the pupil with opportunities to learn both from authority and his own discovery and discussion with his peers.

Obviously these assumptions and purposes are meritorious. However, it is still too early to tell what effect these plans will have on education in the long run.

Kinds of Teaching Teams

As so often happens in education, innovation has resulted in confused terminology. Judson Shaplin defines team teaching as

A type of instructional organization, involving teaching personnel and the students assigned to them, in which two or more teachers are given respon-

---

[1] Leonard H. Clark, Raymond L. Klein, and John Burks, *The American Secondary School Curriculum* (New York: The Macmillan Company, 1965), p. 408.

[2] J. Lloyd Trump, *New Horizons for Secondary School Teachers*, Commission on the Experimental Study of the Utilization of the Staff in Secondary School, National Education Association, Washington, D.C., 1957.

sibility, working together, for all or a significant part of the instruction of the same group of students.[3]

In explaining this definition its author insists that the team must consist of at least two professional teachers "working together for all or a significant part of the instruction." By this insistence he intends to rule out, as not worthy of the name team teaching, teams that consist only of one teacher plus teaching aides and informal *ad hoc* temporary cooperation between professional teachers.[4] Other authorities disagree and so we find in the literature references to teaching teams of many sorts.[5] In general, however, these multifarious types of teams can be categorized into three general types of teaching team organization: (1) the "teacher unit specialist approach, (2) the differentiated role specialist approach, and (3) the informal *ad hoc* approach."[6]

THE UNIT SPECIALIST TEAM.   The unit specialist team approach is meant to allow teachers to become expert on certain phases or units of their courses. In such courses the classes are scheduled so that one teacher can teach his specialty to each of the various sections. This he may do by meeting combined sections for large group instruction or by moving from section to section, period after period, to make his presentation.

One variation of this technique is the plan used in the Long Branch, New Jersey, high school in which three teachers rotate their units so that each teacher teaches his own specialty to each section. In this plan, at the end of the unit, the teachers trade sections and repeat their specialties. Another variation is the interdisciplinary team that uses a block of time encompassing two or three consecutive periods and divides the block of time among the disciplines and teachers as the occasion demands from day to day.

[3] Judson T. Shaplin, *Team Teaching* (New York: Harper and Row, Publishers, 1964), p. 15.

[4] *Ibid.*, pp. 17–18.

[5] For example: (1) Two or more teachers from the same teaching discipline. (2) Two or more teachers from a discipline all teaching at the same grade level. (3) Two or more teachers from different disciplines. (4) Two or more teachers from different disciplines, but all teaching at the same grade level. (5) Two or more teachers from different disciplines who work only with a narrow segment of the school population at one or more grade levels. (6) Teams with paraprofessional aides. (7) Teams that use the services of lay specialists in planning and teaching. (8) Teams with professional members all having the same rank and status. (9) Teams composed of a hierarchy of professional personnel. (10) Teams composed of a hierarchy of professional and nonprofessional members ranging from team leaders through teacher assistants to clerks.

[6] David W. Beggs III, "Fundamental Considerations for Team Teaching," in David W. Beggs, editor, *Team Teaching—Bold New Venture* (Indianapolis: Unified College Press, 1964), p. 42.

THE DIFFERENTIATED ROLE SPECIALIST TEAM. In the type of team teaching just described, all teachers carry equal responsibility and status, each teacher being a specialist in a portion of the content. The differentiated role specialist plan differs from the unit specialist plan in that in it the specialists are specialists in techniques rather than content. Among the team members are presenters or lecturers who teach large groups, instructors who teach small groups, and sometimes nonprofessional or paraprofessional aides who help with clerical, housekeeping, and other tasks that do not require full professional skill. Some teams make use of student or apprentice teachers who work at professional tasks under the supervision of fully certified teachers and so develop teaching skill much as a medical intern practices his profession in a hospital before he sets up on his own.

Under the differentiated role specialist approach lies the assumption that time and effort can be saved by varying scheduling and class size. Its sponsors argue that much of what pupils can learn in high school can be presented in large classes via large-group techniques such as the lecture and the demonstration. Other aspects, they say, must be learned in more intimate groups or through individual study. Discussion techniques, for instance, are excellent for securing certain educational objectives, but, as a rule, they are seldom effective in groups numbering more than fifteen or sixteen. Consequently, technical specialist team plans usually consist of teachers who present lessons to very large groups made up of several ordinary sections, and other instructors who follow up and drive home the lessons in small discussion groups. In addition, further opportunities for study in depth and for following up individual interest and creative urges are provided through independent study. Independent study in this context refers to such activities as project work, reading, drill and practice, writing, and the like.

Some advocates of team teaching recommend that the individual study portion of the plan be supplemented by learning laboratories in which boys and girls will have opportunities to work on programmed material as well as other types of individual and small group activities. As visualized, learning laboratories would consist of large open areas fitted out with carrels for individual study, and teaching devices such as teaching machines, individual projectors, listening booths, and conference areas. To ensure the effectiveness of individual study activities the learning laboratories should be situated near the teacher offices and close to a materials center in which pupils can obtain the materials needed for their work quickly and easily.

In the total school day the time ratio among the three types of activities might be

	Large-group instruction	40%
	Small-group instruction	40%
	Independent study	20% [7]

as exemplified by the following program.

Single-Discipline Team Schedule [8]

TIME	MONDAY	TUESDAY	WEDNESDAY	THURSDAY	FRIDAY
		History 10AB1* (SG)		History 10AB1* (SG)	History 10AB (IS)
8:00– 8:50	History 10AB (LG)	History 10AB2 (SG)	History 10AB (LG)	History 10AB2 (SG)	Project work in library, laboratory, music room,
		History 10AB3 (SG)		History 10AB3 (SG)	art studio, etc.

(60 students, 2 teachers, 1 instruction assistant)
* One History 10AB-SG can be supervised by an instruction assistant, student teacher or student leader. LG = large group, SG = small group, IS = independent study.

Supporters of this type of team teaching advocate it because they believe that it adds much needed flexibility to the curriculum and to instructional methodology. Because the plan calls for individual study and small-group work, they claim that it provides more opportunities for teachers to know individual pupils well than ordinary teaching schedules do. They also feel that this type of plan allows for teachers to do the type or work they can do best. Teachers, like pupils, are individuals with differing abilities, they say. Some of them are good at lecturing, but poor at small-group work; others are good at guiding individual study or several group studies, but are not so effective lecturing to large groups.

Critics of this plan, on the other hand, claim that the large-group aspect of the class is liable to clamp the pupils more firmly into a lockstep. Because large-group instruction requires all the pupils to be at the same place at the same time, these critics see little chance for real provisions for individual differences. Such critics also complain that this sort of team places too much emphasis on teaching by lecture, a method they claim is seldom very effective. Probably this criticism contains much validity. Furthermore, if this type of teaching is desirable, it would seem that the use of television lectures or the use of teaching machines would be more

[7] *This We Believe,* The Decatur-Lakeview Plan, Lakeview Junior-Senior High School, Decatur, Illinois, not dated.

[8] Ira J. Singer, "What Team Teaching Really Is" in David W. Beggs III, *op. cit.,* p. 17.

economical and effective than the large-group lecture. This objection would not, however, preclude the use of large-group instruction for purposes of testing, viewing motion pictures, and other similar activities.

A serious fault of many teaching teams in practice is that they include only the large-group portion of the specialist approach. The major purpose for using large-group lessons is to make time for teachers to guide small-group discussion and individual study. When the team uses only the large-group approach, there is little chance that the overall effectiveness of the teaching will be improved although it may be that the teachers will gain more time for class preparation.

AD HOC TEAMS. The third type of organization Beggs mentions is the informal *ad hoc* type of team. Teams of this sort combine their resources and talents as the need appears. As a rule, teachers of such teams do plan together in a common preparation period. Often they are multidiscipline teams, for example, all the seventh-grade teachers, or teachers of different subjects who have the same pupils. This type of team has much to recommend it, but because of their informality and lack of status and recognition, teams so organized are liable to be temporary and haphazard.

❀

Consider the arguments for and against team teaching. Do you favor it or not? What type of team would you prefer to work on? What strengths do you have to offer to a teaching team?

❀

Lectures and Teacher Talks

The Formal Lecture

The history of the lecture method of teaching is a long and honorable one. Largely because of a reaction against its long years of misuse and overuse, it has been fashionable in some circles to denigrate the lecture, but the lecture has been used with success in the past, is being used with success at the present, and no doubt will be used with success in the future. As a matter of fact, most teachers find lectures almost indispensable for certain purposes. Lectures can be used for introducing activities, for motivating pupils, for summing up at the end of units, and for explaining difficult points. They are particularly useful for bridging gaps between topics to be studied in depth, and for presenting information that would otherwise be unavailable to the pupils. Moreover, as long as the lecture is the predominant form of teaching in our colleges, college-bound boys and girls should have considerable experience with lectures in the last stages of their high-school careers. It goes without saying that this experience with lectures should be accompanied by instruction in how to profit from lectures, most particularly in the art of taking notes.

Just the same, in spite of its many values, the formal lecture is ordinarily a rather ineffective method of teaching secondary-school pupils. Because learning from lectures is relatively passive learning, it may be relatively sterile learning. Except in unusual cases very little of the lecture sticks in the pupils' minds. Pupils seem to learn better when they put themselves into the learning. Unless the pupils do something with the information presented in a lecture, their learning and retention is liable to be rather thin.

The lecture technique sometimes causes discipline problems. Adolescent attention spans for the typical lecture are notoriously short. This statement does not mean that secondary-school boys and girls cannot pay careful attention to a good lecture for a long time. Rather, it means that it takes a good lecturer to hold any audience's interested attention for an hour. In the secondary school a stimulating lecturer, skillfull enough to hold the pupils' attention, and thus able to make them learn, is indeed a rare bird. New teachers who place great faith in their continuous use of the lecture day after day are foolhardy. Remember: Adolescents have a low tolerance to boredom.

PREPARING THE LECTURE. Most secondary-school lectures should be short. A twenty-minute lecture is quite often more than a junior-high-school class can stand. Short talks of about ten minutes' duration are likely to be more acceptable. Senior-high-school classes may be able to profit from lectures that are much longer. The ability of a group to benefit from a lengthy lecture varies, of course, with the maturity of the pupils and the excellence of the lecture.

One reason that many secondary-school lectures are not more stimulating is that good lectures require more preparation than most teachers have time to give them. Very seldom can a teacher lecture effectively on the spur of the moment. If a teacher wants to have a high degree of effectiveness in his lectures, he must plan them meticulously. Not only must he plan what he wishes to say, but he should also plan how he intends to say it. If possible, it might even be wise to practice the lecture before the bedroom mirror.

❊

Why is the lecture considered to be a poor technique for use in secondary schools?

You have been assigned a ninth-grade general science class. This class consists largely of slow learners. It has a reputation of being hard to handle. The youngsters are restless and not much interested. How much would you plan to lecture to such a group? What might you be able to do to hold the attention of such a group?

❂

MAKING THE LECTURE CLEAR. If they are to be effective, lectures must be both clear and persuasive. With this goal in mind, the teacher planning a classroom lecture must guard against attempting too much. Because of its one-way format it is very easy for the teacher who lectures to present ideas quickly and then move on to new ones before the pupils have caught the first ones. Neither secondary-school pupils nor adults are likely to learn much from ideas skimmed over lightly. The capable lecturer limits his talk to a few salient points which he develops and drives home. To be sure that he achieves his purpose, he states clearly what each point is and supports it with illustrations, examples, and other details which, in themselves, may not be important, but which do tend to make the point stand out. And then, after all this has been done, he comes back to his point again, restating it clearly, in order to drive it home and clinch it as firmly as possible in a final summation. As a rule, this type of procedure will carry a lecturer's ideas across to his audience, whereas attempting to cover many points may only confuse his listeners.

Adding illustrations, audio-visual aids, and demonstrations to lectures may help to clarify and point up the desired concepts. Frequently, audio-visual devices can give meaning to what would otherwise remain just a mass of words. Even when the lecture is clear and interesting without them, the use of visual aids can reinforce the learning by adding the impact of another sense. Audio-visual aids are also useful for commanding and holding the attention of listeners whose minds have begun to wander. Teacher lecturers who depend solely on their voices are being unfair to themselves and their pupils.

Clarity also depends on the use of language. Beginning teachers and student teachers are inclined to talk over the heads of their pupils. Concepts and words commonplace to college seniors and recent graduates may be foreign to high-school pupils. Although the teacher should avoid talking down to his pupils, he should be careful to talk to them in language they understand.

The language used should be good English, of course. Some teachers attempt to reach the pupils' level by introducing slang and colloquial expressions into their talks. This is usually a poor policy. Slang and over-informality are more likely to cheapen a lecture than clarify it. Furthermore, the teacher, willy-nilly, is a model of English oral composition whenever he speaks. If his influence on the pupils is to be a good one, he must see to it that his language is the type that he wishes the pupils to imitate.

The use of illustrations and figures of speech often makes lectures clearer and livelier, but their injudicious use can at times defeat their purpose. Particularly treacherous in this respect is the metaphor, which can truly be a two-edged sword. With secondary-school pupils—particularly the younger and duller ones—a teacher should call things by their proper names and leave flights of poetic fancy to others. Certainly if one must use such figures of speech, one must be sure that the pupils understand to what the figures allude. Not to do so may spoil the entire lecture.

Informal Teacher Talks

Much, if not most, of the average teacher's group instruction is done through informal talks to groups or to the entire class. These talks differ from the formal lecture in that they are usually short, *ex tempore* discourses rising out of the needs of the moment. Often they stem from class discussion or pupils' questions. Because these talks are short, teachers do not need to prepare for them as in the formal lecture. Usually they are most effective when interspersed with questions and discussion both from and to the teacher in what is sometimes called the lecture-discussion.

Because this technique will probably be one of his mainstays, each prospective teacher should become proficient in its use. He should also be aware of its dangers and shortcomings.

All of the comments about clarity of language in the lecture are applicable to the short informal talk as well, of course. So too are comments about utilizing the audio-visual aids to make the instruction clearer and more effective. The greatest danger is that the teacher will talk too much. When teachers talk, all too often pupils stop thinking. Remember the Flanders and Amidon study cited in Chapter 1 that indicated that the pupils learned better when the teaching was indirect. Oftentimes teachers must explain, but *they should try to turn many of their teacher talks into indirect teaching by asking questions, posing problems, seeking comments, and entertaining questions.* Also, the teacher should beware of the danger of thinking that pupils have learned something just because he has told it to them. Whenever it is possible to do so, pupils may misunderstand, misinterpret, or miss altogether what the teacher tells them. Teachers who make a habit of following-up their explanations, and other short talks, with questions designed to check the pupils' understanding are well advised. Teachers who try to limit their talks to a minimum and substitute instead questions, discussions, Socratic techniques, and other tactics and strategies which call for the pupils to carry the load of the thinking, are even better advised.

Informal talks are used more often in secondary schools than formal lectures.

✽

For what purposes would you plan to use lectures in your secondary-school teaching? What kinds of lectures are there? How can they be used?

How does one plan a lecture or informal talk? Consider objectives, outline, illustrations, motivations, length, aids, clarity, interest.

How can one tell whether a lecture or talk has been successful?

✽

Large-Class Instruction

In recent years the practice of gathering together very large groups of seventy-five, one hundred, or more pupils for what is called large-group instruction, has become something of a fad. Sometimes these large groups are part of some sort of team teaching plan, but frequently they are not. They may be simply attempts to cut instructional cost.

That some types of learning can take place equally as well in large groups as in small one is a truism accepted by almost all teachers. Certain types of lectures, demonstrations, dramatizations, and other types of teaching in which instruction is a one-way process from the teacher to the pupil, can be just as effective with groups of a thousand as with groups of ten. As a matter of fact, the very size of a large group may cause a teacher to be more effective, or at least to try harder. Sometimes too, large groups can develop a spirit that is catching and which skilful teachers can utilize for motivational purposes.

As one might expect, large-group instruction has both merits and drawbacks. By bringing large numbers of pupils together to be instructed simultaneously, it frees time for the teachers—time that can be used for preparation, individual work, paper correction, and other professional chores. It also makes possible the elimination of much repetition. Many schools today try to take advantage of the talents of outside experts. By using large-group instruction, it is possible to bring the talents of an outside expert to all pupils without asking the guest to repeat himself to several audiences. Similarly, four or five classes can watch a moving picture all at once without tying up the equipment for four or five periods. Incidentally, showing moving pictures to large groups may make it feasible to schedule large blocks of time and procure feature films for use in literature or social studies courses.

The disadvantages of large-group instruction are very serious. Large-group instruction gives little opportunity for pupil-teacher interaction. Except in the most unusual cases, it tends to be merely a period of pouring information into passive, relatively inactive minds. As a result of the size of the group and the type of instruction, the teacher can rarely make allowance for differences in individuals. Whatever is to be done for pupils who have forged ahead or fallen behind, who do not quite understand, or who wish to ask questions must be done at some other time by some other means. All too frequently, large-group instruction tends to chain the pupils in a lockstep more rigid than any before in the history of education.

Also, discipline and control often become a problem. Large groups listening to a full period of dull lecture or poorly planned demonstration sometimes become noisy and unruly. In some situations the extra time teachers were to have as a result of the large-group instruction can turn into periods of policing large classes someone else is supposed to be teaching. Another problem in large-group instruction is psychological noise—the fact that ideas seem to be harder to put across to large groups than to small ones. This difficulty probably results from minds that wander and woolgather during the lectures and large-group demonstrations.

From these advantages and disadvantages one can see that the large-group instruction implies the need for certain special techniques and technology. The problem of psychological noise makes it necessary for much pointing up, repeating and reemphasizing. This problem, plus the problems of control and making contact with so many individuals at once, makes it necessary for teachers to pay particular attention to the use of interest getting and interest holding devices. To help the pupils identify and react as *students,* teachers may use rhetorical questions,

Lectures should be bolstered by the use of diagrams, pictures, blackboard work and other aids, particularly in large-group or television classes.

problems, and other techniques that will tend to arouse, or at least counterfeit, teacher-pupil interaction. Audio-visual devices of many sorts are especially helpful in large-group instruction. Overhead projectors, slides, demonstrations, drama, and similar devices and techniques aid the teacher by giving him another sense by which to make his impact.

Under no circumstances should the large-class instruction be merely a formal lecture or speech, except in the case of assembly speakers or guest lecturers—and even then the unadorned lecture should be avoided if possible. Large-group lecture classes should be supported by other techniques in order to drive the objectives home. As a matter of fact, there can be little justification for straight lecture in large-group classes anyway. If a class is going to be only straight lecture, it would be more economical and more effective to tape or film the lecture and present it to a much wider audience, thus saving the cost of several lecturers. With our new techniques we could then individualize the large class by playing the lecture to individual pupils at the time they need it or are most ready for it.

Instructional Television

Instructional television is a form of large-group instruction. In the following paragraphs we shall discuss briefly the programming of television for classroom use. A more detailed discussion of television teaching and its use in the classroom appears in Chapter 14.

Educational television should deal primarily with the things it can do best. Instead of being just another lecture or lecture with illustrations,

216

the television program should aim to bring into the classroom experiences impossible otherwise, for the television program has capabilities the classroom cannot match. It can take pupils to distant places where they could not otherwise go, show them things and people they could not otherwise see, and bring to them extraordinary events (for example, the President's inauguration) that would otherwise be out of the question. It can take pupils on field trips and present demonstrations in which pupils can really see the inner workings of things. Television programming should take advantage of these capabilities. It should concentrate on opening new vistas and challenges to the pupils and enriching and deepening their concepts and attitudes. Television programming can be especially useful for culminating and tying together the various threads of a unit or course.

Obviously the programmer of educational or instructional television should utilize all the resources available to the medium. Although there is little point in using visual aids simply for the sake of using them, television programming should take full advantage of the television's ability to use film clips, charts, graphs, resource persons, demonstrations, and other materials and techniques to drive home course objectives. Educational objectives, however, should not be sacrificed for technical excellence or dramatic impact. The programs should be accurate and free from anachronisms, false emphasis, prejudice, hasty generalizations, one-sided presentations, propaganda, and other sources of error. Further, the programming should be truly educational, always aimed at furthering school objectives. The content and methodology of the program should be consistent with the educational purpose. For these reasons the program director should be an expert on educational methodology and curriculum. In planning programs he should rely heavily on the opinions and suggestions of the classroom teachers who use the programs.

In order for the programs to be most effective, the television studio should aid the classroom teachers by giving them the opportunity to preview their programs and by providing them with resource materials, suggestions for introducing and following up the programs, and study aids for pupils. From time to time, classroom teachers should have an opportunity to meet with the television programmers to evaluate the programs coming into the schools and to discuss how best to use them.

Using Questions

Uses of Questions

Throughout the course of educational history the question has been one of the most common, if not the most common, of teaching techniques. It continues to be so in spite of modern changes in educational theory, for it is a fine tool both for checking memory and understanding, and getting at higher learning. It has many uses in the modern classroom.

Among these uses we find the following mentioned in textbooks on teaching.

1. To find out something one did not know.
2. To find out whether someone knows something.
3. To develop the ability to think.
4. To motivate pupil learning.
5. To provide drill or practice.
6. To help pupils organize materials.
7. To help pupils interpret materials.
8. To emphasize important points.
9. To show relationships, such as cause and effect.
10. To discover pupil interests.
11. To develop appreciation.
12. To provide review.
13. To give practice in expression.
14. To reveal mental processes.
15. To show agreement or disagreement.
16. To establish rapport with pupils.
17. To diagnose.
18. To evaluate.
19. To obtain the attention of wandering minds.

✿

Can you think of a question to illustrate each one of the purposes mentioned above? After you have formed the questions, test them against the criteria in the following section. How well did you do?

Attend a class in a school or college classroom. Observe the teacher's use of questions. What techniques were used? Were they successful? Why, or why not?

✿

The Good Question

Most of this section refers specifically to oral questions. However, in most cases it can apply just as well to written questions as to oral ones. That is true of the following criteria for the characteristics of the good question. Although these criteria are few in number, if every teacher question lived up to them, teaching, even by master teachers, would improve marvelously.

First of all, *a successful question asks something definite in simple, clear, straightforward English that the pupil can understand.* Therefore one must be careful to avoid ambiguity, confusing constructions, double questions, parenthetical remarks, and other verbiage that might cause the pupil to lose the point of the question.

Vague generalities like, "How about the French?" are usually not very valuable in promoting any of the learning which the lesson is trying to promulgate. In other words, *the good question gets at a definite point consistent with a goal of the lesson.*

A main purpose of questioning is to stimulate learning. A good question challenges the pupil to exert his intellect. To do so the question must make him think. Questions that can be answered by merely repeating some fact from a book can never be as stimulating as thought questions. In fact, as often as not, they are not stimulating at all. *A good question, then, is challenging and thought-provoking.*

A good question is consistent with the aims of the lesson, as well as being consistent with the abilities and interests of the pupils. There is no great point in embarrassing or frustrating a youngster by asking him questions he cannot answer. Neither is there much point in allowing bright youths to slide along on easy questions without stretching their intellects. Moreover, the teacher can harness the interests of various pupils by asking them questions that appeal to their special interests. For instance, the 4-H farm boy who raises stock could contribute greatly to a social studies unit on the country's resources or a general science unit on conservation. He might even be able to make a considerable contribution concerning "the lowing herd [which] winds slowly o'er the lea." In short, *the good question is adapted to the age, abilities. and interests of the pupils to whom it is addressed.*

✿

It has been said that a question should be couched in language considerably easier than the pupils' reading level. Do you agree?

Of what value is a question answerable in one word?

Suppose that one of your purposes is to stimulate the pupils' thinking. How can this be done by questioning? Just how would you word the question? Prepare some examples and try them out.

✿

A Prerequisite to Good Questioning

From the foregoing account it seems evident that questioning requires skill and preparation. Good questioners usually carefully brief themselves on the subject under discussion and prepare key questions in advance. Although some teachers seem to be able to ask well-worded questions at the spur of the moment, to do so is quite difficult. The teacher who prepares in advance will usually be more successful.

Techniques of Good Questioning

The notion of the teacher as a grand inquisitor attempting to catch the recalcitrant pupil should be foreign to the modern classroom. Questioning should be thought of as a way to get at the problems the class is trying to solve—not as an attempt to see how much the pupil knows. An inquisition is not necessary.

Many of the teacher's questions should be quite informal as he tries to help individuals and groups with their various assignments. Questions frequently may be addressed to the entire class, of course, but more often they should be addressed to an individual pupil or a small group. As a matter of fact, in the really live class, the pupils will ask most of the questions.

A teacher should ask his questions in a pleasant, friendly, easy, conversational manner. If he can maintain an atmosphere of easy informality without sacrificing decorum, so much the better. He should always ask his questions in a fashion that indicates that he expects a reasonable answer. If the pupil does not know the answer, or cannot contribute at the moment, there is no point in teasing him about it. Exhortations to think will not bring back a forgotten lesson.

When using questions in a whole-class situation, the teacher usually should first ask the question, wait for the class to think about it, and then ask someone for an answer. In this way everyone has a chance to consider the question before anyone tries to answer it. There is little use in asking thought questions if you don't give the pupils time to think about them.

This technique has another merit in its favor. When the teacher asks the question first, no one knows who is going to be asked. This helps to keep the pupils alert. When the teacher calls on a pupil before asking the question, other members of the class may heave a sigh of relief and not bother to listen to the question.

As usual, there are exceptions to the rule. When one calls on an inattentive pupil, it is probably better to give his name first so that he will hear the question. Otherwise you may have to repeat it and perhaps create an embarrassing situation. By calling his name first, one may recapture his wandering attention and thereby avoid a discipline problem. Similarly, it is sometimes best to name a slow or shy pupil first so that he will know what is coming and prepare himself.

Another technique that may help keep a class attentive is to refrain from repeating questions. If for some legitimate reason the pupil did not understand or hear, then of course to repeat the question is only fair. But if he did not hear because of inattention, the teacher should pass on to someone else. This technique also applies to repeating answers. Repeating answers merely wastes time and encourages inattention.

Distributing the questions about the class fairly equally also helps keep the pupils alert. However, one should not resort to any mechanical system for doing this. Youngsters soon catch on to these devices. The old system, for instance, of going around the class in alphabetical order, row by row, is sure death to pupil attention.

The best way to direct pupil attention to one's questions is to ask really interesting, thought-provoking questions. Leading questions, questions that give away answers, one-word-answer questions, and the like have the seeds of boredom in them. They should be avoided like poison, for they have killed many a potentially good class.

HANDLING PUPIL ANSWERS.   In order to create a permissive atmosphere, i.e., an atmosphere of friendly cooperation, in which the pupils feel free to do their best, even if their best is none too good, the teacher should accept every sincere response appreciatively. Immature thinking and lack of knowledge are not serious faults. If pupils were mature and knew all the answers, we would not need schools. The fault is not to try. Pupils should be allowed to make mistakes without fear of embarrassment, but they should not be encouraged to do careless work. When a pupil does not answer to the best of his ability, the teacher can follow up with other questions which will shake him out of his complacency. Usually he will get the point.

In like manner, teachers should insist that the pupils make themselves understood. An answer that is not clear is not a good answer. If the pupil fails to make a point the teacher can ask him to elaborate. Each answer should be a complete thought unit—although not necessarily a sentence. If the teacher throws the incomplete thoughts back at the pupils, the latter will probably soon learn to answer more clearly.

Although one should listen to all sincere answers, only the good ones should be approved. When his answer is not satisfactory, the pupil should be told why it is incorrect and how he might improve it. Any portion of an answer that is correct should be recognized, of course, but any part of an answer that is incorrect should be criticized. The teacher can do this by pointing out the error himself, or by throwing the question open for discussion by the other pupils.

If the question is answered well, the teacher should express approval. This does not mean that he should be effusive about it. For some questions a friendly "That's right" is quite enough. Other questions, designed to bring out major points, need to be given more emphasis. This can be done by using such questions as a basis for further discussion.

Occasionally, a question brings forth no response other than blank stares from the entire class. In such cases the chances are that the teacher has skipped some steps. Often he can get the desired response by breaking the question down into component parts or by backtracking a bit and asking questions that will lead up to and provide background for the baffling original question. At other times the whole difficulty may be in the wording of the question. When such is the case, restating the question may clear up the problem.

✻

What are the faults of the questioning techniques of teachers you have observed? How can you avoid these faults?

Prepare a list of principles to observe in questioning. Check yourself by these principles in a classroom situation. How well do you do?

✻

HANDLING PUPIL QUESTIONS. Pupil questions should be encouraged. If the pupils leave your class with inquiring minds, you will have accomplished much. But how does one encourage pupil questions? By welcoming them. If the teacher encourages a free, permissive atmosphere in which youngsters know that they will be respected, he can expect pupil questions to increase. Certainly they will if the material studied is interesting and important to them. If the teacher will only ask himself what the youngsters may want to know before he plans the lesson, he can increase the chances of his material's being interesting and important.

Not all pupil questions are as important as others. Some questions are so important that if the class is interested it would be wise to depart from the agenda and consider the question in detail, even if it is not exactly pertinent. Others will be of little importance and can be answered very briefly. Some questions are so trivial that they have no place in the class at all. If the pupil asking the trivial or irrelevant question is sincere, he deserves to be answered, but briefly. The teacher should explain that class time is scarce, that class goals are important, and that there is little time for the trivial. In case the pupil is not satisfied by a brief answer in class, the teacher should arrange to go into the matter more deeply in private sometime later when the discussion would not interrupt the progress of the class. Sometimes the questions may be "smart alecky." Questions of this sort are best turned back on the questioner. If a teacher finds that many trivial or "smart" questions are turning up in his class, he had better check to see if this may be due to his teaching, his material, or both.

At times it is best to turn a question over to some other member of the class or to the class as a whole for discussion. In fact, there seems to be no reason why pupils should not ask each other questions directly as long as they are pertinent to the discussion and asked courteously.

Occasionally, the teacher will be asked questions he cannot answer. In that case he should promptly admit his inability. Perhaps another member of the class does know. If not, the teacher can either find out himself or ask someone to find out for him. If the latter choice is made, the teacher should look up the answer too. Thus he can check to be sure that the pupil reports back correctly.

The Socratic Method

In the fifth century B.C. Socrates, the great Athenian teacher, used the art of questioning so successfully that to this day we still speak of the Socratic method. Socrates' strategy was to ask his pupils a series of leading questions that gradually snarled them up to the point where they had to look carefully at their own ideas and to think rigorously for themselves. In several ways his technique foreshadowed the most progressive teaching of the most ardent progressivists. Socratic discussions were informal dialogues taking place in a natural, easy, pleasant environment. The motivation of the students was natural and spontaneous although sometimes Socrates had to go to considerable lengths to ignite his students' intrinsic interest. In his dialogues Socrates tried to aid students develop ideas. He did not impose his own notions on the students. Rather he encouraged the student to develop his own conclusions and to draw his own inferences. Of course, Socrates usually had preconceived notions about what the student's final learning should be and carefully aimed his questions so that the student would arrive at the conclusions desired. Still his questions were open-ended. The students were free to go wherever the facts led them.

Many modern teachers have tried to adapt the Socratic method to the secondary school. In some cases it has proved to be quite successful. However, it must be remembered that as Socrates used the method it required a one-to-one relationship between the student and the teacher. Some teachers have adapted it for ordinary class use by asking questions first of one pupil and then of another, moving about the class slowly. This technique may work well, but it is difficult because the essence of the Socratic technique is to build question on question in a logical fashion so that each question leads the student a step further toward the understanding sought. When the teacher spreads the questions around the classroom, he may find it difficult to build up the sequence desired and to keep all the pupils with the argument. Sometimes teachers in ordinary-sized classes use the Socratic method by selecting one pupil and directing all the questions at him—at least for several minutes—while the other pupils look on. This is the way Socrates did it. When the topic is interesting enough this technique can be quite successful and even exciting, but in the long run the Socratic technique works best in small-group sessions, seminars, and tutorial sessions with individual pupils.

Problem Solving

Perhaps problem solving should not be called a teaching technique. Nevertheless, teaching by means of problem solving is both useful and popular. It has been used successfully both as an individual and as a group activity. The solving of problems through group activity recently has been used extensively in teaching and in the world of business and research.

The Method of Problem Solving

Whether a problem is solved by an individual or a group, the general technique is about the same. Perhaps this explains in part the popularity of problem solving. It seems to be a natural way to learn.

In a sense, problem solving is a sophisticated form of trial-and-error learning. It provides people a chance to learn from their successes and failures. Furthermore, it leads to real understanding in a way that memorization and drill seldom can, because it provides for the pupils' becoming really involved in their learning. A brief review of the steps will show how actively the pupil participates in learning through problem solving. The steps are

1. The learner becomes aware of the problem.
2. He defines and delimits the problem.
3. He gathers evidence that may help him solve the problem.
4. He forms a hypothesis of what the solution to the problem is.
5. He tests the hypothesis.
6. He successfully solves the problem or he repeats steps 3, 4, and 5, or 4 and 5, until the problem is solved, or he gives up.[9]

SELECTING THE PROBLEM. Although problem solving is a natural way to learn, pupils, as a general rule, do not naturally become expert in the techniques of problem solving. This is particularly true when the class attempts to solve problems by group techniques.

In the first place, pupils need help in finding suitable problems. Sometimes the teacher may find it necessary to suggest problems or to suggest areas in which pupils may seek problems. When suggesting a problem to a group, the teacher might propose the problem directly, or he might set the stage in such a way that the problem will suggest itself to the pupils.

[9] Based on the analysis of the thought process by John Dewey.

For instance, in a social studies class the teacher introduced a problem by telling of the number of people in the country who do not vote. She cited figures showing the lightness of the voting in the local municipal election. This led to a discussion of why citizens do not exercise their franchise. From this discussion the pupils developed two problems: the first, what causes the apathy of our citizens? and the second, what can be done to get people to vote at the city elections? In another class the teacher launched a group problem by asking the following question: How does a plant get its food? After a short discussion the group set out to find the answer to the problem.

No matter what the source of their problem, the pupils will probably need the teacher's guidance in the selection of a suitable one, for, left alone, even the most experienced adolescent, or group of adolescents, may flounder. Sometimes they can find no problem at all; sometimes they select problems not suitable to the course; and sometimes they select problems whose solution requires materials and equipment beyond the school's resources; sometimes they select problems too big and unyielding, blithely setting out to solve in a weekend problems their elders have struggled with for centuries. In view of these considerations, the teacher, or the teacher and pupils cooperatively, should test the problems to be selected against such criteria as: Is this problem pertinent? Is the necessary material available? Can it be completed in the time allotted?

❋

Prepare a complete list of questions you feel should be considered in testing whether a problem should be selected or not.

Prepare a list of eight or ten problems that boys and girls might attempt in the study of a topic in a course in your field of major interest. Where might you advise boys and girls to search for suitable problems for such a topic?

"To be worthwhile, problems should be real and have real solutions." Explain. Do you agree? How are such problems created and carried through to a conclusion?

Why is it often claimed that all secondary-school learning should be of the problem-solving variety?

❋

DEFINING THE PROBLEM.   Once the problem has been selected, the teacher should help the pupils clarify and define the problem. This he can do by means of questions and suggestions. The important thing here is to get the problem sharply defined so that the pupil knows exactly what he wishes to find. Beginning teachers sometimes neglect this step. When they do, pupils find it difficult to know exactly what they are expected to do. This is, of course, a handicap in solving any problem.

Let us suppose that the problem selected has been: Why does an airplane fly? The problem here is quickly and easily defined, for it is obvious to all that we are to find what it is that keeps an airplane up in the air. Yet, even in such an easily defined problem, the teacher may have to make it clear to some pupils that this problem does not refer to helicopters or to rockets.

SEARCHING FOR CLUES.   Once the pupil has defined his problem, he should start to look for clues for its solution. This involves amassing data upon which to base a hypothesis. Here the teacher can be of great help. He can point out areas in which to look for clues. He can provide the necessary materials, or see to it that they are available. He can provide references. He can acquaint the pupils with the tools by which one can gather data.

Even in the solving of group problems, the gathering of evidence may best be done by individuals or small groups. After a period of searching for information, the group can meet to pool the data gained individually and to attempt to find a solution to the problem.

For instance, if the problem should be to prepare a menu suitable for a week's camping trip for a group of teen-agers, the pupils might gather the information necessary for solving this problem individually. Once they had in their possession information concerning what the ingredients of a healthful, well-balanced diet are, what foods contain these ingredients, and any other pertinent data, they might attempt to build suitable menus individually. The final menu could be made during a class discussion using the individual suggestions. Of course, before considering the problem to be solved, the pupils should test it to be sure it meets the criteria for a healthful, well-balanced camp menu.

SOLVING THE PROBLEM.   Preparing the menu in the foregoing example was really an example of setting up and testing a hypothesis. Each individual menu prepared was a hypothetical solution to the problem. These solutions were tested by the pupils until they found one that met the requirements of a healthful, well-balanced diet. When they found such a menu, the problem was solved.

At this stage of solving a problem, boys and girls often need assistance. Many pupils find it difficult to think of tentative solutions. Although the teacher should be careful not to solve the problem for them, he can help put them on the track by pointing out relationships, by asking pointed questions, and by other techniques. Similarly, the teacher can help the pupils test their proposed solutions. Unless pupils establish appropriate criteria by which to judge the worth of a solution, they may think they have a problem solved when they really have not. Consequently, the teacher may need to help the pupil set up criteria that will tell him whether he has actually solved a problem or not, and help him

By learning through his own discovery, the boy will develop clearer understanding than he would through only vicarious experiences.

check his solution against the criteria. Without this aid pupils often
arrive at very poor solutions to their problems.

❋

Select a problem that a pupil might attempt in one of your classes.
Where might he look for clues? What materials should be available
to the pupil? What tools of research might be needed to gather the
necessary data? What skills would the pupil need? How could you
prepare yourself to help a pupil gather the data for this problem?

❋

The Discovery Approach

It should be evident by this time that the basic principle behind the
problem method, the Socratic method, and provocative questioning techniques is to help pupils discover and create their own knowledge and
ideas. The premise underlying all of these techniques is that the pupil
must seek out his own learning rather than just being a receiver of
knowledge. This notion, which has been part of educational theory
for many years, has now become substantiated firmly enough for teachers
to accept it as basic, sound theory. Nevertheless, this theory does not
preclude the teacher from presenting information to pupils. For pupils
to rediscover and recreate all knowledge would be most inefficient. The
principal point in discovery teaching is rather to provide as many
instances as possible for pupils to draw inferences from data by logical
thinking, inductive or deductive, as the case may be. Thus if a child

227

watches a billiard ball bouncing off the cushion at various angles, he may conclude that the "angle of incidence equals the angle of refraction" even though he does not use those words. On the other hand, if he understands the principle, he may be able to apply it to specific practical situations. In either case he utilizes the type of thinking that Dewey had in mind when he stressed problem solving.

Summary

The skilful teacher has many techniques and methods at his command, and so is able to vary his approach according to the instructional problem to be solved. Recently, innovators have utilized the principle of varying the approach according to the situation into various team teaching plans which they hope will allow teachers to teach what they know best by the techniques which they can handle best.

There are many different kinds of teaching teams. In general they can all be placed into three categories. (1) Unit Specialist Teams in which teacher roles are assigned according to the subject matter they teach. (2) Differentiated Role Specialist Teams in which the teachers' roles are assigned according to the type of teaching they do. (3) *Ad Hoc* Teams which combine their resources according to the exigencies of the situation. These teams are often multidisciplinary.

Akin to the teaching team movement is the movement for large-group instruction. This may or may not be part of a team teaching method or of television teaching. At its best large-group instruction can yield great savings of time and effort. Badly used it can result in superficial lockstep learning.

What is true of large-group teaching is also true of television teaching. Instructional television should be treated as one more arrow for one's bow. Its purpose is to help classroom instruction—not to supplant it or hinder it. Well done it can be a marvelous arrangement, but unless it is handled as an integral part of a total program centered around the classroom it can easily become nothing more than a device for spreading poor instruction over great distances.

Among the most important techniques are the lecture, talks, and questioning. Although their use has been severely criticized, each of them has a place in today's schools. Like any other speech, lectures are most successful when they are short and lively. Rather than being just a means of checking whether pupils have learned their lessons, questions are more suitably used as a means of stimulating learning through thinking and problem solving.

Perhaps the most renowned use of questioning is the Socratic method, which is characterized by the logical development of concepts through open-ended, thought-provoking, leading questions. It is chiefly useful in teaching small groups and individuals rather than large classes. Sometimes it is useful in problem solving. In general, the problem-solving method used in schools follows the steps outlined by Dewey as the act of a complete thought. These steps include selecting and defining a problem, gathering data, making hypotheses, and testing conclusions. Pupils need help in carrying out each of these steps. It should be noted that this technique is not the only way of solving problems nor is it always necessary for one to follow the steps in order. The main objective is to seek and discover knowledge for oneself.

FOR FURTHER STUDY

BEGGS, DAVID W. III, *Team Teaching: Bold New Venture* (Indianapolis: Unified College Press, Inc., 1964).

BILLETT, ROY O., *Teaching in Junior and Senior High School* (Dubuque, Iowa: William C. Brown Company, Publishers, 1963), Chs. 7–8.

BRUNER, JEROME, *The Process of Education* (Cambridge, Mass.: Harvard University Press, 1960).

BURTON, WILLIAM H., *The Guidance of Learning Activities,* Third Edition (New York: Appleton-Century-Crofts, Inc., 1962), Ch. 18.

CALLAHAN, STERLING G., *Successful Teaching in Secondary Schools* (Chicago: Scott, Foresman and Company, 1966), Chs. 9, 19.

HOCK, LOUISE, and THOMAS J. HILL, *The General Education Class in the Secondary School* (New York: Holt, Rinehart and Winston, Inc., 1960), Ch. 5.

INLOW, GAIL M., *Maturity in High School Teaching* (Englewood Cliffs, N.J.: Prentice-Hall, Inc., 1963), Chs. 6–8.

KILPATRICK, WILLIAM H., *Foundations of Method* (New York: The Macmillan Company, 1925), Ch. 15.

PLATO, *Meno* (various editions).

RIVLIN, HARRY N., *Teaching Adolescents in Secondary Schools,* Second Edition (New York: Appleton-Century-Crofts, Inc., 1961), Ch. 7.

SHAPLIN, JUDSON T., and HENRY F. OLDS, JR., *Team Teaching* (New York: Harper and Row Publishers, 1964).

TRUMP, J. LLOYD, *Images of the Future* (Washington, D.C.: National Education Association, 1959).

TRUMP, J. LLOYD, and DORSEY BAYNHAM, *Focus on Change: Guide to Better Schools* (Chicago: Rand McNally and Company, 1961).

WELLINGTON, C. BURLEIGH, and JEAN WELLINGTON, *Teaching for Critical Thinking* (New York: McGraw-Hill Book Company, 1960).

ZAPF, ROSALIND M., *Democratic Processes in the Secondary Classroom* (Englewood Cliffs, N.J.: Prentice-Hall, Inc., 1959), Chs. 5–6.

CHAPTER 10

Group Process Techniques

*I*N THE parlance of teachers a group is a number of people working together toward the same goal. A group may consist of an entire class or a small part of a class. Its size does not matter particularly as long as the members work together. In this chapter we shall attempt to discuss some activities whose success depends largely on cooperative group action.

Discussion Techniques

Characteristics of a Good Discussion

A discussion is not just a "bull session." Rather, it is purposeful conversation proceeding toward some goal with a minimum of rambling and bickering. Unlike the "bull session," the discussion is not a pooling of ignorance or unsubstantiated opinion. For a discussion to be successful, the participants need sufficient background to know what they are talking about and to base their arguments on fact. Moreover, the topic must be discussable. The equation $a^2 + b^2 = c^2$ is a fact and so is not a subject for discussion, although perhaps one might discuss its implications.

A discussion is a conversation, not a monologue, or a series of questions. In a really effective discussion, everyone should participate, although it is not always necessary for each person to talk. Sometimes he who only sits and listens participates. In general, however, one can assume that in a discussion the more people who participate actively the better. A discussion is not a place for one person to treat his ego by dominating the conversation, nor is it a place for one person to sell his own point of view. Discussion is not another name for lecture or recitation.

A really successful discussion is not only purposeful; it also achieves its purpose. If it is at all possible, the discussion should lead to some sort of conclusion. Certainly, even if no conclusion is reached, it should always culminate in some sort of summing up. Sometimes the summary may have to include a minority report.

✿

What is a discussion? How does it differ from a recitation?

What values do discussions have? For what purposes are they best suited? What sorts of things can best be learned through discussion? What makes a good discussion?

What can be done about discussions that seem to get nowhere?

✿

Leader's Role in Discussion

If a discussion is to rise above the level of a "bull session," the leader must ordinarily provide active, purposeful leadership. He must get the discussion started and see to it that everyone understands the topic and purpose of the discussion. He must also keep the discussion moving by encouraging all to take part, and by tactfully bottling up any monologuists in the group. He attempts to draw pupils out by skillful questioning. By clearing up errors of fact or judgment and by recalling the group to the problem at hand, he tries to keep the discussion from wandering off into unproductive byways. From time to time he summarizes to be sure that all participants are up to date and helps the group evaluate its progress. Sometimes he may have to suggest next steps. Finally, when all is said and done, he tries to tie together all the ideas, conclusions, and generalizations in the summary.

In spite of his important role, the leader should not dominate the discussion. In the best discussions the leader limits himself to a minor role, for a discussion is an opportunity for participants to share ideas. At the same time, he must not turn the discussion over to the group and let it do as it pleases. *Laissez-faire* leadership seldom leads to profitable discussions. Rather the leader should seek to create a permissive atmosphere in which participants feel free to speak and think freely without fear of embarrassment, but in which all the energies of the group are kept pointed toward the goal.

STARTING THE DISCUSSION. Like any other activity, a discussion requires planning and preparation. Not only must the teacher be well briefed on the topic to be discussed, but he needs a plan for the conducting of the discussion. In the plan, he should include provisions for getting the discussion started and questions for possible use. He should also be prepared with possible conclusions.

Starting a discussion may be something of a strain. It may take a little persuasion, or some special introductory activity. Before starting, the teacher should attempt to arrange the group in a homey, informal fashion. As a general rule, the more pleasant the atmosphere the better chance the discussion has of being successful. If possible, the pupils should be seated so that they can see each other. In actual practice a circle seems to be the best seating arrangement for a discussion, although any other arrangement that brings the participants face to face will do.

If the discussion is to be successful, the pupils must understand what it is they are to discuss and the procedure they will use in discussing it. Sometimes the introductory portion of the discussion needs to be devoted to clarifying the issues. Presenting the topic to be discussed as a problem sometimes makes the clarifying and launching of the discussion easier.

To start a discussion without some activity to develop interest among the participants is quite difficult. People need an opportunity to think and react before they can discuss anything sensibly. Consequently, it is sometimes advantageous to have a discussion develop out of some other activity. "Buzz sessions"—groups of four to six people who discuss the question for four to six minutes—sometimes help to get the discussion under way. Another common device is to start the discussion with a short introductory talk, or for someone to throw some challenging questions (prepared in advance) at the group. A test, quiz, or pretest can sometimes be used to stimulate a brisk discussion.

✿

What can the leader do to start a discussion when the group seems reluctant to participate? Can you suggest at least five approaches which may help the discussion get started?

How would you arrange the physical setting to encourage discussion? Suppose you wished to use the board in connection with the discussion. Would that change your decision?

What can you do with pupils who monopolize the discussion?

✿

GUIDING THE DISCUSSION. Once the discussion is started, the leader must keep it moving briskly in the right direction. Skillful questioning and keeping an outline of the most important points on the chalkboard will help maintain the tempo and hold the group to the topic. So will being sure that all the pupils know and accept the problem under discussion. Should a group digress, the leader can redirect them by restating the question, although the group should be allowed to pursue a digression if it seems to have promise. Occasionally groups that have become confused and cannot agree can be helped by a minute of silent consideration of the problem.

From time to time, the leader should draw the threads together by summarizing, or by asking the recorder to summarize. Such a summary gives the group a chance to stop and look at its progress, to see how it stands, and perhaps to decide in which direction to proceed. To bring out these values, the leader may include any or all of the following.

1. A résumé of the major points made so far.
2. A review of the facts and evidence presented.
3. A synopsis of what has been accomplished and what remains to be finished.
4. A restatement of any conclusions that have been made.
5. An analysis of the course or conduct of the discussion up to this point.

Whatever the gist of the summary, it should be brief, well organized, and to the point. Too many or too long summaries may break up the thread of the discussion and so do more harm than good. Also harmful are summaries which do not represent the thinking of all the group. The final summary at the end of the discussion should pull together all the important ideas and conclusions. To be sure that all points of view are presented fairly, it is often advantageous to elicit the aid of other participants in developing the summary. To note these ideas and conclusions on the chalkboard for all to see will aid to emphasize their importance and to clarify their meaning.

A good summary is essential for the ending of a discussion, but it should not end the consideration of the topic. A suitable follow-up activity that drives home the importance of the things learned or leads into the next activity can increase the value of almost any discussion.

THE ROLE OF THE RECORDER. A recorder is especially helpful in most group discussions. He keeps a record of the important decisions and the trend of the discussion. From time to time, he sums up the status of the discussion upon the request of the leader or upon his own initiative. If necessary, he attempts to resolve conflicts between members of the group by clarifying just what the facts are and just what has been said. He also calls the group to task when it wanders too far afield and sees to it that they tend to the problem at hand. A good recorder can be a tremendous help to the leader of any discussion group.

The recorder's main task, of course, is to keep the record of the discussion. Because this task is a difficult one for many boys and girls, the teacher should take special pains to help the pupil recorder. Usually in classroom discussions verbatim transcripts of the discussion are not desirable. Instead, the group needs to have an account of the major positions taken and the conclusions reached. One method that will help ensure good recording by beginners is to have the recorder keep his record on the chalkboard. This technique makes it possible for all the participants to see the notes and also permits the teacher to coach the recorder if the need arises. The overhead projector can be used similarly with the added advantage that the notes recorded on the transparency can be saved for future reference or for reprojecting. In classes in which the recorder writes notes out on paper at his desk, the teacher might be wise to keep notes himself in order to supplement any lapses of the pupil recorder.

THE ROLE OF THE PARTICIPANTS.   The ability to speak and listen well as participants in group discussions is a rather difficult skill that relatively few adults have truly mastered. When speaking, participants should try to be clear and precise. Although it is difficult to do so during a lively discussion, they should try to organize what they say before they say it so that they can make their points more easily. In this respect they should learn that their presentations will be more successful if they speak clearly and simply without affectation. A simply worded direct argument making one's points one by one in a simple linear order is usually much more likely to be understood than more complicated approaches. The simple technique of taping a pupil's statements and asking him to listen to himself and to try to arrange the ideas he thought he was presenting into a logical outline sometimes helps pupils understand the advantages of direct simple organization.

One danger of placing much emphasis on the way pupils present their opinions is that they may forget to listen to the discussion. Many persons, even participants in television debates and panels, are guilty of being so busy thinking about what they want to say that they never listen to the other participants or to the questions asked them. To train pupils to listen some teachers ask each pupil to repeat the germ of the last speaker's comments before he adds his own.

EVALUATING THE DISCUSSION.   The value of discussion will ordinarily increase as the pupils learn how to carry on discussions and gain experience. Good discussion techniques must be learned and practiced. If we take stock of ourselves and our discussion from time to time, progress in those skills can be expected. An effective way to evaluate a discussion is to tape-record it in its entirety and play it back to the group. If the group has criteria against which to judge the recording, this experience can be very illuminating. Frequently self-evaluations will help to improve discussion skills. Having the group members check a form as simple as the following can be of considerable value.

1. Did the group discussion do what it set out to do?
2. In what way did we fall short?
3. Did we get off the topic?
4. Did everyone participate?
5. Did anyone monopolize the conversation?

Pupils' self-evaluation of their discussions can often be enhanced by letting them listen to taped recordings of the discussions. For evaluating a taped discussion the use of a list of criteria similar to that just mentioned or the one prepared by the A.S.C.D. can be of great help. In spite of its obvious value, the tape recording of group discussions may present something of a problem. To record a large group discussion with an ordinary school tape recorder can be very difficult. For recording, the group needs to be seated in a circle with each person as close to a microphone as possible. Otherwise it may be necessary to turn up the volume so high that the recorder may pick up extraneous noises and spoil the recording. In small groups, of course, the microphone can be passed from speaker to speaker, but in most class discussions this technique is too cumbersome to be practicable. Another danger is the temptation to play the recordings too long or too often. Running through a tape recording may be advantageous for training in group discussion, but overdone it can become a pernicious time-waster. Only parts of the tape should be rerun to illustrate good or poor portions of the discussion, or to reinforce the report of what happened.

THE ROLE OF THE OBSERVER. Sometimes, in order to evaluate the group's discussion, one of the members is asked to act as an observer. The observer's job is to watch the group as the discussion progresses and to report his evaluation to the group. In his evaluation he may use as a guide such criteria as those mentioned above.

Sometimes a second observer follows the discussion by means of a flow chart, an example of which appears as Figure 5. In this flow chart the observer has indicated the flow of conversation by the use of arrows. An arrow pointing from one person to another shows that the participant had addressed his remark to another person. Double-headed arrows indicate an exchange between two people, and arrows pointing into the circle indicate a remark addressed to the group as a whole. By analyzing the chart, it should be possible to tell who in the group was participating and whether the group was participating as a group or as a bunch of individuals. Ordinarily the chart should be made by one of the pupils who comes to the discussion prepared for this assignment. He is sometimes called the second observer or flow-chart operator.

One pernicious problem is the person who dominates the discussion. The flow chart is an especially good instrument for pointing out just who these people are without hurting anyone's sensibilities.

The comments of the observers on the progress of the discussion and the participation of the group members are also an effective means of making the overtalkative person aware of his faults. Frequently the pupils will respond more positively to criticism from one of their peers

FIGURE 5

A Flow Chart

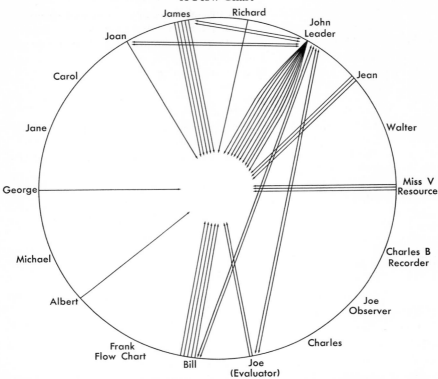

acting as observer than from the teacher. A scheme sometimes used by teachers is to make the overtalkative pupil the observer or flow-chart operator. This assignment may have two merits: it may force the pupil to silence, and it may make him aware of the danger of talking too much.

✿

Make a simple rating scale with which to evaluate a group discussion.

What does the Flow Chart (Figure 5) tell you about the participating group?

Would flow charts be helpful in high-school classes? How would you use them?

✿

THE A.S.C.D. CHECKLIST. The following list[1] is useful for outlining the tasks of the group participants and evaluating their success.

[1] Association for Supervision and Curriculum Development, *1954 Convention Program*, Washington, D.C.: the Association, a department of the National Education Association, 1954, pp. 54–55. Adapted by the 1954 Committee on Conference Orientation and Evaluation from material prepared for the 1950 Convention Program by J. Cecil Parker, University of California, Berkeley.

Each Group Member and the Discussion Leader in Particular

———— Helps decide on specific problems and ways of working as a group
———— Contributes ideas and suggestions related to the problem
———— Listens to what other members say and seeks helpful ideas and insights
———— Requests clarification when needed
———— Observes the group process and makes suggestions
———— Assumes various roles as needed
———— Helps group get acquainted
———— Helps group establish ground rules
———— Reports results of preconference planning for work of group
———— Helps group proceed with planning and deciding
———— Calls on group to clarify, analyze, and summarize problems and suggested solutions
———— Draws out the "timid soul" and keeps the dominant person from monopolizing
———— Knows particular contributions which different persons can make
———— Assists the recorder
———— Summarizes the thinking of the group as needed.

The Recorder

———— Consults with the group concerning the kind of record that is developing as the discussion moves forward
———— Keeps a record of the main problems, issues, ideas, facts, and decisions as they appear in discussion
———— Summarizes the group discussion upon request
———— Requests clarification when his notes are unclear
———— Prepares resolutions and other final reports with other designated members of the group
———— Attends any scheduled clearinghouse or intergroup sharing committee sessions
———— Prepares final group report and is responsible for getting it to proper clearinghouse.

Each Group Member

Pays attention to the way the group:
———— States its goals clearly
———— Permits participation to be easily and widely spread
———— Keeps its discussion clear
———— Assumes leadership responsibility
———— Uses its resources
———— Progresses toward its goals
———— Revises its goals as necessary
———— Participates in evaluation of the group process
————Reports to the group if asked regarding observations on the group process.

Group Members as Resource Persons

Every member of a discussion group is responsible for:

——— Supplying information or other material to the group when requested, or when the discussion seems to call for it

——— Citing his own experience freely when it is relevant

——— Assisting the leader in moving toward the achievement of group goals.

✿

Examine the Association for Supervision and Curriculum Development criteria for discussion groups. How can they be used in a secondary-school class?

How can student leaders, recorders, and resource persons be used in secondary-school classes?

✿

Panels and Symposiums

To discuss any matter well in a large class is quite difficult. Usually such discussion boils down to involving only a few persons, with the rest of the class acting as onlookers. Sometimes some of the benefits of the discussion group can be brought to a large class by using a panel, symposium, or round-table discussion. Here selected members of the group can discuss matters in a fashion similar to the free discussion of the small class. In a panel discussion, participation is open to all members of the panel; in a symposium, each participant makes a set speech, which may be followed by discussion. In either case, people from the floor are given a chance to enter the discussion. Although the panels and the symposiums are usually not suitable for small classes, they may be used to launch discussions in small groups. In both large and small classes the panels and symposiums are likely to be more interesting if they involve questions and discussion from other members of the class.

Role Playing

The Purpose of Role Playing

Role playing consists of an unrehearsed dramatization in which the players attempt to make a situation clear to themselves and to the audience by playing the roles of participants in the situation. Its purpose is to help people see a situation through other people's eyes. To attain this purpose the playing of the roles must be held as closely as possible to the reality of the original situation and yet at the same time allow the players to react to the situation as freely and spontaneously as the situation itself will allow. Because the type of role playing most often used in schools has to do with the understanding of social situations by groups it is called sociodrama. Other types of dramatization also are useful tools for learning to understand the behavior of others, but they do not qualify as role playing unless they meet the criteria of relatively unrehearsed performance, spontaneous reproduction of real situations, and attempts to analyze, understand, and perhaps solve a problem situation. Other dramatizations will be discussed in another section. This section will be devoted entirely to the type of role playing known as sociodrama. Because of the power of drama, it is particularly useful in making clear to pupils the motivation and feelings of others.

For instance, in order to teach how prejudice affects both the prejudiced and the prejudiced against, a group in a social studies class attempted to portray the feelings of a pair of boys who were rejected from a fraternity because of their religious beliefs. The players presented two scenes: the first, the discussion of the candidates at the fraternity just prior to the voting; the second, the scene in which the boys were notified of their rejection. In each of these scenes the players attempted to show the emotions of the characters they portrayed. They particularly emphasized how the boys felt after the rejection. Three different casts portrayed these scenes. After the presentations the entire class discussed the justice of the decision and the probable effect of the incident on the persons concerned.

Another example of role playing is an attempt to make the feelings of the American colonists more real to the pupils. In this class the players represented a group of colonists discussing the news of the "stamp tax." The loyalist tried to show the reason for the tax, but the others shouted him down. From role playing of this sort it is hoped that the pupils will come to understand the tenor of the times being studied.

THE VALUE OF ROLE PLAYING. Role playing may result in other valuable learnings. If Keltner[2] is right, a more complete list of the values of role playing would show that role playing

1. Gives us insight into the effectiveness of the roles we play in real life.
2. Teaches us to examine the roles we play more objectively.
3. Teaches us to perform new roles and to experiment with new roles in order to make more adequate adjustment to the groups of which we are a part.
4. Provides us with a kind of laboratory where we can examine and experiment with roles in situations where we are not "playing for keeps" yet where a semblance of reality is present.

[2] John W. Keltner, *Group Discussion Processes* (New York: David McKay Company, Inc., 1957), pp. 262–263. By permission.

5. Provides us with vivid examples of behavior that are more effective than mere conversation about the situations.
6. Helps us develop clearer communication. When we cannot put an idea about human relations into words we can act it out and thus make it clearer to those who are trying to understand it.
7. Helps us to understand another point of view.

✿   ✿   ✿

For the group, there are several advantages to role playing.

1. It provides a group with a system of communication that is based on action rather than on word symbols. This helps members of the group to understand one another.
2. It helps a group learn the skills necessary for effective group action.
3. It provides techniques of analyzing problems which involve human factors or items of interpersonal relations.
4. It involves the members in a consideration of the problem.
5. It enables a group to pretest ideas that may have significance for the future.

Limitations and Dangers

Role playing is not a magic formula by which to solve all one's difficult teaching problems. It is a difficult technique, the improper use of which can be harmful. Among its limitations and dangers, Keltner lists the following.[3]

a. Participants must be thoroughly prepared for this kind of work. Unless the group is sensitive and open-minded enough to try new ways of working together, the process may meet serious opposition and possibly fail.
b. The cases and the problems must be realistic, practical, and complete enough for clear-cut issues to arise. Unless the role-players know the facts and the backgrounds and conditioning of the characters the whole thing may become superficial.
c. Players often tend to "ham" up their portrayal of the roles. This makes the production a farce and becomes merely a pleasant but frustrating attempt to get at real issues. The players must be cautioned to play the roles as realistically as possible.
d. Role-playing is time consuming. Properly done it takes at least an hour of highly concentrated activity. Unless there are capable leaders and directors available, this time will get away without sufficient use of the method.
e. Role-playing demands some imagination on the part of the group.

[3] *Ibid.*, pp. 277–278.

Unless the group has demonstrated that it has some of this ability to create ideas and use its imagination, the role-playing may be quite sterile.

f. Unless there is an atmosphere of free discussion and inquiry, the role-playing cannot be adequately developed.

g. Role-playing should involve the whole group. There is a tendency on the part of many leaders to dictate all of the conditions and the scenes that are to be portrayed. This is contradictory to the main purpose of the method—that of involving the whole group in the consideration of its problems.

Role-playing is not a device to be used for fun or entertainment. Too many groups today are using it much as they would use a skit or short dramatic production, merely to entertain the members.

h. When the members are not fully acquainted with each other, they may become known in terms of the roles they have portrayed in a session rather than as they really are. It is wise to withhold the use of the method until the members become acquainted. In the large group technique this is not possible nor so important. When stereotype perceptions of people may appear to be forming in a group, the leader should seek an opportunity for the players to be seen in several different roles so that no one role will become associated with the player.

Staging the Sociodrama

PREPARING FOR ROLE PLAYING. Although role playing is usually done without script or rehearsal, it does require preparation. In the first place, the pupils must understand the situation being presented. This necessitates selecting a situation that the pupils can readily comprehend, and carefully briefing both the players and the rest of the class so that they do understand it. The teacher should see to it that each player not only understands the situation but also realizes the purpose of the sociodrama and his part in it. For this reason the players should spend some time discussing their roles with the teacher before the presentation. The teacher must also see to it that the rest of the class understands the purpose of the sociodrama and what they should look for as the drama is presented. Although role playing may be enjoyable, it is not entertainment. The teacher should make every effort to be sure that all the pupils realize this and treat role playing as a serious attempt to clarify a difficult social situation.

SELECTING THE CAST. As one can readily see, role playing requires serious effort on the part of the role player. His job is to attempt to get under the skin of another person and, as far as he possibly can, present that person's actions and emotions. This is no small task. For this reason one should select the players carefully—if possible, from volunteers. Sometimes selecting the cast is complicated by the fact that the most eager volunteers seem quite incapable of carrying out the roles. At times the teacher will have to find understudies for the cast. A helpful procedure is to select several casts and have several presentations. This practice may offset poor presentations and give depth to the understanding of the class as a result of the difference in presentation and interpretation of the roles.

PLAYING THE ROLES.   Role playing is rather taxing for some pupils, and quite often the players are extremely nervous. They may need help and encouragement. Rehearsing the first few lines and preparing a general plan for the development of the dramatization may help the participants to play their parts more confidently. On the other hand, too much planning may stifle the sociodrama's spontaneity and straitjacket the role player's interpretation. Because the purpose of role playing is for the role player to place himself in his role and then, as naturally as possible, enact the role he is portraying, the teacher's part in the planning should ordinarily be limited to giving the pupils the necessary background and enough planning and direction to get started with confidence.

The pattern in most role playing is quite loose. Consequently, there is always a danger that inexperienced role players may lose sight of their roles. The teacher can guard against this eventuality by carefully selecting the role players and thoroughly explaining their roles to them. Sometimes, however, these precautions are not sufficient. On such an occasion, if a player does get badly out of character, the teacher may have to stop the production and re-orient the players. It is better to interrupt the production than to present false information to the class.

PREPARING THE AUDIENCE AND FOLLOWING UP.   As with any other activity, the pupils in the audience should be well prepared for observing the sociodrama. They should understand what is going on and what to look for, or the presentation will be for naught. Similarly, if the pupils are to benefit from the acting, the dramatization must be followed up. A discussion period is excellent as a follow-up after the sociodrama. In fact, it can be the most worthwhile part of the entire presentation.

✧

What should the teacher do if a pupil seems to be badly misinterpreting his role?

What purposes may a sociodrama serve?

What sort of material is best suited to a sociodrama?

✧

Other Dramatizations

Sociodrama is not the only form of dramatization used in teaching. Pupils can bring dramatics to school in all its forms from full-fledged grand opera in the music department to charades in the English classroom. Among classroom dramatic activities one may find such divergent art forms as the ballet, pantomime, pageant, choral readings, cinema, puppetry, shadow plays, and mock radio and television performances.

Such dramatizations have many uses: illustration of an historical scene, portrayal of a literary character, the vitalization of a play, or the representation of a fact or an abstract idea. The impact of a well-done dramatization can drive home concepts and attitudes to both spectators and participants. Especially worth considering are the student-created dramatizations. In addition to the benefit derived from creating the piece, the pupil may learn many facts and figures about the topic to be dramatized as he gathers material for his presentation.

Unlike the sociodrama, dramatizations need to be rehearsed. Before attempting to present a work of art, the players should know pretty well what to say, how to say it, and how to portray their roles. Even if they are only to read a play, the pupils should first read through the parts they are to portray and become familiar with the vocabulary. Impromptu classroom readings of great plays seldom lead to appreciation of the drama. A quick rehearsal in the corridor or in a corner of the classroom will usually increase the effectiveness many times. A more thorough preparation should be even more beneficial.

Only on rare occasions, however, is it worthwhile to spend long periods of time in rehearsal and line learning. For this reason the use of pantomime, pageants, and other activities in which the pupils have few speaking parts may be advantageous. Otherwise, classroom dramatization should probably depend upon the reading of lines. This *caveat* should not preclude the use of such projects as preparing and filming a movie script, or staging a play. It does mean that one should carefully consider the relative values to be derived from the sort of activities that require long periods of rehearsal and memorization.

✼

Criticize the following practice. (Note that "criticize" and "find fault" are not synonymous.) In a junior high school the pupils had been reading plays for outside reading. As a culminating activity the student teacher asked each person to dramatize a scene from his play using his colleagues as actors. Before the presentation the actors consulted with one another for about five minutes and then read their lines all from the same book.

What purposes may dramatizations serve? What sort of material is best dramatized? What types of dramatization are possible? What are the merits of each?

When are dramatizations best used in the teaching-learning cycle?

❊

Teaching Through Committees

The Value of Committees

Quite often teachers divide classes into small groups. Sometimes these groups are based on pupil ability or interest and are designed to provide for individual differences. Such intraclass grouping is discussed in Chapter 7. Here we shall discuss another type of small group—the working committee that has a specific task to perform. Although committee groups are not ability groups, the student should at once recognize that committees do help provide for individual differences in ability and interest. For example, let us suppose a class is studying the family. The class might form one committee to investigate the family life of animals, another to survey adolescent-parent relationships, still another to investigate family life in a polygamous society. A pupil could choose to work on one or another of these committees on the basis of his interests. Within the committee, pupils will be allocated different tasks depending upon the committee's needs and the pupils' interests and abilities. Thus, by using committees it may be possible for pupils to assume various degrees of responsibility and to tackle tasks of varying difficulty, as well as to study things interesting to them.

In addition to providing for differences in individuals, teaching via committees has several other values. This method allows more pupils to participate actively than do the class recitation techniques. It is useful in helping pupils to develop skills of leadership, communication, socialization, cooperation, and thinking. Skillfully used it should be instrumental in teaching pupils how to search out, evaluate, and report on scholarly information. Furthermore, by its very nature committee membership should help pupils accept and carry out roles that will be theirs in adult life, for one skill, as important as it is rare in adult life, is that of organizing and carrying out effective committee work.

Committee work also has the practical advantage of eliminating unnecessary emphasis on reports and other methods. It also makes it possible to combine teaching in depth with wide coverage. Each committee can delve deeply into its area and then share its findings with the rest of the class.

Selecting the Committee

Ideally, a committee should consist of from four to seven members. Whenever a classroom committee grows to include eight or more members it should probably be broken into smaller committees or sub-committees. Committee members can be chosen in many ways. In some situations the nature of the work to be done automatically selects committee participants. When teachers set up committees on the basis of interest, the nature of the pupils' individual interests largely determines the make-up of the committees. Sometimes the teacher should choose the committees himself to suit his own purposes. At other times he will want to allow the pupils to select their own committees.

In the course of time the teacher should probably utilize all these methods of selecting committee members. As a general rule, however, it is probably wise to honor pupil preferences. For that reason, when it seems feasible, the teacher should tend toward allowing pupils to select their own members. Even when he selects the members himself, he should bear pupil preferences in mind.

In every class, pupils tend to form natural groups and follow natural leaders. By observing the class and by using devices such as those described in Chapter 2 the alert teacher can find out who the natural leaders and group members are. He should do so because, as a rule, it is advantageous to make use of these natural groups and natural leaders when forming committees. In this respect the use of sociograms can be particularly helpful.[4]

While forming committees according to natural group lines may be advantageous, several other requirements must also be considered. Among them are the nature of the committee's task and interests of the pupils. One reason for having pupil committees is to allow pupils to work at tasks that seem important to them. The teacher should see to it, insofar as possible, that each pupil works on the committee he is most interested in. Furthermore, each committee calls for members with different abilities. In choosing committee members, provision should be made for these various abilities.

Whenever possible, committees should be made up of volunteers. This is not always feasible, of course, but the teacher may be able to approach this ideal more closely if all the pupils make two or three choices in writing rather than volunteering orally. Making choices in writing allows the more timid to volunteer without embarrassment. Even so, some assignments to committees will have to be made by the teacher or by a pupil steering committee under the teacher's guidance. In either case the

4 See Chapter 2.

Committee members may report their findings in many ways. The oral report is one way; others include panels, symposiums, and dramatic presentations.

teacher should take care to see that the membership of each committee meets the criteria noted above.

No matter how the group members are selected, the teacher should keep a record of the committee memberships and committee assignments. Such a record will give him an insight into the relationships of the pupils in the class. Also, this record will give the teacher information he needs to be sure that all pupils have opportunities to participate to the fullest and to be sure that no one is neglected.

Determining the Committee's Procedure

Every committee should have a specific mission to perform, and the committee members should have a clear understanding of what this mission is before they start to work. This task may be assigned to the committee by a teacher or be the result of group planning. In any case, the work of each committee should further the plan worked out for the entire class.

Once the committee has its mission, it must establish its mode of procedure. One of the first things to be done is to appoint or elect a chairman to lead the committee and a recorder to keep a record of what is done. After these persons are selected, the group should decide on what it is going to do. This means that it must set itself definite objectives in light of its mission. This can be done in committee discussion. Further discussion can develop the methods by which the committee proposes to reach its objectives. At this time specific assignments are given to the various committee members. For instance, the committee may ask one pupil to be responsible for securing certain material, and another responsible for looking up a specific item of information. As soon as this planning is completed, the pupils work together to complete their task. If this procedure is to succeed, the pupils must have a clear understanding of the procedures they can use as well as the mission they are supposed to accomplish.

The Committee Report

After the committee has accomplished its work, it should report to the class in one way or another. An oral report to the class is a common practice. Unfortunately, oral reports can become deadly, particularly if the class must listen to several of them, one following the other. The teacher who wishes to relieve the class from boredom should avoid an unending series of oral reports. Talks by skilled lecturers are difficult enough to sit through; talks by unskilled pupils can become unbearable. Therefore, the teacher should attempt to space the reports between other activities and to see to it that committees report in other different ways. Among the many possible ways to report Hock[5] includes

Dramatic Presentations
   original plays
   role playing
   skits
   parodies of radio or television programs or movies
   monologues
Panel Type of Discussions
   panels
   forums
   debates
   round-table sessions
   town meetings
Written Materials
   newspapers
   notebooks
   scrapbooks
   duplicated material
   creative writing—poems, stories, plays, songs
Visual Depictions
   slides
   maps

[5] Louise E. Hock, *Using Committees in the Classroom* (New York: Holt, Rinehart, and Winston Inc., 1958) p. 32.

Visual Depictions (*cont.*)
   pictures
   graphs
   posters
   models
   exhibits
   murals
   bulletin board displays
Others
   tape recordings
   action projects: open house for parents, party, presentation to P.T.A.
     or civic groups.

✿

In what other ways might a committee report to the class? Give examples of how the examples that Hock lists might be used in your classes.

✿

Helping Pupil Committees

Committees usually require a great deal of teacher guidance. Inexperienced boys and girls will need much help in determining how they should go about completing their work. They need help in determining their goals, the procedures for fulfilling those goals, and ways of reporting the fruit of their labor to the total group. In advising them, the teacher should retain his role as a consultant, not as a dictator. He should point out alternatives open to the pupils and the dangers inherent in some lines of approach to the problem. Since boys and girls, like adults, are likely to take the line of least resistance and stick to the tried and true, the teacher should take special care to make pupils aware of different approaches to committee work.

THE TEACHER'S ROLE. Obviously, then, the teacher's role in committee work is very sensitive. He must encourage the pupils to work on their own initiative, but at the same time see to it that their work is productive. At all times everyone must understand that the teacher is in charge of the class no matter how much freedom he allows the pupils. He must oversee and approve pupil plans and procedures. He will have to be sure that committee work is properly scheduled and coordinated with other class activities. In this respect, one should note that it is poor practice to try to do all the instruction by means of committees. It is seldom desirable to give more than two or three consecutive days to committee work. Rather, committee work should be intermixed with other whole-class and individual activities of various sorts.

MAKING MATERIALS AVAILABLE. Teachers must also be sure that the pupils have suitable materials readily available for their use. At times this duty will require them to make arrangements with the library. At other times, it will mean that the teacher must collect material himself. Occasionally it will mean that he must steer the committee off in some other direction because there is no way to provide them with the material they need. A good procedure may be to require pupils to establish the availability of resources themselves before the committee is allowed to commit itself to any particular problem or course of action. Obviously, teaching by committees requires the teacher to have great knowledge of the content to be covered and the resources available in the area. For this reason, a good resource unit or curriculum guide can be of tremendous assistance to teachers and pupils.

FOLLOWING UP COMMITTEE WORK. Teaching by committees requires the teacher to emphasize follow-up. Pupil reports may do much to tie things together, but by their very nature they tend to leave learning fragmented. The teacher's follow-up is needed to fill in gaps, smooth out rough spots, tie up loose ends, show relationships, and drive home important concepts. Without adequate follow-up the learning of the committee members may stop dead in a frustrating *cul de sac*. All too often teachers' neglect of the follow-up brings the pupils up to the door of understanding and leaves them standing there at the threshold so near to and yet so far from real learning.

Summary

Some of the most effective teaching is group teaching, that is, teaching by and through groups and group methods. By using committee work, sociodramas and other dramatizations, and discussion, teachers can quite often increase their teaching efficiency. This type of teaching is frequently effective in changing attitudes, ideals, and appreciations. It is particularly useful in raising learning above the verbalizing level. Thus, group methods often lead to thorough permanent learning. Teaching by group methods takes considerable time and effort, but the results are usually worth it.

A discussion is not a monologue, a question-and-answer period, or a bull session. Rather, it is a controlled conversation in which participants pool their thoughts on a topic or problem in a purposeful, orderly way. The discussion leader's task is to lead the group into fruitful dialogue without dominating them or allowing them to meander. In this task the aid of a good recorder is extremely desirable. Observers can help the group to learn how to discuss matters more effectively.

One of the most powerful of the new methods, when properly used, is the sociodrama or role playing which consists basically of trying to put oneself in the place of someone else and to act out his point of view. In order to be effective, role playing must be an unrehearsed, spontaneous attempt to analyze and understand real problem situations. Its purpose is quite different from that of the many other types of dramatic representations that may be included in the classroom. These other types should be rehearsed as carefully as the time permits in order to be effective.

Teaching via committees has become quite popular. It is an effective means of providing for individual differences and laboratory experiences. The membership of pupil committees may be determined in several ways, but when feasible, the teacher should take advantage of natural pupil leadership and groups. Although pupil committee members should do the bulk of their own planning and research, the teacher must always be ready in the background with necessary help and guidance. Sharing the results of the committee work with the rest of the class can be a particular problem. The teacher should place considerable stress on lively, original reporting and serious, careful class follow-up of committee work.

FOR FURTHER STUDY

BANY, MARY A., and LOIS V. JOHNSON, *Classroom Group Behavior* (New York: The Macmillan Company, 1964).

BRADFORD, LELAND P., JACK R. GIBB, and KENNETH D. BENNE, *T-Group Theory and Laboratory Method* (New York: John Wiley and Sons, Inc., 1964).

CARTWRIGHT, DORWIN, and ALVIN ZANDERS, *Group Dynamics Research and Theory*, Second Edition (New York: Harper and Row Publishers, 1960).

FLANDERS, NED, *Teaching with Groups* (Minneapolis: Burgess Publishing Company, 1954).

HOCK, LOUISE, *Using Committees in the Classroom* (New York: Holt, Rinehart and Winston, Inc., 1961).

KELTNER, JOHN W., *Group Discussion Processes* (New York: David McKay Company, Inc., 1957).

KEMP, C. GRATTON, *Perspectives on the Group Process* (Boston: Houghton Mifflin Company, 1964).

MILES, MATTHEW B., *Learning to Work in Groups* (New York: Bureau of Publications, Teachers College, Columbia University, 1959).

National Society for the Study of Education, *The Dynamics of Instructional Groups*, Fifty-ninth Yearbook, Part II (Chicago: The University of Chicago Press, 1960).

SMITH, LOUIS M., *Group Process in Elementary and Secondary Schools*, "What Research Says to the Teacher," No. 19, (Washington, D.C.: National Education Association, 1959).

ZAPF, ROSALIND M., *Democratic Processes in the Secondary Classroom* (Englewood Cliffs, N.J.: Prentice-Hall, Inc., 1959), Particularly Ch. 3.

CHAPTER 11

Study, Practice, and Projects

STUDY, homework, practice, and projects are all primarily individual activities. In spite of certain exceptions, these are activities in which the teacher's role should be largely indirect and supervisory, while the pupil carries the burden of the learning load. The following paragraphs are designed to provide teachers with information about how they can help the pupils learn by means of these activities. In carrying out these precepts the teacher should beware of attempting to do the learning for the pupil. In these activities, as in others, the pupil must be free to learn.

Guiding Study

In the past, teachers seemed to take it for granted that pupils just naturally learned to study. Seldom did teachers ever take it upon themselves to teach pupils how. "For tomorrow I want you to study Chapter 14, and you can expect a quiz on it," they would say. But not a word about how one studies, or how one should get ready for the quiz.

More recently, teachers have begun to realize that boys and girls must be taught how to study if they are going to learn how. Left to themselves, few pupils develop good study techniques. If boys and girls reach the secondary grades without having learned to study well, the responsibility for seeing to it that they learn how to study falls on the secondary-school teacher. No pupil can do justice to the secondary-school program unless he has mastered the art of studying efficiently.

Improving Pupils' Study Habits

WHAT STUDYING IS. Some pupils seem to think that studying is the same as reading. This is not the case. Study includes all those activities that have to do with learning through planned effort. Thus, notetaking at lectures, preparation of papers, library work, reference work, problem solving, intensive reading, and skimming should all be considered study

activities. They all are techniques that the pupil needs to learn before he
can become an efficient student.

SUGGESTIONS FOR STUDY. When teachers first became aroused to
the fact that boys and girls needed help in learning how to study, they
developed "rules for study" as guides for the pupils. Among the admoni-
tions often included in such rules are the following.

1. Plan your studying. Make a schedule and stick to it. Have a definite
   place to work. Make your studying routine and part of your routine.
2. Start off immediately. Have your material ready before you sit down
   to work. Be sure you understand the assignment before you begin it.
3. Space your learning. Take two- to three-minute breaks. If possible,
   take your rests at natural breaks in the material you are studying.
   Try to master one lesson or selection before moving on to the next.
4. Study actively. Develop an interest in what you are studying. Try
   to find out something. React to the readings. Ask yourself questions.
   Recite. Work out examples. Illustrate principles. Apply your learning
   as soon as possible.
5. Vary your study technique to suit the subject and your purpose.
   Learn materials in the form you expect to use them.
6. Avoid rote memorization. Memorize those things you need to
   memorize by the meaningful techniques of logical memory. Avoid
   mnemonics.
7. Evaluate your own work and study habits. Try to improve faulty
   habits. Try to increase your vocabulary; look up words you do not
   know. Make use of the aids provided in your books. Do not skip
   headings, marginal notes, questions, prefatory remarks, tables of
   contents, charts, and graphs. Use them.
8. Check your work and proofread your papers before handing them
   in. Take full notes but do not attempt to rewrite the text or copy
   down each word of the lecturer.[1]

On the whole, the advice in these suggestions is good. But the suggestions do not help a pupil's studying, unless they become a part of his
behavior. How to make them part of the pupils' behavior is a problem
that teachers must face.

*

Pick out several of the rules you consider important and try to
devise activities that would make these rules become part of the
pupils' behavior.

*

[1] The student might be wise to examine the list and apply it to his own practice.
Even though each rule is not necessarily an essential, students might do well to
investigate their own study habits if they diverge sharply from these rules.

TEACHING HOW TO STUDY. Instruction in how to study must involve considerable practice in the classroom. In some schools a course in how to study is provided. Such courses are helpful, but they do not relieve individual teachers of the responsibility for teaching study skills. Why not? For one thing, different subjects require different study techniques if study is to be effective. Consequently, in each of his courses, every teacher should try to teach study techniques proper to his course to any youngster who has not mastered them. Furthermore, learning how to study comes only from practicing good techniques, and where else can the pupil practice but in his ordinary courses? Thus every teacher is responsible for teaching pupils how to study for his course. Among the skills with which the pupils may need help are

1. How to read for information.
2. How to analyze a problem.
3. How to plan for study.
4. How to review.
5. How to evaluate materials.
6. How to use charts, graphs, and other audio-visual aids.
7. How to take notes.
8. How to concentrate.
9. How to analyze.
10. How to outline.
11. How to use the library.
12. How to build an adequate vocabulary both general and specialized.

SQ3R. Younger pupils need considerable help in learning how to study. Older ones should have acquired a great deal of this skill and be able to work quite independently at their own level by the time they leave high school. When studying, pupils should utilize the technique of reading for comprehension discussed in the previous section. For the purpose of simplification and for mnemonic purposes these study procedures are often called SQ3R. These cabalistic letters stand for Survey, Question, Read, Recite, and Review—basically the same techniques described in Chapter 12. Skill in these procedures must be developed by direct instruction and much supervised practice in the junior-high-school years.

THE NEED FOR DIAGNOSIS. As in any other teaching situation, one of the first prerequisites for teaching study skills is good diagnosis. By using the techniques of diagnosis described in Chapter 2, the teacher can determine what the pupil needs help with. Much of teaching pupils how to study must be done on an individual basis. As the teacher watches pupils studying, he can suggest ways and means to expedite the process. Questions like the following are often helpful.

What are you doing?
Why are you doing that?
What are you trying to do?
Will this help you?
Is what you are doing worthwhile?
Why do you think this is going to give the desired result?
What might you better be doing now?

TEACHING STUDY SKILLS IN THE ASSIGNMENT. In spite of their great importance, more than diagnosis and individual help is necessary in the teaching of study skills. The teacher can expect little success in this venture unless he teaches the skills directly. Although teachers often neglect it, the assignment offers a golden opportunity for teaching these skills. If the reader will turn back to the assignment discussion in Chapter 3, he will notice that the pupils developed an understanding of what they were trying to do and how they were to go about accomplishing their mission. In similar fashion they might discuss the materials and sources available, the use of the materials, and the relative merits of various study techniques in the performing of this assignment. As one can see, the assignment lends itself to such instruction.

The reverse side of the assignment coin can also be used to teach improved study skills. After an assignment has been completed, the pupils can learn about study skills and their efficiency by discussing the methods different pupils used to study the assignment and the relative success of the various methods.

THE PUPILS' RESPONSIBILITY FOR LEARNING. Although it is true that an assignment, to be good, must ensure that the pupils know how to attack the work to be done, the teacher must also work to convince the pupils to accept the responsibilities of learning. Every pupil should learn quickly that there is no royal road to learning. Teachers should show the pupils how to attack their assignments, but they should not deprive the pupils of their initiative. The idea is to start them off, to encourage them, and to guide them—not to baby them. Rivlin[2] has suggested that the pupils discuss how they would study the material if there were no teacher, then formulate the attack, and work it out under the teacher's guidance. This method has the advantage of helping the pupils find their way under their own initiative yet with the security of the teacher's presence in case of need.

USING A GRADED SEQUENCE. No matter what methods are used to teach study skills, the material taught should be graded according to

2 Harry N. Rivlin, *Teaching Adolescents in Secondary Schools* (New York: Appleton-Century-Crofts, Inc., 1948), p. 276.

complexity and difficulty. Study skills are both difficult and complex. For this reason, they should be taught in sequence; the easier skills should precede the more difficult ones, the simple should precede the complex. The teaching of how to read for information previously cited serves as an excellent example of this point. Here the teacher first teaches the pupil how to extract the meaning from a sentence. This having been mastered, he proceeds to teach how to get the meaning from a paragraph. From there he goes on to getting the meaning from a section, a chapter, and finally the entire book.

Building more complex study skills on simple study skills is a must. To do this successfully requires the cooperative effort of the teachers in the various grade levels, and the teacher's careful diagnosis of each pupil's present level of proficiency.

※

In what ways could teachers of various grade levels cooperate in the teaching of study skills in your field?

In what ways is the studying of algebra different from studying social studies? From home economics? What skills may be used in studying these courses? Do the necessary skills vary from topic to topic within the fields? How?

※

TAKING NOTES ON READING.   Many people recommend that pupils take notes on their reading. Nevertheless, there seems to be considerable difference of opinion about the value of note taking. Certainly the mechanical production of the author's outline cannot be of much value. Neither does there seem to be any particular advantage in making an outline of a textbook when one has the text itself in his possession. On the other hand, to outline an "outside reading" preserves the information so that the pupil can study it later. Outlines consisting of questions with their answers have the additional advantage of highlighting the salient points. In any case, if a pupil does take notes, he should write them neatly, preferably in outline form. Disorderly notes are liable to confuse the pupil rather than to help him.

OUTLINING.   Without any doubt being able to outline well is one of the most valuable skills a pupil can have and teachers in all subjects can help to be sure that pupils master it. Moreover, although having an outline of a text may not be of particular value, making an outline can be very valuable, for by the process of outlining one divides the text into its principal and subordinate points. It follows then that except for the fact that most textbook writers have reproduced the skeleton of their outline in their center heads, side heads and paragraph leads, there is no better vehicle for practicing outlining than one's own textbook.

To teach the pupils to outline correctly, the NASSP has recommended the following techniques which have been well proven over the years.[3]

1. Use easy materials and short selections in teaching pupils the mechanics of outlining. The following steps may be followed in teaching pupils to make outlines.
   a. Teacher and pupils working together select the main topics
   b. Pupils, unaided, select the main topics
   c. Teacher and pupils select the main topics, leaving space for subheads. Teacher and pupils then fill in these subtopics
   d. Main topics are selected by the teachers and pupils and are written on the blackboard. Pupils then fill in the subtopics unaided
   e. Pupils write the main topics and subheads without help
   f. Pupils organize, in outline form, data gathered from many sources.
2. Train pupils to find the main topics and to place them in outline form. Use books with paragraph headings.
   a. Have pupils read the paragraphs and discuss the headings. Suggest other possible headings and have pupils decide why the author selected the headings he used
   b. Match a given list of paragraph headings with numbered paragraphs
   c. Have pupils read a paragraph with this question in mind, "What is the main idea in this paragraph?" Write a number of suggested answers on the blackboard. Choose the best one.
3. Provide practice in filling in subtopics.
   a. The teacher writes the main topics on the board or uses a text that has the main headings. Teacher and pupils then fill in the subheads
   b. Have pupils skim other articles for more information and read carefully when additional material which is suitable for subheads is found. Add these new subheads. Do the same for new main topics
   c. When pupils have gathered sufficient data, have them reread the complete outline and, if necessary, rearrange the order of the topics.
4. Give instructions in making a standard outline form. Many secondary-school pupils do not know how to make an outline. Emphasize

[3] "Teaching Essential Reading Skills," Reprinted by permission from the Bulletin of the National Association of Secondary-School Principals (February 1950). Copyright: Washington, D.C. Based on "How to Teach Pupils to Outline," *Teachers' Guide to Child Development in the Intermediate Grades*. Prepared under the direction of the California State Curriculum Commission. Sacramento: California State Department of Education, 1936, pp. 294–5.

the fact that in a correct outline there must always be more than one item in the series under any subdivision. If there is an "a" there must also be a "b"; if there is a "1" there must also be a "2," etc. . . . A commonly accepted outline pattern is the one given below.

Outline Pattern

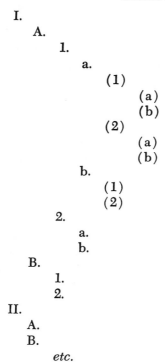

I.
   A.
      1.
         a.
            (1)
               (a)
               (b)
            (2)
               (a)
               (b)
         b.
            (1)
            (2)
      2.
         a.
         b.
   B.
      1.
      2.
II.
   A.
   B.
      etc.

5. Have pupils use this outline form in preparing and giving oral reports.

6. To develop ability to draw valid conclusions, have pupils use facts and ideas which have been organized in outline form, not only as a basis for an oral report or as an exercise in outlining a chapter, but also as the basis for drawing conclusions. To check pupils' ability to make outlines, prepare lessons based on the following suggestions.

   a. List main points and subpoints consecutively. Have pupils copy these, indenting to show subordination of subtopics and writing correct numbers and letters in front of each point

   b. List main topics and subtopics in mixed order and have pupils rearrange and number them

    c. List main topics with Roman numerals. List subtopics (all one value) with Arabic numerals. Have pupils organize subpoints under correct main points

    d. Present short paragraphs of well-organized material and have pupils write main topics and specified number of subtopics

    e. Present part of a skeleton outline and have students complete it

    f. Have pupils outline a problem without assistance. Class discussion is valuable in checking a lesson of this type.

LECTURE NOTES. Similar techniques should be taught to pupils who must learn to take notes from lectures. During early lectures it is wise if the teacher provides a skeleton outline which pupils are to fill in with subheads and detail. During the early secondary-school years the lecturer should stop to point out where he is on the outline from time to time to be sure that everyone is with him. Later this help may not be necessary. As the pupils become more skillful in taking lecture notes the outline skeleton should gradually diminish until at last it finally disappears. After lectures in which pupils have taken notes following their own version of the outline, the lecturer would do well to project his outline on the screen so that the pupils can compare their version with his. Also, lecturers should give pupils plenty of clues to the structure of their lectures as they go on. Such helps as firstly's, secondly's, and so on will not only help to keep the inexperienced lecture-note taker on the track, but may help keep the lecturer on it also. Lecturers who wander are difficult for any note takers—for beginners they are impossible!

Homework

The Problem of Homework

Homework is a problem to all teachers. How much homework should one assign? How much should it count? What does one do to those who neglect it? What kind of homework should one give? The list could go on *ad infinitum*, although these problems tend to become less crucial when one uses unit planning.

HOW MUCH HOMEWORK? How much homework should a teacher assign? The answer to this question depends upon the school, the subject, and the pupils. Quite often the school administration has established some sort of policy concerning homework. If so, the teacher must conform. Should the policy be a poor one, the teacher might work for its improvement, but under no circumstances should he flout it.

When the school has no policy concerning homework, the teacher should probably fall in line with the school tradition, if any. In any case, in schools which have study periods, it is usually good policy to give enough homework to keep the pupils busy at least during the study periods. In this connection, one should coordinate with the other teachers to ensure that pupils are neither overburdened nor underworked. Often a good unit assignment takes care of this problem automatically. At any rate, by giving long-term assignments one gives the pupil an opportunity to adjust his work so that he can avoid being overburdened by time-consuming assignments in several courses. Therefore, even if one does not use the unit approach, it may be wise to give out homework assignments for a week or more ahead. Almost invariably, it is more satisfactory to give long-term assignments in writing to prevent confusion, misunderstanding, and the need for repeating the assignment.

In making decisions about how much homework to give the teacher might want to consider the following points.

1. Although there seems to be no standard practice concerning homework in the United States, it is commonly expected that pupils will do a total of between one and two hours of work at home each day.
2. College-preparatory-class pupils seem to do more homework than others do. Junior-high-school pupils probably should work shorter hours than senior-high-school pupils.
3. The amount of time it takes a pupil to do an assignment depends upon the pupil. An assignment that one pupil can do well in thirty minutes may take another pupil much more than an hour.
4. The amount of time available for study during the school day and for a reasonable period after school hours divided by the number of classes the pupil must prepare for daily represents a fair estimate of the amount of time available for homework for any one class.

From time to time the teacher should check on the length of time his assignments are taking. In addition to asking pupils how long an assignment took them, teachers can check by giving pupils "homework" assignments to do during class periods so as to see how long it takes pupils to complete them.

At this point a word of warning may be in order. Recently there seems to have been a tendency for high-school teachers to illustrate how tough they are and what high standards they hold by piling great amounts of homework on their pupils. Unreasonably long assignments have no place in the secondary school for several reasons. The first is that *the emphasis should be on quality rather than quantity*. By making assignments too long teachers often force pupils to do less than their best, because there is just not enough time for them to do everything well. In addition, overdoses of homework can deprive pupils of the social and physical activities they need if they are to develop into well-balanced individuals. Sometimes unreasonable homework requirements can result in overwork or strain, and so are a threat to pupils' health. It is not necessary for a teacher to be an ogre in order to have high standards.

WHAT KIND OF HOMEWORK? Burton[4] indicates that homework seems to make little difference in the school progress of boys and girls. Perhaps more attention to homework assignments would result in more impressive gains, although studies show little evidence of the efficacy of homework even when accompanied by such aids as questions, study guides, and the like.[5] Probably the reason that homework is ineffective now is not that home study has no merit, but that the present homework assignments, and the lessons they support, are inadequate.

Homework assignments may be of several types. One type calls for reading and studying new or old material. Another type calls for the completion of written work to be handed in. Still another type consists of solving problems, working on projects, or performing other tasks which cannot be done well in school, for example, the surveying of a portion of the community. By far the largest number of assignments at present seem to consist solely of exhortations to read certain pages in the textbook. The exception to this rule is the mathematics class where the assignment is most always to solve certain problems. In general, however, homework is most suitable for activities designed to reinforce old learning. The learning of new techniques and new materials is usually best suited to class situations in which the teacher can guide the pupil and thus guard him from learning the new techniques or new concepts incorrectly. For this same reason homework should be reviewed in class to point out errors, to correct misconceptions, and so on.

Homework assignments can, of course, be used as a basis for a lesson to follow. Moreover, they can provide opportunities for the independent studying that pupils must do if they are ever to learn to think for themselves. However, assignments of new materials for study at home usually place too much emphasis on memorizing as opposed to understanding or thinking. *That is why homework assignments that carry on some activity started in class often result in better learning*, particularly when the activities are the kinds that require library or laboratory work such as digging out information from several sources, analyzing, identifying or defining problems, and doing practice exercises. Furthermore, pupils

[4] William H. Burton, *The Guidance of Learning Activities*, Second Edition (New York: Appleton-Century-Crofts, Inc., 1952), p. 368.

[5] Lloyd McCleary, "Homework," *Educational Leadership* (January, 1960), 27: 217–220, 225.

are less likely to be "forgetful" when the homework stems out of, or continues, an activity they are already working on and is tailored to their interests or needs.

EVALUATING HOMEWORK. Written homework presents several peculiar problems. One of them is that the written homework turned in is not always the work of the pupil, but that of his friends or relatives. Although teachers may condemn it as cheating, for parents to help their children with homework, and for friends to share their work with each other is an accepted part of our American culture which no one else, certainly not the pupils nor their parents, feels to be particularly dishonest. Because of this undoubted fact, teachers should assign written homework mainly as practice material from which the pupil may learn whether someone helps him or not. He should not count it much in making up a pupil's mark. Rather the marks should be based upon papers and tests done during class. Nevertheless, even though written homework should not carry much weight in one's marking, it should always be checked. If the homework is not self-checking, the teacher must check it himself. Unless this checking occurs, the practice value may be entirely lost. In fact, unchecked written homework may serve only to grind erroneous techniques and incorrect concepts into the pupils' minds.

Utilizing Supervised-Study Periods

A supervised-study period is an opportunity both for the pupil to study under guidance and for the teacher to supervise and guide study. This can best be done in the regular class. To a lesser extent it can also be done in study halls. Unfortunately, in some schools study halls are looked upon as merely a means for storing students who have no class at the time. This is hardly efficient. Supervised-study periods need real supervision. Merely to sit and watch the pupils is not the function of the teacher in a supervised-study period. If keeping order in the study hall were the sole function, the school would do better to hire a policeman for this duty.

*

A teacher of English says he corrects homework papers carefully about every fifth assignment. The other assignments he merely checks to see if the work has been done. Is this practice proper? Defend your answer.

In what ways might you as a study hall teacher help boys and girls improve their study hall habits? In addition to the present section you may find some suggestions in Chapter 3.

*

Conducting Practice Activities

Drill, Practice, and Review

Sometimes one can learn something quite thoroughly as the result of a powerful, vivid experience. Unfortunately, such impressive experiences are rare in the classroom. More often the learning must be renewed through drill, practice, or review.

The differences in these words are largely differences of connotation. Drill ordinarily connotes emphasis on unthinking, meaningless repetition, whereas practice seems to connote more purposeful, varied repetition. Review, of course, implies a second look at what has been learned once before. By implication it is often thought of as less intense than drill or practice. For our purposes in this book there seems to be little merit in drawing distinctions between drill and practice. We shall use the word "practice" to denote repetition of this sort.

The Value of Repetition

Repetition is necessary in school learning for several purposes. One of them is to reinforce retention of what has been learned for some things must be learned so well that they will not be forgotten. To be sure that pupils do not forget, learning must be renewed often, much more frequently than is necessary for immediate recall. This extra renewal is called overlearning. Overlearning is essential in memorization, in making behavior automatic, and in creating desirable habits. One major purpose of practice is to provide the overlearning necessary for retention.

Another reason for practice is to develop skill. As the great pianist repeats his concert selections again and again, he continually tries to improve his rendition. He may try to play more accurately, or with more feeling; he may experiment with the tempo, or he may vary his technique. But in each instance he is trying to improve his playing by repeating his performance in a slightly different way. So it is with the learning of all skills. No one can repeat anything exactly as he did it before. Because it allows one a chance to vary his behavior, practice makes it possible for one to improve one's skill.

Practice can also increase one's understanding. As one repeats and renews the learning, the concepts may become much clearer. Just as in the high jump the jumper, through diligent practice, may learn to get his hip up and over the bar, so one may acquire new insights by restudying a topic. This clarifying can be done only if the repetition is meaningful, purposeful, and varied. New skills and new concepts seldom result from dull, dry, aimless repetition.

✽

Why is repetition necessary in school learning? What sorts of things are best learned through drill techniques? Which are not?

Why was the traditional drill class ineffective? How can drill be made effective?

✽

Making Practice Meaningful

In one sense one does not learn through drill or practice. Practice merely consolidates, clarifies, and emphasizes what one has already learned.[6] Therefore, before practice sessions start, the pupil should understand what he is doing and how to do it. Repeating meaningless words or actions is wasteful. When one knows what copper sulphate is, or when one understands the meaning of the verb, this is the time to overlearn $Cu\ SO_4 = $ copper sulphate, or to conjugate the verb *amare*.

Repetition is usually more meaningful in context. Pupils often find it difficult to understand just what they are doing when the material to be learned is isolated from its context. Therefore, practice should occur in as real a setting as possible. For instance, to practice foreign words in sentences and in conversation is probably more effective than to practice them in isolated lists.

Practicing by wholes rather than by parts also makes practice more meaningful. In practicing something very difficult or involved, one may need to practice the difficult parts separately, but, in general, one should practice the whole thing. Then, because no part is learned at the expense of the others, the learning becomes a unit. For example, in practicing the crawl a pupil may need to concentrate on his kick or his breathing separately; he must also practice the entire stroke if he wishes to swim well. In memorizing a passage, one can usually learn most efficiently by the whole or part-whole method. If the selection to be memorized is short, one should memorize the whole thing at once, but if the selection is long, one should divide it into meaningful divisions, each of which can be learned separately. One might learn a sonnet as a whole, but a longer poem stanza by stanza.

For similar reasons practice seems to be most successful when it consists of many different types of activities in many classes. *Making practice part of the regular classwork rather than relegating it to special practice sessions, tends to make practice and the skills or knowledge to be practiced more meaningful.* This procedure also tends to give to the practice its proper proportion and emphasis. When they use special practice sessions as a means of teaching particular skills or knowledge, teachers

[6] This, too, is learning, of course.

tend to treat the practice itself as the end of the instruction. Such distortion of the teaching-learning process can lead only to confusion.

Motivating Practice Sessions

Because of its very nature practice needs to be well motivated. Moreover, practice should always occur under some pressure. The pressure should not be onerous, but it should be heavy enough to be felt so that the pupil will strive to improve. Lackadaisical practice is wasteful practice.

The hunger to learn is probably the most desirable motive, but it does not always seem to be present in pupils. Sometimes the teacher needs to use devices designed to make practice more attractive. The use of games, either individual or competitive, often serves the purpose admirably. Occasionally, someone objects to using competitive games in the classroom. However, if the teacher takes care to make them fun for all and to eliminate petty glory-seeking, such games have a place. Individual games that can be used include such things as anagrams, authors, crossword puzzles, and other puzzles of all sorts. These can be played as "solitaire"; but some of them can be competitive as well. Group games such as charades and "baseball" and "basketball" in which the questions take the place of base hits and field goals are also effective. In fact, almost every parlor game can be adapted for classroom use.

In utilizing such games, the teacher should be careful to include only the pertinent and important. He should be particularly wary of pupil-developed questions. Pupils too often search for the trivial and the obscure. Games which feature such questions help very little and should be avoided. Teachers should also avoid games which eliminate those who make errors. The old-fashioned spelling bee is not very useful because the people who need the practice most are eliminated early.

Using the Principle of Spaced Learning

Partly because of motivation factors, learning is usually more efficient when practice is spaced over a period of time with rather frequent breaks than when it is concentrated in long, continuous practice sessions. This phenomenon is known as the principle of spaced learning. Psychologically speaking, the principle seems to operate because of several reasons. One of them is that a person can keep motivation and effort at a high level for only a short time before he begins to tire. By keeping the practice periods relatively short and interspersing them with rest periods, one can do all one's practicing at or near his top performance level. In this way he is able to get maximum benefit from his performance. Also, the shortness of the practice sessions, plus the opportunities for rest, prevent the pupils from developing incorrect habits from practicing when over-tired. Another reason for the spacing of practice is that the intervals of rest between practice give the learner a chance to forget his mistakes before he goes on to the next practice session. Because after each rest period the pupil concentrates anew on learning correctly, spaced learning tends to reinforce correct learning and to cause mistakes to drop out.

As the learning becomes more firmly entrenched, the practice periods should become shorter and the intervals longer because not so much time is needed to renew the learning. This also helps to keep the practice from becoming too deadly.

Eliminating Unnecessary Drudgery

Practice can be dreadfully boring, as we all have learned to our sorrow. To keep it from becoming so, the teacher should eliminate as much unnecessary work as possible. If the exercise is to punctuate a paragraph, to copy the entire paragraph is pointless. Indicating the words preceding the punctuation should be enough. It is better still to mimeograph the paragraph and punctuate directly on the mimeographed sheet.

For this very reason practice or drill should not be used unnecessarily. Teachers need to bear down on some things but not on others. If a teacher emphasizes the drill aspect too much, he runs the risk of making the class unnecessarily boring. *Hard practice should be reserved for important learning which needs to be habitualized or to be retained a long time.* In other words, one should concentrate practice on a few skills. Also, since memorizing is at best a dreary pastime, teachers should not demand that pupils memorize things that they need not remember. There are quite enough things a person should know by heart without loading pupils up with unnecessary memorization.[7]

WHEN DRILL IS NEEDED. In spite of the warning in the previous sections, teachers should not expect to eliminate all rote learning from their teaching. Some facts and abilities simply must be developed by direct attack and repetition. Among these are such things as idiomatic expressions, conjugations, chemical formulas, and mathematical facts. Historical dates provide an excellent example of such facts. Most dates in history can be taught by always associating the event with the date during the discussion. Other techniques, such as making time lines and time charts, are also available and valuable. However, in order to have a skeleton on which to hang historical events, pupils must learn key dates. These key dates must be taught directly once the pupils have learned their significance. To ensure that pupils learn them and retain

[7] By this we do not imply that pupils should never have an opportunity to learn a poem by heart for the pure pleasure of knowing it.

them, a few minutes at the beginning or end of the period might well
be given to practice on key dates several times a week.

✻

How might one adapt a spelling bee to give everyone plenty of
practice?

How can one avoid the poor attitudes that often accompany drill?

Why is it recommended that practice should always be under some
pressure?

✻

Individualizing Practice

If practice is to be really valuable to pupils, it should be individualized.
To find a practice exercise valuable and important to every teen-ager in
your class is virtually impossible. Almost invariably some of the pupils
will have mastered the skill to the point where it would be better for
them to move on to something else. On the other hand, other pupils
probably do not understand well enough so that they can truly benefit
from the practice at all. So, except for such things as military drill and
similar mass group exercises, group practice should be used sparingly.
Instead, practice should be tailor-made for each pupil.

To individualize practice is easier than it sounds. Since practice
ordinarily consists of experiences designed to strengthen learning that has
already been acquired, the teacher can leave much of the teaching to the
pupils themselves. By providing self-administering and self-correcting
materials and arranging situations in which pairs and small groups can
work together correcting and helping each other, the teacher can make it
possible for each pupil to arrange his own work so that he can concentrate on the practice most important to him.

For this reason diagnosis, particularly self-diagnosis, is an important
aid to effective practice. As the pupil realizes his weaknesses, he is more
likely to see the necessity for practice. Then, if his practice is rewarded
by visible progress, he may willingly redouble his efforts. Nothing is so
encouraging as success.

An example of such a practice technique was one used in the teaching
of ninth-grade grammar. In this class the teacher supplied the pupils with
a multitude of exercises designed to give practice in each of the areas
studied in grammar. Before studying each grammatical topic, the pupil
took a pretest to see how well versed he was in the area. If he scored
very high in the pretest, he could skip that topic and go on to another; if
he did not, he practiced the exercises for that topic until he thought he
had mastered the material. As he finished each exercise he corrected his
own work, sometimes consulting a teacher or a neighbor about why such

and such was so. When he thought he was ready, he tried another test. When he had demonstrated by the test scores that he was the master of that topic, he was allowed to move on to the next one. Of course, the teacher administered the tests and made himself available to help and guide the pupils with their practice. The result was a busy class working on those exercises which most concerned them.

The Project

A Definition

A project is a natural, lifelike learning activity involving the investigation and solving of problems by an individual or small group. Ideally it should consist of a task in which the pupil sets out to attain some definite goal of real value to him. As originally visualized, this goal seems to have been something tangible. Although this connotation is perhaps no longer essential, projects frequently involve the use and manipulation of physical materials and result in tangible products.

A classic example of such a project may be found in the agriculture projects in which pupils conduct farming enterprises such as raising a calf or a crop. A less ambitious project in an academic class might be making a scrapbook anthology for an English class, or an illustrated history of the life of the honeybee. An unusual group project reported from a Western high school is the building and selling of a house by a group of high-school apprentice pupils.

Selecting the Project

Ordinarily, the pupil should plan, execute, and evaluate the entire project himself. Even so, the teacher's role is important. He must help and guide the pupils. One of the more important ways he can guide them is in selecting a suitable project. Sometimes the teacher will find it necessary to provide a list of possible projects from which pupils can choose. Or he might suggest readings in which the pupils might find project ideas. Occasionally, he may be able to stimulate ideas for projects by a discussion of possible projects, or by a teacher talk about what others have done, or by a demonstration of former projects. An interesting device is to have members of previous classes act as consultants and tell the class about some of the projects completed in past years. Sometimes the teacher may need only to approve the plans formed by a pupil.

In any case, the teacher should approve a project before the pupil attempts it, for selecting projects requires sound judgment. The following criteria may help in selecting useful projects. The first of these is that *the project should consist of real learning activities.* Unless one is careful, projects sometimes may turn out to be mere busywork. Scrapbooks and picture collections quite often fall into this category. An example of a supposed project which was little more than busywork was a notebook for an English class which consisted of biographies of authors, copied from the appendix of the English textbook. Teachers should guard against this danger by continually asking themselves, "What learning will result from this project?"

Not only should the learning be valuable, *it should be pertinent to the course*. Because of their very nature, projects often include materials and activities from other subjects. Consequently, there is a constant danger that the project may get out of the field completely.

Another important criterion in the selection of projects has to do with time. The teacher should consider whether or not the *learning to be gained from a project is worth the time spent on it*. Not only must the amount of time be considered, but one must also decide whether the learning might be gained more economically in another way.

Other criteria the teacher and pupil should consider include *the availability and cost of materials and equipment necessary*.

Conducting the Project

Once the project has been selected and approved, the pupil is ready to proceed with it. As in any other activity, the teacher will find it necessary to help and guide the pupil as the latter attempts to carry out his plans. However, the pupil can carry a great deal of responsibility for executing them. He is also in a particularly good position to evaluate his own progress and its results. Consequently, the teacher should allow the pupil to accept a good share of this responsibility. Although the teacher should always be ready to help, he should be careful not to be too solicitous and thus stifle the initiative and ingenuity of the pupil.

An Example of a Good Project

One of the best examples of the project is one which took place in a science class in a Vermont school. In this class, the pupils were attempting to study the stars, although they had no telescope. One day, during a laboratory session, a pupil asked if it might be possible to build a telescope. The teacher answered that it could be done although it would be difficult. A conference followed and the pupil, with some friends, decided to attempt to build a telescope as a project. The first thing that they had to do was to find out how to construct a telescope, i.e., they had to find out how a telescope works, what materials are necessary in making one, and how these materials can be put together. Once they had acquired this information, the boys decided on the kind of telescope they wished to build and gathered the necessary materials. Then they put it together. Hours of work and seemingly insoluble problems were part of this project, but finally the boys assembled a usable telescope. After they got through using it, they presented the telescope to the school for use in science classes. The telescope is now being used by the pupils of that high school.

This project has all the essentials of a good project. The result was well worth the effort; it was realistic and lifelike; it consisted of problem-solving situations; and it was conceived, planned, and executed by the pupils under the guidance of the teacher.

✲

How might you use individual projects in your class? Group projects? Why is it sometimes said that directions for pupils may be too explicit?

✲

Summary

The activities described in this chapter are ones in which the pupil learns independently under the teacher's guidance, but not his domination. Nevertheless, the pupils need the teacher's help.

Most secondary-school boys and girls need to be taught how to study. The teachers of the various subjects are responsible for seeing that each pupil learns how to study his discipline. To this end each teacher will have to show pupils how to perform a number of scholarly skills, such as analyzing problems, taking notes, and picking the meat out of lectures. Much of this teaching can be done in giving the assignment.

Homework is a problem. One seldom knows how much and what kind of homework will be best. There is no virtue in giving too much homework. Some of the problems of how much homework to give can be solved by means of term assignments in writing. Probably the best kind of homework is that which reinforces old learning or which follows up work which has been well started in class. Giving brand-new work for homework may result in incorrect learning which must be untaught in class later. Because of friends' and parents' tendency to share in the homework process, the teacher should not place too much weight on it in evaluating the pupil. Still, written homework should always be checked.

Practice makes perfect. Secondary-school classes should allow plenty of opportunity for the repetition necessary to drive learning home. To be most effective, practice should be meaningful, varied, and as free from boredom as possible. To eliminate drudgery and to make practice efficient, one should individualize practice exercises and activities as much as possible after carefully diagnosing the needs of the individual pupils.

Ideally a project should consist of a task that the pupil sets for himself and then carries through to completion himself under the teacher's guidance. It should have intrinsic value to the pupil as well as being pertinent to the teacher's educational goals. Sometimes the projects are group projects, but whether group or individual, each project should be realistic, lifelike, and of innate value to the pupils, and it should be conceived, planned, and executed by the pupils under the teacher's guidance.

FOR FURTHER STUDY

BURTON, WILLIAM H., *The Guidance of Learning Activities*, Third Edition (New York: Appleton-Century-Crofts, Inc., 1962), Chs. 12, 19.

GRAMBS, JEAN D., WILLIAM J. IVERSON, and FRANKLIN PATTERSON, *Modern Methods in Secondary Education*, Revised Edition (New York: Holt, Rinehart and Winston, Inc., 1958), Ch. 11.

LEE, JAMES MICHAEL, *Principles and Methods of Secondary Education* (New York: McGraw-Hill Book Company, Inc., 1963), Ch. 10.

RIVLIN, HARRY N., *Teaching Adolescents in Secondary Schools* (New York: Appleton-Century-Crofts, Inc., 1961), Chs. 9–10.

STRANG, RUTH, *Guided Study and Homework*, "What Research Says to the Teacher," Number 8 (Washington, D.C.: National Education Association, 1955).

STEEVES, FRANK L., *Fundamentals of Teaching in Secondary Schools* (New York: The Odyssey Press, Inc., 1962), Ch. 7.

CHAPTER 12

Reading

Reading Activities

Books have two major functions in the school, as they have in life itself. They provide a source of information and ideas and, equally important, they are a source of enjoyment. The teacher should seek to emphasize both of these aspects in his teaching, for to be truly educated, pupils must learn to value books as a great treasury of learning and a great source of pleasure.

Every Teacher a Reading Teacher

THE READING PROBLEM. Every secondary-school teacher, no matter what his subject, must face up to the necessity for the teaching of reading in his classes.

Reading is a difficult skill that takes years to master. For most of us it is a skill we must continue to learn well into our adult lives. Even then, almost no one reads as well as he could. In the secondary schools, if Elizabeth Drews is correct, about one third of the pupils cannot read their textbooks.[1]

The reading problem becomes really acute in the junior-high-school years, because then the pupils are faced with more and more reading to do and less and less time to do it in. As the reading level becomes more difficult, the problem becomes greater. Faced with great amounts of reading material too hard for them to read, the pupils tend to become frustrated and bored. Some of them cope with this problem by dropping out of school as soon as they can. More than three times as many poor readers as good readers drop out of high school before graduation, most of them during the tenth grade.[2]

[1] Cited in *Reading Instruction in Secondary Schools*, Perspectives in Reading Number 2, International Reading Associates, Newark, Delaware, 1964, p. 32.
[2] Ruth C. Penty, "Reading Ability and High School Drop Outs," in M. Jerry Weiss, *Reading in the Secondary Schools* (New York: The Odyssey Press, Inc., 1961), p. 180.

DEVELOPMENTAL READING. It follows, then, that programs to continue the development of reading skill in junior and senior high school are necessary. To meet this need, secondary schools all over the nation are inaugurating reading programs. Presently these programs are of three kinds.[3]

One is the program that provides training for slow boys and girls who are doing as well as can be expected considering their ability and who need continued coaching in reading to develop their limited potential to the utmost. The second type of reading program is the program for boys and girls who for some reason have not learned to read properly, although their potential ability is average or even better than average. As a result of corrective programs some of these pupils make phenomenal gains and soon learn to read at their normal ability level. The third type of reading program is for the already good readers. This program attempts to improve pupils' already adequate skills and to carry each pupil along to higher competencies so that he will be a highly efficient reader who can make the utmost of his potential abilities.

It is the third of these types that has come to be known as the developmental reading program.

Remedial reading classes are usually taught in special classes or in reading laboratories; developmental reading programs are usually taught by classroom teachers. Probably the most satisfactory arrangement for developmental reading programs is a team approach in which one teacher, be it the reading teacher, the core teacher, or the English teacher, teaches the skills common to reading in all fields; the librarian teaches the library skills, and the various content teachers teach the reading skills necessary for their various subjects. In this connection, one should note that the block-of-time program lends itself well to developmental reading programs, because the block teacher has more time to learn the strengths and weaknesses of his students and teaches in a flexible organization, which lets him group his pupils, differentiate his material, and organize class time for various reading activities.[4]

M. Jerry Weiss has outlined five characteristics of a good developmental program.

1. Reading instruction must aim at individual students, taking into account their different backgrounds, abilities, and interests.
2. Flexibility of instruction depends upon the availability of a wide range of reading materials of all kinds and on all sorts of subjects. In an effective program much of the initiative passes to the student and the teacher's role changes to that of a guide, a "listener," a resource person, a critic.
3. Reading instruction means paying attention not only to the basic skills of

[3] Leonard H. Clark, Raymond L. Klein, and John B. Burks, *The American Secondary School Curriculum* (New York: The Macmillan Company, 1965), p. 197. By Permission.
[4] *Ibid.*

reading, but also to the general end which education should serve; the widening of the student's intellectual, emotional, and moral horizons.

4. Reading instruction is completely successful only when the student has acquired the habit of active continuous reading and can read with ease in all of the subject areas which, by necessity or choice, he faces.

5. The reading program is not the product of one teacher, but demands the involvement of the entire faculty and administration in a wholehearted and single-minded concentration on drawing the best possible work out of each student.[5]

SUBJECT MATTER READING. Specialized subject matter teachers should expect to do their share in the teaching of reading, because each discipline presents a reading program of its own. Each discipline has its own language with its own vocabulary. Moreover, reading in different disciplines requires different approaches. Reading a page of an algebra text differs markedly from reading a page of a novel! In addition, reading in certain disciplines requires specialized skills. Reading in history or geography requires some fluency with maps; mathematics reading assumes the ability to read equations. The only person competent and available to teach these special skills is the specialized subject matter teacher concerned. Of course, reading teachers may carry on part of the developmental reading programs by conducting classes in developmental reading designed to help the average pupil as well as special remedial classes for pupils who need special help in reading. Nevertheless, in almost any school under almost any system the brunt of a successful program of developmental reading—that is, the program designed to better the skills of normal readers—must fall on the subject-matter teachers for whose courses most secondary-school reading is done. Ordinarily the subject-matter teacher should teach these skills through the regular reading material used in the course.

Selecting a Textbook

Textbooks have always had an important place in the classroom. Because this is the case, the selection of good textbooks is essential. In some schools, the teachers choose the texts for their own classes. In other schools, committees of teachers select the texts. Only rarely do superintendents, principals, or boards of education select the textbooks. Even when texts are selected by state or city authorities, the teacher may have a choice among various possibilities. Consequently, he should be aware of what makes a good textbook, even though, at first, he will probably have to use texts that have been selected by his predecessors. The following questions may serve as a guide.

[5] M. Jerry Weiss, *Reading in the Secondary Schools* (New York: The Odyssey Press, Inc., 1961), p. 10. By permission.

1. What is the date of the copyright? Is the information and interpretation presented up to date?
2. Who is the author? Is he competent in the field? Does he write clearly and well?
3. Is the book suitable for the objectives of your course? Does it cover the proper topics with the proper emphases?
4. Are the topics arranged in a desirable sequence? If not, can the sequence be altered or portions omitted without disrupting the usefulness of the book?
5. Is the content accurate and accurately presented? Is the book free from bias?
6. Are the concepts presented clearly? Are they adequately developed with sufficient detail or is there a tendency to attempt to jam in too many ideas too compactly?
7. Is the vocabulary and language appropriate for the pupils of the class?
8. Does it presume background knowledge and experiences that the pupils do not yet have?
9. Does the author make good use of headings, summaries, and similar devices? Does he give opportunity for the readers to visualize, generalize, apply, and evaluate the content?
10. Are the table of contents, preface, index, appendices. and glossary adequate?
11. Does the book provide suggestions for use of supplementary materials?
12. Does it provide a variety of suggestions for stimulating thought-provoking instructional activities?
13. Are these suggestions sufficiently varied both as to level and to kind?
14. Does the author document his sources adequately?
15. Is the book well illustrated? Are the illustrations accurate, purposeful, and properly captioned? Are they placed near the text they are designed to illustrate?
16. Does the book have suitable maps, charts, and tables? Are they clear and carefully done? Does the author refrain from trying to cram too much data onto his maps and charts?
17. Is the book well made? Does it seem to be strong and durable?
18. Does the book look good? Is the type clear and readable? Do the pages make a pleasant appearance with enough white space?

ONE TEXT OR MANY READINGS? In many schools the basic problem in selecting a textbook is whether to use a single textbook, or to use several readings.

In general, the weight of the argument seems to favor the use of several readings. A single text can lend organization and order to a course. Frequently it is the sole source for a course plan readily available to the new teacher. On the other hand, the teacher should know his own class better than any authority writing behind the ivy-clad walls of a university. Therefore, the teacher is in a better position to select and organize the material for a particular group of pupils in a particular school than the textbook writer. In addition, when a teacher adopts a single text the class is limited to a single point of view, a single reading level, and a single style.

The use of several readings has the advantage of making it possible for pupils to read material suited to their abilities and needs. If a youngster is attempting to learn the contribution of Samuel Gompers to the labor movement, it matters little whether he searches for his information in the *Encyclopaedia Britannica,* a biography of Gompers, or a history of the labor movement, as long as he learns it as efficiently and effectively as he can. Since this is true, the teacher can help boys and girls pick books to study which are most suitable for their abilities and which may appeal to their interests. It is very difficult to provide adequately for individual differences if one limits the readings to one text only.

Another important possibility that presents itself in using many readings is the opportunity to read original sources. Textbooks often tell about things superficially. In many instances this treatment is justified because of the limitations of time and space, but certainly the pupil should be allowed to meet some of the originals face to face. The use of many readings makes this easily possible, especially now that much first-rate material is available in paperbacked editions.

Some teachers find it difficult to organize courses when many readings are used. If a teacher uses unit techniques and follows the procedures outlined in Chapters 5 and 7, this difficulty should be reduced. Another solution to this problem is to adopt one textbook as a basic reader and to supplement it with other readings. In any case, the key to the technique, when one uses many texts or readings, is to be sure that each youngster knows what he is seeking in his reading. For instance, in the example above, if the youngster does not know what he wants to find out about Gompers, his search in any book is likely to be fruitless. When many readings are used, the use of study guides such as the one appearing in Chapter 6, usually helps give the pupils direction.

*

How can one determine the suitability of a book's reading level for a particular pupil?

Why do authorities often condemn the use of only one text in the classroom? What is your position on this question?

If the pupils in your class do not all read the same readings, how can you ensure that they all have an opportunity to acquire the important learnings?

✼

USING LIBRARY MATERIALS. In order to teach in the way we think one ought to teach, pupils must have plenty of material to read. To make this supply of reading material readily available, each classroom should be a library. In this classroom library, all sorts of reading matter should be readily accessible to the pupil—periodicals, pamphlets, brochures, and the like, as well as books. For record-keeping a self-charging system with pupils acting as librarians from time to time may suffice. Usually one needs worry little about loss of material if such a system is used.

In addition to the classroom library one should make good use of the town and school libraries. While it is true that in some communities these libraries are rather scantily supplied, the librarians are almost invariably eager to cooperate with teachers. Teachers should make the most of this opportunity.

Few boys and girls, or men and women for that matter, use libraries well. Although instruction in the use of the library may ordinarily be the English department's responsibility, the teacher whose pupils use the library is also responsible to see that they use the library facilities efficiently. Librarians usually welcome the opportunity to explain library techniques either in the classroom or in the library. A visit to the library early in the year might well increase the efficient use of its facilities by the pupils.

Individualized Instruction

It has been said that the purpose of the textbook is to bridge the gap between the pupils' experience and knowledge and the concepts that they are going to have to master. Textbooks that can do this job are hard to find. No single textbook can do it for every member of a class. Therefore, it would seem that the only valid approach for a reading program is to match the readings and the readers in an individualized reading program. Where a truly individualized reading approach does not seem practical, then the next best thing would seem to be to divide the class into reading groups. The techniques for conducting such groups are discussed in Chapter 7. The reader may wish to consult that section at this point in order to fill out his understanding of the present discussion.

AN EXAMPLE OF INDIVIDUALIZATION. Individualized reading is based upon the assumption that pupils differ in reading ability and in background, and that pupils can acquire much the same information and

At best, reading is an individual matter and so most reading assignments in secondary-school subjects should be individualized.

concepts even though they may not read the same books or articles. Thus in the study of Ancient Man pupils with low reading ability might read such easy reading material as the Abramowitz pamphlet *World History Study Lessons,* while others read such difficult and esoteric material as the final chapter of Von Koenigswald's *The Evolution of Man.* Others might be reading in such varied works as Chapters 2 and 3 of Van Loon's *The Story of Mankind,* Ashley Montagu's *Man: His First Million Years,* a *National Geographic Magazine* article (e.g., Cynthia Irwin, Henry Irwin, and George Agogino, "Ice Age Man vs Mammoth," June, 1962, 121:828–836, or Thomas R. Henry, "Ice Age Man, the First American," December, 1955), *Life Magazine* articles on Ancient Man, or the Dell Visual paperback *Prehistory.* Or they might be reading the first unit "Days before History" in Hartman and Saunders text *Builders of the Old World,* or Chapter I of Black's textbook *Our World History.*

GIVING INDIVIDUALIZED READING DIRECTION. In any unit just what it is pupils read does not really matter as much as that they read

TECHNIQUES OF TEACHING

to attain certain objectives. These objectives are all grouped around the same theme—in this case prehistoric man. Each pupil is guided toward these objectives by the teacher's assignment, which should set for the pupil definite directions. In the above instance, he may have asked the reader of Von Koenigswald to find out how man developed his culture and what his first tools were like. He might ask similar questions of the pupils reading the Abramowitz material or of those reading Ashley Montagu. The pupils reading the *Life* or *National Geographic* articles might be searching for information about life among ice-age people— what the people ate, their hunting techniques, and more about their tools and weapons. And so on with the pupils reading other selections. The teacher could present the questions to the pupils orally as he gives the pupils their assignments or in conferences while they are working. Another way would be to prepare a dittoed or mimeographed study guide which would list the questions that the pupils ought to look for and suggest readings in which the answers might be located. Pupils could use these guides both to direct their study and as reference lists from which to select what they would read. An example of such a study guide appears in Chapter 6.

The teacher should act as a guide for individualized readings. On the basis of his knowledge of the pupils' reading ability, interests, background, and academic needs the teacher should suggest readings appropriate to individual pupils. Insofar as possible he should match pupil reading ability with the reading level of the selection to be read. However, he should not debar a pupil from reading or attempting selections that he might enjoy and profit from merely because the selection seems to be too hard or too easy. Pupils who bite off more than they can chew should be allowed to change if they find the work frustrating. The teacher should not let good readers make a habit of working below their level; it is better to suggest challenging assignments to them rather than to forbid them access to easy reading. After all, sometimes the easiest, simplest reading is the best. Common interests and purposes may cause considerable overlap in the reading of able and less able pupils.

✳

Using the criteria listed on page 274 as a basis, review several textbooks in your field. In what ways are they good? In what way bad? If you had a choice which would you adopt?

What advantages does the use of multiple readings have in the subject you wish to teach? What disadvantages? How would you use such a technique in the study of mathematics?

Prepare a list of readings for pupils of different reading levels for a topic in a course you might teach.

✳

Using Books Properly

Teaching the Use of Books

The effective use of books is not a skill that comes naturally. Pupils often seem to think that books are merely to be read, but the really effective use of books is not that simple. As Bacon says, "Some books are to be tasted, others to be swallowed, and some few to be chewed and digested."

Pupils need to learn how to determine which books to taste and which to chew, and how to perform each of these operations well. The criteria suggested in an earlier section should be helpful in choosing one's reading material. Boys and girls can learn how to use such criteria by class discussion and by application of the criteria to various books. They may even develop their own criteria as a group project. In general, let it be said here that reference works usually are designed to be scanned, fiction and some supplementary reading may deserve only to be skimmed, and that most textbooks must be chewed. In this connection, one should note that reading in science and mathematics texts almost always requires careful word by word concentration, whereas fiction quite frequently benefits from a blithe general overview in order to catch the flavor.

Learning to Skim

Some books should be chewed and digested; others should be merely tasted. We have tried to explain how to chew and how to digest a book in the section entitled Developing Reading Comprehension. The pupil should also learn how to taste, that is, skim, for skimming allows one to sample, to skip the old and become familiar with the new, to concentrate on the pertinent and brush over the irrelevant.

To learn to skim one needs to have, in the first place, a good background in the subject so that he can recognize the pertinent and the novel when he sees them. Having such a background, the pupil can glance through the preface and table of contents to see what the book is about. Perhaps he need go no further. Such a quick perusal may tell him that this book is not what he wanted. If the book seems pertinent to his problem, he may scan the book, reading the headings, introductory paragraphs, chapter summaries, and sample the opening, middle, and final paragraphs. When he finds a topic that seems provocative, he can read it carefully. Sometimes he will find that he must go back to read a previous section, but no harm is done because he is still reading only what is most essential or interesting.

To teach boys and girls to skim books effectively, teachers should first teach the techniques involved directly, and then follow up this teaching

with practice. An example of the type of practice useful for this purpose
follows.

1. In a class discussion decide what the class would like to learn from
   the chapter.
2. Let each pupil skim the chapter to see what it has to say on these
   points.
3. Discuss what the class has found in the chapter.

*

How does one determine when to skim and when to read carefully?
Can you think of any exercise games that one might use to teach
skimming?
Of what importance is the ability to skim in mathematics, in social
studies, in science?
Build some exercise games you might use to help pupils better to
understand a text in your field.

*

The Parts of the Book

Authors and publishers of textbooks go to considerable effort to provide the reader with help in using their texts. You might check through
your college texts to see what aids to learning have been included.
Among them you may find tables of contents, prefaces, chapter summaries, chapter introductions, chapter headings and subheadings, problems to be solved, charts, graphs, illustrations, sign-post sentences,
indexes, glossaries, and footnotes. Properly used, these devices can make
textbook study more efficient. Every pupil should know how to use them
and use them well.

TEACHING THE PARTS OF THE BOOK. One of the best ways to
teach pupils to use the parts of a book is actually to practice using them
in class when the class starts a new book. The teacher might develop the
lesson with questions and exercises such as the following.
"Where does one find what the book contains?"
"Examine the table of contents and see what the book is about."
"Now that we know what the book contains, what was the author's
purpose in writing it? Where can we find out?"
"What else can one find out in a preface? Let us read it and see. Does
this book seem good for our purposes?"
"How can the information we learned in the table of contents or the
preface help us in the study of this text?"
"Does it seem that this book is better for our purposes than other texts
available? How can you tell without reading the book?"

"Let us compare this book with some others we might use."

Similar exercises may be used to introduce the index and the glossary, until the teacher is sure that the pupils not only know how to use them but have acquired the habit. This, of course, means recurrent practice sessions. In each unit the pupils should have plenty of opportunities to look up things in the index. More than occasionally the teacher will find that the pupils have difficulty in using the index because they do not know the alphabet. For these pupils, special instruction and practice are necessary.

A good type of practice for pupils having trouble with alphabetizing consists of scrambling the words from a page in the dictionary and asking the pupils to put them in correct order. If the words are on cards it makes it much easier and saves time while being fully as effective. Pupils can also make their own lists and test other pupils. In such cases the pupil should first demonstrate his own ability to arrange his list properly before testing his peers. The teacher may have to teach directly how to find such things as "questioning, techniques of" and items that do not appear under the expected category but are listed in another.

THE PARTS OF THE CHAPTER. The parts of the chapter can be taught in a similar fashion. The teacher can ask the pupils to find· out what the chapter is about. This they can do by checking the subheads, and by reading the introductory section or paragraph, the summary, and the marginal notes. On the basis of this information the pupils can be expected to formulate questions of their own concerning what they might learn from the chapter and similarly from the sections. Continued practice with this sort of activity should help create a habit of reading with an inquisitive open mind.

✻

What skills and information does a pupil need in order to learn to use the library effectively?

If your school provided no classroom library, what would you do to provide suitable reading materials?

How much time should a biology teacher take to teach pupils how to use the parts of the biology textbook?

✻

CHARTS, GRAPHS, ILLUSTRATIONS. When reading, pupils frequently skip charts, graphs, and illustrations. This is unfortunate because the author includes these aids for a purpose. At times, they contain the meat of what the author is trying to say. They can clarify complex ideas and obscure points. Consequently, pupils should be taught to use these materials.

Many times the reason the pupils do not use charts, graphs, illustrations and similar materials is that they do not know how. When this is true, the teacher must correct the situation. Ordinarily he can best teach the use of such materials in the usual units of his courses rather than by introducing a separate unit on this topic. In his regular classwork the teacher can ask questions that require the pupils to refer to graphs, charts, or illustrations. Sometimes the questions can be pupil-made. When a pupil does not know how to use the chart, graph, or other aid, the teacher should show him how. At first much of this instruction should probably be group instruction; later it probably will become individual and remedial. In either case exercises like the following will prove useful.

Using the graphs taken from *Americas* as a basis (p. 283), answer the following questions.

1. Approximately how many Mexican movies in 1961 were produced entirely by Mexicans? How many by Mexico in collaboration with others?
2. Same for Argentina.
3. Same for Brazil.
4. In 1961 the U.S. produced 254 movies. How long would the bar representing U.S. film production be if we should add it to this graph? (The length of the bar representing Cuban movie production is one eighth of an inch. Cuba made three feature movies in 1961.)
5. According to the Inter-American Institute the information contained in Figure 6 is not strictly comparable. Why not?
6. How many times a year do you go to the movies? Do you go more or less frequently than the average American did in 1962?
7. In what country did the average person attend movies the fewest times? How often did he go? How could the average be less than one? Why do you suppose the people do not go to the movies more frequently in that country?

Vocabulary Building

A Responsibility of All Teachers

Every teacher is responsible for helping each pupil in building his vocabulary. This is true for science and mathematics teachers as well as for teachers of English. In order to ensure that their pupils' vocabularies are adequate, teachers should introduce the study of important key words early in the course and discuss other key words as they appear. The use of vocabulary lists and word games is helpful in building an adequate vocabulary.

FIGURE 6

Facts and Figures of the Americas*

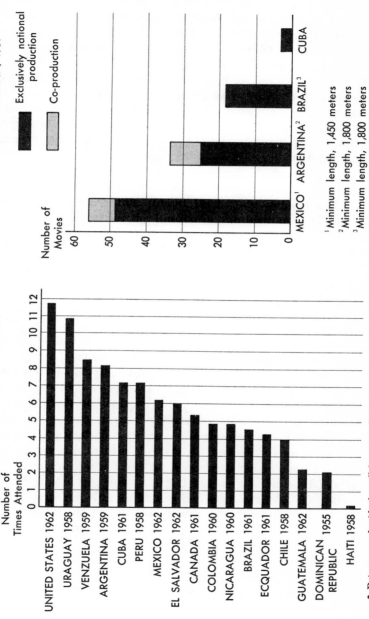

AVERAGE ANNUAL MOVIE ATTENDANCE
IN THE AMERICAS PER INHABITANT

PRODUCTION OF FULL LENGTH
MOVIES IN LATIN AMERICA, 1961

Exclusively national production

Co-production

Number of Times Attended

Number of Movies

MEXICO[1]   ARGENTINA[2]   BRAZIL[3]   CUBA

[1] Minimum length, 1,450 meters
[2] Minimum length, 1,800 meters
[3] Minimum length, 1,800 meters

UNITED STATES 1962
URAGUAY 1958
VENZUELA 1959
ARGENTINA 1959
CUBA 1961
PERU 1958
MEXICO 1962
EL SALVADOR 1962
CANADA 1961
COLOMBIA 1960
NICARAGUA 1960
BRAZIL 1961
ECQUADOR 1961
CHILE 1958
GUATEMALA 1962
DOMINICAN REPUBLIC 1955
HAITI 1958

* Data prepared with the collaboration of the PAU Department of Statistics and the Inter-American Statistical Institute, a professional organization coordinated with the OAS.

Reprinted from *Americas*, monthly magazine published by The Pan American Union in English, Spanish, and Portuguese, Vol. 16, October 1964.

USING WORDS IN CONTEXT. A common practice in vocabulary building is for the pupil to keep a notebook in which he compiles a glossary of terms useful in the course. If the teacher uses this technique, he should see to it that the pupils do not merely copy words and definitions in their notebooks. This practice usually amounts to little more than transferring the word from one page to another. What we want to do is to transfer the words into the pupil's mind. Consequently, exercises that force the pupil to use the word in context and to learn its meaning are preferable. Defining a word in one's own words is a difficult feat which sometimes serves these purposes admirably. Similarly, acting out words is sometimes a pleasant way to bring out the meaning. So are games and exercises in which one tries to find the closest synonyms. The best practice of all, however, seems to be actually to use the words frequently in the classroom in their natural context. With strange words one should, of course, check to see that each pupil knows what the word means. This can be done by asking pupils to explain the word's meaning. The really important part in any of these exercises is that they consist of meaningful practice.

＊

How can a teacher make a vocabulary notebook into a worthwhile learning experience?

＊

INTRODUCING NEW WORDS. Few teachers realize how many new words face the pupils in their assignments. Teachers of the various subjects must pay particular attention to teaching the new vocabulary of the lesson to come before the pupils begin to read it. In this respect the teachers must be sure not only that pupils recognize the word, but that they can attach the right meaning to the word as well. Quite frequently boys and girls can not match any reality to key words that teachers use in their lessons. Therefore, if pupils are to read these words with any understanding at all, teachers must see to it that the words are well explained before the pupils begin reading them. In this process the teacher should emphasize relationships and be sure that the pupils become familiar with the words both orally and visually, so that the words will have meaning to each pupil. There is no point in vocabulary study that is just a memory exercise.

DIRECT TEACHING. There should be direct teaching of vocabulary, however. Particularly important is the teaching of the technical meaning of words in the various disciplines. The word *root,* for instance, has greatly different meanings in language study, biology, and mathematics. Considerable attention should be placed on teaching pupils how to use suffixes, prefixes, and roots to analyze words and to build up meaning. Skill in this sort of word analysis is necessary in developing good meaningful science vocabularies since much of the nomenclature in scientific classification is a matter of considering roots with suitable prefixes and suffixes, for example, lepidoptera, hymenoptera, hemiptera, and homoptera are classes of insects whose wings (*ptera*) are scale (*lepido*), membrane (*hymen*), half (*hemi*), or all the same texture (*homo*).[6] In another instance Bamman points out that a boy who understands the *trans* of *transparent* has already won half the battle of understanding *translucent*.[7] Similar direct instruction is needed to help pupils identify words made up of two other words.

Particular care should be given to qualifying and transitional words, for these words set up the relationships in sentences and paragraphs. Soon, however, the pupil should be able to assume the burden for identifying and using such clues independently. On the other hand, idiomatic expressions and foreign words do not lend themselves to easy transfer. Teachers will always have to teach them directly, almost by rote.

Sometimes the direct teaching of the meaning of words can be made more interesting and meaningful by teaching the history of the words. Geneological charts showing the words' etymology can make interesting subjects for pupil bulletin boards. So can cartoons showing how suffixes and prefixes change the meanings of words. Other devices useful for making vocabulary study interesting are anagrams, crossword puzzles, and double crostics.

USING THE DICTIONARY. Probably the best aid to good vocabulary development, however, is the dictionary habit. Every pupil should have a dictionary of his own. Now that good, inexpensive editions like *The New American Webster Handy College Dictionary* are available in paperback editions, teachers should encourage each pupil to have a dictionary of his own, to carry it around with him, and to use it. In addition, teachers will find it necessary to teach junior-high-school pupils and some senior-high-school pupils how to use the dictionary. Among the skills one must teach, according to Jan Tausch, are the following.

The secondary student should be able to recognize alphabetical sequence, use guide words, identify root words in both inflected and derived forms, select the definition that fits the context, and realize the differing purposes of comma and semi-colon as used in dictionary meanings. He should be capable of using

[6] Henry A. Bamman, "Reading in Science and Mathematics," in *Reading Instruction in Secondary Schools*, Perspectives in Reading No. 2, International Reading Association, Newark, Delaware, 1964, p. 64.

[7] Henry A. Bamman, Ursula Hogan, and Charles E. Greene, *Reading Instruction in the Secondary School* (New York: David McKay Company Inc., 1961), p. 196.

the pronunciation key, the etymology key, and responding correctly to the accent mark. He should know that geographical and biographical information can be located in some dictionaries and understand also the limited nature of this information so that he uses it appropriately.[8]

Only when the pupil becomes familiar with the dictionary can one feel that he is well on his way to literacy.

Teaching Word Attack Skills

Because pupils in junior and senior high schools face a much larger vocabulary than that with which their elementary-school texts have made them familiar, they need to know how to decipher new and unfamiliar words. That is to say that they need skill in the use of phonetical and structural analysis and the use of context clues. Even though instruction in all of these skills is part of their elementary-school instruction, most boys and girls need additional instruction and practice before they are expert in them. Secondary-school teachers must provide this additional instruction. If you have not had professional training in the use and teaching of these skills, it would be wise for you to study the manuals and handbooks which accompany the basic reading series used in elementary schools, or a good text in the teaching of reading. The following discussion can do little more than hint at the ways in which the secondary-school teacher can help pupils learn to attack new words.

PHONETIC ANALYSIS.[9] Phonetic analysis refers to the processes of determining the sounds in words from an analysis of the letters of the words. Pupils possessing skill in phonetic analysis will be able to

1. Hear and recognize initial, final, and medial consonants.
2. Hear and recognize consonant blends.
3. Hear and recognize consonant digraphs.
4. Hear and recognize diphthongs.
5. Hear and recognize vowels.

Boys and girls who do not have these skills should practice them. For this purpose teachers should use elementary-school practice materials. In these exercises the pupils should first master the simple skills and then move to the more complex ones (for example, single consonants before blends). To ensure that the benefit of these exercises is not lost, teachers

[8] Evelyn Jan Tausch, "Teaching Developmental Reading in the Secondary School" in *Reading Instruction in Secondary Schools*, Perspectives in Reading No. 2, International Reading Association, Newark, Delaware, 1964, p. 52. By permission.

[9] This section is largely based on Henry A. Bamman, Ursula Hogan, and Charles E. Greene, *op. cit.*, pp. 94–102.

should take particular care to ensure that pupils have a chance to use the skills being developed in actual reading situations. Also, teachers should make provision for enough review and practice to maintain the skills once they have been mastered.

STRUCTURAL ANALYSIS. Structural analysis has to do with the parts of words that go together to make up each word's meaning. These parts include inflectional endings, prefixes, suffixes, roots, syllables, and so on.

Inflectional endings are particularly troublesome for some pupils. The often-encountered omission of inflectional endings from words in their writing and oral reading is evidence of the prevalence of this difficulty. Pupils who make such errors need to have their direction focused on inflectional endings through exercises in locating, pronouncing, and hearing them.

All pupils should understand how prefixes and suffixes are combined with roots to make new words. They should also recognize the most important prefixes and suffixes. Bamman, Hogan, and Greene[10] list two techniques that have been used very successfully for developing skill in using prefixes and suffixes and recognizing derived forms.

1. Select a root form and build a "family" of words, substituting and adding various prefixes and suffixes. Call attention to the fact that the meaning of the root form *does not change:*

voice	convocation
vocal	vocation
vocabulary	avocation
invoke	provoke
evoke	vociferous

2. Select a derived form and examine its components, calling attention to the meaning of each part. Ask the students to name other words which contain the components:

philosophy

*phil*anthropist	theo*sophy*
mis*anthropy*	pan*the*ism
*mis*ogamist	*Pan* American
big*amist*	anti-*American*
*bi*sect	*anta*gonist

In this connection perhaps it should be noted that the most common prefixes include, according to Stauffer, *ab, be, com, de, dis, en, ex, in* (into),

[10] *Ibid.,* p. 99.

in (not), *pre, pro, re, sub, un.*[11] The secondary-school teacher should be sure that his pupils know these prefixes. Diagnostic tests for this purpose would certainly seem to be in order.

SYLLABICATION. Similar analysis can be used to bring out the meaning of compound words to break words into syllables. Understanding of syllabication is essential for word attack skill. Boys and girls who can recognize syllables control knowledge that shows them how to break up words into components, and so to look at their various parts. Syllabication also gives pupils a key to pronunciation and so directly to meaning. To teach this skill teachers should make ample use of the dictionary and instruction on determining which syllables to stress. Much of this practice must of course be done orally. Hearing the syllables may be quite as important to the pupil as seeing them.

THE CONTEXT CLUE. Skillful adult readers probably identify most of the strange new words they encounter by the *context clues* which give away their meaning. Among these clues Bamman, Hogan, and Greene include the following, all of which the reader will undoubtedly recognize as old friends and allies.

1. Inference: the reader's experience helps him to infer the meaning:
   The heat from our big fire came in and we were as warm as *toast.*
2. Direct explanation:
   The specialist on snakes, a *herpetologist,* showed us the poisonous and nonpoisonous snakes.
3. Use of an antonym:
   Everyone was to travel light; *excessive* weight of baggage would handicap the expedition.
4. Figures of speech:
   I watched with dismay as I observed in his face a rush of *volcanic* violence from which I had seen strong men withdraw.
5. Situation, attitude, tone, or mood of a particular writing:
   They at first thought that the snakes were wooden ones, and there was a noticeable *recoil* when they realized the reptiles were really alive.
6. Summary statement:
   Windows buckled and splintered, walls tottered and crumbled, a roof sagged weirdly, and a terrifying sheet of flame crept greedily upward and upward toward the adjacent walls of the covent; it was a *holocaust* unparalleled in my childhood experiences.[12]

[11] Russell G. Stauffer, "A Study of Prefixes in the Thorndike List to Establish a List of Prefixes That Should Be Taught in the Elementary School," *Journal of Educational Research*, XXXV (February, 1942), pp. 453–58.

[12] Henry A. Bamman, Ursula Hogan, and Charles E. Greene, *op. cit.*, p. 101.

Teachers should point out to pupils how these context clues can be used and give them opportunities to use them. Usually, however, it will be difficult to provide exercises that can be used successfully with a large number of pupils. In the main these skills should be learned in the context of one's ordinary reading. When pupils run up against hard words they can apply these skills to them. Exercises in which pupils individually spot words they don't know as in the example by Elkins cited on page 295 are useful for this purpose.

✧

How can one make a vocabulary notebook a worthwhile learning experience?

Examine a few high-school textbooks. What helps do you find for teaching the vocabulary? Do you find many words that seem difficult for normal pupils? For slow pupils?

✧

Developing Reading Comprehension

One of the most difficult of skills seems to be to read a selection in such a way as to glean the ideas the author was trying to present. William G. Perry[13] tells us that out of 1500 Harvard and Radcliffe freshmen assigned to read a certain chapter in a history book only one in one hundred was able to glean the sense of the chapter well enough to write a short statement on what the chapter was about. *Ninety-nine per cent of these Harvard and Radcliffe freshmen had not learned to read for comprehension well enough in their twelve years of college preparation to complete this simple task.* That secondary-school teachers should exert more effort to teach pupils to read for comprehension more skillfully seems self-evident.

READING COMPREHENSION SKILLS. One uses many skills in reading. The lists of comprehension skills that appear in professional books and articles are frequently long and sometimes overwhelming. Niles, however, says that these skills can be reduced to "three skills, or abilities, which, . . . clearly differentiate between the reader who comprehends well and the reader who does not."[14] These skills are "(1) the ability to

[13] William G. Perry, Jr., "Students' Use and Misuse of Reading Skills: A Report to the Faculty," *Harvard Educational Review*, Summer, 1959, 29:193–200; cited in Olive S. Niles, *Improvement of Basic Comprehension Skills: An Attainable Goal in Secondary Schools*, A Scott, Foresman Monograph on Education (Chicago: Scott, Foresman and Company, 1964), p. 4.

[14] Olive S. Niles, *op. cit.*, p. 5.

observe and to use the various and varied relationships of ideas," for example, time, listing, comparison-contrast, cause and effect, "(2) the ability to read with adjustment to conscious purpose, and (3) the ability to make full use of the substantial backlog of real and vicarious experience which almost every reader, even the beginner, possesses." Many exercises for teaching skill in reading comprehension are available. Usually the regular textbook can and should be used for such practice exercises. The following are only a few of many possibilities. The teacher should ask the pupil to read a paragraph and then tell what it means. He should explain the meaning of key words and key sentences, paragraph leads, and topic sentences, and give the pupil practice in finding them. As soon as the pupil has learned to get the meaning out of paragraphs, the same procedure should be repeated with sections and later with chapters. Exercises of this sort can be made more interesting by using, among other things, games in which one attempts to reproduce the author's outline, by dramatizing the main ideas of a selection, by turning a book into a TV drama, and by boiling down a paragraph or section into a telegram with, of course, a penalty for any word over the limit. Sometimes these activities should be made to include the entire class. However, boys and girls who have mastered these skills and use them well should not be required to do the same exercises as pupils who have not yet learned them. The teacher can expect to find both good pupils and poor ones among those who need help in these skills.

READING IN QUESTIONS. The question is the key to learning reading comprehension skills. To learn to comprehend we must learn to read with open, inquisitive minds. It is because of the need to encourage this frame of mind that the following procedure is recommended for studying a chapter or similar reading.

1. Survey the chapter.
2. Determine what one can expect to learn in the chapter. State as questions or a question outline.
3. Read the chapter to find the answers to the questions.
4. Evaluate what has been read.
5. Apply the information to specific situations or problems.
6. Review by asking oneself the original questions.
7. Reread quickly (skim).

The heart of the method just discussed is asking oneself questions before, during, and after one's reading. Teachers should encourage such self-questioning in their pupils. At first, however, the teacher may need to do the questioning directly, either orally or by means of a study guide. If the reading were to be about the prehistoric men mentioned earlier in the chapter, for instance, one might ask the pupils to look for the answer to such questions as the following.[15]

On page 8 the author implies that prehistoric man was probably just as smart as modern man. What evidence do you find to support that statement?

What does the author think of prehistoric art? Do you agree with him?

In what respect do prehistoric man's achievements seem to foreshadow those of modern man?

What kinds of religious beliefs did prehistoric man seem to have? How can you explain why he had these beliefs?

Trace the development of his tools. What do the types of tools tell us about prehistoric men of various periods?

If you were to pick the one general idea as the main idea presented in this selection, what would it be?

Another technique that may be useful for developing searching attitudes in pupils is to develop the questions together in a discussion before starting on the readings. Such a discussion might be launched by the teacher's asking a question like "What do you think you want to find out from this reading?" or "What do you think that the reading might tell you?" In the case of the prehistoric men again, pupils might want to know about such things as

What did prehistoric men eat?
How did they get their food?
Where did they live?
Did they believe in God?
What did they wear?
What did they do for recreation?

As such questions are developed in class discussion they could be put on the board by a pupil recorder. Then, if one wishes, these questions could be made into a formal list or study guide. In some instances at least, it would probably be better to let individual pupils adapt these questions to their own use, each one taking as many, or as few, as seems desirable for him for his own questions, adding other questions if he wishes.

Another approach would be for the pupils to write down what they expected to learn from the reading. Their lists would be used as the basis for class discussion, or could be checked over by the teacher for approval and possible additional suggestions, before beginning the reading. This approach is good when pupils' reading is individualized. Or-

[15] These questions are based on Paul Hogarth and Jean-Jacques Salomon, *Prehistory—Civilization Before Writing*, Visual Series No. 6 (New York: Dell Publishing Company, Inc., 1962), pp. 7–9, 40–81.

dinarily, pupils should get the teacher's approval of their questions before they start reading. It is not wise, however, to hold up a pupil who is ready to read just because the teacher has not had time to approve his questions. When he is ready to go, let him proceed under temporary clearance. The checking can come later. In determining the questions to be asked the pupil can benefit much from knowing how to use the guides and aids put in the text by the author.

The questions asked should not be just questions of fact. Let them instead put emphasis on relationships: Why? How? So what? Of what importance is this? What's the point? These are the kinds of questions that will bring out ideas. Aim the questions at the big ideas, not the details. Perhaps the first main question in every list should be "What was the idea that the author wanted to get across?" And probably the second question should be "What details did he use to try to get this idea across to his readers?" These same questions should be asked in the pupils' tests also, because it is by test questions that pupils determine what learning the teacher really values.

Questions are useful for developing comprehension skills only when they are asked *before* the pupil starts reading. One of the reasons that pupils do not learn to comprehend better is that neither they, nor their teacher, think to ask the questions beforehand. Asking questions afterward will merely tell whether or not one has understood; it will not help pupils develop skill in comprehending. The time for the reader to be active and alert is during the reading.

SIX STEPS FOR IMPROVING COMPREHENSION. Fehr[16] has suggested six steps for improving comprehension in mathematics. Bamman[17] has adapted these steps to include both mathematics and science. In the latter form the steps make a good summary of the measures necessary to teach reading comprehension in any subject. They are

1. Help the student adopt a problem consciousness.
2. Develop wide experience and broad background in mathematics and science situations.
3. Activate the problem.
4. Help students ask meaningful questions.

[16] Howard F. Fehr, "Teaching High School Mathematics," *What Research Says to the Teacher,* Pamphlet No. 9, Department of Classroom Teachers and American Educational Research Association (Washington, D.C.: National Education Association, 1955), pp. 24–25.

[17] Henry A. Bamman, "Reading in Science and Mathematics" in *Reading Instruction in Secondary Schools,* Perspectives in Reading No. 2, International Reading Association, Newark, Delaware, 1964, pp. 66–67.

5. Become sensitive to the student who is using an unsuccessful attack on the problem.
6. Generalize the solution to every problem.

✿

Do the six steps developed by Fehr and Bamman apply to social studies or literature? Why, or why not?

Try reading a college assignment with the use of questions and without them. Which seems more beneficial?

✿

Reading Critically

EVALUATING WHAT ONE READS. "All that glitters is not gold," and all that is printed is neither true nor good. Unfortunately, many young people seem to have considerably more respect for the written word than is warranted. More than one high-school pupil bases his faith on the fact that it is "in the book." Often these pupils become sadly confused when they find that what the book says is not necessarily true. Teachers should take it upon themselves to ensure that their pupils learn to read critically and to evaluate what they read.

HOW TO EVALUATE ONE'S READINGS. How does one teach pupils to evaluate their readings? One technique is to give the pupils plenty of practice. When several readings are part of each pupil's task in the various units, he soon becomes aware of the differences of opinion that exist. So perhaps the first step is to give the pupil different readings about the various topics, to consider carefully the differences of opinion, and to discuss why these differences exist.

Another step in evaluating one's reading is to try to establish the difference between fact and fancy. Early in life pupils should learn that some things are fact and some are fiction. Teachers can teach pupils how to determine the difference between fact and opinion by asking them such questions as: Is that so? How do you know? How can you check? Is this true or does the writer merely think so?

In their attempts to distinguish fact from fancy, pupils also should learn to look for signs of bias in the writer. Assignments asking them to check their reading for such things as sensationalizing, emotionality, easy sweeping statements, disregard for facts, and loaded words will help familiarize the pupils with some of the signs of bias. Another check is to examine the writer's documentation. If the writer refers only to old works or works that are in disrepute, probably he has not documented his work carefully. The writer who argues from anecdotes should also be distrusted. Single, isolated cases introduced into the context with the implication that they are typical are often false documentation.

Arguing from anecdote is an example of writing that violates the rules of logic. When teaching pupils to evaluate their reading, teachers should teach them to apply the test of logic to all they read. A technique useful in introducing the application of the rules of logic is to discuss violations of logic in their reading or in television materials. For instance, a television commercial implies that one gasoline is better than another because it is made in a refinery that can make its entire product 100 plus octane gas. Why does this not make good sense? Or again, one reads that a certain athlete smokes Bippos. Is this any reason why anyone else should? What does he know about it? Material of this sort can be used to teach the more obvious breaches of logic. As pupils become familiar with these errors, they can apply these tests to magazine articles and other readings.

DANGER OF POLEMICS. Pupils should also be wary of polemics, propaganda devices, and other attempts to persuade. Newspapers "Letters to the Editor" and editorials often provide excellent examples of political polemics that lend themselves to classroom instruction in critical reading. Examples of such slanted material can be found in almost any newspaper any day. Teachers can utilize them by giving pupils individual study assignments or by projecting them via the opaque projector or, after making a transparency, the overhead projector. In either case the teacher might ask the pupils to analyze the selections and to answer such questions as: Do they contain any of the faults of logic? Is the presentation just? If not, why not? Can you find instances of loaded words and other propaganda devices?

Exercises of this sort and others that the teacher may devise should help give pupils skills in evaluating. Moreover, they can be expected to encourage a questioning attitude in the pupil. It is hoped that after such teaching he will not swallow things, but will read with an active awareness of the snares of misinformation and poor logic, and also be inclined to test any idea before he gulps it down.

STYLISTIC CRITICISM. Reading critically also includes being alert to style and skill in writing. Does the style serve the thought? Is it appropriate? Does the writing bring out or obscure the meaning? Does it bring out or obscure the feelings? Does the author use symbolic language? If so, how does he use it? What does he mean to imply by means of his symbols? Are his methods effective? Any reading that brings out the answers to such questions is critical reading.

So also is any reading that results in the pupils' questioning or actively thinking about the values or implications of what they read.

Especially important is the reading experience that helps to make the pupil react creatively—by drawing an illustration, by acting out the scene, by being the catalyst for making up an original poem, story, or ballet. Teachers should provide for such reactions by giving the pupils plenty of opportunity to evaluate, question, discuss, and think about what they read to encourage creative responses of all sorts.

Oral Reading

Reading aloud is considerably neglected by teachers in modern secondary schools. This neglect is unnecessary and unwise, particularly in view of the amount of excruciatingly painful oral reading that we find in some classrooms. Subject-matter teachers of all subjects who use oral reading in their classes should take time to help pupils to read better orally. Such help is necessary no matter whether the purpose of the reading is artistic (as in the reading of poetry or drama), or practical (as in reading a passage from a geography textbook).

Oral reading is not synonymous with sight reading. It is quite doubtful whether anyone really benefits from the agonizing attempts of unprepared pupils to plow through difficult material they have not read. Oral reading requires reading for effect. Therefore, pupils should always have an opportunity to read the material through silently first, so as to get some idea of the phrasing and to master the pronunciation of the strange words. Once they are ready, they should be encouraged to read in front of the class.

Before they are really prepared to read orally, however, the pupils need considerable practice. Narrative material seems to be best suited for oral reading practice. Most pupils need to have considerable help in learning to read naturally, in smooth thought units. In this respect the tape recorder can be used to a great advantage. From it a pupil can hear how he sounds naturally and how he sounds when reading. Thus he can get cues to help him improve his phrasing, emphasis, and cadence. Another common device to help pupils improve their phrasing is to have them underline the thought units in the selection they are to read. Sometimes the oral reading practice can best be done by pairs. An example in which the use of the first five minutes of each core class was routinely used for oral reading in duets is reported by Deborah Elkins.[18]

There are times when children can share something with only one other classmate. This became evident in one routine procedure which teachers found very fruitful—the use of the first five minutes of every core session for oral reading in "duets." Each child had an outside reading book on his own level,

[18] Deborah Elkins, *Reading Improvement in the Junior High School* (New York: Bureau of Publications, Teachers College, Columbia University, 1963), p. 41.

whether it was on the Westward Movement or fantasies for young children or an adventure story. In the adventure-story sequence children were trying to come to some conclusion about what constituted adventure. Did you have to risk your life? Was there adventure in every-day life? Was the same experience adventure for everyone? A standard homework assignment was reading from that book every night. Each child had a mimeographed chart on which he made certain entries.

Then he prepared the paragraph he liked best for reading to his classmate. After reading to his classmate he entered two or three words in the proper column, words he would like to be able to recognize more readily. This work was begun as soon as the children entered the classroom, even while the teacher was on hall duty. Any questions were referred to the teacher. As soon as the teacher returned he circulated around the room, listening, advising, noting progress, making comments of encouragement on the charts wherever this was warranted. In other words, at the start of each day, every child had a chance to read aloud and be heard, and the time consumed was only five minutes.

Speed Reading

For the last few years there has been much flurry about reading rapidly and efficiently. As a result many schools are conducting training in speed reading for their pupils. Possibly they should, because the average pupil does not read as rapidly as he might and the amount of print one has to get through in our modern society is staggering. On the other hand, the criterion for judging one's reading effectiveness is not so much how fast he reads, but how well he understands what he reads.

Good readers adapt their reading speed to what they are reading and their purpose in reading it. Poor readers tend to read everything at about the same rate. Classroom teachers, then, should concentrate on helping pupils learn how to adapt their reading attack to the situation. Most reading in science and mathematics, for instance, requires slow, careful study. So does studying the rule book in the physical education class, but reading in mathematics classes seldom calls for skimming or scanning, while in physical education classes one might well want to use these skills frequently to spot rules applicable to specific situations.

Summary

In spite of many changes, reading remains the heart of the secondary-school curriculum. Therefore, every teacher should consider himself to be a teacher of reading. Although reading specialists may teach remedial programs and courses for slow learners, the subject matter teacher must assume responsibility for developmental reading in his subject.

Selecting the proper reading material is essential. Probably no one text can ever be adequate. To utilize many readings in their classes and to develop techniques for individualizing instruction would usually be more satisfactory. For this reason, full use of the library and the development of classroom libraries is essential.

Boys and girls must be taught how to use books effectively and efficiently. They need to know how and when to skim, how and when to read closely, and how to use the aids provided by the author and publisher. The subject teacher must also help pupils to develop their vocabularies and to read for comprehension. Part of his job is to point out new words and ideas and to suggest methods by which the pupil can get the most from his reading. But most important of all is his obligation to teach pupils to read critically with open minds. For pupils to learn to evaluate what they read is just as important as their learning to read with understanding.

Oral reading has been neglected in the secondary schools. If pupils are to be asked to read orally, they should be taught how. On the other hand, teachers must be wary of fads which cause us to emphasize the wrong objectives in our teaching. A recent example is the fad for speed reading. Going through a book quickly is not always a valid goal. Rather, the pupil should learn to adapt his reading attack to the material to be read.

FOR FURTHER STUDY

BAMMAN, HENRY A., URSULA HOGAN, and CHARLES E. GREENE, *Reading Instruction in the Secondary School* (New York: David McKay Company, Inc., 1961).

BARBE, WALTER B., *Teaching Reading: Selected Materials* (New York: Oxford University Press, 1965).

BLAIR, GLENN MYERS, and WILLIAM POWELL, *Diagnostic and Remedial Teaching*, Second Edition (New York: The Macmillan Company, 1967).

BUTMAN, ALEXANDER, DONALD REIS, and DAVID SOHN, *Paperbacks in the Schools* (New York: Bantam Books, Inc., 1963).

ELKINS, DEBORAH, *Reading Improvement in the Junior High School* (New York: Bureau of Publications, Teachers College, Columbia University, 1963).

GUNN, AGNELLA (editor), *What We Know About High School Reading* (Champaign, Illinois: National Council of Teachers of English, 1958).

HAFNER, LAWRENCE E., *Improving Reading in Secondary Schools: Selected Readings* (New York: The Macmillan Company, 1967).

HENRY, NELSON B. (editor), *Development In and Through Reading*, Sixteenth Yearbook of the National Society for the Study of Education, Part I (Chicago: The University of Chicago Press, 1961).

KARLIN, ROBERT, *Teaching Reading in High School* (Indianapolis: The Bobbs-Merrill Co., 1964).

NILES, OLIVE S., *Improvement of Basic Comprehension Skills: An Attainable Goal in Secondary Schools*, A Scott, Foresman Monograph on Education (Chicago: Scott, Foresman and Company, 1964).

Reading Instruction in Secondary Schools, Perspectives in Reading No. 2, International Reading Association, Newark, Delaware, 1964.

WEISS, M. JERRY, *Reading in the Secondary Schools* (New York: The Odyssey Press, Inc., 1961).

PART V

The Materials of Instruction

CHAPTER 13

Audio-Visual Materials

MARK HOPKINS could conduct a school merely by sitting on one end of a log. Most teachers need more material than that. In fact, for most teachers the more materials available the better they can teach. This chapter and the one following will discuss some of the materials that are available and how they may be used to aid instruction.

The Use of Audio-Visual Aids

Among the host of materials waiting to be used by the teacher are audio-visual aids of all sorts—films, film strips, pictures, maps, globes, charts, models, graphs, mock-ups, terrain boards, snapshots, slides, opaque projection, microprojector, overhead projectors, microscopes, chalkboards, phonograph records, sound tapes, radio, television, dramatizations, and *realia*. This list is not exhaustive. Perhaps you can add to it. With such an abundance of material, the problem becomes how to find what is best for our uses and how to best use what we select.

Purpose of Audio-Visual Aids

The term "audio-visual aids" is an appropriate one because it describes just what they are—aids to teaching and learning. Audio-visual aids cannot substitute for real teaching, however. They have an entirely different role, a powerful role, it is true, but a role in support of teaching. If one thinks of them and uses them as teaching tools, he will not go far wrong.

Audio-visual aids can help make ideas and concepts clear. As an earlier chapter points out, verbalism is one of the banes of the American secondary school. Audio-visual aids can help raise learning from verbalism to true understanding. The words "rubber bogey buffer bumper" may mean little to the reader, but, if he should see a picture or model of one, or watch one in operation in a moving picture, the words would probably become meaningful. Making words and phrases real is the greatest potential of audio-visual devices.

Audio-visual aids can also make learning interesting and vivid. A Chinese proverb tells us that one picture is worth a thousand words. Whether or not this is true, good audio-visual aids have eye and ear appeal. By snaring our attention they make learning more effective. Audio-visual aids can be invaluable in promoting motivation and retention.

Using Audio-Visual Aids Properly

In a suburban school a beginning teacher surprised the supervisor by asking, "Is it all right to use film strips for my American history class?" "Of course," he replied, "Why not?" "Well," she said, "I tried one last week and the class gave me a lot of trouble. They seemed to think the film strip was kid stuff and they acted up something terrible." Yet that same day the supervisor had visited a class—supposedly a class of the toughest youngsters in the school—where the teacher, who was using a film strip in science, had excellent interest and attention. The difference seemed to be that one teacher expected the film strip to teach itself; the other was really teaching with the film strip as an aid.

Audio-visual aids cannot teach by themselves. They need skillful teaching to make them effective. Just like any other instructional activity, audio-visual aids should be an integral part of the total plan selected because they seem best suited for that point in the lesson. And, as with any other activity, the teacher must prepare the class for the audio-visual activity, guide the class through it, and follow up after its completion.

*

Why is it impossible to substitute audio-visual aids for good teaching?

A certain school always presents moving pictures to all its children on Friday afternoon. Criticize this practice.

*

SELECTING THE AUDIO-VISUAL AID. In selecting an audio-visual aid, a teacher should consider, in addition to its suitability, such things as visibility, clearness, level of understanding, ease of presentation, and availability of material. To be sure that the aid is effective and appropriate, the teacher should try it out before using it with the class. This is particularly important in selecting films, film strips, and recordings and in presenting demonstrations. Sometimes films and recordings seem to have little resemblance to their descriptions in the catalog, and a demonstration that does not come off is literally worse than useless.

PREPARING FOR THE AUDIO-VISUAL ACTIVITY. Before using an audio-visual activity, the teacher must prepare the pupils for it. This he can do by introducing the audio-visual material. Sometimes a short

Moving pictures like other audio-visual materials must be introduced, explained, and followed up.

sentence identifying the aid and its purpose will suffice. At other times, he should spend considerable time discussing the purpose of the activity and suggesting how the pupils can get the most from it. The introduction to a moving picture or a film strip, or a recording should point out this purpose and suggest points that pupils should watch for in their viewing or listening.

Not only must the teacher prepare the pupils for the activity, he must also prepare the activity itself. Nothing can be more embarrassing or more disruptive than movies that do not move, demonstrations that do not demonstrate, and other audio-visual fiascos. The competent teacher checks the little things. Does he have enough chalk? Are there extra fuses? Can everyone see the poster? Will the machine run? Attention to detail is particularly important in preparing for an audio-visual activity. More than one class has been upset by the lack of a piece of chalk, an exciter lamp, or an extension cord.

Care in preparation is particularly necessary when using projectors and other audio-visual machines. This type of equipment is effective and convenient but hardly foolproof. Before using such devices, the teacher should be sure to check everything possible. If he is going to use slides or transparencies, he should be sure that they are all there and in order. If he is going to use a tape recorder or movie projector, before the class starts he should check out the machine, be certain that it runs properly, and that it is properly adjusted. To be sure that the pupils can see and hear, he should try everything out under conditions similar to those he expects in the class.

GUIDING PUPILS THROUGH AUDIO-VISUAL ACTIVITIES. Instead of relieving the teacher of his responsibility for guiding pupils' learning, the use of the audio-visual aids gives him an opportunity to make his guidance more fruitful. In order that the pupils get the most from the audio-visual aid, the teacher should point out to the pupils what to look for and what to listen for. Often it may be necessary for the teacher to explain to the pupils what they are seeing or hearing. To do this, the teacher would do well sometimes to provide the pupils with a list of questions or a study guide to direct their attention. On other occasions, he should stop to discuss vital relationships on the spot.

✿

Suppose you order a film from an audio-visual center and when it arrives it turns out not to be what you had expected. What would you do?

If you were to order a film for a class in your field, what criteria would you use in your selection?

✿

FOLLOWING UP AUDIO-VISUAL ACTIVITIES. In spite of the appeal and vividness of audio-visual aids, they cannot prevent some pupils from misunderstanding or missing part of the instruction. The teacher should follow up the activity to bridge the gaps and to clear up misunderstandings. Follow-up also renews the learning and thus increases retention. Furthermore, it has motivational aspects. One danger in using films, film strips, television, and radio is that pupils sometimes think of these activities as recreational, and so give scant attention to them. If a teacher follows up activities featuring such audio-visual aids with discussion, review practice, and testing, he can usually correct this misapprehension and also point up and drive home the learning desired.

Using Different Kinds of Aids

Chalkboards, Bulletin Boards, Flannel Boards, and Charts

Now that we have discussed the proper use of audio-visual material in general, let us consider how to use some of them in particular. Perhaps the most commonplace of all audio-visual aids is the old-fashioned blackboard or its brighter modern counterpart, the chalkboard. This device is so omnipresent that many of us fail to think of it as an audio-visual aid at all; yet most teachers would be hard put if they had no chalkboards available.

Closely akin to the chalkboard are bulletin boards, flannel boards, and charts. The chalkboard and flannel board are more flexible and versatile than the bulletin board and charts, although charts can be made more flexible by covering them with transparent acetate and writing on the acetate with china marking pencils. Similarly, large pieces of newsprint, cardboard, or wrapping paper can be used to draw and write on in the same manner as on a chalkboard. Chalkboards and flannel boards can best present material to be exhibited for a short time, while bulletin boards and charts may be used for more permanent exhibits.

CHALKBOARD TECHNIQUES. Perhaps because the chalkboard is so familiar, teachers seem to be careless of their chalkboard techniques. Good chalkboard techniques do exist; they apply also to bulletin boards, flannel boards, and charts. Teachers should remember to use these tools properly.

The first point in the use of the chalkboard is that people cannot learn much from a visual aid they cannot see. It is important for teachers to write legibly, to use portions of the board within the pupils' range of vision, to write large, and to stand out of the pupils' line of sight. In passing, one might add that pointers are useful tools. They do not obstruct the view nearly as much as an arm, a shoulder, or a back.

A second point is that a neat, orderly board aids learning, whereas a cluttered board can be distracting. To get the best out of a chalkboard, bulletin board, or chart, it should be neat and orderly with plenty of "white space" so that the material to be learned or studied will stand out. Crowding materials on a board makes it unattractive and confusing. In the use of bulletin boards, neatness and attractiveness are extremely important, and here especially the teacher should strive for an uncluttered look. Bulletin boards and charts are more effective if they are arranged simply and tastefully.

To achieve a neat, uncluttered appearance and to reduce distractions, teachers should remove things from the chalkboards and bulletin boards as soon as they are no longer necessary. Courtesy demands that when you vacate the room for another teacher, you leave the chalkboards clean and orderly. Most teachers object to cleaning up after others. Can you blame them? If one must leave something on the board, the courteous thing is first to ask the permission of any other teachers who use the room, and then to use a panel that would not be in their way. When one wishes to use the chalkboard it is most irritating to find a panel or two covered with "Please do not erase" signs.

EMPHASIZING THE IMPORTANT. In order to capture the pupils' interest and direct it toward the salient point, teachers should try to arrange each bulletin board and display so that the observer's eye automatically travels toward the center of interest around which the display is focused. One can facilitate this focus by keeping the board or display free from extraneous material, by centering the most significant portion of the display, and by using lines, real or imaginary, to direct the attention from the subordinate items to the central items. Titles and captions are also extremely helpful in putting the central idea across.

Another technique that keeps down distraction is to cover material prepared for display later in the lesson. When this is not done, pupils are liable to pay more attention to aids planned for later use than to the lesson in progress. This procedure can be made even more effective by covering the different sections of a chart or display in such a way that one can uncover one section at a time as it is needed. With a little imagination the teacher can make the procedure highly vivid and dramatic. One can get the same effect with an overhead projector by gradually uncovering the transparency or by adding flip-ons. Another variation is the flip chart which consists of a large pad of sheets that can be flipped over out of the way to reveal new material as the class proceeds.

The same effect can also be obtained by proper use of the flannel board or the hook-and-loop board. With these devices the technique is to prepare materials ahead of time, and then at the propitious moments in the class presentation magically stick them onto the board.

In any case it should be axiomatic that one must avoid covering the boards with vivid material and then lecturing in the face of this distraction. On the other hand, in a classroom laboratory the material should be available so that pupils can consult it whenever necessary.

MAPS, GRAPHS, AND OVERLAYS. Among the charts we may use in our classes are maps and graphs. Although techniques for teaching with maps and graphs are the same as for other types of charts, their use is often ineffective because the pupils do not understand how to read them. The teacher must be sure to teach the language and symbols of graphs and maps to the pupils who do not understand, or the aid will be worthless to them.

The use of overlays can also make the use of charts and maps more effective. An overlay is simply a sheet of transparent material that can be laid over the map or chart so that one can write on it without injuring it. Good ones have been made out of plastic bags such as those used by dry cleaning establishments,[1] old plastic table cloth covers, plastic drop

[1] Very thin plastic sheets such as those used by dry cleaners are difficult to cut. To avoid this trouble, place the plastic on a sheet of paper—newspaper will do—and then cut both with shears. The paper adds enough bulk and stiffness so that the shears will cut the plastic easily.

cloths, and the like. Individual overlays may be used with the maps and charts in books and magazines. The overlay may be preprinted or developed as the class moves along by writing on the plastic with a china marking pencil (grease pencil), or with a felt-tipped marking pen.

Similar results can be obtained by projecting maps and charts on to a chalkboard. Then additional detail can be filled in on the chalkboard itself. This technique is not quite as flexible as the overlay in the opinion of some practitioners.

✻

Observe the board work of your teachers and fellow students. What makes it effective? What keeps it from being more effective?

What advantages can you see in the flannel board or hook-and-loop board over an ordinary blackboard? Why is this type of board often used in television commercials rather than the chalkboard?

✻

Use of Projectors

Many types of projection equipment are available. Among them are opaque projectors, slide projectors, film strip projectors, overhead projectors, microprojectors, as well as the ubiquitous motion picture projectors. These machines can bring to the entire class experiences that would otherwise be impossible, or possible only on an individual basis or at great cost. For example, if a teacher wishes to show English money to a social studies class, he can project the images of a sixpence, shilling, florin, and half crown on a screen by means of an opaque projector so all can see at once. This technique allows everyone to see the coins without interrupting the presentation, something impossible if the coins should be passed around. Or, if a teacher wishes to show pupils what actually happens during the making of steel, he can show them a film or film strip. By using these techniques a teacher can avoid a costly field trip and at the same time actually show pupils by means of annotated drawings, exploded drawings, and magnifications much about the making of steel that the pupils could not see in a real field trip.

THE OPAQUE PROJECTOR. The opaque projector is an extremely valuable tool. It will project on the screen the image of opaque surfaces which are too small for all pupils to see readily from their seats and it will do so in color. With it a teacher can project not only *realia* like the coins mentioned above, but also pictures and pages from books, pamphlets, and magazines. Unfortunately, most opaque projectors require almost complete darkness to be effective and even then they are hard to focus and rather awkward to use.

THE OVERHEAD PROJECTOR. Overhead projectors are also extremely useful and versatile. It is not too much to say that every classroom should contain one. They can be used in lighted classrooms without darkening the room, thus allowing pupils to take notes or do other activities not possible in darkened classrooms. Some teachers, for instance, use overhead projection to present quiz questions rather than mimeographing them or writing them on the chalkboard. Moreover, they are so constructed that one can write, draw, and point things out from the front of the room without turning his back on the class and obstructing the pupils' lines of sight.

The versatility of the overhead projector makes it particularly valuable. Not only are the transparencies easy to make, but they can be prepared in advance and used over and over, thus avoiding the tedious job of copying material on the chalkboard and tying up the board with "Do Not Erase" signs. In addition, transparencies can be placed on top of one another so as to present information in almost any combination one desires. Thus, to an outline map of Europe one could show and compare the national boundaries in 1914, the changes in boundaries after the Versailles treaties, the land grabs by Nazi Germany, and the present boundaries simply by adding and subtracting *flip-ons,* that is, other transparencies. On the other hand, the overhead projector can be used effectively for on-the-spot recording and illustrating. In one class during a discussion the recorder outlined the course of discussion on a transparency. Later, when a question arose concerning what had been said in the discussion, he was able to project the notes on to the screen for all to see. Such characteristics are valuable for making teaching more effective and at the same time reducing the amount of tedious busy work which sometimes interferes with more important teaching tasks.

SLIDE AND FILM STRIP PROJECTORS. Slide projectors and film strip projectors can be discussed simultaneously because the two are often combined into one machine. After all, a film strip is little more than a series of 2×2 slides joined together on a strip of film. The film strip has the advantage of having been put together by an expert in a ready-made sequence. Slides are more versatile, but using them requires more careful planning by the teacher. Just one slide out of order or upside down can throw a well-conceived lesson out of step.

Some film strips come with recorded commentary and sound effects. Although these are usually quite impressive, often teachers would rather provide their own commentary as the film strip progresses. Of course, if he wishes, a teacher can prerecord his own commentary and sound effects and synchronize them to a film strip or to a series of slides. Utilizing sound with slides is usually enhanced by the use of an automatic projector. If the teacher can influence the choice of slide projectors to be furnished him, he would do well to insist on a projector that will operate both manually and automatically.

Thirty-five millimeter film strip projectors and 2 × 2 projectors are small enough and simple enough to operate for small group or individual use. For individual or small-group viewing the image can be thrown onto a sheet of cardboard no larger than the projector itself. It seems surprising that more teachers have not taken advantage of this capability of the thirty-five millimeter film strip and slide projectors.

Another machine, which seems to have been lost in the rush onward to new technology, is the 3 × 4 magic lantern. This machine was a mainstay of the audio-visual department of years ago and still has great potential. Its glass slides give very good fidelity and can be made easily. Those machines should not be left to gather dust in storerooms.

MICRO-PROJECTION. The number of pupils who never see what it is they are supposed to see through the microscope is probably astronomical. The microprojector can eliminate for practical purpose much of this difficulty by enlarging and projecting the image in the microscope's field onto a screen so that all the pupils can see the image and so that the teacher can point out salient features to everyone at once. Another technique that gives much the same result is to take pictures of the slide through the microscope. This technique is not difficult. It is merely a matter of screwing a compatible thirty-five millimeter camera to the microscope and taking pictures by means of the optics of the microscope. The resulting 2 × 2 slides can be projected on a screen. In much the same way transparencies for overhead projection can be made with a Polaroid camera.

Preparing such materials takes time, but almost always they are worth the effort. In many instances much of the preparation of such aids can be done by pupils, thus giving them valuable learning experiences and saving time for the teacher.

A Word About Moving Pictures

At present, along with television, motion pictures are the most glamorous of audio-visual aids—so much so that many teachers depend upon films to do what these aids cannot do. To be effective, motion pictures must be selected with care, previewed, introduced, and followed up. Remember, a darkened classroom is an excellent place for older students to sleep and for younger pupils to commit mischief.

PRESENTING THE FILM. Checking on the equipment is essential when using motion pictures because the motion picture projector can

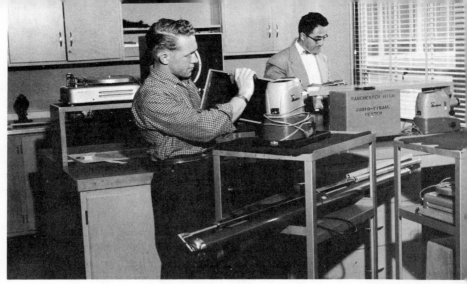

A key to successful use of audio-visual aids is careful preparation. Here a teacher and a pupil get the equipment in order.

be a particularly cranky machine. Running a little of the film immediately before the presentation to be sure all is working is a wise precaution. Once the film is in progress, projectionists should not sit back and relax; supervision of the film by checking the tension, loops, and the like can pay dividends.

In this day of sound movies and television we sometimes forget that the silent motion pictures can also be an effective audio-visual aid. As a matter of fact, the silent picture is sometimes more useful than the sound movie because the teacher can comment as the movie progresses, thus bringing out the salient points.

It is never wise to try to comment on a film by outshouting a sound track. Pupils cannot listen both to their teacher and to the moving picture. Nine times out of ten such comments will confuse, rather than clarify, the point a teacher wants to make unless he stops the machine before he speaks. Good planning calls for taking care of such explanations before starting the projector. In this respect the silent film has another advantage over the sound film. A teacher can emphasize and clarify by stopping the film and repeating a particular sequence as he explains and amplifies it much more easily with silent than with sound film.

TWO RECENT INNOVATIONS. In the past the use of the motion picture in the classroom has been plagued by two distinct disadvantages. One was that the projection was designed solely for large-group instruction; the other that the films had to be shown in darkened classrooms. Neither condition needs to obtain any longer. New self-threading individual eight millimeter projection devices make motion picture projection a means for providing for individual differences, and new rear projection arrangements allow moving picture projection in lighted rooms. Increased use of these devices can make motion picture projection considerably more effective.

❁

What misconceptions are liable to rise from the use of aids such as the moving pictures? How can these be avoided?

What steps should you as a teacher go through before presenting a film to a class?

❁

Other Audio-Visual Material

USE OF PICTURES. Pictures of all sorts are available for classroom use. Pictures can be found in many places. Especially useful are the pictures in textbooks. In addition, teachers should collect as many pictures as they can. Not only are the pictures useful aids, but collecting them can also be fun. Specimens and other *realia* having to do with one's subject can be equally valuable and likewise fun to collect. In fact, numerous teachers have developed picture and specimen collecting into lifetime hobbies.

No particular technique is necessary in the use of these materials. However, if he uses a visual aid, the teacher should remember to display it in such a way that each pupil can see it clearly. He should also remember to point out whatever the pupils are to learn from the aid. One danger to avoid is that of exhibiting pictures just because one has them. Although showing pupils a collection may be splendid fun, even for the pupils, one should be sure that the material is pertinent before using precious class time on it.

Another practice to avoid is passing pictures and other materials around the room so that pupils may look at them while the lecture, recitation, or discussion continues. Pupils cannot pay attention to two things at once. While pupils are examining the audio-visual aid they cannot concentrate on the lesson. A much better practice is to utilize the opaque projector to throw an image of the picture or object on the screen where all can see it at once. Another alternative is to display or to pass the material around during a laboratory or work session when it is less liable to disrupt the learning process.

MODELS AND REPLICAS. Models, replicas, and sand tables also make admirable audio-visual materials, and pupils can help in constructing them. In using pupil help in building aids of any sort, teachers should be wary of two dangerous faults: one, that the pupil may spend so much time creating the aid that he neglects the things he can learn from it; and two, that inaccurate models may give pupils erroneous concepts. Teachers should be particularly on guard against incorrect proportions, historical anachronisms, and other details that can mislead pupils. Whenever it is necessary to distort in order to be effective, as is often the case in preparing three-dimensional maps, the teacher should be sure to warn the pupils of the inaccuracies.

TAPE RECORDERS AND RECORD PLAYERS. By means of recording one can bring to class the voice of an eminent mathematician discussing mathematical theory, a famous actor reading an ancient or modern play, a statesman discussing foreign policy, or a symphony orchestra playing Rimski-Korsakov. Additionally, with modern equipment, one can record a class discussion and in a play-back use the recording as a basis for analyzing and evaluating the effectiveness of the discussion. Pupils with difficulties hearing their own errors can sometimes identify and correct them after hearing and evaluating tape recordings of their own voices. The language laboratory is based on this technique. Teachers interested in providing for individual differences and individualizing classes can prerecord assignments and lessons for certain individuals to do with the tape recorder while the teacher is busy with other groups and individuals. Truly, the possibilities of tape recording are almost limitless.

*

What audio-visual aids are available to you? What aids can you create? How could you use them? Survey the situation. You will undoubtedly find a wealth of material you had not thought of before. Consider such things as pictures, moving pictures, slides, microprojectors, chalkboards, bulletin boards, charts, graphs, diagrams, demonstrations, schematic representations, opaque projection, records, tapes, models, maps, globes, film strips, radio, television, felt boards, overhead projectors, tachistoscopes, displays, exhibits, aquaria, terraria, stereoptican slides, sand tables, and *realia*.

How can *realia* be used? Is the real object, if available, always the best aid to learning? Justify your answer.

Television and Radio

An Unrealized Potential

Schools have yet to utilize the full potentialities of television and radio. Perhaps this is not to be wondered at, because so far the remarkable possibilities of the motion picture are far from realized in our schools. The potential of these devices is tremendous—at first glance almost limitless. Through these techniques the pupil can be present at the critical moments of history, he can see government in the making, he can watch great experiments in science, he can visit the farthest corners of the earth, he can hear famous symphonies, and see great plays and operas. All these can be brought to him through television, radio, motion pictures, and recordings. These devices can bring to the pupils great experiences, but these experiences cannot take the place of teaching.

Certain school systems are conducting interesting experiments in which master teachers teach large classes by means of television. In such classes it is possible to bring to pupils teaching that they would not otherwise get. Still, television teaching does not relieve the classroom teacher of his responsibility for instruction. Even when a master teacher conducts a television lesson, the classroom teacher still has to go through his standard routine. He must plan, he must select, he must introduce, he must guide, he must follow up, in order to fill in the gaps, correct misunderstandings, and guide the pupils' learning.

ROLE OF EDUCATIONAL TELEVISION. Probably educational television's basic role should be to augment, enrich, and point up the curriculum by bringing to the school, and to the general public, experiences beyond the scope and capabilities of the ordinary classroom. According to a committee of the Northern Region of the New Jersey Association for Supervision and Curriculum Development:

. . . only in unusual circumstances should educational television attempt to take on the role of classroom instruction. Rather, it should concentrate on making available to the schools and to the general public the things which it can do best. In general, these are the programs of general and special interest which are valuable to the homeviewer as well as being useful to teachers of various disciplines and grade levels to enhance their instruction. In the majority of programing, the programs should not be aimed at specific classes but should consist of experiences of more general nature from which teachers may dip as seems necessary and desirable to them.

In certain cases instructional television is necessary and desirable. Examples of such programs are television courses for adults and other persons not regularly enrolled in school programs, and courses which are beyond the capabilities of the ordinary curriculum because of lack of facilities, competent teaching personnel, or sufficient number of pupils to justify a class.[2]

THE WASHINGTON COUNTY REPORT. The school authorities of Washington County, Maryland, the school district with perhaps the

[2] John Farinella, Robert Frazier, and Leonard H. Clark, *Guidelines for Educational Television,* Report of The Committee on Staff Utilization, Northern Region, New Jersey Association for Supervision and Curriculum Development, Spring 1963, unpublished. By permission.

longest experience with closed circuit instructional television, is more sanguine regarding instructional television. In their 1963 report they list the following conclusions derived from a study of closed circuit instructional television in their schools during the period from 1956–1961.[3]

1. Pupil achievement can improve significantly when television is consistently used as a teaching aid.
2. Television accelerates the teacher's professional growth.
3. Television makes it possible to upgrade the curriculum and enrich the educational program more easily and economically than before.
4. Television is especially useful as an instructional aid to add new learning experiences to the school program. It does not "replace" the teacher or "substitute" techniques and procedures which would eliminate regular classroom learning activities and personal teacher-pupil relationships.
5. The operational costs of television can be met without increasing the normal school budget.
6. The problem of finding and retaining top quality teachers is eased.
7. Television changes the role of the classroom teacher and makes him—along with the studio teacher—part of a teaching team.
8. Television brings greater equality of opportunity for all pupils.
9. Television increases vocational training opportunities.
10. School television facilities can serve the public in a variety of ways —for adult education, community projects and the dissemination of many kinds of information.

Using General Educational Television Programs

When matters of great national or international significance are being telecast, it may be wise to stop other class activities and witness the event. When Lieutenant Commander Shepard and Lieutenant Colonel Glenn made their first space flights, in many schools all other activities ceased while the pupils viewed the telecasts of these events. Such activities are well worthwhile particularly when the telecast is skillfully introduced and followed up.

Often telecasts of significant events occur at times which do not allow direct classroom viewing. This difficulty can be circumvented by recording the program and playing significant parts during school hours. Recent advances in video-tape technology are making it possible for schools to do their own video recording relatively cheaply. However, much of the material telecast by commercial and educational television stations is copyrighted and may not be available for rebroadcast to schools without permission of the copyright holder.

[3] *Washington County Closed Circuit Television Report*, Hagerstown, Maryland, pp. 2–3. By permission.

Another technique is to assign home viewing of telecasts. Because not all pupils have television sets available to them, it may be necessary to make such assignments selectively, with certain individuals or committees responsible for reporting them. At times, in order to get wider experiences to share in class, it may be wise to ask different pupils to view the coverage on different channels. As with other assignments, television viewing assignments should be clear so that the pupils know what to look for and what they are trying to do. The use of a bulletin board to list assignments with attendant problems, questions, and projects, has proved successful for many teachers.

Determining how best to use educational and cultural television programs can be something of a problem. Television sections of local newspapers and television magazines carry descriptions of featured programs that the teacher can use as a basis for lesson planning and assignments. Frequently, professional magazines carry study guides for exceptional programs. Sometimes teachers can secure information about both the proposed scheduling and the content of coming programs in advance by writing to local television stations or to the television networks. When such information is available, classroom activities can be planned around certain television programs, or the planned class sequence can be altered in order to take advantage of exceptional television opportunities.

Instructional Television

Too many pupils have learned well in television classes for anyone to continue to doubt whether television can be used to teach. The question now concerns what the most efficient and effective ways to teach are and where television classes should fit into the picture, if at all.

The television staff and the classroom teachers represent a team. The classroom teacher represents the heart of the team. The television teacher, if there is one, should be a consultant and resource person. The classroom teachers should determine how the television should be used and, as far as classroom-beamed telecasts are concerned, what the aims and content of the telecast should be. In other words, the classroom teacher should enter into the planning and evaluating of the television offerings. Teachers should inform television presenters and directors of program effectiveness and let them know what they want and expect from future programs.[4]

The Anaheim (California) City School District *Instructional T.V. Guide* gives a good example of the television teaching team in action.[5]

[4] John Farinella, Robert Frazier, and Leonard H. Clark, *op. cit.*

[5] James D. Brier, editor, *Instructional T.V. Guide,* Anaheim City School District, Anaheim, California, 1961, p. 18. By permission.

Much of the following discussion of the duties and responsibilities of television and classroom teachers has been adapted from this excellent manual.

. . . The studio teacher indicates by the way questions and ideas are presented, the type of response that is expected of pupils observing. (He may say, "What famous man, that we have heard about before, died at the Alamo?" He may say, "Can you *think* of other types of plants that adapt to their environment in a different way?" The first question should be answered audibly by pupils in the classroom with the teacher guiding and encouraging the response. The second question requires a covert response from each pupil which the class-room teacher may wish to bring up after the telecast for further discussion.) Types of response that detract from the intimacy of the studio teacher-pupil relationship should be avoided. (The studio teacher might state, "Let's *think* about why the pioneers went west." The classroom teacher responds, "Mary, what do you think?" Mary may or may not give a correct response. The teacher in the studio cannot anticipate the timing for an oral response to this type of question and the attention and rapport existing between studio teacher and pupil is divided during the discussion in the classroom.) *Participation is an important factor in learning;* it must be developed, encouraged, and con-trolled by both studio and classroom teacher working together during the telecast.

DUTIES OF TELEVISION TEACHERS. The television teacher should be a person of exceptional competence in his field, who possesses special talents suitable to the medium. Because of his strategic role, much of the planning of the television course falls on him. Study or lesson guides for the use of the pupils and teachers, and studio scripts for the actual television lesson must be prepared well enough ahead so that the class-room teachers can make full use of them. Planning television lessons is more critical than planning ordinary lessons. They require much atten-tion to detail. The television teacher cannot afford to leave loose ends dangling to be picked up on the way, nor can he leave his lesson plan loose so as to feel his way from the class response.[6] He must be espe-cially careful about his timing and pacing. The lesson should not be either too fast or too slow. Somehow it should give the pupils a chance to react and give at least the appearance of teacher-pupil interaction. Until new techniques that will allow for real interaction between tele-vision teacher and individual pupils are developed, the television teacher must rely on such devices as rhetorical questions and pauses for this purpose.

The television teacher must also allow for the possibility that some pupils may not understand the first time. In a large class or a television audience the teacher must cope with the problem of psychological noise

6 Not being able to feel the class reaction is a hardship to at least some television teachers. To try to overcome this problem, some of them pretape their lessons and then during the telecast sit in the back of the classroom to watch pupils' reactions to their presentation. Because classes differ, this technique, although valuable, is not entirely satisfactory.

—that is, the tendency of people in large groups not to hear all that is presented. To mitigate this problem the teacher must find ways of repeating points again and again without boring the pupils who have already caught on. Clever use of visuals will often help solve this dilemma. In any case, television teachers should make optimum use of visuals. After all, the medium is television.

In addition to planning and teaching, television teachers must support the classroom teachers in other ways. They should listen carefully to the classroom teachers' suggestions, criticisms, and comments, and attempt to put teacher suggestions into the television lessons. As often as they can they should get into the classroom in order to become better acquainted with the teachers and pupils and to get something of the feeling of the classroom.

Finally, the television teacher has the important job of building public support of the television teaching program. In this role he must be a public relations agent going out to meet the parents, teachers, and the public in general so as to inform them of the program and solicit from them their support.

THE ROLE OF THE CLASSROOM TEACHER. All in all, the television teacher's role is an exacting one, but it is not as important as that of the classroom teacher, for it is he who carries the real load.

Before the television class begins, the classroom teacher prepares the setting. He must see to it that the classroom environment is arranged properly, that the necessary provisions for easily carrying out the routines of classroom management and administration have been made, and that the pupils are psychologically and intellectually ready for the lesson to be telecast. To accomplish these missions the classroom teacher must be familiar with the television teacher's plan. He should, therefore, study carefully the study guides, studio scripts, and course of study well before each lesson. The information in these documents will tell him what materials he needs to have ready and give him clues on how to best prepare the pupils for the class.

Any materials needed during the telecast must be ready and waiting before the telecast. So that the pupils will be ready also, the classroom teacher should discuss the lesson to be televised with them. In this discussion the pupils should learn something of the purpose of the television lesson—what they can expect to see and hear and what they can expect to learn. At this time the teacher can teach the pupils new vocabulary they may need and fill in any serious voids evident in their background. This last responsibility implies the necessity for the classroom teacher to continually analyze and evaluate the present knowledge and abilities of his pupils both individually and collectively.

During the telecast the classroom teacher must continue his role as guide to learning. He must circulate among the pupils to determine whether they understand and are proceeding correctly. Sometimes he will have to supplement the television teacher's instruction, especially in "work-type" lessons during which the classroom teacher may need to correct and help pupils. More frequently he will prefer to take notes of pupil reactions—particularly evidences of lack of understanding or misunderstanding—for use in follow-up activities after the telecast.

Part of his follow-through during the telecast is the handling of questions put by the television teacher. Some of the questions asked will require no overt response, of course. Others should be answered aloud. The classroom teacher's plan for the television lesson should include provisions for handling these questions. A common approach is for all pupils to answer them in unison since calling on individual pupils creates a problem of timing.

AFTER THE TELEVISION CLASS. The follow-up after the television class is fully as important as the class itself. One of the most common faults in all teaching is the failure to follow through to clinch what was to be taught. The classroom teacher should check the pupils' learning against the objectives of the lesson and reteach if necessary. He should also provide additional experiences to enrich and carry forward the learning in the television class. Since creative activity is so necessary to effective learning and since television lessons are liable to be largely passive, classroom teachers should consider the desirability of utilizing many projects, discussions, experiments, investigations, writing, and similar activities that allow pupils to engage actively in their own learning.

Physical Set-Up for Television Class

Pupils can benefit from television only if they can hear and see clearly. Both picture and sound must be kept at a reasonably high fidelity, free from interference. For that reason, teachers must pay particular attention to the tuning of the receivers and do everything in their power to see to it that the sets are properly maintained. Except in extremely unusual circumstances one should not attempt to use television in classrooms located where the reception is marginal.

To ensure good viewing one needs to observe a few rules of thumb for the physical arrangement of the classroom whether large or small. The following rules are more or less generally accepted by experts in the field.

1. Use 21- to 24-inch screen television sets with front directional speakers.
2. Place the sets so that each pupil has an unobstructed line of sight.
3. The screen should not be more than thirty feet from any pupil.
4. The set should be about five and one half feet from the floor (that is, about the same height as the teacher's face).
5. The vertical angle of sight from any pupil to the set should never be more than 30°; the horizontal angle, never more than 45°
6. The room should be kept lighted so that pupils can see to take notes.
7. No glare should reflect from the screen. To reduce glare one can
   a. Move the set away from the windows.
   b. Tilt the set downward.
   c. Provide the set with cardboard blinders.
8. The sound should come from front directional speakers. If several sets are in use in one room, it may be better to use the sound from only one set than to have it come from several sources. In large rooms for large-class instruction it may be more satisfactory to run the sound from one set through a public address system.
9. Pupils should have adequate surface space for writing.
10. To allow for quick, easy transition from the telecast, television classrooms should be fitted out with adequate audio-visual equipment, display space, filing and storage space.

✣

What seem to you to be the arguments for or against the use of instructional television?

Criticize the position taken by the committee of the Northern Region of the NJASCD.

What methods could you take as a classroom teacher to keep television instruction on a personal basis? What could you do as a television teacher?

✣

Sources of Audio-Visual Materials

Occasionally, teachers defend dull, humdrum teaching on the grounds that the school administration will not give them adequate materials. Usually such complaints are merely "buck-passing," although they may be signs of incompetence; for at the expense of a little ingenuity and initiative, boundless supplies of audio-visual materials are available in even the poorest schools. The following paragraphs attempt to show how audio-visual materials may be acquired. Of course, to show what is available in each of the various subjects and fields, and how to obtain it, is beyond the scope of this book. Therefore the discussion will attempt to point out only some sources which may be of general interest. The student desiring more specific information should consult texts and periodicals concerning his own subject field.

FREE AND INEXPENSIVE MATERIAL. As pointed out in an earlier section, building a file of pictures is relatively easy and can be considerable fun. In addition, such a file is so useful that the prospective teacher can hardly afford not to build one. He can start by collecting pictures from periodicals. Picture magazines, such as *Life, Look, The National Geographic Magazine,* and *Holiday,* are full of potentially useful pictures. So are the special-interest magazines such as those devoted to popular science and history. He can also obtain pictures from commercial sources such as museums and publishing houses both by purchase and rental. Many libraries have pictures to lend to teachers for short or long periods.

Not only pictures but other materials, such as slides, specimens, souvenirs, models, and the like, are readily available for the asking. Many museums will send such material to schools free of charge. In almost every hamlet in the United States some villager has a collection of interesting materials that could be used with profit in the classroom. Usually he will be pleased to let the pupils see it. Quite often the most avid collectors are other teachers, particularly college professors.

Stores, factories, commercial concerns of all sorts are usually willing, and in some instances anxious, to give samples of raw and processed materials to the schools. At times such material is accompanied by pernicious advertising, but usually the objectionable material can be eliminated. Likewise, many firms offer films, slides, film strips, and other similar audio-visual materials free upon request. Many of these materials are very good, although each should be carefully screened before using. The amount of excellent material available from local, state, national, foreign, and domestic government agencies, is almost boundless.

FILMS FOR RENT. Most of the more valuable classroom films are not lent to the school gratis. Since films are usually too expensive to be purchased by any but the largest school systems, most films used in the classroom are rented from film libraries. Your school will probably have a clear policy and procedure about renting films. This policy, of course, should be followed to the letter. The critical thing is to order films early. Good films are in demand; a late order may mean that you will have to do without.

Each renting library publishes a catalog of its films. In addition, film companies and other agencies publish catalogs and announcements of films. Hints about useful films can also be found in textbooks, curriculum guides, and resource units. Through these sources teachers can usually find films suitable to their purposes. Perhaps the list of sources in Chapter 14 may help the teacher. In using the list one should note that the list is not limited to films or even to audio-visual material alone.

USING COMMERCIAL FILM. Commercial motion pictures too are a potential teaching resource of great value both as an art form and as a source of subject matter useful in English, social studies, art, music, and other courses. Therefore, the alert teacher scans the notices of coming attractions to spot likely productions suitable for exploiting. In this connection pupils can be a great help. When exceptional productions come to town, perhaps a theater party with definite assignments would be worthwhile. Or perhaps it would be better to list it as an optional activity. In any event, the teacher should call the film to the pupils' attention and suggest how it might fit into their program. Sometimes films make excellent subjects for pupil reports either oral or written.

Many old motion pictures are classics that can add greatly to the ordinary course of study. In some instances, if asked, local theater operators will arrange to bring these films back to town. Also, quite a large number of these classic motion pictures have been reissued as sixteen millimeter films and are available for school use in both the original film length and in shorter cut versions. The shorter versions can be used in the classroom; if the film is worthwhile enough it may be possible to reschedule the periods so that one can show the full-length feature straight through at one sitting during school hours or in the evening.

Source of Information About Television Programs

Information about television programs slated for local viewing can be obtained in much the same way as information about the theater. Much information is readily available in professional journals, for example, the *NEA Journal* and *NEA Reporter,* specialized magazines such as *T.V. Guide,* the television sections of newspapers and magazines, and from the television stations and networks themselves. A teacher will usually find more programs suitable for school use than he might expect. One issue of the *NEA Journal,* for instance, listed some twelve programs that were potentially useful for social studies classes.[7]

Since it is almost impossible for any teacher to keep himself well informed concerning all the television programs that might be poten-

[7] The February 1964 issue. Cited in Leonard H. Clark, "The Mass Media and the Social Studies," in Jerome L. Miller, editor, *Mass Media in Secondary Schools,* 1965 Yearbook, New Jersey Secondary School Teachers Association.

tially useful, it may be wise for the teacher to enlist the aid of the pupils to scout out and report on programs of value. Many teachers regularly post billings of such programs on the chalkboard or bulletin board. These billings may be enhanced by the adding of commentary and suggested aids for viewing.

Television programs that seem to have no direct bearing on the course of study can sometimes be useful. All television dramas have plots, most of them have music, they all take place in time and space, and so almost any one of them can be used for some purpose in English, social studies, art, or music classes. The ubiquitous wild-western television drama, for instance, can be used in a study of the customs and mores of the times, and to bring home the difference between historical fact and fiction, to illustrate plot structure, or flat versus round characterization, the use of music in the theater, and so on. Particularly useful are the many documentaries and educational programs that commercial television stations use to fill in blank periods during their off hours and that make up much of the bill of fare of educational television programs. Instructional television courses telecast for adults are often good sources of enrichment and a means for providing for individual differences. Sometimes they require high-level ability from the viewer, but usually they do not. The educational television stations telecasting such programs usually publish program schedules, reading lists, and study materials that can be purchased for a relatively small fee.

Homemade Visual Aids

Many visual aids can be made easily by the teacher or the pupil. One of the simplest to make is the flannel board which can be constructed quickly by stretching a piece of felt across a board of the desired size and tacking it down securely. Signs, pictures, letters, and so forth can be stuck on the flannel if their backs are covered with strips of sandpaper or felt. A similar device can be constructed quickly out of a sheet of iron or steel on which material can be displayed by means of magnets. Housewives use such magnetic boards in the kitchen or family area to remind themselves and their families of things they ought not forget. Their use can be just as effective in the classroom.

SLIDES AND FILM STRIPS. Two by two (35 millimeter) film slides and film strips, the large glass slides, and transparencies for overhead projection are readily available from commercial sources and quite easy to make locally.

Thirty-five millimeter photography is an excellent source of slides. Thousands of slides are for sale, as one can see by thumbing through the photography magazines on display at any newsstand. Furthermore, excellent 35 millimeter slides can be made locally. The teacher can usually find someone to make the slides for him, if he is not equipped to make them himself. The school camera club would probably welcome such a project; if not, certainly one of the teacher's friends or pupils would be delighted to serve. Color slides are usually made by sending the exposed film to commercial concerns.

To produce film strips is more difficult than to make individual slides. Ordinarily the process involves copying from other slides by means of an expensive adaptation of a 35 millimeter camera. However, the same effect can be achieved with slides, and the slides are more versatile. Of course, camera clubs and other local personnel can develop film strips and even motion pictures, if they wish.

With surprisingly little extra effort it is possible to provide synchronized tape recordings for a film strip or series of slides. All that one needs to do is to write a script with clues, noting when the operator should change slides, and then transcribe the script on a tape recording. Not only is it fairly easy, but it is fun to do. Homemade sound-film strips of this sort can be used for large-group instruction in an assembly or lecture hall or for individual instruction in the classroom utilizing earphones and a miniature screen.

Making glass slides is not at all difficult. Commercial firms sell kits for making them. With these materials it is possible to make slides by typing on a special film or by writing or drawing directly on the glass. Such slides can be used with "magic lantern" projectors and overhead projectors.

MAKING OVERHEAD TRANSPARENCIES. There are many ways to make transparencies for the overhead projector. A number of photo-copying or dry copying office machines will make transparencies of printed, typed, or written material or drawings. Preparing transparencies on some of these machines is something of an art. On others all one does is push a button and wait a few seconds. One can also make transparencies by using a special carbon paper or by using a china marking pencil or india ink. The popular felt-tip marking pens, for example, a Magic Marker, can be used to make transparencies in color. One can also make transparencies directly with a Polaroid camera. With all these sources, and acetate sheets so inexpensive (any clear acetate can be used to make transparencies by hand—the machine-made transparencies require specially treated film), there seems to be no reason why one should not have all the transparencies one needs. In order to preserve them and to keep them accessible it is recommended that one frame his transparencies and file them. Commercial frames are readily available for transparencies.

Flip-ons, which are simply additional sheets that can be placed on the original transparency to add further detail or information, are made in exactly the same way as any other transparencies. If one wishes one can fasten these to the frame of the original transparency with little metallic foil hinges. The use of frames and hinges has the advantage of keeping the transparency and its flip-ons together in proper order.

*

What sources of audio-visual material are available to you in your community?

What materials are available for use in your college classes? What could you do to make more material available if you were one of the teachers?

Pick a college course and see what audio-visual materials you could develop for it.

*

Summary

Good teachers can be better teachers when they have plenty of materials to work with. Fortunately, American teachers are blessed with materials galore. although some may have to search a little to find them. Prominent on the list are audio-visual aids—films, pictures, maps, globes, charts, models, graphs, mock-ups, terrain boards, radio, television, chalkboards, and tack boards. All of them are excellent aids to teaching if they are used well, but they are not miracle drugs. They alone cannot do the job of teaching. The same teaching techniques—introducing, explaining, problem solving, follow-up, and evaluation—used in other teaching are also needed to get the most from audio-visual aids.

Some audio-visual materials are expensive and hard to get. This is true of other materials also. But this fact should not discourage the teacher. Much material is available for the asking. Much more can be made or improvised. Hints of how to obtain and create such materials can be found in the catalogs, curriculum guides, source units, and periodicals on the subject. Today no teacher has an excuse for not having a supply of suitable materials.

Recent advances in mass media have created many opportunities for teachers to capitalize on commercial cinema and television. Teachers who do not utilize these commercial media may be missing opportunities to harness their undoubted appeal to youth. The use of new media, particularly television, film, and tapes, has also proved valuable as a means of bringing to the classroom outstanding experiences and personalities not otherwise available. But teachers should not expect miracles of them. Television, film, and recorded presentations like anything else need to be introduced and followed up properly. On their own, they may be nothing; carefully handled they can work wonders. This is, of course, true of all tools. Perhaps the answer to the problem of effective and efficient teaching in the future lies in the building of man-machine systems that allot to each person and tool the most appropriate role.

FOR FURTHER STUDY

BOTTRELL, HAROLD R., *Teaching Tools* (Pittsburgh: The Boxwood Press, 1957).

CASSINER, HENRY, *Television Teaching Today* (New York: UNESCO Publications Center of Columbia University Press, 1961).

CROSS, A. J., and IRENE CYPHER, *Audio-Visual Education* (New York: Thomas Y. Crowell Company, 1961).

DALE, EDGAR, *Audio-Visual Methods in Teaching*, Second Edition (New York: Holt, Rinehart and Winston, Inc., 1954).

deKIEFFER, ROBERT, and LEE W. COCHRAN, *Manual of Audio-Visual Techniques* (Englewood Cliffs, N.J.: Prentice-Hall, Inc., 1962).

DENT, CHARLES H., and ERNEST F. TIEMANN, *Felt Boards for Teaching* (Austin: University of Texas, Visual Instruction Bureau, 1955).

EBOCH, SIDNEY C., *Operating Audio-Visual Equipment* (San Francisco: Chandler Publishing Company, 1960).

ERICKSON, CARLTON W. H., *Fundamentals of Teaching with Audiovisual Technology* (New York: The Macmillan Company, 1964).

FREEDMAN, FLORENCE B., and ESTHER L. BERG, *Classroom Teachers' Guide to Audio-Visual Material* (Philadelphia: Chilton Company, 1961).

HOLLAND, BEN F., H. C. HARTSELL, and R. L. DAVIDSON, *Audio-Visual Materials and Devices*, Revised Edition (Lubbock, Texas: Rogers Litho Printers, 1958).

HORN, GEORGE F., *Bulletin Boards* (New York: Reinhold Publishing Corporation, 1962).

MILLER, JEROME L. (editor), *The Mass Media in Secondary Education*, 1965 Yearbook/30, New Jersey Secondary School Teachers Association, 1965.

New Teaching Aids for the American Classroom, OE-34020, Office of Education, U.S. Department of Health, Education and Welfare (Washington, D.C.: U.S. Government Printing Office, 1960).

SHORES, LOUIS, *Instructional Materials: An Introduction for Teachers* (New York: The Ronald Press Company, 1960).

SMITH, MARY HOWARD (editor), *Using Television in the Classroom* (New York: McGraw-Hill Book Company, Inc., 1961).

TARBET, DONALD G., *Television and Our Schools* (New York: The Ronald Press Company, 1961).

THOMAS, R. MURRAY, and SHERWIN G. SWARTOUT, *Integrated Teaching Materials* (New York: David McKay Company, Inc., 1960).

TROW, WILLIAM CLARK, *Teacher and Technology* (New York: Appleton-Century-Crofts, Inc., 1963).

WITTICH, WALTER A., and CHARLES SCHULLER, *Audio-Visual Materials: Their Nature and Use*, Third Edition (New York: Harper and Row Publishers, 1962).

CHAPTER *14*

Other Materials of Instruction

*A*UDIO-VISUAL materials make up only a small portion of the teacher's arsenal of instructional materials. Materials of instruction include everything the teacher uses in his classroom presentation—textbooks and other books, pamphlet material, newspapers and magazines, mimeographed and dittoed material prepared locally, workbooks, self-instructional material, teaching programs and machines, and much more. This chapter will discuss the use of some of these materials. Some materials having been treated elsewhere will be treated here only briefly, or not at all, but the basic principles pertaining to the materials discussed here pertain to them also.

Printed and Duplicated Materials

Pamphlets, Brochures, and Other Reading Matter

Reading materials are discussed in another chapter. Let it suffice here for us to point out the tremendous amount of materials that are available for the asking or for a small fee—one particularly rich source being the Federal and state governmental agencies. The Government Printing Office lists thousands of pamphlets and books for sale, and the various federal agencies distribute great amounts of interesting informative material for the asking. Other sources are large industrial and commercial firms; foreign governments; supragovernmental agencies, such as the United Nations, UNESCO, and NATO; civic organizations, such as the League of Women Voters; and professional organizations, such as the National Education Association.

Newspapers and magazines are a constant source of material for every one of the curriculum fields. Pertinent articles in them should be included in reading assignments. In addition, newspapers and periodicals can furnish the material for bulletin board displays and other visual aids. Gathering suitable material of this type of display can well be delegated to a class committee. Sometimes this committee can combine its efforts with those of the bulletin board committee to search out pertinent material and display it effectively.

Workbooks and Exercises

Many textbook publishers provide workbooks for use by pupils in secondary-school classes. Lately these books have suffered from an ill repute that is often well deserved. Workbooks need not be bad, however. Properly written and well used, they can be very helpful. Whatever is true of them can also be said of teacher-prepared exercises.

When properly used, workbooks and duplicated exercises make it possible for teachers to allow pupils to pace themselves and so provide for the differences in pupils. There is no need for all pupils to do the same exercise at the same time. As a matter of fact there is no real reason why all pupils need use the same workbook. It is quite possible to use a workbook designed for use with one text with another one. However, when so doing the teacher should take care to see that the selections used are compatible. When differences between the text and a workbook may cause confusion in the pupils, a little editing and cutting will usually make the content of various workbooks match well enough to avoid any serious difficulty.

One of the complaints against workbooks is that they encourage rote learning and discourage creative thought. These criticisms are often justified, particularly so when the workbook consists of sentences from the text which the pupil completes by searching the book until he finds the missing words. Such workbooks and workbook assignments should be avoided. However, workbooks can also present problems, review material, and study guides which elicit much more than simple rote learning.

As with anything else, assignments in workbooks and locally produced materials must be followed up. Reinforcement is probably better if the follow-up is immediate. In some instances good results can be achieved by providing answer sheets so that the pupil can check his own work himself. In other cases the workbook problems lend themselves better to follow up in classroom discussion or by the teacher's going over the problem in class. *In no case should the teacher leave the workbook work unchecked until he can find a propitious moment at some later time to collect and correct it.*

Mimeographed and Dittoed Material

In the better school systems, the teachers seem to provide their pupils with great amounts of duplicated materials. These materials should be used in just the same way as printed materials of the same type.

Teachers often give such material to the pupils to keep, or to use up at the time. In a good many cases this practice is desirable. On the other hand, preparing mimeographed and dittoed material costs time and money. There is no reason why duplicated exercises and supplementary reading materials should not be used again and again if the teacher takes precautions. Therefore, the teacher may wish to have the pupils write their answers to exercises and problems in a notebook, or on a separate piece of paper, rather than on the materials directly. If one binds the duplicated, supplementary reading matter in some sort of stiff cover, it will be quite durable. Construction paper or manila file folders are excellent for this purpose. Pamphlets made this way will last longer if the copy is stapled to the cover rather than fastened with paper fasteners.

Some schools provide teachers enough secretarial service to prepare stencils and run off everything that teachers can wish for. More usually the job of preparing supplementary materials falls to the teacher himself. Consequently, as soon as he can, the prospective teacher should learn how to prepare and run off mimeograph stencils and spirit duplicator masters. Neither the mimeograph machine nor the spirit duplicator is very difficult to operate and the latter is frequently made available for teacher use in the teachers' workrooms of many schools. One merit of the spirit duplicator is that master copies can be made easily by hand. This characteristic makes it a boon for the nonexpert typist and for the teacher who needs to reproduce drawings, figures, and other devices not easily done on a typewriter.

✿

It is not too soon for you to start collecting material for the classes you may sometime teach. The student who picks up and saves all the pertinent material he can find will have a start toward becoming a well-equipped teacher.

Examine several workbooks. Do they seem to encourage independent learning or rote memorizing? Examine teacher-prepared material in the same way. How can these materials be made to encourage independent thought, if they do not?

✿

Teaching Machines and Programmed Learning[1]

Recently educators seem to have become somewhat disenchanted with teaching machines and programmed instruction. If this reaction curbs the

---

[1] The state of confusion concerning programming is illustrated by the disagreement concerning the spelling of the word. Some authorities double the *m;* others do not.

wild enthusiasm of the late '50's and early '60's, it may be a good thing. For although teaching programs can teach, the commercial firms sponsored the boom of the past years before anyone really understood why the programs worked or how to design and use them. One result of this too early exploitation is that it has stabilized the movement at a moment when it should have remained dynamic and daringly experimental. Perhaps now the professional climate will encourage researchers to experiment with new designs and ways of utilizing teaching programs and machines in the schools.

The Teaching Machine

The teaching machine differs from the ordinary audio-visual aid in that it actually does some of the teaching. In effect, what the machine does is to present and to follow up a series of lessons, that is to say, teaching programs. In this sense the machine is a mechanical tutor that works with the pupil in a one-to-one relationship, although in reality it is the teaching program that does the actual teaching.[2]

Teaching Programs

Preparing a teaching program is an extremely slow process requiring great skill and knowledge. To do the job adequately usually requires the collaboration of several experts—a classroom teacher who knows the pupils for whom the program will be aimed, a programming expert who understands the art and science of programming, a subject-matter specialist who knows the content to be programmed, and perhaps a curriculum expert who knows where the subject matter fits into the entire curriculum. In practice, some of these roles can be combined in the same person, but ordinarily preparing programs is too difficult and time-consuming a task for teachers to attempt alone.

Selecting a program from those already published is not an easy task either. The nature of programming precludes a teacher's merely thumbing through sample programs to find a suitable one. Further, there are no adequate standards to consult for guidance in making a selection. At the present time the only reliable method of selecting a program is to first survey the literature to see what is available and then to try out the likeliest programs on a small sampling of the pupils to be taught. Should a program publisher not be willing to meet this test, his program should be automatically eliminated from consideration.

[2] Students interested in the various types of machines should consult one of the numerous works on the subjects, for example, Chapter III of Lawrence Stolurow's *Teaching by Machine*, Cooperative Research Monograph No. 6, OE-34010, Office of Education, U.S. Department of Health, Education and Welfare (Washington, D.C.: U.S. Government Printing Office, 1961).

TYPES OF PROGRAMS.   There are many types of teaching programs. A few of them are listed here.

1. Linear types in which the pupils proceed by small steps through preset programs by recalling or inventing answers to questions. (Constructed response.)
2. Linear types in which the pupils proceed by small steps through a preset program of multiple-choice items. In both types 1 and 2 the program tells the pupil whether he has answered a question correctly or incorrectly and then goes on directly to the next question in the pre-set sequence.
3. Linear programs combining constructed and multiple-choice responses.
4. Linear programs utilizing large steps and constructed responses.
5. Intrinsic branching programs in which the next step is determined by the pupil's response to the present one. In case of error the machine reprograms the pupil on a remedial course that will show him his error and put him straight again.
6. Language laboratory programs in which the pupils repeat correct foreign pronunciation presented by the machine or answer questions presented by the machines.
7. Programs in which the machine demonstrates a skill by means of filmstrips or motion pictures so that the pupil may learn the skill by imitation.
8. Programs in which the machine gives the pupil instructions to follow in order to learn a skill.
9. Programs that present a situation either verbally or visually and then ask the pupil questions about the situation described.

ESSENTIAL CHARACTERISTICS.   The essential characteristics of a teaching program, common to all of the above, are set down here.

1. The objectives, that is, what is to be learned, must be carefully defined.
2. The pupil progresses toward these objectives by means of a carefully planned logical sequence of relatively small steps.
3. The sequence and its items have been rigorously tested and revised to ensure that the program does in fact lead to the desired goals.
4. The pupil is active; it is he who does the learning. The machine allows him no time to relax or be inattentive.
5. The pupil assumes the responsibility for learning and sets his own pace.
6. The pupil learns of the results of his activity in each step immediately before going on to do anything else. If programming

enthusiasts are right, programs hold an advantage over other types of learning materials in that they can teach pupils individually more quickly, more thoroughly, and more pleasantly. Furthermore, they open up possibilities for individualizing instruction so that pupils can learn according to their own talents and needs without being bound to the "lockstep" of the common classroom recitation.

SKINNERIAN PROGRAMS. Most teaching programs on the market are Skinnerian linear programs. These programs, which are based on Skinner's theory of operant conditioning, bring the pupil to the desired goal by a series of successive approximations. Each step is an attempt to bring the pupil a little closer to the goal by asking him a question that he can answer correctly. Then, when the pupil does answer, the program reinforces the correct response by confirming that the answer is correct. Of course, if the response was incorrect, the program lets the pupil know that he has erred, although in good Skinnerian programs pupils are not given much chance to answer questions incorrectly for fear that they might reinforce errors and so learn the wrong thing. For this reason, the Skinnerian programs use exceedingly small steps and cue the learner to the correct responses. As a rule, in a Skinner program all pupils must follow the same route and complete all of the items in the order prescribed. Although some Skinnerian programs have been built with multiple-choice response items, Skinner himself has been insistent that the pupil should construct his response by writing it down. The illustration on page 332 is an excerpt from a linear program.[3]

INTRINSIC PROGRAMMING. Norman Crowder has advanced a quite different approach in what he calls intrinsic programming. Basically, Crowder's technique is to take relatively large steps, to use longer frames, perhaps several paragraphs at a time, and to reteach the pupil if he errs. Crowder's idea seems to be that a pupil can and must learn from his own mistakes and that not all pupils need the same program. Therefore, he provides branches that offer the opportunity for reteaching, or review, or depth teaching to those who seem to need it. The answer to each frame determines what the next frame will be.

SELECTING THE BEST PROGRAM. Just which of the various types of programs is best for classroom use is hard to determine at this time. The experimental evidence is contradictory and frequently at variance with what one sees in practice. Some evidence indicates that different types of programs are most effective for different people and different subject matter. It seems, for instance, that the very small steps and rigidity of

[3] Leonard H. Clark, *Resource Units: A Teaching Program,* Unpublished manuscript.

RESOURCE UNITS: A TEACHING PROGRAM

	1. Many school boards provide teachers with source or resource units to help them with their planning. Source units and _____ units are different names for the same thing.
1. resource	2. While the term source unit is sometimes used, the more common name is _____ unit.
2. resource	3. The term *resource unit* is very appropriate because the resource unit is a _____ to which teachers can go for suggestions when they are building teaching units and lessons.
3. resource	4. Source unit is also a very appropriate name for the resource unit because it is a _____ of suggestions teachers can use in building their lessons and teaching units.
4. source	5. Resource units are designed to help teachers plan lessons and teaching _____ .
5. units	6. Teaching units are units that are meant to be taught. Resource units are not meant to be _____; rather they provide resources from which a teacher can build teaching units that can be taught.
6. taught	7. A resource unit is simply a resource that a teacher can use for planning teaching units and lessons. It is _____ a plan for a teaching unit.
7. not	8. The resource unit is useful in _____ teaching units because it provides suggestions that may be used in the teaching unit.

❖   ❖   ❖

the linear program may tend to bore and frustrate older and brighter pupils. Branching can avoid some of this difficulty and so may, in this one respect at least, have an advantage in secondary-school instruction. Linear programs to be used in secondary schools should provide opportunities for pupils to "test out" of portions of the program so that they can skip material that would repeat previously learned subject matter.

❖

What advantages does programmed learning have in providing for individual differences?

What place does programmed instruction have in overall strategy?

The library is the heart of the school and a major source of material for secondary-school classes. Every pupil should learn to use it effectively.

What reply would you make to the critics who complain that programmed learning is too mechanistic and impersonal?

What types of programs seem best to you for use in your classes?

❊

Sources of Teaching Materials

Where to Find Materials

Materials for learning can be found almost everywhere. Among good sources of information telling where to find and how to use materials of instruction are curriculum guides and source (resource) units, and references such as those cited below. Note that this list is not complete, but simply suggestive.

Association for Supervision and Curriculum Development, *Using Free Materials in the Classroom*. The Association, Washington, D.C.

The American Film Review, The American Educational and Historical Film Center, Eastern Baptist College, St. Davids, Pennsylvania.

Bureau of Educational Research, *Sources of Teaching Materials,* The Bureau, Ohio State University, Columbus, Ohio.

Civil Aeronautics Administration, *Sources of Free and Low-Cost Materials,* United States Department of Commerce, Washington, D.C.

Committee on Scientific Aids to Learning, *School Recording Techniques,* National Research Council, 41 East Forty-Second Street, New York.

DEVERS, ELIZABETH, *Sources of Free and Inexpensive Materials,* The Author, P.O. Box 186, Grafton, West Virginia.

Division of Surveys and Field Services, *Free and Inexpensive Learning Materials,* George Peabody College for Teachers, Nashville, Tennessee.

Educators Progress Service, *Educators Guide to Free Curriculum Materials,* Randolph, Wisconsin.

———, *Educators Guide to Free and Inexpensive Material,* Randolph, Wisconsin.

———, *Educators Guide to Free Films,* Randolph, Wisconsin.

———, *Educators Guide to Free Filmstrips,* Randolph, Wisconsin.

———, *Educators Guide to Free Guidance Material,* Randolph, Wisconsin.

———, *Educators Guide to Free Science Materials,* Randolph, Wisconsin.

———, *Educators Guide to Free Social Studies Materials,* Randolph, Wisconsin.

———, *Educators Guide to Free Tapes, Scripts, and Transcriptions,* Randolph, Wisconsin.

Field Enterprises, Inc., *Sources of Free and Inexpensive Educational Materials,* Chicago.

H. W. WILSON COMPANY, *Educational Film Guide,* New York.

———, *Film-Strip Guide,* New York.

Institute for Communications Research, *New Teaching Aids for the American,* (Stanford, California: Stanford University, 1960).

JEWETT, ARNO, *Recordings for Teaching Literature and Language,* Bulletin 1952, Number 19, United States Office of Education, Washington, D.C.

Materials List for Use by Teachers of Modern Foreign Languages, Modern Language Association, Foreign Language Program Research Center, 70 Fifth Avenue, New York.

MILLER, BRUCE, *Sources of Free and Inexpensive Teaching Aids,* Box 369, Riverside, California.

———, *Sources of Free Pictures,* Box 369, Riverside, California.

National Association of Secondary-School Principals, *Free and Inexpensive Teaching Aids for High School,* Washington, D.C.

National Education Association, Department of Audio-Visual Instruction, *National Tape Recording Catalog,* Cumulative Edition, The Department, Washington, D.C., 1963.

———, Music Educators National Conference, *Film Guide for Music Educators,* The Conference, Washington, D.C., 1961.

NELSON, LESLIE W., *Instructional Aids . . . How To Make and Use Them*, William C Brown Company Publishers, Dubuque, Iowa, 1958.

PEPE, THOMAS J., *Free and Inexpensive Educational Aids*, Dover Publications, New York, 1960.

SILVERSTONE, DAVID M., and LIONEL BRANDON, *Instructional Materials Primer*, Educators Publishing Service, Cambridge, Massachusetts.

Teacher Tested Ideas, Department of Education, State of New Jersey, Trenton, New Jersey.

U.S. Government Films for Publications Use, U.S. Department of Health, Education, and Welfare, Office of Education, Government Printing Office, Washington, D.C.

U.S. Government Printing Office, Catalogs available on many subjects, Washington, D.C.

————, *A Directory of Film Libraries*, Washington, D.C.

WILLIAMS, CATHARINE M., *Learning from Pictures*, Department of Audio-Visual Instruction, National Education Association, Washington, D.C., 1963.

The following periodicals are a sampling of those which carry information about instructional materials and how to procure them.

Audio-Visual Instruction
A V Communication Review
Educational Screen and Audio-Visual Guide
The English Journal
Film and A.-V. World
Journal of Business Education
Journal of Health Education, Physical Education and Recreation
Journal of Home Economics
Music Educators' Journal
The Newsletter
The Personnel and Guidance Journal
The Mathematics Teacher
School Arts
The Science Teacher
Social Education

Value of Resource Units and Curriculum Guides

As we have said, resource units are excellent sources of information concerning materials of instruction. A resource unit is designed not to be taught but to serve as a source from which the teacher can build a teaching unit for classroom use. It contains suggested objectives, learning activities, lists of materials of instruction, teaching aids, and other information valuable in unit building. Some resource units are gauged for a definite grade level, but others may be used as a source for units at many levels and include tremendous amounts of material.

When such units are provided by the school system, the teacher should make use of them. If, however, none has been prepared in his school, the teacher can borrow from those available in other communities. Collections of resource units may be found in the curriculum libraries of many schools and school systems, schools of education, and state teachers' colleges. Sample copies are sometimes exhibited at conventions of educational associations. Many of them are available for purchase. Sometimes they may be obtained free. Information concerning them may be obtained from your supervisor, the state department of education, and such professional organizations as the Association for Supervision and Curriculum Development whose annual bulletin, Curriculum Materials, is a treasury of the best resource units and curriculum guides.

Curriculum bulletins, curriculum guides, and courses of study are also excellent sources of materials and ideas. Frequently they contain lists of materials available, addresses of places from which materials can be obtained, and other useful information. If they are provided by your school, use them. Don't let them gather dust; they are too valuable.

✿

Look at a sample resource unit. Note the amount of material it presents. How could you use such a resource unit for your own teaching?

✿

Finding Free and Inexpensive Material

Much teaching material is free or inexpensive. Many teachers seem not to be aware of this fact. To illustrate, some science teachers have been known to bewail unnecessarily a shortage of equipment. Science teachers should have equipment, of course; yet the lack of equipment should not completely hamstring them. The titles of Carleton J. Lynde's books, *Science Experiences with Ten-Cent-Store Equipment, Science Experiences with Inexpensive Equipment,* and *Science Experiences with Home Equipment* suggest that teachers can find plenty of materials for science experiences even if equipment is scarce. Similarly, teachers can find materials for the other subject fields, if they look.

A word of caution concerning free and inexpensive material is in order. Although much free material is available, some of it is hardly worth cluttering up one's shelves with. Consequently, one should cull the material quite thoroughly before presenting it to the pupils. In his examination of such material the teacher should be particularly alert for material that is merely advertising or propaganda.

Writing for Material

When writing for free material, the teacher should use official school stationery. The letter should state exactly what you want, and why you want it. Many firms like to know just how the material will be used and how many persons will see it. Sometimes teachers ask pupils to write the letter. Although doing so is excellent practice for the pupils, some firms will honor only letters from the teacher. Of course, one can sidestep this program by having pupils prepare letters for the teacher's signature or by having the teacher countersign the letter.

Making One's Own Materials

Frequently teachers need to make their own materials, particularly practice materials and study guides. Modern methods of duplicating written and typed materials are easy to use, and very versatile. With relatively little effort and ingenuity, teachers can duplicate exercises, diagrams, reading materials, assignments, study guides, and a multitude of other things. Once prepared, materials of this sort should be shared with other teachers. To hoard valuable teaching materials is wasteful.

An interesting technique used by a social studies teacher is to tear chapters out of old books and rebind them into pamphlets by stapling them into folders or notebook binders. By this technique the teacher amassed a considerable library of short articles on many topics pertinent to his social studies courses from discarded textbooks, *National Geographic Magazines,* and other books and periodicals at practically no expense. Not only was this a cheap method of securing reading matter, but reducing the books and periodicals to pamphlet form made a large number of different readings accessible at the same time. The scheme had the additional advantage of cleaning out numerous school closets and family attics.

A certain English teacher uses the same procedure to provide exercises in grammar. She cuts up old textbooks to make files of exercises for use in grammar classes. Another English teacher collected exercises for punctuation study by having pupils submit sentences to be punctuated. She collected them until she had a large number of exercises which she reproduced for pupil use. A science teacher makes a habit of going around to garages and junk shops to pick up old switches and other materials which, with the help of his pupils, he turns into demonstration equipment for his laboratory. Another science teacher allows brilliant boys and girls to prepare microscope slides for class use. An art teacher prepares his own clay for ceramics classes by processing, with the help of his pupils, clay dug from a bank near a river a few miles from the school.

❋

These incidents illustrate a few examples of the myriad sources of materials open to the ingenious teacher. What materials could you use for a class of your own? Where might you find these materials? How might you use them?

❋

Federal Funds for Instructional Materials

The problem of securing adequate materials of instruction is being alleviated greatly for many school districts by the provisions of recent federal legislation. Because regulations and budgeting for federal funding are likely to change with each Congress, teachers should keep alert for opportunities that apply to their schools and subjects. Keeping up with the provisions of the National Defense Education Act, the Elementary and Secondary Schools Act, the "Poverty" act and other similar Federal legislation as well as state and local implementing regulations is an important part of the teacher's professional responsibility.

Using the Community

The Community As a Resource

Extending the classroom into the community can make a course exciting and forceful, for every community is a gold mine of resources for teaching. The experiences of the pupils as they get out into the community are not only a welcome change but also potent learning activities. Similar benefits can also come from bringing the community into the classroom. For this reason every school should have a file of community resources available. Individual teachers sometimes keep such files for use in their own classes, but probably a well-kept central file is more efficient, although the teacher will need to keep additional information applicable to his own classes. In this file the teacher should be able to find information concerning resource persons, instructional material that can be obtained locally, possible field trips, and projects.

Using Resource People

Undoubtedly the most important resource of a community is its people. Even in a poor rural community the number of people who have special knowledge and talent that they can share effectively with a class is amazing. Often these persons can bring to a class new authority, new interest, new information, and a new point of view. Among the people who might be good resource persons are town, county, state, or federal government employees, hobbyists, travelers, businessmen, college teachers, specialists, clergymen, and people from other lands. Alumni, and parents and relatives of the pupils are frequently available and usually interested in visiting the schools. A certain chemistry teacher aroused class interest by featuring a visit by a metallurgist from a local brass mill. A source we sometimes forget are the other teachers and school officials of our own or neighboring school systems.

Resource persons can be used for many purposes. They can provide pupils with help in specialized projects. If a pupil needs help in constructing a rocket as a science project, perhaps an officer from a nearby air defense battery would be willing to help show him how. Resource persons can also provide information not otherwise readily available. Who would know more about soil conservation in your county than the local Soil Conservation Service agent?

PREPARING FOR THE GUEST SPEAKER. Resource persons are frequently used as speakers. Before inviting a layman to speak to his class, the teacher should check to be sure that there is a reasonable chance for the success of the activity. Quite often one can find out a lot about the potential speaker from other teachers and friends. In any case, you should visit him and talk to him about his subject. In your conversation you can probably determine whether he is the type who understands and can get along with young people. You can also probably determine whether he can speak at the young people's level. If his field is engineering and he discusses reaction motors only in the language of the professional engineer, he will not contribute much to the class.

When inviting a person to speak, you should brief him carefully on what he is to talk about and the purpose of the talk. A suitable agreement should be made concerning the length of the talk, the asking of questions, visual aids, and so forth. It is wise to remind the speaker of these agreements, the time, place, and topic in a letter of confirmation. The letter should be written diplomatically. Perhaps as good a form as any is to state the agreements as you understand them and ask him if he concurs. You can also remind him of these commitments when you introduce him to the class.

The public announcement that he is to speak for ten minutes and then answer questions often has a desirable effect on a long-winded, rambling guest. Such precautions may seem far-fetched but they are sometimes necessary. It is most discouraging to have a speaker talk for forty minutes of a forty-five-minute period without letting the pupils ask one of the questions they have prepared.

The teacher should also prepare the pupils for the meeting. As with other instructional aids, they should know what to expect and what to look for. Quite often, making up questions they would like answered is good preparation for listening to the speech and for the discussion period after the speech. Pupil questions may also be given to the speaker as a guide for his speech.

As a rule, speakers cannot be counted on to hold the attention of a class for a whole period. The guest appearance is usually much more successful if the formal speaking is kept quite short and the bulk of the program devoted to discussion and pupil questions. Sometimes it is more rewarding to bring in resource persons to act as consultants for pupil discussion groups.

Conducting Field Trips

Particularly vivid learning experiences sometimes result from going out into the community. One of the most common devices used for extending the classroom into the community is the field trip. This method is a time-honored one having been used with great success for centuries. Field trips can take many forms. A nature walk is a field trip. A visit to the museum is a field trip. So is a period spent on the athletic field searching for specimens of insects.

Conducting a field trip is much the same as conducting any other instructional activity. The pupils must be introduced to it, they must be briefed on what to look for, and the activity should be followed up. However, field trips do present certain special considerations such as scheduling, permissions, transportation, expense, and control.

Early in his planning, the teacher should talk the trip over with his principal or supervisor. Bringing the principal into the planning early will help in eliciting his support. Moreover, the teacher will probably need the principal's assistance in arranging the administrative details as well as his authorization of the trip.

Before planning the trip, the teacher should make the trip himself, if possible, to see whether it would be worthwhile for the pupils and how it can be made most productive. He must arrange the details at the place to be visited. Many museums, factories, and other places of interest provide their own tour services. If they do, the teacher must be sure to let the proper persons know the purpose of the visit and what the pupils should see. He must also arrange for the necessary permissions, schedule changes, transportation, and so forth. Pupils can often help considerably in the planning and arranging of a field trip. However, the teacher should be careful to double- and triple-check himself on the details. He must also double-check to be sure that everyone has a mission to perform on the field trip. The trip should not be a joy ride or an outing but a real learning experience.

✵

What are the advantages of taking pupils on field trips? What are the disadvantages?

Why must field trips be planned? What particularly must be considered in the planning? To what extent and in what ways can the pupils participate in planning and carrying out the plans?

Many field trips are not worth the time, trouble, and expense. How can you ensure that your field trips are not merely outings?

✵

Studying the Community

A field trip is one way to study an aspect of the community. There are other ways, of course. One of them is to read and study. A surprisingly large amount of printed information is available about almost every community. This material may include reports of the federal, state, and local governments; releases by the Chamber of Commerce and similar agencies; stories in the local press; advertising and promotional literature from local concerns; publications of local civic and fraternal organizations; and, sometimes, articles in state and national publications. Unpublished material can sometimes be used to advantage. A pupil in a New England community was allowed to use old school records to write an historical account of the founding of the local school system in the early nineteenth century.

Another common method by which to study a community is to interview its prominent citizens. This method is not always fruitful because many persons find interview techniques difficult to use. If pupils are to apply it in a community study, they should be properly instructed in how to carry out a successful interview. The teacher should provide demonstrations of good interview techniques, and the pupils should practice on themselves before practicing on adults. Of course adults, particularly important adults, will make allowances for the errors of pupils who interview them. Nevertheless, you will want pupils to make a good impression on the people interviewed. For this reason, if no other, the pupils should be well rehearsed in their roles before leaving for the interview.

Another excellent method to use in studying the community is observation. The familiar device of keeping a record of the foods pupils eat, so often used in health, hygiene, biology, and home economics classes, is an example of this type of study. Counting the number of cars that do not come to a full stop at a stop sign is another. Ordinarily, for observation to be successful, the observer needs to be well briefed in what he is looking for. He needs to have criteria by which to objectify his observation and some system of recording it. Usually a checklist, or rating scale, or similar form is helpful to observers both for recording and for objectifying the observations. Since accurate observation is rather difficult, pupils who engage in such techniques should be instructed in their use. Quite often practice sessions will be beneficial.

CONDUCTING A COMMUNITY SURVEY. Another technique sometimes used successfully in studying a community is the survey. A community survey is a study of the status of something in the community. It might consist of a study of the opinions of citizens regarding a forthcoming election, or a study of sanitary conditions in a certain ward. Thus a survey can be a two-edged sword. Well planned, it can bring pupils face to face with the realities in the community. Poorly planned, it can result in erroneous learning and impaired public relations. Therefore every community survey should be prepared thoroughly and planned carefully. Before the pupils begin, they should be well versed in the topic to be investigated and the techniques they are to use. A poorly prepared survey is seldom worth the pupils' effort.

Gathering and interpreting the data of the survey can be troublesome. The actual gathering of the data may be done in many ways. Among them are the interview, the questionnaire, observation, and combinations of these and other techniques. Planning for the use of these techniques should be done carefully so as not to waste the time of the respondents and so that the data gathered are really useful. The interpretation of the data should be approached with even more caution. One should set up criteria to differentiate between important and unimportant data, and meaningful and meaningless data. Moreover, one should set up criteria to determine the meaning of the data. This can often be done by inspection, but in some classes one may wish to apply simple statistical procedures. High-school pupils can learn to use these procedures readily. Information concerning their use may be found in any textbook on educational measurement or statistics. Many of the newer high-school mathematics texts discuss these procedures as well.

Teachers and pupils are sometimes tempted to make public the results of their survey. In most cases the temptation should be resisted, and the survey should be reported to the class only. If it seems desirable to make the report public, the teacher should consult his administrative superior before releasing anything. In addition, he can sometimes consult with a group of laymen in collaboration with his superior. In any event, the report should be made public only if it is outstanding and if its public release will enhance the relationship that exists between the school and the community.

With the possible exception of requiring a little more imagination, this type of activity is not particularly different from any other. As in any other activity involving the community, the planning should be exceptionally good. If the project involves meeting the public, the pupils should be well versed in their roles.

CONDUCTING COMMUNITY SERVICE PROJECTS. One evening in a suburban city a group of teen-agers went from house to house ringing doorbells. They were social-studies pupils conducting a campaign to inform voters of the issues in the coming elections and to persuade them to vote. Such service projects are another effective way to extend the classroom into the community. Quite often such activities get at objectives which the more usual classroom activities fail to reach. The techniques for preparing pupils for community study are equally efficacious in preparing them for a service project.[3]

Securing Administrative Approval

Projects like the one mentioned in the last paragraph can lead to complications if they are not carefully managed. One can well imagine that the school administrators were particularly concerned with the conduct of this activity. So it is with almost every activity involving the community. Projects of this sort have been known to upset school-community relations. For that reason the teacher should always secure the advice and consent of his administrative and supervisory superiors before attempting such activities. In communities where the climate of opinion is not right, these activities will have to be forgone. The administration may find it necessary to withhold permission for other reasons also. Perhaps the proposal would interfere with other activities or classes; perhaps the timing would not be propitious; perhaps the community has had a surfeit of school surveys or service projects; perhaps the budget would not stand the expense. The decision about whether the activity should or should not be attempted is the administrator's prerogative.

✻

What might be a community service project suitable for use in your community? If you were to attempt to use this project, what preparations and precautions would you take?

In your own circle of friends and relatives, how many of them have special skills and knowledges which they might share with secondary-school pupils? How might you use the resources of these people in a secondary-school class?

[3] Techniques for conducting group projects are discussed in Chapters 10 and 11.

How would you go about preparing a group of pupils to interview the mayor of your community?

✳

Summary

There is no shortage of material for use in the schools. Free or inexpensive reading matter on almost any subject is available from governmental and business agencies. Still, most teachers will find it advantageous to make their own dittoed or mimeographed readings and study guides. They will probably want to duplicate their practice materials and exercises. When they do, it may be wise to consider methods by which one can preserve homemade materials for reuse.

Exercises and practice materials are also available commercially in workbooks. Workbooks have earned a bad reputation by encouraging the rote learning of inconsequential facts. Still, they can be useful for practice and review and for providing for individual differences.

The teaching program is an adaptation of the workbook utilizing scientific principles. Whether presented by machine, book, or some other means, the program acts as a mechanical tutor which presents and follows up lessons. As a rule, teachers should not attempt to build their own teaching programs. Nevertheless all teachers should understand how the programs are constructed so they can select and use them knowledgeably. At the present there are many types of programs, the two major types being the linear and the intrinsic. Just which type is best we do not yet know. So far the only really dependable way to judge a program's worth is to try it out with pupils.

Many publications list sources of materials of instruction. For specific courses and units the best sources of information are curriculum guides. Although many materials can be procured by simply writing and asking for them, many teachers find the best materials are the ones they make themselves.

Perhaps the best resource the teacher has is the community itself. It is both a source of subject matter and a source of instructional material and resource persons. Community lay persons can be used as classroom speakers and as consultants and guides. Field trips, community surveys, and community service projects are time-proven ways to utilize the community for instruction. Community activities should be planned and followed through very carefully so that the activity may be worthwhile and to save the school from embarrassment. In activities of this sort the teacher must always bear in mind their possible effect on school-community relations. Therefore, it is especially important that all such activities be cleared with all the authorities concerned.

FOR FURTHER STUDY

The readings listed for further study at the end of Chapter 13 as well as the references cited within the present chapter under the heading "Sources of Teaching Materials" are suitable for further study of the topics presented in this chapter. In addition you may wish to consult references on programmed learning such as the following.

CRAM, DAVID, Explaining "Teaching Machines" and Programming (San Francisco: Fearon Publishers, Inc., 1961).

DETERLINE, WILLIAM A., An Introduction to Programed Instruction (Englewood Cliffs, N.J.: Prentice-Hall, Inc., 1962).

GLASER, ROBERT, and ARTHUR A. LUMSDAINE (editor), Teaching Machines and Programed Learning (Washington, D.C.: Division of Audio-Visual Instruction, National Education Association, 1960).

GREEN, EDWARD J., The Learning Process and Programed Instruction (New York: Holt, Rinehart and Winston, Inc., 1962).

LYSAUGHT, JEROME P., and CLARENCE M. WILLIAMS, A Guide to Programed Instruction (New York: John Wiley and Sons, Inc., 1963).

MARGOLIES, STUART, and LEWIS D. EIGEN, Applied Programed Instruction (New York: John Wiley and Sons, Inc., 1962).

SCHRAMM, WILBUR (editor), Programed Instruction (New York: The Fund For the Advancement of Education, 1964).

————, Programmed Instruction—Today and Tomorrow (New York: The Fund for the Advancement of Education, 1962).

————, The Research on Programmed Instruction, OE-34034 Bulletin 1964, No. 35, Office of Education, U.S. Department of Health, Education, and Welfare (Washington, D.C.: U.S. Government Printing Office, 1964). (An annotated bibliography.)

STOLUROW, LAWRENCE M., Teaching by Machine, OE-34010, Cooperative Research Monograph No. 6, Office of Education, U.S. Department of Health, Education, and Welfare (Washington, D.C.: U.S. Government Printing Office, 1961).

PART VI
Evaluation

CHAPTER 15

Evaluation and Testing

A Basis for Next Steps

In order to guide his ship in its proper course, a navigator must know where he is. He therefore keeps a running record of his approximate position and frequently checks to fix his exact position. He must do so in order to know in what direction to lay his course. If he does not know where he is, how can he tell in what direction to go? So it is with teaching. We must know where we are in order to know in which way to go. We must continuously appraise and reappraise our position. This appraisal of the teaching-learning situation is called evaluation.

Evaluation is also used to ascertain a pupil's status and the worth of his schoolwork. In short, it is used as a basis for school marks, reporting to parents, and promotion. Although this role of evaluation has its place, it should not be evaluation's primary role. When our navigator finds his position, he may be elated to know that the day's run has been satisfactory or chagrined to find that he is considerably off course. But that is not the end of it. He lays a new course that will take him where he wants to go in the light of the new information. Evaluation is much too dynamic a process to be limited to pronouncements concerning the value of something. In teaching, its primary purpose should be diagnosis and finding one's bearings as a basis for deciding the next steps to take.

The Need for Definite Goals

To evaluate, one must know not only where he is but where he wants to go. This destination is his goal. One can judge one's progress by finding out how close one has come to it. In teaching, the goals are the learnings the teacher is trying to teach his pupils. These goals should be specific and definite. Unless they describe specific learning products and indicate standards of excellence, there is no way to tell how well the pupils are progressing. Effective evaluation depends upon definite goals. For this reason it is recommended that for each lesson and unit the objectives, which are the teacher's goals, be stated specifically in simple declarative sentences.

Evaluation versus Measurement

The basis of evaluation is judgment. This is the quality which makes evaluation differ from measurement. Measurement describes a situation; evaluation judges its worth or value. For instance, the score of a student's test may be 70. This in itself does not tell us much of anything. Is 70 good or bad? No one can say until he has more information. If 70 represents the highest score of all the students of our school, that may indicate one thing; if it represents the lowest score, it may indicate another; if it is the lowest score, but the work of a brilliant student, it may indicate something else; if it is the lowest score, but the best effort of the slowest pupil, it may indicate something else again. Evaluation is the judgment or interpretation that one draws from the information at hand about a pupil's work. It is the basis upon which a teacher determines what to do next.

Measurement is also essential for evaluation. Only by measuring can we hope to ascertain the status of the pupil's learning at the moment. Measurement can also give us information about the approximate status of other aspects of the pupil's personality. From these measurements we can evaluate the learning or other personality trait in light of our goals. Measurement is only a tool to be used in evaluation. Used by itself it is meaningless, but without it evaluation is likely to be very erratic indeed.

✳

What is the difference between measurement and evaluation?

What can test results be used for? What are the most valid uses of test scores?

✳

Evaluative Devices and Techniques

The Right Instrument

Teaching objectives are of various sorts. Bloom, Kratwohl, and their associates[1] have set up taxonomies in which they list six different types of "cognitive" objectives and five different types of "affective" objectives. In order to measure these different types of learning products, one must use different types of measuring devices. The type of test item that will

---

[1] Benjamin S. Bloom (editor), *Taxonomy of Educational Objectives, Handbook I, Cognitive Domain* (New York: David McKay Company, Inc., 1956); Kratwohl, David R., Benjamin S. Bloom, and Bertram B. Masia, *Taxonomy of Educational Objectives, Handbook II, Affective Domain* (New York: David McKay Company, Inc., 1964).

ascertain whether a pupil knows a fact will seldom be useful for determining his ability to analyze, and will almost certainly be useless for finding out his values. So each measuring device and test item should be selected to do a particular job. Teachers and test builders must be very careful in building tests to select the types of items that can do what they are meant to do.

Limitations of Tests

Although paper-and-pencil tests are the commonest tool used in measuring pupil progress, they often fail to give us the most important information we want in the evaluation of a pupil. By their very nature, paper-and-pencil tests are more likely to test knowing-about than knowing, verbalizations rather than the ability to do, or platitudes rather than changes in attitude or behavior. Since understandings, abilities, and changes in attitudes or behavior are the essential goals of the unit, teachers must use other devices and techniques to supplement the formal tests and get at these important learnings. The following paragraphs will endeavor to point out how some of these devices can be used to advantage.

Evaluation by Means of Observation

Perhaps the most common basis for judging the behavior of another person is to observe him. This technique is as old as mankind. Unfortunately, it has several limitations. Observers are notoriously unreliable. The behavior of the pupil is often different when he knows he is being observed. However, to a degree, these limitations can be reduced by careful observation. A helpful technique is to determine in advance what to observe and how to observe it. Another is to set up a checklist, rating scale, or some other written guide to help objectify one's observation. Rating scales and checklists are especially helpful in judging skills and changes in behavior.

Rating scales and checklists can also be used to help objectify the evaluation of products of the pupil's work, such as a lamp made in an industrial arts class, or a composition or theme. Such devices have the advantage of showing the pupil an analysis of the rater's evaluation and also of preventing the rater from being unduly influenced by any one aspect of the work being evaluated.

In using such tools, the final evaluation can be made dependent upon a numerical score. However, one must always remember that the evaluation of literary and art works and other creative activities cannot be reduced safely to numerical scores. To avoid cul-de-sacs, the rater should allow for the possibility that a simple aspect of a creative work might

Check lists and rating scales are useful to objectify the evaluation of skill activities such as these boys must learn in mechanical drawing.

outweigh all others, and that some items may be completely inapplicable to certain works. Consequently, subjective rating after an inspection using a rating scale may be considerably superior to mechanical rating on the strength of a total score or average of the ratings.

PREPARING A RATING SCALE. One can make rating scales and checklists quite easily. To make a rating scale, merely decide what characteristics you wish to rate. Then arrange a scale for each of these characteristics. Since a five-point scale is about all a rater can handle, there is little point in making finer distinctions. If each point of the scale is labeled, the rating is much easier.

To illustrate this process, suppose we wish to build a scale to use as a guide for judging the excellence of some posters which pupils have prepared. First we must decide what to consider in judging the posters. Let us say that among other things we wish to include neatness, lettering, eye appeal, and design. We then provide a rating scale similar to the one on page 353. In this rating scale, the gradations are indicated by descriptive words encompassing the gamut from best to worst. These descriptions help make the teacher-ratings somewhat more objective than they might be otherwise.

Rating Scale for Posters

DESIGN	Crystalline beautiful perfect	Clear well-balanced pleasing	Mediocre	Confusing poorly balanced crowded	Hodge-podge
NEATNESS	Meticulous	Excellent	Average	Fair	Sloppy
LETTERING	Superior	Excellent	Average	Fair	Poor
EYE APPEAL	Overwhelming	Intriguing	Catchy	Dull	Insipid

Another plan is to use numbers as in the following scale for evaluating themes. Five equals the highest rating and one the lowest. "NA" means "not applicable." The scale is used by circling the number desired.

Rating Scale for Written Work

(Circle number indicating rating. Code: 5, highest; 1, lowest; NA, not applicable)

1. Originality
         5   4   3   2   1   NA
2. Vividness of expression
         5   4   3   2   1   NA
3. Clearness
         5   4   3   2   1   NA

           *   *   *

11. Spelling
         5   4   3   2   1   NA
12. Sentence structure
         5   4   3   2   1   NA

PREPARING A CHECKLIST. Checklists are prepared in much the same way as rating scales. However, instead of making a scale we prepare a list on which the rater can indicate the presence or absence of certain qualities or characteristics by checking.

For instance, in checking some plastic letter openers that the pupils had made in his industrial arts class, the teacher might make up a checklist like the following.

Checklist for
Plastic Letter Opener—General Shop I

Check each item if the letter opener is up to standard in this particular:
( ) 1. The blade is properly shaped.
( ) 2. All saw marks are removed.
( ) 3. The plastic is free from warping and pitting.

As the teacher inspects the letter openers, he will check the applicable items. This will give him a firm basis for evaluating the product.

In the following device, used for rating the speech of college students preparing for teaching, spaces are left blank so that the rater can either check or make some comment for each of the various items.

Speech Qualification Rating Sheet

	EXPLANATION	READING	QUESTIONING
Poised			
Direct			
Animated			
Distinct			
Audible			
Fluent			
Clear (ver)			
(vis)			
Pronunciation			

RECOMMENDATION

✲

Is it really possible to objectify observation? Explain.

Compare the various types of rating scales and checklists given above. What are the strong points and weak points of each? Why?

✲

USING BEHAVIOR LOGS AND ANECDOTAL REPORTS. As Chapter 2 points out, observation is particularly important for gaining information about the attitudes, behavior, and abilities of pupils. The anecdotal reports and behavior logs described in that chapter are excellent devices for systematically recording such observation. Because they are records of the everyday behavior of pupils, they can be very revealing.

Use of Problem-Situation Tests

The teacher does not always have an opportunity to observe how his pupils act in certain situations. To fill this lack, the problem-situation test has been developed. In this test the examiner confronts the pupil with a problem situation. The test is to see what the pupil will do. In some cases the teacher can face the pupil with an actual situation, and observe what he does. For example, a common procedure in an auto-mechanics course is to give the pupil a motor that will not run and tell him to find out what the trouble is. Similarly, in a class in which one is attempting to teach pupils how to conduct a meeting according to Robert's Rules of Order, the teacher might set up a meeting and see how well various members preside.

To set up situations of this type may be quite difficult. However, teachers can create pencil-and-paper problem-situation tests to serve the same purpose. If a teacher wished to observe each member of the class demonstrating his skill in handling a meeting, too much time might be consumed. He therefore might devise a situation test consisting of questions like this one.

You are senior class president. You have just called to order a special meeting of the class to discuss the class trip, the senior ball, commencement activities, and the class gift. What should the order of business be for this meeting?

In the case of the broken engine, the teacher might devise a problem situation with questions like this one.

A farmer's tractor will not start. What steps would you take to find out what the matter is with the motor?

The items used in a problem-situation test may be either the essay or objective type. Usually, however, some type of free recall item is better than an item that suggests possible solutions to the problem.

Use of Themes, Notebooks, Homework, and Recitation

Of course, themes, homework, papers, and oral recitations are also evidence of pupil progress. They should be checked carefully. A good rule is never to assign anything that is not going to be checked by someone. Practice material, however, need not always be checked by the teacher. Sometimes pupils can check their own and each other's work quite effectively. In order to provide an objective basis for evaluating such work, one can utilize rating scales, checklists, and standards. Both the rating device and the exercise should be used mainly as aids to instruction. The emphasis should be on diagnosis, practice, and learning rather than on rating.

❁

What devices other than tests does the teacher have available for estimating the progress of pupils? How can each be best used?

What would be the best way to test a pupil's honesty? His ability to swim? His appreciation of a poem? His freedom from prejudices? His understanding that "all men are created equal, with certain inalienable rights"? What do your answers imply as far as a testing program is concerned?

Of what uses can a behavior log be to a classroom teacher? To a guidance worker?

❁

Self-Evaluation of Pupils' Work

Too many teachers think of themselves as sitting in judgment on the work of the pupils. The purpose of evaluation is to determine where the class is and to decide where it should go. The person most concerned in any teaching-learning situation is the pupil. *If evaluation is to be fully effective, and the pupil is to set his goals correctly, the pupil should participate in evaluating his own progress.*

Pupils can cooperate in evaluating their own progress in many ways. First, they can participate in formulating the goals for the unit. Second, they can cooperate by checking their own work. Third, they can inspect their own work to find their strengths and weaknesses. Fourth, they can often decide when they have reached the point where they should go on to something else.

For example, in a certain English class one of the major concerns was the improvement of oral language skills. Each pupil was given a small roll of recording tape to use during the semester. Every pupil learned how to run the tape recorder and could, if he so desired, use the tape during out-of-class hours. On the tape each pupil could record conversations, class discussions, oral reports, and practice material. The recordings were criticized both by the pupils and the teacher. Pupils noted their own errors and worked on them individually. They also practiced by themselves on material provided by the instructor until they thought they had improved enough to record their voices again and to listen to the playback. The other work of the class was largely individualized, so that pupils could use the tape recorder whenever they were ready. In this way the pupils were able to see their errors, and with the teacher's aid set up a program for improvement. Thus they were able to see their progress and to judge whether they had improved enough to go on to other work. The teacher felt that the class improved much more than if he had tried to teach these skills directly and had made the criticisms himself.

Another evaluation technique used in the same English class was to let the pupils criticize both their own themes and those of other pupils. The primary goal was clarity, so the teacher let the pupils read each other's themes and point out what was not clear in them. Then the teacher, or on occasion another pupil, told the writer where in the text or the supplementary readings he could find a discussion of the particular error. Sometimes the teacher gave the pupil self-correcting exercises to help remedy his fault. Ordinarily, the pupils worked on these exercises until they thought they had conquered the problem. Since the pupils knew these exercises were not to be counted into their marks, they felt no need to cheat. Again, the teacher felt that the pupils learned much more efficiently than they would have if he had corrected each paper himself and had doled out marks.

AIDS TO SELF-EVALUATION. Pupils can keep anecdotal reports and behavior logs to measure their own work. For instance, a pupil working on a project can keep a daily log or diary of his progress and a record of his successes and difficulties. In a unit a pupil might submit short reports on himself at the culmination of different aspects of the work, and estimate the worth of his product and the benefits he has gained from the activity. If marks are not overemphasized, pupils can evaluate much of their own work and keep many of the records.

The use of cameras and tape recorders may make it easier for pupils to judge their own progress. They also make it possible for teachers to analyze pupils' actions, to diagnose errors, and to measure progress. Teachers can also use these devices to show pupils how well they are getting on and what their faults and strengths are. Motion pictures are commonly used by coaches and physical education directors for these purposes. Similarly, tape recorders are often used in speech classes and in the evaluation of discussions, panels, and other group activities.

The pupil may also participate in the evaluation of his own work through conferences with the teacher. In the conference the pupil has an opportunity to ask the teacher for help on difficult points, while the teacher has an opportunity to evaluate the pupil's work, to point out errors, to encourage him, and to diagnose his performance. The conference need not be formal. A few words at the teacher's desk or at the pupil's work station may serve just as well as a full-dress interview. In fact, the more informal the conference, the more valuable it is likely to be.

Testing

Four Criteria of a Good Test

When considering the worth of any measuring device, be it standard test, teacher-made test, or rating scale, four things need to be considered.

1. How valid is it?

2. How reliable is it?
3. How objective is it?
4. How usable is it?

The most important of these criteria is validity, that is, the extent to which the device measures what it is supposed to measure. A measuring device that is not valid is worthless. Validity is dependent on several things. In the first place, the instrument must be suitable to the nature of what is to be measured. A paper-and-pencil test would hardly be a valid measure of a baseball player's ability to bat, for instance. Furthermore, the instrument must measure all the significant aspects of what is to be measured in an amount proportional to their importance. If, in testing batting ability, one tested the batter's stance, but not his ability to hit the ball, the test would give a false result because of poor sampling. Moreover, to be valid the test must also discriminate. In testing batting ability, of what use is a test that does not differentiate between the good batters and the poor batters?

A particularly important criterion for establishing the validity of an achievement test is curricular validity. Curricular validity indicates the extent to which a test measures what was taught in the course. Without it, an achievement test cannot be valid. When the items of an achievement test are concerned with learning that was not part of the course, the test will give incorrect results because of its lack of curricular validity. Commercial achievement tests sometimes give an inaccurate picture of the achievement of pupils in a particular school because the curriculum of the school may differ from that for which the commercial test was designed.

The second test of the worth of an evaluative device is reliability. A test is reliable if it can be trusted to give the same results when repeated or when different forms are used. In general, a long test is more likely to be reliable than a short test, and an objective test more reliable than an essay test. These are about the only criteria readily available for the average teacher-built test, although statistical methods are used to determine coefficients of reliability for standardized tests. Reliability, to a large extent, takes luck out of the picture. When a test is truly reliable, a teacher can be quite sure that he has a good estimate of whatever is being measured. And if what it measures is what it is supposed to measure, the test is a good one, for a test should be both reliable and valid. However, if one or the other must be sacrificed, it should be reliability because validity is much more necessary than reliability in a test.

Another criterion of a good test is objectivity. By objectivity educators mean that the personality of the scorer does not affect the scoring of the test. Thus a truly objective test will be scored in exactly the same way by every scorer. For this reason objectivity in a test helps make the scoring fair and the test reliable. As long as validity is not sacrificed, the more objective the test the better. However, a valid test is often a good test even though it is not objective, while an objective test that is not valid is always worthless.

A fourth criterion of a good evaluative device is its usability. Obviously a two-hour test is not suitable for a forty-minute class period. Everything else being equal, teachers should avoid tests that are hard to administer, difficult to score, and expensive.

✿

Objective-type tests are not always objective. Why not? Why might a truly objective test in composition be a bad test?

What are the most important criteria for judging the worth of a test? Rate these criteria in order of importance. Why did you choose that order? When would you use an objective test? Apply these criteria to a test in one of your college courses.

✿

Building an Objective Test

As in all other teaching, the first step in test construction is to plan. Every teacher should set up objectives for each lesson or unit he teaches. He should use these objectives for the basis of his test plan. To a large measure they should determine what kind of test to give and what items to include. Some learning products may be tested best by performance tests, some by essay tests, some by objective tests, and some by observation. The test builder attempts to pick the type of item that will best suit the objectives of a particular lesson. After consideration he may find it advisable to use several types of test items and devices. Whatever choice he makes usually depends upon the time and materials available as well as the objectives to be tested. In the following paragraphs we shall first discuss the building of an objective test and then the building of an essay test.

THE OBJECTIVE-TEST ITEM. Both essay-test items and objective-test items have their good and bad points. In several ways the objective-test item is the better of the two. With it teachers can provide a relatively adequate sampling quite easily. Furthermore, since objective-test items limit the pupil's choice, the answers do not wander from the point in the way essay answers sometimes do. Also, they are not likely to include irrelevant material or be affected by environmental conditions. For these reasons, objective tests are often more reliable than essay tests. In addition, the use of scoring keys makes the objective test easy to score. In fact, the scoring is often so easy that it may be farmed out to clerks or other nonprofessionals. Moreover, the use of keys and automatic scoring devices can make the objective test really objective. It is only when the scorer departs from the key that the test becomes subjective. Objective tests have the additional advantage of being less time-consuming than essay tests. As a matter of fact, objective tests can often do in a single period more than an essay test can do in a double period.

In spite of their virtues objective-type tests have many serious faults. In the first place, good objective-test items are difficult to write. Even in carefully built tests some items are liable to be ambiguous or to contain clues that may give away the answers. Second, to test high-level learning with this type of test is difficult. Although objective-test items can test the ability to organize, the ability to use what has been learned, the ability to show relationships, and the ability to evaluate, such items are extremely difficult to build and frequently even more difficult to key. The objective-type test often tests only isolated facts with a resultant emphasis on verbalism rather than true understanding.

DESIGNING THE OBJECTIVE TEST. The first step in building an objective test is to design the test. It should be done with care, for the task is to build a test that will allow the pupils to show just how well they have progressed. The test builder should avoid any extraneous influences that might affect the test score. In designing the test, he should bear the following rules of thumb in mind.

1. All teaching objectives should be tested in proportion to their importance.
2. The test should include items easy enough for the slowest pupils and items difficult enough to challenge the brightest ones.
3. To avoid confusion, only a few types of items should be used in the test.
4. All items of the same type should be placed together.
5. Items should be arranged from the easiest to the most difficult so as not to discourage the less bright at the beginning of the test.
6. Directions, format, and wording should be crystal clear. There is no room for trick questions or obscurity. A test is neither a joke nor a puzzle.

❊

Of what value are the objectives of a lesson or unit when one is devising a test?

Why is it sometimes stated that there is no such thing as an objective test?

In constructing a teacher-built test, what procedure would you follow? Outline what you would do step by step.

❊

SELECTION OF THE ITEMS. Once the teacher has developed his test plan, he is ready to select the test items. In order to ensure curricular validity, without which an achievement test is of little value, the teacher should see to it that each item selected is directed toward a specific teaching objective. Moreover, he must be careful to select items that point up the objectives in proportion to their importance. A test that emphasizes some goals at the expense of others is not valid.

If the teacher has taught the unit or lesson before, he should have a file of test items. Good test items are too difficult to build to be thrown away. Consequently, whenever a teacher gives a test he should save the good items and file them away for future use. Keeping such a file is easy, since all the teacher needs to do is to clip the good items from his test as he uses them, paste them to cards, and file them. A little painless filing may save much laborious item building. It goes without saying that the teacher will find it desirable to construct additional new items for every test. Fortunately, the item builder has many types of items from which to choose.

Types of Objective-Test Items

Probably the most familiar type of objective-test item is the alternate-answer item. Alternate-answer items are items in which the pupil has a choice between two possible responses, for example, true-false or yes-no. Items of this sort have had great popularity, but they are looked on with disfavor by some authorities because they encourage guessing. Some examples are

Circle the correct answer (or underline the correct answer).

True-False	1. Milton was a sense realist.
Right-Wrong	2. Reliability is the degree to which the test agrees with itself.
Yes-No	3. Most early scientific discoveries were made by university professors.
Were-Were not	4. Girls _____ allowed to attend school beyond elementary level in Colonial New England.
Forward-Rearward	5. The clutch lever of the Bell and Howell projector must be in the _____ position before it will run.

This type of item can be found in many forms. An interesting variation is the following in which the pupil must identify synonymous words.

In the following, write S in the space provided if the words are essentially the same; write D if they are different.
( ) 1. reliability-consistency
( ) 2. scoring-grading
( ) 3. measuring-evaluating
( ) 4. norm-average.

A more familiar alternate-answer item is the true-false item. True-false items can be set up in many ways. The following examples, for instance, call for decision concerning whether an item is probably true or probably false.

In the proper space below, write plus (+) if true or probably true. Write minus (−) if false or probably false.
(   ) 1. Validity is the most important characteristic of a good examination.
(   ) 2. The split-half method is used in estimating the reliability of a test.
(   ) 3. Reliability is frequently expressed by the use of coefficient of correlation.

Other variations of the true-false item, as in the example below, call for a third alternative response.

Write plus (+) if true, minus (−) if false, 0 if only an opinion.
(   ) 1. Hartshorne and May found a positive correlation between honesty and intelligence.
(   ) 2. The intelligence test is the best contribution of psychology to education.
(   ) 3. The A.Q. is more reliable statistically than the I.Q.

Another variation calls for four alternatives. In this variation the pupil is supposed to indicate whether a statement is true, probably true, false, or probably false. Variations of this sort help to take guessing out of the true-false test. Another variation designed for the same purpose requires the pupil to correct false statements.

Write plus (+) if true, minus (−) if false. If false, show why.
(   ) 1. The school superintendent usually heads the board of education.

Checklist items are much like alternate-answer items. Usually these items consist of fairly long lists from which the pupil checks the items which apply. In the following example the list might well consist of ten items.

Check the duties of the local board of education that appear in the following list.
_____ 1. Hire teachers.
_____ 2. Adopt school budget.
_____ 3. Select superintendent.
_____ 4. Etc.

MULTIPLE-CHOICE ITEMS. Multiple-choice items have the advantage of being relatively free from guessing if four or more alternative responses are used and if reasonable care is used in picking the incorrect responses. However, if these distractors (i.e., incorrect answers) do not seem reasonable, they can easily give the answer away. Two types of multiple-choice questions appear below.

Select the best answer and write its letter in the space in the margin.

———— 1. The U.S. Commissioner of Education is
   a. selected by the people.
   b. elected by the Senate.
   c. appointed by the President with the approval of the Senate.
   d. elected by the House of Representatives.
   e. appointed by the Secretary of Health, Education, and Welfare.

Underline the right answer (or circle or cross out the right answer).

1. The first college in the colonies was
   a. Harvard   d. Yale
   b. Columbia   e. Brown
   c. Princeton

These variations differ in form only. A variation of the multiple-choice item which differs in substance as well as form is the category or identification item. Usually these are used with long lists.

Mark the items which result from action of the sympathetic nervous system, S; those which result from action of the parasympathetic nervous system, P; if neither of these systems controls an item, leave it blank.
   (   ) 1. Increases heart beat.
   (   ) 2. Dilates pupils of eyes.
   (   ) 3. Increases sweating.
   (   ) 4. Checks flow of saliva.
   (   ) 5. Movement of forearm.
   (   ) 6. Secretion of adrenalin.
   (   ) 7. Etc.

MATCHING-TEST ITEMS. Another common type of objective test is the matching test. Again we find several variations of the basic form which consists of two unequal columns of items to be matched as in the following.

With one exception each of the phrases in column II has to do with one of the items in column I. Place the letter preceding the phrase in the parentheses preceding the appropriate item in column I.

I	II
( ) 1. Carnegie unit.	a. A life goal.
( ) 2. Course.	b. The total offering.
( ) 3. Program of studies.	c. The relationship between present tendencies toward, and capacities for, behavior and the immediate goal toward which he is working.
( ) 4. Curriculum.	
( ) 5. Aptitude.	

I	II
( ) 6. Ability.	d. A developed capacity for behavior.
( ) 7. Core activity.	e. The structural basis upon which the capacity of *d* above is developed.
( ) 8. Aim.	f. In the unit assignment something which everyone must do to some extent at some time.
( ) 9. Transfer of training.	g. Using the experience of one situation or series of situations to meet other situations more successfully and efficiently.
( ) 10. Subjects.	h. English I.
	i. A quarter of a full year's work.
	j. A subdivision of subject matter.

Another variation of the matching question is the following in which the pupil must find the words that would fill the blanks in a paragraph. Care in making these items is necessary or the answers may give themselves away, as in some instances in the example.

All words omitted from the following paragraph appear in the column at the left of the page. Indicate the word or phrase that best fits the blanks by placing the letter representing the blank in the appropriate parenthesis.

( ) 1. Problem solving.	The goals for American democracy were set up by the founding fathers in (a). The goal which is all-inclusive and most important for modern educators is probably (b). To help achieve this goal, schools should represent (c) of society. Schools should be (d) and (e).
( ) 2. Promote the general welfare.	
( ) 3. Strata.	
( ) 4. Memorization.	
( ) 5. Coeducational.	
( ) 6. Declaration of Independence.	
( ) 7. Cross sections.	
( ) 8. Bill of Rights.	
( ) 9. The needs of youth.	
( ) 10. Comprehensive.	High-school teaching should be evaluated in terms of its success in meeting (f).
( ) 11. Preamble to the Constitution.	
( ) 12. To insure the blessings of liberty.	In a democracy, learning activities must be largely (g).
( ) 13. College entrance requirements.	

ORGANIZATION AND EVALUATION ITEMS. Skillfully made organization and evaluation items can test a high level of learning and the ability to use knowledge. Items that require the pupils to organize are especially useful in testing learning above the verbalization level. The following item in which the pupils are asked to place a list of events in chronological sequence requires more than mere verbalization on the part of the pupil.

Place the following in chronological order by numbering the first event 1, the second event 2, and so on.

——————— The Declaration of Independence.

——————— The Articles of Confederation.

——————— The battle of Lexington.

——————— Washington's assumption of command of the Continental Army.

Items that ask pupils to evaluate and rate practices can not only test knowledge, but can also test the ability to draw fine distinctions. Questions of this sort are excellent for getting at the higher mental processes.

Rate the following techniques according to the following scheme: E, excellent; D, doubtful; X, poor. Place your responses in the parentheses.

( ) 1. In questioning, accepting any answer that can be used at all.

( ) 2. Asking questions that can be answered by monosyllables.

( ) 3. Encouraging pupils to ask questions of the teacher and of each other.

( ) 4. Reviewing for purposes of examination.

( ) 5. Etc.

SITUATION-TEST ITEMS. Situation items also demand that the pupils be able to use their knowledge. In this example the pupils must know how to do an item analysis in order to answer correctly.

What does the following item analysis tell you about the items in the text? Put your answer in the space below.

STUDENTS	ITEMS						TOTAL SCORE
	1	2	3	4	5	6	
John	+	0	0	+	0	+	111
Mary	+	+	0	+	0	+	109
Susan	+	+	0	+	0	0	100
Mike	+	+	0	+	0	+	96
Don	+	0	+	+	0	+	94
Harry	+	0	0	+	0	0	60
George	+	0	+	0	0	+	58
Anne	+	0	+	+	0	0	57
Tom	+	0	+	0	0	0	42
Sally	+	0	+	0	0	0	40

1. Item 1 ——————————————————————————

2. Item 2 ——————————————————————————

3. Item 3 ——————————————————————————

4. Item 4 ——————————————————————————

5. Item 5 ——————————————————————————

6. Item 6 ——————————————————————————

Free-Response Items

Free-response items which provide the pupils with no suggested responses also test a high level of learning. The most common representative of this type of item in objective tests is the completion item. In the completion item the pupil merely places the correct answer in the blank.

> Fill in the blanks.
> 1. The first permanent secondary school in this country was founded at _____.
> 2. The Committee of Ten recommended that the elementary schools be limited to grades _____ through _____ .

To make scoring easier, teachers often require that the answers to the completion questions be placed in an answer column.

> Place the answers in the blanks in the space provided in the margin.
> _____ 1. American high schools average about _____ pupils per school.
> _____ 2. I.Q. = _____ × 100.

When using completion items, teachers should be wary of ambiguous questions and unexpected correct responses. Good completion items that call for more than isolated, pinpointed facts are difficult to build.

Short-answer questions are exactly what the name implies, questions that can be answered in a word or phrase, as in the following. They are extremely useful, but, as with completion questions, it is difficult to write the items so that they will rule out undesirable responses.

> Place the answer to each of the following questions in the space provided.
> _____ 1. A boy is 10 years old; on a Stanford-Binet test his score is similar to that of the average 12-year-old. What is his I.Q.?
> _____ 2. Approximately what percentage of local school money is furnished by the federal government?
> _____ 3. What is considered to be the best size for a local school board according to Crow and Crow?

✣

> For what may the various types of tests be best used? Criticize the items used as illustrations. In what ways might they be improved?
> What are the characteristics of a good objective-test item?

✣

Building an Essay Test

THE ESSAY-TEST ITEM.   The essay item has several distinct advantages over the objective-test item for testing certain types of learning. Being a pure recall type of item, it tests a higher level of knowledge than do many objective-test items. It can also test the ability to organize, to use materials, to show relationships, to apply knowledge, and to write—abilities that are not easily tested by objective-test items. Furthermore, pupils seem to put more effort into studying for essay tests.

On the other hand, the validity of an essay test is liable to be low. This lack of validity stems from the fact that in essay tests it is very difficult to get an adequate sample of the pupils' knowledge of what was to be learned. Irrelevancies are likely to enter into the essay item. The validity and reliability of the test are lowered by the tendency of some pupils to wander off the subject, to "throw the bull," and to speak in vague generalities. The validity of the essay test is also lowered by the tendency of scorers to mistake skill in expression, style, glibness, hand-writing, neatness, and other irrelevant qualities for knowledge of what was to be learned. Scoring essay items, when done properly, takes considerable time and hard work. This greatly reduces the test's usability.

Because the essay-test item is prone to these faults—low objectivity, low reliability, and low usability—the teacher should use such items with discrimination. As a rule, the essay test should be reserved for occasions in which the teacher wishes to test a high level of recall and in which he wishes to test the ability to organize material, to apply what has been learned, to evaluate, to show relationships, and to write well. In determining whether or not to use such items, the teacher should also consider whether or not essays instead of essay tests might not be a better measure. The pupil who has time to sit and develop his thoughts in a theme or essay may demonstrate his skills in these areas more accurately than in the rush of an examination.

DESIGNING THE ESSAY TEST. Designing an essay test is much like designing an objective test. The object is to find out the pupil's progress. The teacher selects items that will ascertain what that progress is. Because of the time factor, the problem of adequate sampling becomes extremely important. As a rule of thumb, one should use many short essay items rather than a few long ones.

Here are some other rules of thumb to keep in mind in constructing essay tests.

1. Limit the questions to something the pupil can answer adequately in the allotted time and be sure each question is worded so that the pupil realizes these delimitations.
2. Be sure the sample is adequate and that the test will actually show how well the pupils have acquired the learning products that were the goals.
3. Be sure each question tests specific learning products and that the information necessary for the correct answer was included in the course.

4. Be specific. Be sure each question indicates just what the pupil is to write about. To do this, it may be necessary to write several sentences explaining the question. Avoid "discuss" questions. They are too vague and general.
5. Decide what the standards are for scoring the answers before you commit yourself to any question.
6. Be clear.

Administering and Scoring Teacher-Built Tests

Giving the Test

At first glance it would seem as though there was nothing at all to giving a test. This is not the case, however. Both essay and objective tests must be administered carefully. Once the test and key have been prepared, the first thing to do is to check the test to be sure it contains no errors. Little slips in typing may cause items to turn out quite differently from what was intended. The teacher should also note any directions that may be unclear and any items that need to be explained. A good way to spot unclear items and directions is to ask another teacher to read the test critically.

If possible, any errors or obscurities should be corrected before one takes the test to class. Announcing and correcting errors in class take valuable time away from the test itself, and there is usually someone who misses the correction and is thus penalized. Since correcting the test before class is not always possible, the teacher may have to explain items and procedures to the class orally. If so, he should do so before the class begins. If in addition he writes the explanation or correction on the chalkboard, the pupils can refer to it as the test progresses and thus will not be penalized if they forget or miss the announcement. Interrupting the test to make announcements is a poor practice because it may break into a pupil's train of thought and upset him.

To avoid distracting the pupils once the test has started, the teacher should be sure that each pupil has everything he needs before the test begins. It is important that the pupils check to see that each one of them has a good copy of the complete test. Even the most carefully prepared test may have poorly mimeographed, blank, or missing pages, so the teacher should have extra copies of the test to substitute for defective ones, if necessary. If this checking is completed before the test starts, it will eliminate confusion and interruptions during the test itself. Confusion and delay may also be minimized by setting up a routine for distributing and collecting the tests.

Preparing the Classroom for the Test

The physical condition of the classroom makes a tremendous difference in the test situation. The comfortable pupil can do his best work, the uncomfortable pupil often cannot. For this reason the teacher should consider the light, heat, and ventilation in the room. If possible, he should prevent any noises, interruptions, or other distractions. Common practice when giving standardized tests is to post a notice, "TESTING: PLEASE DO NOT DISTURB." There is no reason why such a practice should not be used for ordinary teacher-built achievement tests also. Many teachers are guilty of carrying on conversations with pupils or other teachers during a test. Some leave the classroom doors open while other classes are moving in the corridors. Such disturbances are liable to distract the pupils and reduce the reliability of the test.

Scoring the Essay Test

After the test has been given, it must be scored. Ordinarily, the test should be scored immediately. Otherwise the teacher loses the opportunity to capitalize on the test's motivational and diagnostic aspects.

Essay tests are notoriously hard to score. To score them objectively is almost impossible. However, the teacher must try to score them as objectively as he can. This is no easy task, but the following procedure can somewhat reduce the difficulty.

1. Before giving the test, answer each question yourself. (*Sometimes you will not want to use the item after you try to answer it.*) Note all the acceptable points and the relative importance of each. If you wish, give each point a numerical value or weight. This is the key.

2. After the test has been given, read the first essay question in each of the papers and assign scores on the basis of the key. If a pupil has mentioned an acceptable point not in the key, add the point to the key and reread the papers already scored to be sure that everyone gets credit for the point.

3. After completing the first question in all of the papers, repeat the process with the second question. It is much easier to read one question in all of the papers at once because the scorer can concentrate on that one question.

Scoring the Objective Test

The objective test is considerably easier to score than the essay test. The questions lend themselves to easy automatic scoring. In fact, scoring such questions is often so automatic that they can be scored more profitably by a clerk or pupil than by the teacher.

As in the essay test, the key should be made out before the test is given. A good method is to indicate the acceptable answers as the test is being made out. Then the teacher should let the test sit for a day or so, after which he should retest himself to see whether he still believes that the answers are acceptable. If they are, the teacher is ready to make his key. One of the easiest methods of making a key, if the test is arranged so that the responses are in a column, is simply to take an extra copy of the test and fill in all the responses correctly. The key can be placed against the test and the answers compared. Often, the teacher will find it easier to cut off the text of the test so that his key will be a strip which can be laid along either side of the answers on the test being corrected. This makes it easier to correct answers listed on the left side of the page if the scorer is right-handed. Some teachers find it easier to score by simply checking all correct items, that is, items which agree with the key. Others prefer to mark the wrong answers. Of course, if one intends to correct for guessing, one must indicate both right and wrong items.

Example:

key		*test*
—— a		(a) John Smith was an: (a) explorer, (b) merchant, (c) captain, (d) general.
✗ c		(a) Pocahontas married: (a) John Smith, (b) Myles Standish, (c) John Rolfe, (d) John Winthrop.

USING THE MASK.   Another common type of key is the mask. Masks are stiff pieces of paper or cardboard which, when placed over the test, cover up all the incorrect responses and allow only the correct responses to appear. They can be made easily. All one needs to do is to cover the test with the paper and then make holes in the mask where the correct answer should appear. With this type of key all the scorer needs to do is to mark correct all answers that show through the mask.

Example:

TEST

1.	a b c d	John Smith was an (a) explorer, (b) merchant, (c) captain, (d) general.
2.	a b c d	Pocahontas married (a) John Smith, (b) Myles Standish, (c) John Rolfe, (d) John Winthrop.

MASK

1.	O	
2.		O

CORRECTING FOR GUESSING. Since in testing one is attempting to determine progress toward the desired learning products, one should not conduct a guessing contest. When items have fewer than four responses, pupils can guess the answers relatively easily. Consequently, some teachers correct for guessing when scoring items with fewer than four responses. This is easily done. The formula is

$$S = R - \frac{W}{(C - 1)}$$

S is the corrected score, R is the number of correct responses, W the number of incorrect responses, and C the number of choices provided for each item. Substituting in the formula we find that for alternate-answer items the formula becomes Rights minus Wrongs.

$$S = R - \frac{W}{(2-1)} \qquad \text{or} \qquad S = R - W$$

For items having three choices we find that the formula becomes Rights minus ½ Wrongs.

$$S = R - \frac{W}{(3-1)} \qquad \text{or} \qquad S = R - \frac{W}{2}$$

These are the only two instances in which the formula is used.

Many teachers and writers in the field of measurement prefer not to use the correction formula at all. They feel that the correction is not worth the trouble because it seldom changes the relative rating of the pupils. Besides, pupils do not understand it very well and do not like it. Perhaps the best answer to the problem is to use items with at least four choices as much as possible. If it is necessary or advisable to use alternate-answer questions, the teacher should probably make the test long enough to accommodate several items directed at each learning product. This will tend to compensate for guessing without using the formula.

Evaluating Teacher-Built Tests

Much of the evaluation of a test can be done before it is given. The most important criterion of a test's worth is its validity. Does it test what it was supposed to test? Perhaps the easiest and best way to check the validity of a teacher-built achievement test is by inspection. Do the items test the goals of the course? Does the test cover the various goals in proper proportion? Is it free from catch questions and ambiguous items? Is the physical format correct? Are questions of the same type grouped together? Are the test items arranged from "easy" to "difficult"? Is the test free from format blunders such as matching items that go over the page? In other words, is it valid, reliable, objective, and usable?

After the test has been given, it can be evaluated more fully. Things that can be checked are

1. Length.
2. Directions.
3. Item discrimination.
4. Difficulty of items.
5. Clearness.
6. Balance.

RUNNING AN ITEM ANALYSIS. An item analysis can be very helpful in evaluating a test. The procedure for such an analysis is quite simple. On a sheet of graph paper list the pupils' names on the stub at the left, and items of the test in the heading. We are interested only in the upper and lower quarters, but it is best to list all the pupils in rank order because the chart can also be used for diagnosis. By using plus (+) and minus (−) signs, indicate whether each of the pupils answered each of the items correctly or incorrectly, as in the chart below.

UPPER QUARTER

	1	2	3	4	5	6	7	etc.
Jerry	+	+	+	−	−	+	−	
John	+	+	+	+	−	+	−	
Sally	−	−	+	+	−	+	−	

LOWER QUARTER

	1	2	3	4	5	6	7
Mike	+	−	−	−	−	+	−
Susy	+	−	+	−	−	−	+
Tom	−	−	−	+	−	−	+
George	+	−	−	+	−	−	+

By studying this chart one can learn how well the items discriminated and how difficult they were. The chart also gives clues to items that are not well written, are ambiguous, or were not learned.

Any good test should have some items that very few people can answer and some that almost everyone can answer. The first are needed to find out who the high achievers are; the second, to encourage the low achievers. Ordinarily, most items should be answered correctly by about half of the pupils. An item that is answered correctly by fewer than 20 per cent of the pupils may well be a bad item. One should examine it to see if it is not too difficult, if it tests any of the objectives, if it is pertinent to the course, or if it is poorly written. On the other hand, if the item is answered correctly by more than 80 per cent of the pupils, one should check to see if it is too easy or if the wording gives the answer away.

By comparing the answers of the upper-quarter pupils with those of the lower-quarter pupils, one can find other things that help to evaluate the items. If the upper quarter of the pupils answered an item correctly and the lower quarter of the pupils answered it incorrectly, the item discriminates between them. If both upper-quarter and lower-quarter pupils answered the question equally well, it does not discriminate. If an item is answered correctly more frequently by the lower-quarter pupils than the upper-quarter pupils, something is very wrong indeed. Perhaps the key is wrong, or perhaps the item needs to be rewritten.

✿

Often you hear it said that an achievement test on which pupils make perfect scores is a poor test. Discuss the merits and faults of such tests.

Compare this item-analysis chart with that used in the section on diagnosis. How could you combine both of these into one procedure? What, if anything, would this sample portion of the item analysis show about the items?

✿

Standardized Tests

Although the teacher-built test will always remain the mainstay in the teacher's tool kit, standardized tests are important supplementary measuring devices. In general, there are three basic types: achievement tests, character and personality tests, and aptitude and intelligence tests. They differ from teacher-built tests in that they are carefully built to provide a common unit of measurement just as the yardstick provides a common measure for length. To this end, the procedures for administering, scoring, and interpreting the tests have been standardized so that the results may be compared all over the country.

Standardized Achievement Tests

The standardized achievement test is a most useful tool. It comes in two basic types: (1) that which shows strengths and weaknesses of pupils as a basis for diagnosis and (2) that which shows the status of individual pupils as compared with boys and girls throughout the nation. Standardized tests are useful for these purposes, but they are not valuable for determining achievement in any particular course, or for evaluating the effectiveness of any particular teacher's teaching. In the first place, they rarely measure exactly what was taught in the course. Second, since standardized tests are liable to emphasize facts rather than understandings, abilities, attitudes, and skills, they frequently fail to indicate achievement in the most important aspects of the pupils' learning. Moreover, if a course or course sequence differs markedly in content from the courses in the schools which were used for standardizing the test, the latter will not measure the true achievement of the pupils or report accurately how their achievement compares with other pupils.

Personality and Character Tests

Personality and character tests are also important tools for the teacher. That they can be a useful source of information about pupils has been pointed out in an earlier chapter. Tests of this sort are not only useful for such purposes, but they can also help ascertain to what extent such teaching goals as attitudes, ideals, and other personality and character traits have been achieved. They are essential, of course, as a source of information in the guidance program.

Aptitude and Intelligence Tests

Aptitude tests are another source of information for the teacher. They attempt to show what a person's aptitudes or innate abilities are. Among the aptitude tests available are intelligence tests that seek to show one's aptitude for intellectual work, and tests designed to show one's aptitude for music, art, and various types of tasks. Probably the best known type of aptitude test is the intelligence test. Tests of true intelligence are extremely difficult to construct. It is doubtful that any intelligence test really measures intelligence. However, the scores from such tests are extremely helpful in understanding the individual, and should be used— but with caution. Similarly, tests for other aptitudes, such as musical, artistic, and vocational aptitudes, give important contributions to the teacher's knowledge of the pupil and are a great aid in guidance.

Selecting a Standardized Test

Standardized tests should be selected with care. There are many of them. Some are excellent, others are far from satisfactory. In searching for a suitable test, the teacher can receive considerable help from such sources as curriculum laboratories and test files maintained by local and state departments of education and by colleges and universities. Textbooks on tests and measurements often list and criticize several tests both in the text and appendices. Catalogs of the various test publishing houses tell what they have to offer. Critical analyses may be found in the *Mental Measurement Yearbooks* compiled under the editorship of O. K. Buros, probably the most dependable sources of information concerning standardized tests. In these books the various tests are discussed without fear or favor by competent analysts. New tests are frequently listed in such journals as the *Education Index, Psychological Abstracts, Review of Educational Research,* and *Educational and Psychological Measurement.* Textbooks in specific methods courses often discuss standardized achievement tests in the field with which they are concerned. Another source is the various bibliographies of tests.

These references will usually provide considerable information about the tests' validity, reliability, and usability. By using these references it should be relatively easy to eliminate the instruments that are patently not appropriate for one's purpose and thus narrow down the number which one should examine most carefully in making the final selection.

In the final selection the test buyer should carefully consult sample copies of the test and its manual. (Any test that lacks a manual should be viewed with particular caution.) The first thing one should check for is the validity of the test. Is it designed to do what you wish it to do? If it is an achievement test, does it fit in with the philosophy and objectives of the school and courses concerned? How was the validity established? From what type of population were the norms derived? If the population was greatly different from the type of class you have, the test will not be valid for your group. How were the items selected? Does a careful, logical, and psychological analysis of the test and its manual indicate that the items measure what they purport to measure?

If the test is valid, then one may go on to check the test's reliability and usability. In so doing, the teacher should bear in mind that a test bearing a reliability coefficient of less than .70 is probably a bad risk, and that ease in administering, scoring, and interpreting can lighten what is at best a difficult job.

Administering a Standardized Test

Any standardized test worth its salt will give clear, detailed directions for the administering of the test. Teachers should follow these directions exactly. Failure to do so may give false scores. As much as possible, standardized tests should be treated as routine classroom activities. A great to-do about the giving of a standardized test may cause tensions and upset the purpose of the test. Particularly reprehensible is coaching pupils for the test. A standardized test is a sampling. If boys and girls are coached on the sample the test will be much in error and it will be impossible to find out what the test might have told you. The only sure way to give a test a chance to do what you wish it to do is to administer it exactly as the manual prescribes.

✻

If you were to select a standardized test to measure the achievement of pupils in one of your classes, how would you go about it?

How would you find out if a standardized achievement test was valid in your situation?

In what ways might poor administering of a standardized test upset the test results?

*

Interpreting Standardized Test Scores

The value of a standardized test comes in the interpretation of the scores. Consequently, a standardized test should provide norms that permit the comparison of one group with other groups. Norms should not be confused with standards. A standard is a level of achievement or ability required for some purpose. A norm is quite a different thing. It is an average. Usually we deal with grade norms or age norms. A ninth-grade norm, for instance, is simply the average or mean score of the ninth-graders. It is a theoretical point at which the average of the scores of all the ninth-graders falls. Similarly, an age norm is the average of the scores of all the pupils of that age. This means that in an average group at any particular level, half of the pupils should be higher, and half of the pupils lower, than the norm. Thus any pupil who is reading at the tenth-grade level is reading as well as the average tenth-grader. Without further information one cannot tell whether this is good or bad.

USING DERIVED SCORES.   Norms are really derived scores provided by the test makers to aid the user in the interpretation of the test. Grade norms and age norms, however, are not the only types of derived scores that may be used. One of the most familiar types is the ratio intelligence quotient. This score represents the ratio between the mental age of a child and his chronological age, i.e., $IQ = MA/CA \times 100$. It is, in effect, a refinement of the age norm. In interpreting the intelligence quotient, 100 is average, and the range from 90 to 110 is considered to be normal. Persons whose I.Q.'s range from 80 to 90 may be considered slow, while persons having scores from 110 to 120 may be considered bright. Persons below or above these points may be considered quite slow or quite bright, as the case may be.

In interpreting I.Q.'s, one must be cautious. Different tests of intelligence do not yield the same scores. Also, scores from the same tests vary considerably. I.Q.'s may be accepted as general indices of brightness, but they cannot be accepted at their face value. A good rule might be to assume that the chances are good that the actual index of brightness would fall within a range of five points above or below the I.Q. derived from the test. To judge how bright a particular youngster is requires the use of other criteria in addition to the intelligence quotient.

Another type of derived score is the centile or percentile norm. The percentile score indicates the percentage of the sample population who reached that score. For example, if a youngster receives a percentile score of 10, ten per cent of the group did less well than, or as well as, he, and 90 per cent did better. The fiftieth percentile, of course, is average.

Other derived scores are the sigma score and the T score, which are based upon the normal curve of probability and the standard deviation from the mean. A sigma score is often called a Z score. It tells the number of standard deviations a person's score is above or below the mean. For instance, a score of +0.5 sigma means that the person's score was one half of a standard deviation above the mean of the scores of all persons taking the test. In order to eliminate fractions and plus and minus signs, McCall has invented the T scale in which the mean is represented by 50 and each standard deviation is given the value of 10. In this scale +0.5 would become 55. The sigma or Z score itself has been varied to eliminate the signs by taking 5 or 10 as the mean and expressing the deviation from the mean as a multiple of the standard deviation. Thus our score of +0.5 may become 5.5 or 55, or 110, depending upon the values used. The chart below is an attempt to compare these scales.

Comparison of Various Derived Scores

Standard deviations	−3	−2	−1	0	+1	+2	+3
Z scores	−3.0	−2.0	−1.0	0	+1.0	+2.0	+3.0
Converted Z scores	70	80	90	100	110	120	130
T scores	20	30	40	50	60	70	80
Percentiles	0.1	2.3	15.9	50	86.1	97.7	99.9

From this table we see that a T score of 70 can be interpreted to mean that the pupil is rated at two standard deviations above the mean or within the top 3 per cent of those taking the test. Presumably this is a good score, but one cannot really tell until he knows more about the pupil and the test situation. To make decisions on the basis of test scores alone can be very dangerous.

USING TEST NORMS. Norms are useful in that they provide a basis for comparing pupils from different school systems. They are valuable in evaluating school programs, and they can also tell the approximate standing of pupils with respect to their peers. Thus they can be extremely useful in developing individual programs for pupils and in providing for individual differences. For instance, if a teacher finds that an eighth-grader seems to have ability at the tenth-grade level, he should investigate the feasibility of giving him work that would be challenging at that level.

❖

In a certain seventh grade a test indicated that 25 per cent of the pupils were reading below the seventh-grade level. The teacher claimed that there was no cause to worry. Would you agree? Why, or why not? Do you need more information on which to decide?

The parents of a brilliant boy have just been informed that their youngster has achieved his grade norm in all areas and is slightly above norm in one area. They are well pleased. Should they be?

Some schools segregate boys and girls into homogeneous groups on the basis of an I.Q. score alone. After reading this short discussion do you think this practice is proper? Why, or why not?

❖

Summary

If we are to keep from drifting aimlessly like so much flotsam and jetsam in the surf, we need to determine where we are and where we should go. This process is evaluation. It differs from measurement in that it involves judgment of worth, while measurement merely describes the pupil's status. Many devices can be used to measure the status of the learning of boys and girls. We should use more of these devices than we ordinarily do, but evaluations can be made only by the evaluator himself. Consequently, goals and standards must be established to give the evaluator touchstones against which to compare the value of what he is judging.

But the purpose of evaluation is not merely to determine a pupil's worth. Evaluation should be the basis for determining what comes next, or where to go on to. Evaluation can also be useful as a basis for remedial action, or as a basis for deciding whether retention or promotion will be better for a pupil. Evaluation is a concomitant of good teaching.

Tests stand or fall on the basis of their validity. If a test is reliable, objective, and usable, so much the better. But a test that is not valid is worthless. The key to test building is to choose items that will ascertain whether or not the pupils have attained the teaching objectives. Consequently, the test builder should aim his items at specific goals. The same criteria that hold for teacher-built tests also hold for standardized tests. Although statistical procedures and other esoteric techniques are useful for the professional tester, the basic ingredients necessary for the classroom user and builder of tests are good judgment and careful thought.

FOR FURTHER STUDY

ADAMS, SAM, and FRED M. SMITH, *Educational Measurement for the Classroom Teacher* (New York: Harper and Row, Publishers, 1966).

ADKINS, DOROTHY, *Test Construction: Development and Interpretation of Achievement Tests* (Columbus, Ohio: Charles Merrill Books, Inc., 1960).

AHMANN, J. STANLEY, and MARVIN D. GLOCK, *Evaluating Pupil Growth* (Boston: Allyn and Bacon, Inc., 1963).

BLOOM, BENJAMIN S. (editor), *Taxonomy of Educational Objectives, Handbook I: Cognitive Domain* (New York: David McKay Company, Inc., 1956).

CHAUNCEY, HENRY, and JOHN E. DOBBIN, *Testing—Its Place in Education Today* (New York: Harper and Row Publishers, 1963).

DAVIS, FREDERICK B., *Educational Measurements and their Interpretation* (Belmont, California: Wadsworth Publishing Company, Inc., 1964).

DUROST, WALTER N., and GEORGE A. PRESCOTT, *Essentials of Measurement for Teachers* (New York: Harcourt, Brace and World, Inc., 1962).

EDUCATIONAL TESTING SERVICE, *Making the Classroom Test,* A Guide for Teachers, Educational and Advisory Service, Series No. 4, Second Edition, Princeton, N.J., 1961.

————, *Multiple Choice Questions: A Close Look,* Princeton, N.J., 1963.

GARRETT, HENRY E., *Testing for Teachers* (New York: American Book Company, 1965).

GRONLUND, NORMAN E., *Measurement and Evaluation in Teaching* (New York: The Macmillan Company, 1965).

GROSE, LOIS M., DOROTHY MILLER, and EDWIN R. STEINBERG, *Suggestions for Evaluating Junior High School Writing,* National Council of Teachers of English, Champagne, Illinois, not dated.

KRATWOHL, DAVID R., BENJAMIN S. BLOOM, and BERTRAM B. MASIA, *Taxonomy of Educational Objectives, Handbook II: Affective Domain* (New York: David McKay Company, Inc., 1964).

LINDWALL, C. M., *Testing and Evaluation: An Introduction* (New York: Harcourt, Brace and World, Inc., 1961).

McLAUGHLIN, KENNETH F., *Interpretation of Test Results,* Bulletin 1964, No. 7, OE-25038, U.S. Office of Education, U.S. Department of Health, Education, and Welfare (Washington, D.C.: U.S. Government Printing Office, 1964).

MORSE, HORACE T., and GEORGE H. McCUNE, *Selected Items for the Testing of Study Skills and Critical Thinking* (Washington, D.C.: National Council for the Social Studies, 1964).

STANLEY, JULIAN C., *Measurement in Today's Schools,* Fourth Edition (Englewood Cliffs, N.J.: Prentice-Hall, Inc., 1964).

THORNDIKE, ROBERT L., and ELIZABETH HAGEN, *Measurement and Evaluation in Psychology and Education,* Second Edition (New York: John Wiley and Sons, Inc., 1961).

WOOD, DOROTHY ADKINS, *Test Construction* (Columbus, Ohio: Charles E. Merrill Books, Inc., 1960).

CHAPTER *16*

Marking and Reporting to Parents

MARKS hold an extremely high position in our school system. They are used as a basis for reporting pupil progress to parents and to other interested persons, and as a basis for promotion, graduation, and honors. Teachers frequently use marks as a means of motivating pupils to greater effort. Guidance personnel use marks in guiding boys and girls for college entrance or employment.

To perform these tasks, most school systems use a marking system based on a five-point scale. The most common version is the A B C D F scale. Variations of this scale use the numbers 1 2 3 4 5 or the terms "Superior," "Above Average," "Average," "Below Average," and "Unsatisfactory." Some schools use a scale based on 100 per cent, while others merely indicate the work to be passing or failing, or in some cases outstanding, passing, or failing.

Criticism of Marking Systems

Unfortunately none of the variations mentioned has been quite satisfactory primarily because marks and marking systems are based on certain fallacious assumptions. According to Wrinkle[1] these fallacies are six in number.

1. The belief that anyone can tell from the mark assigned what the student's level of achievement is or what progress he has made.
2. The belief that any student can achieve any mark he wishes—if he is willing to make the effort.
3. The belief that the student's success in his after-school life compares favorably with his success in school.
4. The belief that the student's mark is comparable to the worker's pay check.
5. The belief that the competitive marking system provides a worthwhile and justifiable introduction to competitive adult life.

[1] William L. Wrinkle, *Improving Marking and Reporting Practices* (New York: Rinehart and Company, Inc.), copyright 1947, permission of Rinehart and Company, Inc.

6. The belief that school marks can be used as a means to an end without their becoming thought of by students as ends in themselves.

The truth of the matter is that these beliefs have little or no basis in fact. The errors contained in some of them are quite plain. Obviously the ordinary school marking system does not allow adequately for individual differences in pupils. That school marks and worldly success do not always correlate well is a commonplace. That learning rather than marks should be the object of education is self-evident. However, the average student may find it difficult to realize that marks do not tell what a student's level of achievement is or what progress he has made.

Marks As an Indication of Pupil Progress

Marks do not tell one as much about a pupil's progress as one might suppose. For example, if someone says that Johnny received an A in ninth-grade social studies, what does that tell you? Does it mean he worked hard or that he is a bright loafer? Does it mean that he has mastered some particular bit of subject matter, or does it mean he has a charming personality?

Letter and percentage marks do not give the answers to such questions. They do not show what skills, concepts, attitudes, appreciations, or ideals the pupil has learned. They give no indication of the pupil's strengths or weaknesses in a subject, nor do they tell how much he has progressed. In fact, as often as not, they hide information. For instance, because of his excellence in literature, reading, grammar, or written composition, Jack receives an A in English. However, he may be quite poor in conversational skill. The mark of A, therefore, hides the fact that he is deficient in one area of English. Such a marking system is of little value to anyone who really wants to know much about the pupil's progress in school. Still, it does predict fairly well a pupil's continued success in a subject and does give a rough index of his teacher's estimate of his worth.

Even as an indication of the teacher's estimate of a pupil's worth, marks are not always very valuable. Teachers' marks are often influenced by extraneous matters such as sex, effort, extracurricular activities, neatness, school behavior, attitudes, and attendance. Obviously, such inconsistencies may result in many inequities.

Particularly futile are marking systems that attempt to give precise marks. No human being can make the fine distinctions in the schoolwork of pupils that the percentage system requires. Neither have we been able to develop testing instruments capable of such fine distinctions. Since the data on which pupil marks are based are so rough, the computing of percentage marks hardly seems worth the trouble.

Marks As a Mental-Health Hazard

A frequent criticism of marks is that they are a mental-health hazard. Some critics feel that marks place an undue emphasis on competition and success. This emphasis, they believe, endangers pupils' mental health. Others feel that these pressures represent nothing more than the ordinary give and take in life, so that these objections should not be taken seriously. However, it is certainly true that marks often cause anxieties and worries out of proportion to their importance in pupils' lives. It seems, therefore, that the advisability of using marks is at least questionable from a mental-health standpoint.

Marks As a Motivational Device

Probably the only valid argument for using letter or percentage marks is that they have a certain motivational effect, particularly with the better pupils. Even this effect, however, may be illusory. If marks really motivated effectively, would not fewer pupils fail?

As a matter of fact, sometimes marks have a very poor motivational effect. This is true when the mark rather than the learning becomes the major goal. In such circumstances the pupils concentrate on getting marks rather than on learning something worthwhile. The result often is cheating, cramming, electing easy courses, and expending only enough energy to pass.

❖

Of what value are marks? Do they serve the purposes to which they pretend? If they do, how do they do it?

What do you think of competitive marking? What value does it have? What weaknesses?

For what purposes should marks be used?

❖

Marking Tests and Papers

"Marking on a Curve"

At best, assigning marks is a thankless task. In the following paragraphs several ways to do this job will be suggested. However, the teacher must remember that no procedure can relieve him of the responsibility for making decisions, some of which will be difficult.

According to the theory of the normal curve, which is based on the laws of chance, any continuous variable will be distributed according to a perfectly smooth bell-shaped curve (Figure 7), if no factors are present to throw things off balance. Thus, according to the laws of chance,

FIGURE 7

The Normal Curve of Probability.

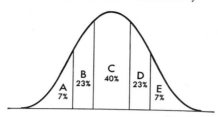

in a large group marks should tend to fall according to the normal curve. In other words, letter marks would, according to this theory, be distributed about as follows: A, 7 per cent; B, 23 per cent; C, 40 per cent; D, 23 per cent; E (or F), 7 per cent. Just what the exact percentages should be is debatable.

Marks based on this theory have had considerable vogue. Unfortunately, in ordinary practice the theory does not apply to secondary-school marks.

The theory of the normal curve assumes that the variable varies according to pure chance. Ordinarily, this is not true in secondary-school classes. For one thing, a secondary-school class is not a normal, but a select, group of people. Many of the slow-learning pupils have been dropped. Therefore, because of the selection that has taken place, the marks of secondary-school pupils would not ordinarily correspond to a normal curve, but would fall instead in approximately the following proportions: A, 15 per cent; B, 25 per cent; C, 40 per cent; D, 15 per cent; E (or F), 5 per cent.

Second, few classes are large enough to warrant using the normal curve. In order for the theory of the normal curve to operate, one needs at least fifty pupils to be marked against the same criteria. To use the normal curve as a basis for marks in a group smaller than fifty may lead to errors in marking. Therefore, when marking, the teacher must depend largely upon his own judgment. Statistical procedures such as using the normal curve are seldom worthwhile.

Using Relative-Growth Groups

In spite of its faults, the normal curve can be used to indicate the relative growth of pupils with respect to each other. Teachers can do this by setting up a five-point, relative-growth scale. In such a scale the percentage of members in each of the relative-growth groups will be distributed in the same proportion as when marking by the normal curve, i.e., I = 7 per cent; II = 23 per cent; III = 40 per cent; IV = 23 per cent; V = 7 per cent. These groups do not represent marks, however, but comparisons within the class. They merely show each pupil's progress in relation to that of his classmates.

The following method of determining relative growth within class groups has been used with some success.[2]

1. Subtract the lowest score from the highest and add 1 to find the range.
2. Determine the approximate standard deviation by dividing the range by 5.
3. Find the mid-score.
4. Add ½ the approximate standard deviation to the mid-score and subtract ½ approximate standard deviation from the mid-score to find the boundaries of the middle group.
5. Find the other group boundaries by adding (or subtracting) the standard deviation from the group limit already established.

For example: We have a test whose scores range from 63 through 117. The mid-score of the test is 89. Seventy-three pupils took the test. The range of the test is 117 minus 63 plus 1, or 55. The approximate standard deviation is 55 divided by 5, or 11. The middle relative-growth group falls between 94 − 84; the next higher relative-growth group ranges from 95 − 105; the highest ranges from 106 up. The other two groups become 83 − 73 and 72 − 62. However, if the scores fall so that there are natural breaks at places near the end of the groups, one might use these natural breaks for group limits instead of the limits computed.

Although the relative-growth groups can be quite useful, pupils and parents have become so mark-oriented that they do not always willingly accept this practice.

Using Raw Scores Instead of Marks

Another effective device is to give the results of objective tests in raw scores, telling the pupils the range of the scores and the range of the relative-growth groups. By comparing their scores, high-school pupils soon realize how they stand in comparison with their classmates. If the scores are accompanied by comments such as, "I think you have missed the point of . . . , and should reread it," or "You did not provide enough illustrations," or "You have not differentiated between major and minor points," and so on, the pupil can learn how he stands in relation to his own potential and the standards of the course. Conferences also help make these points clear.

Assigning Marks to Tests

Both this plan and the relative-growth plan avoid giving actual marks to tests. However, if one must give marks, the only satisfactory solution

[2] See Roy O. Billett, *Fundamentals of Secondary School Teaching* (Boston: Houghton Mifflin Company, 1940), p. 634, for a fuller explanation.

is to establish certain criteria for each mark and then mark on the basis of those criteria. In marking tests, teachers should remember that the purposes of tests are primarily to evaluate pupil progress and to diagnose pupil learning rather than the giving of marks.

✿

How does a teacher grade a test if his school uses the five-letter system of marking?

Why do authorities generally condemn the percentage system of grading tests?

What are sigma scores, T scores, and Z scores? What are their good and bad points? How might they be used in marking tests?

✿

Assigning Marks to Compositions and Other Creative Work

Compositions and other creative work are difficult to mark. Perhaps the following technique used by a veteran teacher of English is as good as any in marking original written work:

First, he selects a comfortable chair with plenty of floor space around him. Then he reads each paper carefully, making notes as he reads them. On the basis of this reading he judges whether the paper is "Superior," "Excellent," "Average," "Fair," or "Poor." Then, without placing any mark on the paper, he places it on a portion of the floor designated for papers of that category. After reading all the papers, he places them into piles according to their categories and lets them lie fallow for a while. Later, refreshed, he rereads each paper in each group to test his previous judgment, and moves from pile to pile those papers which he feels he has rated too high or too low. He then assigns marks to the papers in the piles. Although this technique is not foolproof, with a little ingenuity it can be adapted for marking various types of original work.

Other devices particularly useful in the marking of compositions and themes are rating scales and checklists. The use of these devices was discussed in an earlier chapter.

Term and Course Marks

The Basis of Term Marks

Term marks should be based on achievement. No other basis for granting marks is valid. The amount of energy the pupil expended, his attendance, and his classroom behavior should not be included in his mark. That such things should be noted and reported to school officials, guidance persons, new teachers, and parents is axiomatic, but they should be reported as separate entities, not as part of a mark. A mark should be *an index of achievement* in a course, nothing more, nothing less.

Some teachers and theoreticians have proposed the theory that a person should be marked on the amount of progress he has made during a year. On the face of it, progress is an admirable criterion for marking. However, if the mark is also to be an index of the pupil's level of achievement, then a mark based solely on the amount of progress made during the period is misleading, as the following case demonstrates.

When they arrived at the first class of their drawing course, John already had great—almost professional—skill in drawing, while Jim had no skill whatsoever. After a year in class, John has progressed very little, although he can still draw much better than anyone else in the class. Jim, however, has become interested in drawing and has made swift progress. He is now slightly better than the average pupil in the class, although still not nearly as good as John. How should one mark the two boys? If one bases the marks on progress, then Jim should get the higher mark, but this would lead to the ridiculous situation of giving the higher mark to the less skilled student. To be fair and to give a reasonably accurate picture in a mark the criterion must be achievement rather than progress.

Criteria for Term Marks

In marking boys and girls, the teacher should know exactly what each mark means. Many of the better schools provide careful descriptions and definitions of the various marks or grades. The following is copied from the *Junior High School Quarterly Report* used in the Seattle Public Schools.[3] As you read the criteria try to evaluate them. Are they valid? Are any extraneous criteria included? Are any necessary criteria omitted?

Description of Marks Used in Junior High School
Quarterly Report

A. Superior:

Pupil is careful, thorough, and prompt in the preparation of all required work.

Is quick and resourceful in utilizing suggestions for supplementary activities.

Works independently and has sufficient interest and initiative to undertake original projects beyond the assigned work.

Uses time well.

Does not guess.

Is careful to express thoughts clearly and accurately.

Shows leadership in classroom activities.

Has excellent self-control and effective study habits.

[3] Seattle Public Schools, *Junior High School Quarterly Report*. Description of marks used by permission.

B. Above Average:
>   Pupil prepares all assignments carefully.

Is conscientious and dependable.

Requires no urging to have work done on time.

Responds readily when called upon.

Makes a practice of doing all work assigned and makes some suggestions for supplementary work.

Has good study habits of routine assignments.

Is loyal, dependable, and helpful in class activities.

C. Average:

Pupil does good work, but requires considerable direction and stimulation from the teacher.

Is usually dependable and cooperative.

Has good intentions, though interest is not always keen.

Does not show a great deal of concern in following his subject beyond minimum requirements.

Responds to encouragement and guidance, though sometimes inclined to be careless or slow in accomplishment.

Needs to be prompted by frequent questions in reports or discussions before the class.

Should develop more independent habits of study.

D. Passing:

Pupil indicates that more growth will result from advancement than from repetition of the subject.

Should improve concentration in study.

Should make more careful preparation and respond more frequently.

Requires special help and encouragement constantly.

Is irregular in his attention and application.

E. Unsatisfactory:

Pupil has study habits that are poor and ineffective.

May lack adaptability for specific study.

Either will not, or cannot hold his attention to his work.

Fails to work reasonably near the level of his ability and does not meet class requirements.

Obviously, such definitions and explanations help teachers mark fairly. If definitions are not provided for the school, individual teachers should provide them for their own classes. As a matter of fact, even when school-wide criteria are provided, teachers should supplement the established criteria with additional ones designed to meet the need of individual classes.

Determining Term Marks

Probably the best way to determine term marks for a course is to give the pupils marks for each unit. The final mark can be computed by taking an average of the unit marks, making due allowance for those units that

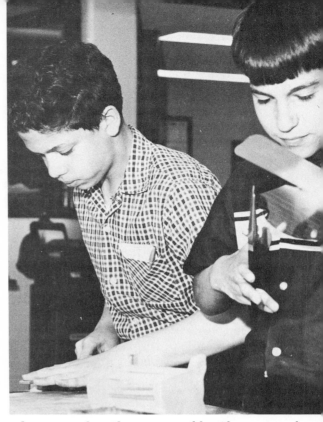

Term marks should be based on as much evidence as possible. Observation of these boys' skills may be fully as important as their test scores in determining their achievement.

may be more important than others. Unit marks can be arrived at quite easily. Since marks should be based on as much evidence as possible, throughout the unit the teacher should rate all the test results, oral reports, written work, observation, and other pupil activities on a five-point scale as described in preceding sections. Then the teacher can determine the unit mark by inspecting all the evidence recorded for each pupil and weighing each according to its importance. No attempt to derive an average arithmetically need be made. Obviously, the resultant mark will be based on largely subjective considerations, but then, marks are always subjective, no matter how one marks. A mark arrived at by this procedure is probably as fair as a mark arrived at by any other.

Some schools require that marks be recorded and reported as percentages. This presents a problem to the conscientious teacher because percentage scores often require judgments finer than the human mind can make. However, such scores may be approximated by assigning values to the unit marks. For instance, if the passing grade is 70 per cent, then the teacher can assign the following values: A, 95 per cent; B, 87 per cent; C, 80 per cent; D, 73 per cent; F, 65 per cent, or less if you wish.

To attempt to give finer evaluations for the various units would be merely deceiving oneself and one's clientele.

✻

> Suppose you are an eleventh-grade English teacher. What should you wish to know about a pupil coming to you from the tenth grade? Would the fact that he got a B help you? If not, what information would be more helpful?
>
> Is it possible to devise a means whereby all teachers' marks will mean the same thing? If not, why not? If so, what do you advise?

✻

Reporting to Parents

The Right to Know

Every parent has the right to know how his children are progressing in school. In fact, he probably is obligated to know whether he wants to or not. Following is a list of what a parent should know about the progress of his child in school.

1. How well is the pupil progressing in each of his subjects?
2. How does his progress compare with that of the other boys and girls in his age group and in his class?
3. What are his potentialities? Is he developing any particular talents or interests?
4. How does his progress compare with his potentialities?
5. What specific difficulties does he have, if any?
6. In what has he done well?
7. How does he behave in school?
8. How does he get along with his peers? With his teachers?
9. Is there any way the parent can help him?
10. Is there any way the parent can help his teachers?

Such information should be passed on to the parent at regular intervals in some fashion or other. This process is called reporting to parents. It is an important part of the school's program for many reasons. In the first place, it is through this reporting that the school can fulfill its responsibilities of telling parents of their children's status in school. Second, it gives the school an opportunity to enlist the parent's help in educating his child. Third, it gives the school an opportunity to explain its program to the parent and to solicit his understanding and assistance. All of these things are done by various means. The most common are report cards, parent conferences, and letters to parents.

Report Cards

By far the most common medium for reporting to parents is the report card. Different types of cards are used, but most schools report pupil progress by means of the ubiquitous A B C D F marking system in one guise or another. Because of the inadequacies of A B C D F marks, there is a definite trend toward supplementing these marks by adding to report cards marks in such things as effort, behavior, study habits, and attitudes. Also, many schools provide considerable opportunity for the teacher's comments and, increasingly, an opportunity for parents to comment in reply.

The report card is a vital link in the teacher's relationship with pupils and parents. Improper marking can upset pupils' morale and destroy home relationships. However, if a mark is consistent with what has been going on in class, the pupils will usually accept it without question. So will most parents if they are forewarned.

At any rate, the teacher must be careful in making out report cards. Quite often the school provides definite instructions for preparing them. When this is done, the teacher should follow the instructions to the letter. If instructions are not available, the teacher should be sure to find out from a supervisor or experienced teacher just what the procedures are. It is always better to find out before one makes a *faux pas* than afterward.

✻

Some examples of report cards used in secondary schools follow. Note the difference in procedure. Note what is included on each card. Criticize the cards. Which do you think is most satisfactory? Attempt to fill out the report for some youth. Doing so may point out several things you had not thought of. Which do you prefer? Why?

Look at the report card files in your curriculum library. Consider the merits of the various pupil progress cards and marking systems.

✻

FIGURE 8

Wethersfield Junior High School Report Card.

Grade 9 Home Room Subjects	Teachers	First Quarter			Second Quarter			Third Quarter			Fourth Quarter			Year's Average
		Subject	Effort	Citizenship	Subject	Effort	Citizenship	Subject	Effort	Citizenship	Subject	Effort	Citizenship	
Algebra														
Ancient History														
Art														
English														
General Business														
Home Economics														
Industrial Arts														
Latin														
Mathematics 9														
Music														
Science														
Social Studies														
Days Absent														
Times Tardy														

Name_____ Wethersfield Junior High School   Year 196__ — 196__
Last First Middle

Used by permission of the Superintendent of Schools, Wethersfield, Conn.

FIGURE 9

Manchester High School Quarterly Progress and Activity Report (Front)

PUPIL'S NAME GRADE

The letter grade is a mark of scholastic achievement and should be interpreted as follows: A — Very superior quality, B — Above average quality, C — Fair, average quality, M — Marginal, below average but passing, D — Failure, no credit allowed.

In spaces 1-12 a check means *improvement is desired.*

	English																																																	Physical Education					
	1	2	3	4	AVG	PT	1	2	3	4	AVG	PT	1	2	3	4	AVG	PT	1	2	3	4	AVG	PT	1	2	3	4	AVG	PT	1	2	3	4	AVG	PT	1	2	3	4	AVG	PT	1	2	3	4	AVG	PT	1	2	3	4	AVG	PT
GRADES																																																						
1. Does not appear to be working to best of ability.																																																						
2. Does not complete a reasonable amount of work on time.																																																						
3. Does not work neatly.																																																						
4. Takes little or no part in class discussion.																																																						
5. Fails to follow directions.																																																						
6. Does not proceed independently.																																																						
7. Has little interest in work.																																																						
8. Takes no initiative in making up missed work																																																						
9. Does not work well with others.																																																						
10. Does not appear to profit from constructive criticism.																																																						
11. Is discourteous and poorly mannered.																																																						
12 Destroys or mutilates school property.																																																						

Used by permission of Manchester High School, Manchester, Conn.

FIGURE 10

Manchester High School Quarterly Progress and Activity Report (Back)

MANCHESTER HIGH SCHOOL

MANCHESTER, CONN.

QUARTERLY PROGRESS

and

ACTIVITY REPORT

OF

GRADE

YEAR 19———-19———

This report is to inform the parent of the general progress the child is making in school.

No formal report of this nature can give a complete picture. Each parent is cordially invited to visit teachers for a more complete report and for discussion of matters of mutual concern.

In general, approved absences from school are those caused by illness of the student, severe illness or death in the family. In general, all other absences are unapproved unless advance approval has been secured from the school. Students will be given zeros for work missed because of unapproved absences. Demerits will be issued in case of truancy and unapproved absence.

ATTENDANCE RECORD	QUARTER			
	1	2	3	4
Number of Days Absent				
Number of Times Tardy				
Number of Times Dismissed				
DEMERITS				
Total number of Demerits Accumulated.				

TEACHERS' COMMENT	TEACHERS' COMMENT	TEACHERS' COMMENT	TEACHERS' COMMENT

SIGNED (Parent — First Quarter)   *SIGNED* (Parent — Third Quarter)

SIGNED (Parent — Second Quarter)

Used by permission of Manchester High School, Manchester, Conn.

Report to Parents

To the Parents of Junior High School Students:[4]

This report of your child's progress will be sent to you four times during the school year. The report is our attempt to acquaint you with your child's growth and development in the whole school program. It is not our intention to provide a comparison of any child's achievement with that of other members of his class. The grades report each child's progress in relation to what we can reasonably expect him to accomplish in the light of his own ability. We will try to emphasize the factors which we feel are producing the behavior and achievement, for it is this analysis of causes which will enable you to help in the guidance and development of your child's learning experiences.

We will welcome your comments and your personal visits to school. Both will help to bring about the greatest possible personal, social and scholastic growth of your child during this school year.

CHARLES W. WILLIS,

Superintendent of Schools.

H—Honor
S—Satisfactory
U—Unsatisfactory

[4] Instructions to Parents from Harford County Junior High School Report to Parents. Used by permission of Board of Education of Harford County, Bel Air, Maryland.

JANUARY 31[5]

Core   _____

Science   _____

Mathematics   _____

Arts and Crafts   _____

Home Economics   _____

Industrial Arts   _____

Agriculture   _____

Music   _____

Physical Education   _____

Attendance { Days Present   _____
              { Days Absent   _____

Parent's Comment

Teacher's Comment

Parent's Signature

[5] Sample Page from Harford County Junior High School Report to Parents. Used by permission of Board of Education of Harford County, Bel Air, Maryland.

395

Unsatisfactory Progress Report[6]

Guidance Department, Wethersfield High School

Student _____ Grade _____ Date _____ 196 __

Subject _____ Subject Teacher _____

Analysis of the Student's Effort

————Course is difficult, but student is working faithfully.

————Can master subject only if willing to make necessary effort.

————Having difficulty right now, but it should prove temporary.

————Fails to submit assignments regularly. Must constantly be reminded.

————Prepares daily assignments, but does them carelessly.

————Neglects to ask questions or seek help from teacher.

————Gives up when encountering slightest difficulty in assignment.

————Effort is confined to study period; dashes off a written assignment, just to get it finished. Neglects to do any real studying and tells parents homework was completed in school.

————Apparently does not spend enough time studying at home.

————Tries to bluff in class, and depends on last-minute cramming for tests and examinations.

————Needs parental supervision of home study. To obtain satisfactory grades, should spend an hour and a half to two hours of study at home—without radio, television, telephone, or other distractions.

————Does not review unless class is specifically directed to do so.

————Lacks order and system in work and method of study.

————Fails to record homework assignments, then doesn't know what to do.

————Comes to class without pen, notebook, books, or other equipment needed; then disturbs others by trying to borrow from them.

————Usually takes home only one textbook—sometimes none at all.

————Lets assignments go until the last minute.

————Makes a half-hearted attempt to do assignments, then submits incomplete work.

————Fails to check own work.

————Turns in examination papers that are untidy, carelessly written, or incomplete.

————Daily work is usually untidy, carelessly written, or incomplete.

————Advisable for parents to inspect regularly all homework assignments.

Analysis of the Student's Discipline

————Frequently absent; does not make up assignments.

————Frequently late.

————Social activities seem to take precedence over school duties.

[6] Used by permission of Superintendent of Schools, Wethersfield, Conn.

————May be led by others much too easily.

————Is obviously too tired during school day to put forth best effort—may be suffering from too much out-of-school work, or social activity, or television, etc.

————Is indolent; works only if checked closely by teachers.

————Is inattentive in class—inclined to daydream.

————Is always quick with an alibi.

————Frequently requires disciplinary attention—is talkative in class, childish at times; distracts and disturbs other students; likes to show off.

————Sometimes careless of personal hygiene and appearance.

————Undisciplined and immature—sometimes defies school regulations.

————Resents correction and effort of school staff to train and help.

————Is sometimes disrespectful to teachers.

————It would be advisable for parents to check on student's outside work, school activities and companionship.

————Should be checked to see that associates are schoolmates rather than older adult companions, especially if the latter are not improving the student's character, morals and ideals.

————Reason for student's working after school should be carefully reviewed by parents.

————Student has too much spending money, is selfishly concerned only in hitting a social pace far beyond that suitable and to the neglect of school duties.

————Does not realize that study must come before pleasure.

Analysis of the Student's Attitudes

————Seems to be indifferent to success or failure in school work.

————Thinks school work is unimportant; just aims to "get by."

————Takes no pride in doing work well.

————Can be counted on to take the line of least resistance.

————Shows excellent home training at all times.

————Is respectful and polite with teachers and companions.

————Has ability to do better work, but lacks determination and interest.

————Is not responsive in class; fails to participate in class discussion.

————Lacks loyalty to the school—lacks interest in extracurricular and athletic activities; is seldom seen attending school functions with other students.

————Lacks pride in upholding reputation of school, teachers, parents, and fellow students.

————Has clearly indicated a wish not to be attending this school.

————Has indicated a wish to be following a different course.

————Wants to quit school and go to work.

————Has no appreciation of the value of an education or of the effort

---

Student _____   *Grade* _____ *Date* _____ 196 __
Subject _____   *Subject Teacher* _____

    and sacrifices of others to make an education possible.
————Evidences good intentions at times, but may lack the strength of
    character to carry them out.
————Disturbing home conditions may create psychological factors that
    interfere with study and interest in school.
————Is unconcerned about displeasing parents with a poor report card.

His Present Grade of Scholastic Achievement Is

Other Remarks or Recommendations:

Interviewed by _____ *Date* _____ 196 __

Supplementary Reports

Many schools find the report card alone insufficient as a basis for
reporting pupil progress, even when some information over and above
marks is supplied to parents. To meet this need, several schools issue
supplementary progress reports from time to time. Preparing these reports
may be the responsibility of the classroom teacher, the homeroom teacher,
or the guidance personnel. More often than not, supplementary reports
take the form of warnings of possible failure or reports of unsatisfactory
progress. In a few school systems such reports are sent on other occasions,
for example, to notify the parent that the pupil is doing well. These
reports may be made as notes to parents, warning slips, checklists, conferences, and letters of commendation. A typical form used at the Wethersfield Connecticut High School appears on pages 396–398.

Letters to Parents

Letters to parents are of two types: (1) routine letters used as reports
to parents in addition to, or in place of, report cards; (2) letters for
special occasions—requests to see the parent, invitations to class func-

tions, letters notifying the parent about the pupil's work, and letters calling the parent's attention to some abnormality in the child's behavior.

Letters to parents—no matter what their purpose—should be carefully written. They should always be correct as to form and style. Errors in spelling, composition, grammar, and sentence structure should be avoided at all costs. Errors that might never be noticed in the letter of a lawyer, doctor, or dentist may be very embarrassing if made by a teacher. This is particularly true in the so-called better neighborhoods. Teachers should not take offense at parents' expecting such high standards in English usage. It is the price of being a teacher. "Teachers *should* know, you know."

Letters used as progress reports should be short and to the point. Unless one is careful, such letters soon become stereotyped. If possible, each letter should be a personal message to the parents, but even a stereotyped letter is better than one that is not clear. In writing to parents, teachers should remember that parents may not be familiar with the professional jargon of teachers. Consequently, the teacher should attempt to write in clear, idiomatic English. Sentences like, "Mary seems to have difficulty adjusting to the group," may be crystal clear to you but mean little to some parents. In a report concerning a seventh-grader, the statement that "Lucy seems to be a little immature" may seem appropriate enough to you and your colleagues, but it can make you the laughing stock of the country club set.

In writing such letters it is usually best to start and end on a pleasant note. A frequent recommendation is always to commence by reporting something favorable about the pupil and ending in an optimistic vein. This is sound advice. However, the effort to be pleasant must not outweigh truthfulness. The parent is entitled to an accurate report which reflects the teacher's best judgment concerning the child. Sometimes teachers are so careful not to hurt the parent's feelings and so eager to establish amicable relations with the parent that they fail to point out clearly the pupil's failings. This is not fair to the parent. While the teacher should not be tactless, he should let the parent know the facts about his child. The best rule is to decide what you wish the parent to know and then say it simply and pleasantly.

The body of the report should estimate the progress of the pupil as accurately as possible. This estimate should indicate the pupil's progress in relation to his ability and also in relation to the normal achievement for pupils at his grade level. It should point out the pupil's strong and weak points, and show where he needs help. The report should not be limited to achievement in subject matter alone, but should also provide information concerning the pupil's social behavior and other aspects of his activities in school. At times, the teacher will wish to ask the parent for his cooperation in some specific way. Certainly he should always ask the parent for his comments.

An Example of a Letter to a Parent

When writing a letter to a parent, be brief, clear, pleasant, honest, and factual. An example of a homeroom teacher's letter to a ninth-grader's parents follows.

Dear Mr. and Mrs. Smith:

Joan's teachers have reported to me the results of her first quarter's work. They are quite satisfactory except for algebra, in which she is experiencing some difficulty. Her difficulty seems to be caused by a lack of understanding of mathematical principles. Mr. Courtney, her algebra teacher, feels that she should have extra help in his course. In all other respects, Joan seems to be making an excellent start this year.

If you have any suggestions or comments to make about Joan's school work, we should welcome them. Also, we should very much like to have you visit our school whenever it is convenient for you.

Cordially yours,
Jennie Jones

✵

Compare the merits and faults of the following as a means of reporting to parents:

letter marks
percentage marks
pass-fail marks
letters to parents
conferences with parents
descriptive marks

✵

Conferences with Parents

Parent-teacher conferences are an increasingly popular method of reporting pupil progress to parents. This procedure has many advantages. It allows the teacher and the parent to discuss the pupil face to face. The conference should serve to create better understanding between parents and teachers and to obviate parental misunderstandings that sometimes result from teachers' letters and report forms. The conference gives the parent an opportunity to ask questions and to make suggestions. It also gives the teacher an opportunity to solicit additional information from the parent and to suggest ways in which the parent can cooperate to improve the child's work.

Conferences can be very helpful as supplements to the written reports of pupil progress to parents. It is doubtful whether they should be the sole medium for reporting, although some elementary schools rely almost wholly upon them. In secondary schools, conferences are more likely to be arranged to meet certain definite problems.

In spite of their many advantages parent-teacher conferences have certain inherent drawbacks. They are often time-consuming and difficult to schedule. Sometimes they must be scheduled at hours that are inconvenient for the teacher. Occasionally, instead of clearing up misunderstandings between parents and teachers, conferences add to them. At times the parent may be difficult to deal with. Some parents are emotional, domineering, or excessively talkative. Some are opinionated and overly critical of the school. The competent teacher attempts to plan and conduct parent-teacher conferences so as to avoid these difficulties as much as he can.

Some suggestions for conducting parent-teacher conferences follow.

1. Plan what you wish to say and how you wish to conduct the conference. Do not make a fetish of your plan, but do try to keep to the purpose of the conference at least. If possible, keep the conference moving. On the other hand, do not rush the parent. In your planning allow enough time to talk things over thoroughly and leisurely.

2. Be pleasant, courteous, tactful, and patient. Remember that the visit to the school may often be upsetting to the parent. Listen to him and try to understand his point of view. Remember that he has much information valuable to you. Let him tell it to you. If he is running hot, keep cool and let him talk it out. This is often an effective way to calm an irate parent. However, do not be obsequious. One does not need to agree with a parent to be polite. If the parent is severely critical of the school, arrange for him to talk to the principal or someone else in authority. Remember at all times that a conference is serious business and should be conducted with care and dignity.

3. Be clear and specific. Try to be sure the parent understands you. Talk to him in simple English and avoid technical terms. Make specific points and back them up with specific examples. Avoid vague, unsubstantiated generalizations which may lead to misunderstanding. Summarizing at critical points during the conference and at its end may help eliminate confusion and ensure a common understanding of what has transpired.

4. Avoid criticizing other teachers and school officials. First, it is unethical. Second, it will surely hurt your standing with your colleagues. Third, it will probably cause the parent to form a poor impression of you.

5. Solicit the parent's cooperation. The school is as much his as it is yours, and he has as much at stake in its success as you do. His interest in his own children is presumably greater than yours. Many parents would be eager to help if they only knew how. On the other hand, the teacher should be cautious about making suggestions which the parent might resent as intrusions on his own privacy, home life, or social life. If any suggestions of this sort need to be made, the teacher should be sure that his suggestions are constructive and that the parent is ready to act upon them. Frequently the better part of discretion is to leave such suggestions to guidance personnel, an administrator, or a supervisor.

6. After the conference the teacher should note down what has been said, what suggestions have been made, and what conclusions have been reached. This should be done as soon as possible lest some of the information be forgotten.

7. Ordinarily there should be some follow-up on every teacher-parent conference.

✻

Marks quite often become a bone of contention between parents and the school. Why? How can this be avoided?

In a conference the parent strongly criticizes the school administration or another teacher. You wholeheartedly agree with the parent. What should you do?

Describe what you consider the best system of marking and reporting to parents.

✻

Promotion

Desirability of Continuous Promotion

Promotion is an exceedingly difficult problem. Most logically promotion should be based on readiness. Pupils should progress through their course work in orderly fashion, staying with a particular course or unit only long enough to learn the material well and then moving on. In other words, the pupil should be promoted when he is ready. Promotion based on readiness is called continuous promotion.

Unfortunately, the secondary school is seldom organized in a manner suitable for continuous promotion. The difficulty preventing continuous promotions is that our schools are graded. At the end of a year the youngster must go on to the next grade or return to the beginning of his present grade. This system makes little sense. Our present pass-or-fail promotion policies may either make the pupil repeat material he has already learned, or force him ahead to more difficult material before he is ready. The establishment of nongraded high schools may foreshadow the end of this perplexing problem. Continuous promotion is the heart of the nongraded high school idea.

Setting Standards for Promotion

Although continuous promotion is not usually feasible in our secondary schools, the principles behind it do apply to promotion in general. The basic criterion for deciding if a pupil should be promoted is whether or not he is ready to profit from the next higher course in the subject. Even though the pupil does not intend to go on to the next course, the principle still holds in general, although perhaps it need not be applied quite so stringently in this instance. In other words, teachers should have standards of minimum achievement for their courses, and these standards should represent what is required of the pupil before he is ready for the next higher course.

The Role of Social Promotion

Although a teacher should ordinarily promote only those pupils who are ready, on occasion pupils are promoted whether they are ready or not. Usually when this is done, it is an attempt to keep the pupil in a social group with which he is compatible. This practice is called social promotion. On occasion, it is justified. The old practice of keeping sixteen-year-olds in third-grade classes was cruel. An example of a well-justified social promotion follows.

A junior-high-school boy was reading well below his grade level. Although evidently of at least normal intelligence, he was quite incapable of doing junior-high-school work. The boy also suffered from an acute speech defect and certain other emotional problems. The school psychiatrist examined the boy and recommended a social promotion as a means of helping him find himself. In this case the promotion was justified. But automatic promotions are never justified. Too often the young people are promoted to free the classrooms and because of a mistaken attempt to be democratic. Fortunately, such promotion is usually confined to the elementary grades and less usually to the junior high school. One rarely encounters either social or automatic promotion in the high school.

*

To what extent can one apply the principles of continuous promotion in the ordinary secondary school?

Do you agree that social promotion was justified in the example cited above?

A boy is completing his second year in Latin I. He is definitely not yet capable of doing the work of Latin II. What do you recommend the teachers do as far as promotion is concerned?

✲

Two Final Considerations

Although the teacher should maintain standards, these standards should be flexible. The fact that a pupil has not mastered the material of a course may not be a sufficient reason for keeping him back. On the other hand, merely spending a year in a classroom is not a sufficient reason for promoting him either. Some pupils should repeat courses. Each problem of promotion should be decided on its own merits. In applying promotion standards to a particular case, one should bear in mind two main questions: (1) How will the decision affect the pupil concerned? and (2) How will the decision affect the other pupils? Probably the final criterion should be: Which would benefit the pupil more? If it seems that the youngster would benefit from repeating the course another year, let him repeat it; if, on the other hand, there seems to be no reason to think that another year would be beneficial, let him move on. However, one should also consider the other pupils. How will promoting this pupil affect them? How will it affect pupil motivation? and morale? Will promoting him be fair to the others? If promoting a pupil will injure pupil motivation and morale in any way, one should weigh the case carefully before deciding to promote the pupil.

To Pass or Not to Pass

Deciding if a pupil should pass or fail often calls for difficult decisions. To illustrate the complexity of the problem let us consider the following situation. In your Algebra I class you have a youngster who has done poor work. It is your considered opinion that he just is not a mathematician. He is unable to do the work, no matter how hard he tries—and he seems to have tried very hard. He and his family are determined that he go on to college and insist that he continue with mathematics. Presumably, if he passes Algebra I, he will try Algebra II for which he is definitely not ready. What should you do? What would be best for the boy? To pass and attempt Algebra II? To fail and to repeat Algebra I? Is there some other way out? What about the effect on the other pupils? What information do you need and what must you consider to answer this problem intelligently?

As you can see, if you try to think this problem through, it probably has no truly satisfactory answer. Fortunately, many schools help the teacher in making this decision by establishing quite definite school policies concerning promotion. When they do, the teacher should try to follow the policy. Other schools have no formal policy, although there may be an informal one. Even if there is no policy at all, the principal can advise what one ought to do. Even so, the decision of whether or not to promote must be made by the teacher on the basis of what is best for the pupil himself and for other pupils in the school within the limits set by school policy.

Summary

Parents have a right to know how well their children are doing in school, and teachers have a duty to keep the parents informed. For years teachers have used marks to meet this obligation. Although many parents, pupils, and teachers do not realize it, marks, unfortunately, do not inform anyone of much of anything. Moreover, present-day marking systems tend to emphasize the mark rather than the learning. About the only value they have is a certain amount of incentive value, and even that seems to be overrated.

As teachers have come to recognize these facts, they have made numerous attempts to create better methods of evaluating and reporting pupils' progress. So far none of these attempts has been completely successful. Probably what is needed is a system that explains in writing how well a pupil is doing in relation to the standard for the group and to his own potentialities. In reporting to parents and pupils, such devices should undoubtedly be supplemented by conferences. Modern systems of reporting to parents seem to be moving in that direction. However, in many cases they still have a long distance to go. In the meantime, we shall have to do the best we can with what we have.

Promotion has always been a problem for the conscientious teacher. Promotion should be based on readiness, but this principle of continuous promotion is not readily feasible in the secondary school as now organized. The need for continuous promotion is one of the major arguments for the establishment of non-graded secondary schools.

There is no truly satisfactory answer to the problem of promotion. The final decision, however, should rest with the teacher, and his decision should be based on what is best for the student himself and for the other students in the class and school.

FOR FURTHER STUDY

The references cited for further study in Chapter 15 are also suitable for Chapter 16. In addition the following references may be of interest.

BROWN, B. FRANK, *The Non-Graded High School* (Englewood Cliffs, N.J.: Prentice Hall, Inc., 1963), Ch. 9.

BURTON, WILLIAM H., *The Guidance of Learning Activities*, Third Edition (New York: Appleton-Century-Crofts, Inc., 1962), Ch. 2.

CUMMINS, ROBERT E., "Evaluating and Grading," *Education*, September 1961–May 1962, *82:* 403–405.

DOUGLASS, HARL R., *Modern Administration of Secondary Schools* (New York: Blaisdell Publishing Company, 1963), Chs. 17 and 25.

FOX, WILLARD, and ALFRED SCHWARTZ, *Managerial Guide for School Principals* (Columbus, Ohio: Charles E. Merrill Books, Inc., 1965), Ch. 10.

JANSEN, V. H., *Marking and Reporting Procedures in the Secondary Schools of Texas* (Austin, Texas: Texas Study of Secondary Education), 1966.

JOHNSON, MAURITZ, JR. "Solving the Mess in Marks," *New York State Education*, November, 1961, *49:* 12–13, 30.

JOHNSON, R. RICHARD, "Better Ways of Measuring and Reporting Student Achievement," *The Bulletin of the National Association of Secondary School Principals*, September, 1962, *46:* 94–97.

KUMPF, CARL H., "Social Promotion—A Misnomer?", *The National Elementary Principal*, May, 1961, *40:* 35–37.

McKEAN, ROBERT C., *Principles and Methods in Secondary Education* (Columbus, Ohio: Charles E. Merrill Books, Inc., 1962), Ch. 8.

OVARD, GLEN F., *Administration of the Changing Secondary School* (New York: The Macmillan Company, 1966), Chs. 5, 10, 12, and 18.

ROLLINS, SIDNEY P., and ADOLPH UNRUH, *Introduction to Secondary Education* (Chicago: Rand McNally and Company, 1964), Ch. 10.

TERWILLIGER, JAMES S., "Self-Reported Marking Practices and Policies in Public Secondary Schools." *The Bulletin of the National Association of Secondary-School Principals*, March, 1966, *50:*5–37.

WILES, KIMBALL, *Teaching for Better Schools*, Second Edition (Englewood Cliffs, N.J.: Prentice-Hall, Inc., 1959), Ch. 12.

PART *VII*

Non-Instructional Duties

CHAPTER *17*

Classroom Management

Responsibilities for Management

The responsibilities of teaching involve more than instruction or guiding learning. A great deal of the teacher's time is spent with the management of his class. The keeping of records, reports, requisitions, the routine of the classroom itself, all occupy much of his school day. While the experienced teacher may consider it a matter of course, classroom management can and does present problems for the beginning teacher. The quicker he learns to master the routine, and the quicker he realizes the effect of classroom management on learning, the quicker the beginning teacher will become master of the situation.

Too seldom are new teachers properly oriented to the routine of a particular school, the records and reports that must be kept or filed, and the physical environment that should prevail. This chapter, therefore, will try to clarify some of the problems of classroom management and will attempt to outline procedures that will aid the teacher in managing the classroom more effectively.

✧

Think back over your own high-school days. What jobs did your teachers do that were not strictly teaching? In what ways did the performing of these tasks make the learning process easier or more enjoyable for you?

✧

The Physical Environment

The Appearance of the Classroom

The physical facilities of the classroom play an important part in setting the stage for instruction. Checking such things as lighting, windows, temperature, ventilation, and decor is part of the teacher's job.

Of course, a teacher can do little about the size and shape of his classroom, but he should do his best to make it as pleasing and comfortable as possible. In doing this, he should enlist the aid of his pupils. Untutored boys and girls are inclined to be disorderly, but, like everyone else, they prefer pleasant surroundings. If appealed to properly, they will often spend much time and effort in improving the orderliness and appearance of the classroom. This is particularly true of the classroom in the junior high school, where the teacher can often enlist pupil aid by creating a feeling of proprietorship in the pupil. Such feelings are more difficult to arouse in the highly departmentalized senior high school. There the teacher may have to do much of the work himself, although an appeal to the maturity and good sense of the pupils may enlist considerable cooperation from them. On both the junior- and senior-high-school levels, pupils have been eminently successful in beautifying their classrooms.

Cleanliness and Orderliness

Perhaps the first thing to do to make a classroom attractive is to see that it is clean and orderly. To be sure, it is the custodian's job to keep the classroom clean, but his work can be made much easier if the pupils and teachers cooperate. If possible, the teacher should have a place for everything, and everything should be in its place. In classrooms that have a scarcity of closet, cupboard, and other storage space, this will require considerable improvising. However, it is well worth the effort. So is cleaning up after oneself. To spend the last few minutes of a class period cleaning the chalkboards, putting materials away, and rearranging the room is an excellent practice. It should make the class that follows more pleasant. Nevertheless, the teacher should not try to be so antiseptically clean and orderly that he kills all the germs of learning in the classroom. A certain amount of disorder must be tolerated sometimes so that work may go on.

Brightening Up the Room

Color can also add tremendously to the pleasantness of a room. The days of the dingy, drab "schoolhouse brown" should be over. Modern schools are usually decorated in cheerful pastels—cool greens and blues for the warm, sunny side of the building, and warm orange and yellow for the cool, shady side. Whether the school has seen fit to brighten the walls or not, the teacher can add color through his own efforts.

The ingenious teacher can make even the dingiest classroom colorful. Displays on the tackboard, murals on the chalkboard, exhibits on the window shelf, all these and more can be called upon to lend life to the classroom. In classrooms that lack bulletin boards and display areas, a teacher can extemporize. Perhaps he can use some of the new adhesive devices to display pictures and posters directly against the wall. Perhaps he can run rolls of paper across a wall to create a display surface, or create a temporary tackboard from corrugated paper. Any table or desk can masquerade as a showcase. The possibilities for the ingenious and ambitious teacher are virtually unlimited and, with a little encouragement, the pupils will usually be more than willing to help.

❊

One school suspends all classes for a day so that the entire effort of the student body can be devoted to cleaning the grounds and building. Is this time and effort justified?

A young teacher assigned to a particularly dingy classroom asked permission to suspend classroom activities in that room for a day so that he and the pupils could wash the woodwork and the windows, rearrange the furniture, and beautify the room in general. What might some of the arguments pro and con be for such activities?

❊

Pictures are excellent for adding life to a room. Preferably, classroom pictures should be pertinent to the topic being studied. However, nothing should prevent the teacher from hanging a picture merely because it is beautiful or adds to the appearance of the room. A certain teacher of social studies used to make a hobby of collecting color prints of old masters. Partly for his own enjoyment, and partly as a method of instruction, he made it a practice to hang prints pertaining to the topics his world history classes were studying. These pictures, though not pertinent to mathematics, also added significantly to the mathematics classes which shared the classroom.

One can enhance the value of exhibits, displays, pictures, and other eye-catching materials by changing them from time to time. Variety and novelty in themselves tend to make a classroom brighter. Consequently, teachers should see to it that the materials on exhibit in their classrooms are of current interest. Even the plaster bust of Cicero and the monochrome of President Grant are not sacred and may be moved from time to time. Committees of pupils can be formed to keep the exhibits up to date. A common device is to have such a committee as part of each unit to be studied. Of course, duties of this sort should be passed around the class. Although the pupils will need some guidance, they themselves can often collect, arrange, and display exhibits that the teacher would be hard put to match.

The Classroom As a Laboratory

The modern classroom is a busy place. Since pupils learn through their own activities, the classroom should be arranged as a laboratory of learning. To be a laboratory in this sense, a room must have many work areas and much material and equipment with which to work. In such a laboratory the teacher is blessed with all the tables, files, cabinets, cupboards, easels, exhibit cases, tackboards, chalkboards, and other equipment necessary to carry on a full, rich, varied program.

In one corner one should find a well-stocked classroom library for research and reading. Here books, magazines, reference works, texts and vertical files may be arranged for easy classroom use.

Other areas of the classroom may be similarly arranged for other purposes. The furniture should be movable so that the class can arrange it in rows to watch a motion picture or dramatization, or in a circle for a discussion, or in a hollow square to allow for an arena stage.

Improvising a Classroom Laboratory

Unfortunately, many classrooms are far from being classroom laboratories. Many have the seats bolted to the floor. Few have all of the equipment mentioned in the preceding paragraph. This fact, although unfortunate, should not discourage the teacher. Rich instructional programs can be carried on successfully in situations far from ideal. If the room has immovable furniture, an eager committee may be able to group together in one corner of the room, sitting sideways and backwards in the immovable chairs; they can gather round the teacher's desk, or worktable, or, if necessary, even move into the corridor. If there are no file cabinets, paper cartons can often be arranged to hold quite a sizable collection of file folders. A coat of paint or a covering of wallpaper can make such homemade filing cabinets quite attractive. With a little ingenuity one can often improvise substitutes which, although perhaps not the best, will do until something better can be obtained. Occasionally, the substitute turns out to be superior to the real thing.

In many schools, organization of classroom laboratories is a problem because one classroom must be shared by many teachers. This problem, however, is not insurmountable. The teacher who uses the classroom most should have priority, but all the teachers should share in planning the arrangement. If the teachers are reasonable and considerate, they should be able to agree on an arrangement satisfactory to all concerned.

Providing for Adequate Lighting

The classroom should not only be attractive, it should also be comfortable and conducive to good health. In this connection lighting is, of course, extremely important. In general, it is safe to say that a teacher will not be much troubled about lighting problems if he uses common sense. Still, it may be worthwhile to mention a few precautions about lighting.

The principal problem, as far as lighting is concerned, is to direct the light toward the pupil's work area so that it will be free from glare and shadows. No pupil should be seated so that he is directly facing a source of light. Nor should any pupil be seated so that his shadow falls on his work. To this end, boys and girls should sit so that the light comes over the left shoulder when they are writing. (This rule, of course, does not hold for left-handed writers; they should sit so that the light comes over the right shoulder.) Since brightness contrast seems to be one of the greatest causes of eye strain, the classroom should be evenly lighted and free from bright or dark spots. This is one reason that designers of school rooms have replaced blackboards with green chalkboards. For the same reason, the walls next to the windows in some schools have been painted white or a very light pastel. The teacher, of course, cannot do much about the decoration and construction of the room, but he can do much to reduce glare, shadows, and brightness contrast if he makes the most of the lighting, windows, and shades in the classroom.

The key to the problem seems to be to keep alert to what is going on in the classroom. On a bright, sunny day it is often necessary to draw the shades in order to reduce brightness and glare. If the sky should cloud over, it may become necessary to raise the shades and turn on the light on the far side of the room. As the day gets darker, one may have to turn on all the lights in the classroom to get enough light into every corner. To expect any teacher to be continuously alert to such changes is unreasonable, so the teacher should make it clear to his pupils that they should feel free to draw the shades, change seats, or make whatever other adjustments may be necessary if they are bothered by the lighting in any way.

✿

Suppose you have an unruly class. Would you allow them to adjust lights and shades as they see fit? If not, what would you do?

College classrooms are quite often drab. Pick one that is particularly bare and plan how you might brighten it up even though you have no funds for this purpose.

Suppose one teacher wants the room set up as a classroom laboratory; another who uses the same room wishes the room to follow the traditional pattern. What would you suggest as a solution to this problem?

✿

Heat and Ventilation

Heat and ventilation are also important in making a class comfortable. Rooms that are too cold distract pupils' attention from their work. Rooms that are too hot slow pupils down. The ideal temperature is somewhere in the vicinity of 70° F. Sixty-seven to 73° seem to be acceptable. The teacher should check the thermometer from time to time to be sure that the classroom is within that range.

Usually one can do little about a cold classroom other than to complain to the office. However, if the room is too hot one can regulate the heat by

adjusting windows or the heat valves. Of course, if a teacher turns off
the heat, he should be sure to turn it on again before leaving the room;
common sense dictates that one should check to see if the heat is turned
on before he complains about there being no heat in the classroom.
Some schools have strict rules about teachers adjusting the heat. When
this is so, the teacher should abide by them, as his interference may
affect the heat in other rooms and also the amount of drain on the
heating system.

The teacher should also attempt to keep the classroom reasonably
humid. The desirable classroom humidity is about 50 per cent, but in the
ordinary classroom, humidity is difficult to control. However, the teacher
can take care to keep the air as fresh as possible and to prevent drafts.
Stuffy classrooms are unpleasant; drafty ones are health hazards.

Flexible Seating Arrangements

Most modern schools are equipped with movable chairs rather than
fixed furniture. This being so, the teacher should resist the temptation to
place the furniture in serried ranks, as was done with the old fixed
furniture. Although arranging chairs in rows has some advantages from a
control and convenience point of view, it has relatively few advantages
from an instructional standpoint. As a matter of fact, no classroom seating
arrangement is perfectly satisfactory for all activities and all classes. The
teacher should arrange the class according to the classwork the pupils
are to do. For watching a movie, working individually, or listening to a
lecture, some variations of the ordinary row set-up may be desirable; for
committee work, small circles of chairs may be best; for a discussion, a
circle or some segment of a circle may be suitable.

Some teachers like to seat the pupils in alphabetical order or with the
larger pupils in the back. In the traditional class these practices may
make the routine easier, but if one uses flexible methods, such plans are
pointless. To let the pupils select their own seats is probably as good a
plan as any. However, for at least the first few days, the pupils should
keep the same seats so that the teacher can identify them by means of a
seating chart.

Modern textbooks sometimes recommend placing the teacher's desk
in the back of the classroom. This serves the purpose of removing the
teacher from the front of the room and, to a degree, tends to make the
class less teacher-centered. However, the position of the teacher's desk is
not particularly important. The important thing is to arrange the entire
room so that it will be useful and comfortable.

Some examples of possible class arrangements are shown in Figure 11.

*

Some teachers recommend breaking up boon companions, cliques,
and troublemakers by seating them so that they can not talk to each

FIGURE 11

Diagrams of Possible Room Arrangements.

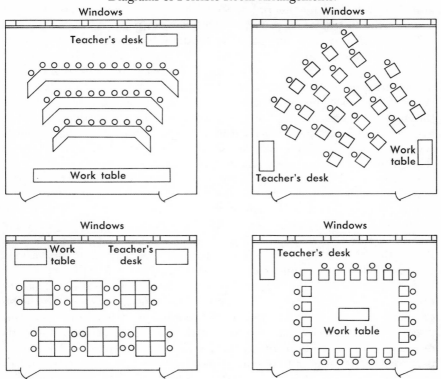

other easily. Others say this is a useless procedure and creates more harm than good. What is your opinion on this problem?

❋

Handling Classroom Routine

As a general rule, classes will make better progress if the more usual tasks are routinized. Routines make it possible for boys and girls to know what to do without being told over and over again. For instance, there should be no question about whether to write on both sides of a paper, or whether a pupil should give his oral report from his desk or from the front of the room, for we *always* write on only one side of a sheet and we *always* give oral reports from the front of the classroom.

Time is critical in any class. Routinization of housekeeping activities is an effective way to save time. The more time we can save for active instruction the better. However, too much routinizing can lead to boredom and loss of interest. A good rule is to routinize as many of the administrative and managerial aspects of the classroom as possible but to leave the instructional activities free from routine.

Routinization can be applied to such administrative matters as attendance, tardy slips, and excuses. In handling these, the teacher must, of course, carry out the school regulations. However, in order to save time and interruptions, all of this work should be completed before the class starts. Attendance should be taken by some quick method such as noting the unfilled chairs. Calling the roll is a time-wasting procedure. In order to take attendance quickly it is usually a good practice to have pupils start off at the beginning of the class in their assigned stations, even though they move to other work stations later.

In order for the class to get started with a minimum of confusion, the teacher should routinize the issuing of equipment and materials. The issuing of papers and books can often be delegated to pupils. Before the class starts, materials to be used during the period should be ready for instant distribution. A good way to keep confusion to a minimum is to list on the board those things which will be needed during the various periods. Thus the pupils can equip themselves with the necessary materials without asking a single question. A similar routine can be set up for putting things away at the end of the period. In some classes the teacher will want to routinize the collection and distribution of pupil papers. This is usually done by passing the papers to, or from, the ends of rows, or to the head of the table. However, in a classroom laboratory perhaps a better way is to circulate unobtrusively about the class and to collect or distribute the papers without interrupting the pupils' work.

One should never become a slave to routine, but if certain tasks must be done again and again, a properly used routine can make the class more efficient and pleasant.

Administrative Duties

Administrative Procedures

Administrative procedures are designed to aid instruction and to make life more pleasant in the school. By following these procedures, the teacher can usually make things easier for everyone. Occasionally, administrative details become somewhat oppressive and at times downright ridiculous. These are the exceptions that prove the rule. In any case, the teacher has no choice; if he is to do his job properly, he must follow administrative procedures exactly.

Preparing Paper Work

Many of the teacher's administrative duties come under the heading of paper work. It takes a considerable amount of paper work to run a school; teachers sometimes think there is too much of it. Just a few of the forms on file at the University of Hartford Curriculum Library indicate the amount of administrative paper work—attendance reports, absence reports, book inventories, book lists, book requisitions, cafeteria forms, conference reports, custody requests, and detention slips. However, if budgets are to be prepared, materials of instruction to be purchased, pupils to be accounted for, teachers to be hired and paid—in short, if school is to keep at all—teachers must be prepared to do their share of paper work.

The secret in dealing with paper work is to do the job carefully and to do it on time. Properly submitted reports filed in plenty of time endear the teacher to the administrative staff, particularly if nothing is omitted from the report or form submitted and all the information is accurate and exact.

Preparing Requisitions

The requisition provides a good example of administrative paperwork. A requisition should state exactly what is wanted in such a way that there can be no mistake. Vague requests such as "a cupboard for the music room" are almost useless to the purchasing agent. When he receives such a request, he must either send the requisition back for more information or try to guess what the teacher has in mind. In either case, if the purchase is delayed or the wrong material ordered, the fault lies with the teacher, not with the principal or purchasing department.

When requesting the purchase of an item, it is best to give an example of exactly what you want by giving a catalog reference. A catalog reference explains what you are talking about and also enhances your chance of getting exactly what you want rather than something "of equal quality."

Not only should requisitions be accurate and specific, they should also be on time. One late requisition may hold up an entire program. There is always a time lag between ordering and receiving supplies. Furthermore, some items are in short supply. So, if a teacher wants something, he should requisition it early. Many of the best films, for example, are booked solid for months in advance; if the teacher does not request them early, he should be prepared to substitute some other activity.

Keeping Accurate Records

Among the duties involving paper work is the keeping of records. Records accounting for pupils and their attendance, and records accounting for equipment and supplies, are essential to the running of the school. Without them money, time, and equipment would be lost. Usually the amount of record-keeping involved is relatively small if one keeps his records up to date. However, if one neglects one's records for a time, putting them back into proper shape can become quite a job. The solution, of course, is not to let the recording get ahead of you.

Keeping Accurate Inventories

Teachers should inventory their books, supplies, and equipment from time to time. The school frequently provides the forms and sets the time for inventories. In some classes, however, the teacher must maintain a running inventory to ensure keeping proper amounts of material on hand. When inventorying books and equipment, one should note the condition as well as the presence of each item. The key to maintaining a running inventory is, as in any other kind of record-keeping, to keep the records up to date. When one removes something from stock, he should note it at once or his records will soon become incorrect. Remember that if your records say you have plenty of HCl, when the bottle is actually empty, your classes will suffer.

Keeping Personnel Records

Particularly important are records that deal with pupils. Pupil records must always be filled out accurately in fairness to the pupil and to other teachers. In fact, the accuracy of some records such as those having to do with attendance may have importance which transcends the classroom. In more than one instance they have been used as evidence in court cases involving pupils, and of course, they provide the basic data from which the state allocates its grant to the local school district.

In some states pupil accounting is done through the daily register. The school office maintains all the registers in many school systems, but other systems require that each teacher keep the register for his own class. In the register one can usually find the following information.

1. Name and address of each student.
2. Age as of a particular month and birthdate.
3. Name and occupation of parent or guardian.
4. Daily attendance record of each student (absence, dismissal, tardiness).
5. Average and aggregate attendance (monthly, semester, and yearly).

Keeping this record properly is particularly important because of legal implications and because state financial grants may be based upon such records. To illustrate the importance of these records, one need only say that in some systems the teachers do not receive their June checks until the register is turned in properly filled out. As with other records, daily attention to detail is the only way to ensure accurate pupil accounting.

✻

What legal complications could result from an improperly filled out register?

What materials and supplies would you need to keep records of in your classes?

What pupil personnel records would you expect to work with as a teacher?

✻

The Teachers' Manual

The preceding paragraphs have mentioned only a few of the administrative responsibilities of teachers. There are many more. Early in one's career one should make a special effort to learn the administrative procedures of one's school. The regulations and directions for the various administrative tasks may often be found in the teachers' manual or handbook. Study the manual carefully before you attend your first class. If the school does not furnish a manual, make one of your own. When in doubt of what your procedure should be, consult the principal. Doing so may save you much embarrassment, confusion, and delay.

Classroom Management and Recent Innovations

The recent birth of new technologies and the resurrection of old ones have had little real impact on classroom management except to make attention to detail more important. Since we have already discussed these technologies, we shall not discuss them here except to point out how they effect classroom management. In many schools the problem of heating and ventilating rooms used for large-group instruction is difficult, particularly during warm weather and especially if the room must be darkened. Because of the one-way nature of most large-group and television instruction, and the size of the group, distractions can become much more bothersome than in ordinary classes. Also in large-group classes discomfort and distraction can increase the "psychological noise" attendant upon any large-group presentation, and worse yet, may lead to the real noise of collapsing discipline. For this reason, too, the teacher should carefully check sight lines and acoustics before large-group instruction. Routines for passing and collecting things, moving in and out of the room, and so on, need to be worked out carefully and carried out quite formally in order to avoid confusion and the wasting of time.

The small group and individual study require far less formality than the large group. However, they do require adequate surroundings suitable to the task before them. Work groups and individual researchers need to have materials readily available so that they may go to them with the least amount of difficulty. In some cases they can be best served by classroom libraries and laboratories, and at others, by central sources such as libraries and materials' centers. In any event, the processes for getting materials and equipment for use should be simple and quick. When pupils have to wait around to draw a tape or program with which they should be working, the system may break down.

Considerable attention needs to be given to work space for small groups and individual workers. Small discussion groups should be housed where they can discuss freely without disturbing others—a situation that does not always obtain when groups are separated by movable partitions. Work groups and individuals need adequate provision for storage and sometimes space in which to leave work in progress so that they can come back to it. Not many schools have really adequate facilities for the encouragement of independent study. To improvise good work space may be difficult, but teachers and administrators should be alert to the need so as to take steps when the opportunity offers.

Flexible schedules and no-bell systems present no great problem to the teacher except that he may have to learn to be a clock watcher. To keep from disturbing others it will, however, be necessary to keep good order and quiet in groups that move about the corridors at odd times. Although control of pupil movement is really an administrative problem, the teacher must be ready to help keep these movements under control.

Summary

To many teachers housekeeping has a particularly disagreeable connotation, but careful housekeeping is necessary in the well-run classroom. Because uncomfortable boys and girls do not learn well, the teacher should take particular care to make the classroom as pleasant as possible physically. To do so, he must pay particular attention to heat, lighting, and ventilation, as well as the room's appearance.

The efficient classroom is usually a flexible one. Probably no particular room arrangement of the furniture is the best arrangement. The classroom should be a laboratory for learning, replete with all the supplies and equipment necessary and adaptable to any of the activities one can reasonably expect.

The careful planning of routine activities can help speed the learning process. The competent teacher will consider routinizing any activity which is repeated day after day, such as paper distribution and collection. However, one should not allow routinization to become a fetish or let it interfere with effective instruction.

Administrative functions are also necessary for good housekeeping. By using meticulous care and promptness in handling administrative duties, the teacher will help the entire school to run more smoothly.

The recent popularity of new technologies such as team teaching, television, programmed instruction, and flexible scheduling have had little effect on classroom management and administration except to make care for detail more important. Because most secondary schools were not built to house such technologies, teachers and administrators should be awake to opportunities to facilitate their use by adjusting the means already available.

FOR FURTHER STUDY

BURRUP, PERCY E., *Modern High School Administration* (New York: Harper and Row Publishers, Inc., 1962), Chs. 12–13.

BURTON, WILLIAM H., *The Guidance of Learning Activities*, Third Edition (New York: Appleton-Century-Crofts, Inc., 1962), Ch. 23.

BROWN, EDWIN JOHN, and ARTHUR THOMAS PHELPS, *Managing the Classroom— The Teacher's Part in School Administration*, Second Edition (New York: The Ronald Press Company, Inc., 1961).

GRAMBS, JEAN D., WILLIAM J. IVERSON, and FRANKLIN K. PATTERSON, *Modern Methods in Secondary Education*, Revised Edition (New York: Holt, Rinehart and Winston, Inc., 1958), Ch. 12.

OVARD, GLEN F., *Administration of the Changing Secondary School* (New York: The Macmillan Company, 1965), Ch. 13.

RISK, THOMAS R., *Principles and Practices of Teaching in Secondary Schools*, Third Edition (New York: American Book Company, 1958), Ch. 20.

RIVLIN, HARRY N., *Teaching Adolescents in Secondary Schools* (New York: Appleton-Century-Crofts, Inc., 1961), Ch. 13.

WILLIAMS, STANLEY W., *Educational Administration in Secondary Schools* (New York: Holt, Rinehart and Winston, Inc., 1964), Chs. 16–17.

CHAPTER *18*

The Teacher and
Extra-Class Responsibilities

*A*LTHOUGH the teacher may think that the multitudinous tasks and responsibilities of classroom teaching are quite enough, his work is not limited to the classroom. It also includes extracurricular responsibilities, guidance functions, and, as we have seen, administrative duties.

The Teacher and the Extracurriculum

The Importance of the Extracurriculum

In a sense the extracurriculum is part of the curriculum. To be quite accurate, extracurricular activities should be thought of as variables in a constants-with-variables program, or, to use less technical terminology, as elective parts of the total educational program. The skills, concepts, and attitudes learned through such activities may be fully as valuable as those gained in formal courses. If these activities deserve a place in our school programs, each teacher must expect to contribute to the extracurriculum in some way.

The Teacher's Role in the Extracurriculum

Conducting extracurricular activities is much the same as conducting any other learning activity. The principal difference between extracurricular activities and class activities is that the coercive element is removed. Because of this lack of coercion, most pupils in an extracurricular activity are there because they want to be. Thus extracurricular activities afford unusual opportunities for utilizing natural motivation and interest.

On the other hand, because there is no coercion, activities that do not appeal to pupils are doomed to a marginal existence, if not to extinction. Such activities should be dropped in favor of activities the pupils want.

An extracurricular activity that seems worthless to the pupils certainly has little valid reason for existing.

This fact imposes an increased burden for leadership on the activity sponsor. The appeal of any activity often depends upon the way the activity is conducted as much as on the activity itself. Good leadership and good planning have made more than one faltering extracurricular activity a success in every sense of the word.

CONDUCTING EXTRACURRICULAR ACTIVITIES. The job of the sponsor or coach is to guide or direct the pupils as they conduct the activity. Delegation of responsibility is an important key in the guidance of any extracurricular activity. Guidance implies helping pupils over the hard parts by advising them on what to do and showing them how to do it. It also implies checking up on the pupils to be sure that they are carrying out their responsibilities properly. If the activity is a good one, group pressure can usually be counted on to help force "do-nothings" to produce. In any event, the principal duties of the sponsor, once the plan has got under way, are to see to it that the right assignments get to the proper persons, to help the pupils where they need help, and to keep checking to see that things are done and done well. If, in doing all this, the sponsor can keep in the background, so much the better.

In certain types of extracurricular activities, such as theatrical productions, athletics, and musical performances, the sponsor may have to accept a more important role in planning and direction in order to maintain high standards of performance. Even in such activities the sponsor does not need to become the dictator some teachers appear to be. The pupils can be of real help in planning them cooperatively. Still, if the pupils are ever to have the thrill of really first-class performance, much of the planning and direction must be assumed by the sponsor, director, or coach.

THE QUALITIES OF LEADERSHIP. How does one provide good leadership for extracurricular activities? Having the right kind of personality certainly helps. Adams and Dickey[1] list the following fifteen "attitudes of a good sponsor." They say that the list is "not all-inclusive." Perhaps you can find other attributes to add to the list.

1. Vitality in guiding and directing the activities of boys and girls.
2. Enthusiasm and ability to create enthusiasm for others' own interests.

[1] Harold P. Adams and Frank G. Dickey, *Basic Principles of Student Teaching* (New York: American Book Company, copyright 1956), pp. 230–231. Quoted by permission of American Book Company.

3. Tact in associating with boys and girls to prevent familiarity, but to maintain their confidence and respect.
4. Interest in many things.
5. Ability to get along well with people.
6. Awareness of problems of social living.
7. Desire to associate with boys and girls.
8. Adaptability in being able to change carefully made plans as needs arise.
9. Ability to guide without domineering.
10. Possession of a sense of humor.
11. Possession of ability and/or training in the area of at least one activity.
12. Acceptance of all boys and girls regardless of personal attractiveness or social position.
13. Understanding and appreciation of the needs and problems of pupils.
14. Resourcefulness and interest in exploring new and different fields and problems.
15. Ability to derive satisfaction in pupil accomplishment, rather than from results of one's own efforts.

✿

In what ways do these attributes differ from the attributes of successful classroom teachers? What attributes are more necessary for good classroom teachers? For good sponsors? How can prospective teachers develop these attributes?

In some schools extracurricular activities are held during the school day as activity periods; in others they are held in after school hours only. Can you justify giving up school time for extracurricular activities?

✿

Planning Extracurricular Activities

One needs more than a good personality to lead an extracurricular activity well. As in any other teaching, planning is the key to success in conducting an extracurricular activity. In some extracurricular activities the planning can be done informally, for by their very nature many extracurricular activities lend themselves exceptionally well to teacher-pupil planning. Club activities are especially suited to such techniques. But in no activity can planning be skipped if the activity is to be successful for very long.

COOPERATIVE PLANNING. Pupils, as a rule, need help in planning extracurricular activities. Usually the pupils are eager to do things well, but they need to be shown how. Consequently, the teacher must coach the responsible pupils in their duties and help them evolve good plans. For instance, club officers usually need to be taught how to conduct meetings, and school-paper editors need to be taught how to edit and proofread. Moreover, the teacher may need to suggest things for the pupils to do. Because of their lack of experience, boys and girls seldom have enough ideas concerning the things they might do to make their program successful. Part of the sponsor's task is to fill in the gaps.

Not only does the teacher need to help with ideas, but he must help the pupils set up criteria of excellence by which to judge the ideas and to maintain high standards. A case in point is the selection of a play for production. At times, youngsters are tempted to select a hackneyed farce with no literary merit whatsoever. They can usually avoid this pitfall if they work out standards of excellence before reading the plays. Extra-curricular activities should always be of high caliber.

At the same time, the teacher must keep the pupils from attempting more than they can manage. The enthusiasm of youth often bites off more than it can chew readily. When the teacher thinks the pupils are considering a project that will be too much for them, he should warn them. A good method for doing this is to consider the possibilities and probabilities in a group discussion early in the planning. However, one should not be too quick to condemn plans as being too ambitious. Condemning the plans may raise the hackles of the planners; besides, what pupils can do, when they really want to, is amazing.

Because of the audience appeal of these activities, many communities have come to demand almost professional standards. These demands place great pressures on the coach or director and the pupils. Although high standards are always desirable, they should not be maintained at the expense of the total educational program or the needs of the boys and girls. When any extracurricular activity interferes with the total educational program of the school, it is time for a change.

CRITERIA FOR PLANNING EXTRACURRICULAR ACTIVITIES. In planning any extracurricular activity, the teacher should bear in mind one criterion above all others: schools are maintained by our citizens for the education of youth. This being so, all school-sponsored activities should be learning activities. It is not the schools' business to entertain the populace, or to provide recreation for boys and girls. These worthwhile activities are the province of other agencies. This does not imply that the schools should ban all recreational activities, nor eliminate sports. But it does mean that each activity the school sponsors should lead toward some goal appropriate to the purposes of the school. If any activity as planned leads to no such purpose, it has no place in the school and should be dropped or changed. In other words, a dance for purely recreational purposes is probably not a proper school activity, but a dance whose purpose is to develop the social graces in boys and girls has its place, providing that it is expressly arranged for that purpose.

Another criterion is that the pupils should feel that the activities are worthwhile. Pupils quickly drop out of activities that are not worthwhile. Even such high prestige activities as football suffer from this. In order for an activity to be really successful, it must have high intrinsic value or important incentive. True cooperative planning is one way to ensure such value. In extracurricular activities it should be utilized to the utmost.

Who Should Participate in the Extracurriculum?

The answer to this question is *everyone*. Schools are provided to educate everyone enrolled. Therefore, all school activities should be open to all boys and girls. Each pupil should be given a chance to participate, enjoy, and exploit his interests to the best of his ability. Of course, certain extracurricular activities require skills and abilities that some pupils do not have. After a fair trial these pupils may be guided into some other activity, or perhaps some other job within the same activity. For instance, the boy who cannot hit the basket will not add much to the basketball team as a player but may make a good manager or publicity agent; similarly, the girl whose dramatic ability is nil but who is good at make-up can find an important place in the dramatics club.

This principle of making extracurricular activities open to all has been most seriously violated in school social activities. There is no room in the school for activities that bar boys and girls on the basis of social position, class, or wealth. Junior proms, sororities, clubs, and parties that require a considerable expenditure of money by pupils cannot be justified in a public high school because the expense automatically rules out participation by the less wealthy pupils. Equally out of place are secret societies, fraternities, and sororities whose membership is determined by social favor and secret ballot. Such activities do not belong in the program of the modern public secondary school. The sponsor should guide the pupils into desirable social habits and see to it that no pupil is barred because of wealth, race, religion, or social status.

THE DANGER OF OVERPARTICIPATION. While it is true that every pupil should be allowed to pursue his interests, many pupils must be protected from overparticipation. Even for teen-agers the day is limited to twenty-four hours. To do all the things some high-school youngsters attempt to do is impossible. Many youths spend so much time and energy on the extracurriculum that they have little or no time left over to spend on their classwork. To prevent these pupils from attempting too much, it may be necessary to limit their participation in extracurricular activities.

Besides causing pupils to neglect their studies, individual overparticipation in extracurricular activities tends to limit participation to a relatively small group of pupils, thus preventing other equally talented pupils from participating. Particularly troublesome is the fact that the positions of leadership are frequently monopolized by a small group of pupils. Such situations are common because both teachers and pupils tend to select those who have already shown themselves willing and able. Properly guided, extracurricular activities can involve many youngsters in positions of trust, responsibility, and leadership, thus developing these qualities in a larger part of the student group.

USE OF POINT SYSTEMS. In some schools individual overparticipation and concentration of the choice positions are prevented by the use of some sort of point system. Under this plan each extracurricular position is allocated a number of points: e.g., student council president, 12 points; class president, 10 points; newspaper editor, 10 points; football player, 8 points; member of the science club, 1 point. Each pupil is permitted to carry only a certain number of points during any school term. Thus, if the maximum number of points were set at 25, a boy who was both president of the student council and editor of the school paper would not be permitted to hold another major office.

OTHER WAYS TO AVOID OVERPARTICIPATION. Limiting overparticipation by point systems and similar devices is usually a matter of overall school policy. When such policies do not exist, the teacher needs to find some other way to distribute the honors among the pupils. Rules forbidding leaders to succeed themselves, vesting control in an executive board with a revolving chairmanship, and similar arrangements may be helpful. Delegating responsibilities is another way to involve more pupils.

*

What do you think of point systems? Would you agree with the point allocation for the above position if 25 points are to be the limit? What values would you recommend?

What would you do to make sure that all boys and girls had an opportunity to participate in the extracurriculum?

As an activity sponsor how could you see to it that everyone had a chance to participate fully?

*

Business Management

The business management of any pupil organization should be carefully supervised by the teacher. Usually the school authorities will have set up explicit procedures for the collecting, expending, and accounting of money. These regulations should be followed to the letter. Carelessness in this matter can lead to embarrassment and to outright financial loss. Even though pupils may collect the money and a pupil treasurer may be charged with keeping the books, the teacher cannot escape his responsibility for safeguarding any funds in the treasury.

Money for extracurricular activities may be obtained in several ways. An allocation may be requested from the student council or some other central agency upon the basis of a budget, or money may be raised through membership dues or fund-raising projects. In general, one should keep dues and fund-raising campaigns to a minimum. Dues may embarrass some pupils; fund-raising campaigns may take too much of the pupils' time, besides being a source of annoyance to the people who must contribute the money. In any case, before venturing on such a project, the sponsor should get the principal's permission. In fact, soliciting the principal's advice on all matters concerning the financing of extracurricular activities is a wise precaution.

Ordinarily, all money is placed in the hands of the school treasurer. To leave cash in teachers' desks or pupils' lockers is very risky. In order to ensure proper accounting, most schools insist that all payments be made by check by the school treasurer on presentation of suitable vouchers by the officers and sponsors of the activity. The wise sponsor has as little to do with cash as possible and is very careful to stick to the letter of the law as far as money matters are concerned.

Suggestions Concerning Handling Money

Most sponsors must handle money at one time or another. Consequently, a few words of precaution may be advisable.

1. Set up a system of accounting for funds before collecting any.
2. Give receipts for all money received. Be sure to keep a duplicate or a stub.
3. Record all transactions immediately.
4. Deposit all funds with the school treasurer, safe, or bank immediately after receiving them. Get a receipt.
5. Do not keep money in your desk or on your person.
6. Do not keep school money with your personal money.
7. Do not commit the school or extracurricular activity to any indebtedness without official approval.
8. Do not authorize payments of any bills until they have been approved.
9. Do not pay any bills by cash. If possible, always pay by school check. Be sure to get receipts for any payments made.

10. Always follow to the letter school regulations concerning handling of funds.

The Teacher and the Guidance Program

Every Teacher a Guidance Worker

In recent years the need for guidance and guidance services has grown enormously. The great increase in secondary-school enrollment and the consequent diversity in the student population has made the problems of providing adequate secondary-school curricula for individual pupils much more complex than in the college-oriented school of a half century ago. To date, American secondary-school educators have not been able to solve these problems satisfactorily. About one third of our American youths do not finish their secondary-school courses, while others who keep on to the bitter end find that, after all, their secondary-school years have given them little of value. In 1958, the Congress recognizing the seriousness of pupils' need for help and direction provided federal support for programs to improve guidance, counseling, testing, and the training of counselors.

Every teacher's job includes guidance duties. If he does no actual formal counseling or homeroom guidance, he must cooperate with the persons charged with such responsibilities. If he teaches in a school which, as yet, has no specialized guidance personnel, he will undoubtedly have to perform some of the duties ordinarily assigned to the specialist. No matter where he teaches, the good teacher finds it necessary to guide pupils in his classes in ways not included in the course of study. Every teacher should contribute eagerly to the guidance program, for it can be extremely helpful to him and his pupils. As a matter of fact, *the functions by which a classroom teacher contributes to the guidance program are pretty much what a good teacher would expect to do anyway*. Since there is a trend toward broadening guidance activities in the secondary school, new teachers will be more and more likely to find guidance duties formally recognized as part of their assignment. But whether there is a guidance program or not, the good teacher will engage in many guidance activities as part of his normal teaching responsibilities.

The Guidance Program

What, then, is the guidance program? It is not, as many people seem to think, designed to provide a place where troubled pupils can go to have a counselor solve all their problems and make their difficult decisions for them. Rather, it is a program designed to help pupils to understand themselves and to direct their own lives more efficiently. At the same time, the guidance program attempts to provide the information necessary for efficient teaching of each individual and for improvement of the total school program. *Through the guidance program the school tries to help all pupils shape for themselves fuller, happier, more useful lives, and become better students and citizens.*

To accomplish these purposes the complete guidance program provides the following services: individual inventory service; occupational and educational information service; counseling service; placement service; and follow-up service.[2]

These services are not separate offices or departments of the guidance program. In actual practice, no formal distinction is made between the services. Many guidance workers engage in all the services every day and would be hard put to tell when they are providing one service or another. These services are similar to those the teacher uses in his teaching, but much amplified in scope.

THE INDIVIDUAL INVENTORY SERVICE. The individual inventory service includes all the data-gathering devices and records by which the school gets to know the pupils. Included in this service are cumulative records, anecdotal reports, health records, reports of home visits, intelligence and other psychological test scores—in short, all the information the school has been able to gather about the pupils. Among the information gathered here are personal statistics, home environment, preschool history, health information, school history, aptitudes, abilities, personality traits, nonacademic and out-of-school activities, and plans and interests. To gather this information, the guidance workers use the same devices that teachers use to learn about pupils in their classes, plus data from other sources not readily available to the classroom teacher. Among them are previous school records, school testing programs, case studies, interviews with pupils, their parents and others, questionnaires, autobiographies, and routine and extraordinary reports from teachers and other sources. The data gathered through the individual inventory service are used as a basis for counseling by the guidance workers and are made available to teachers for use with their pupils.

A good school testing program is an essential part of an adequate individual inventory service. Properly used, modern tests provide much information indicative of pupils' potentialities. When misused, however, test results can be harmful. They should never be considered the final authority in making decisions or in studying an individual. To avoid misuse and misunderstandings teachers and counselors should use test scores for only well-defined purposes. When dealing with pupils and

[2] Harold Mahoney, "The Guidance Program, Bulletin 45," Connecticut State Department of Education, 1948, pp. 19–28.

The guidance counselor helps pupils to help themselves. Here a guidance counselor conducts a pupil interview.

parents, teachers should be particularly careful to explain and interpret test results to them. Failure to do so may allow parents and pupils to come to erroneous conclusions.

THE INFORMATION SERVICE. The occupational and educational information service is a repository for information of all sorts. In addition to occupational and educational information, this service might also make available information about oneself (collected through the individual inventory service), boy-girl relations and extracurricular opportunities. The following description of the Wichita, Kansas, program illustrates the type of information made available to pupils.

1. Information concerning educational requirements and opportunities beyond the secondary school.
   a. Current catalogues available for colleges, universities, and special training institutions.
   b. Current information regarding financial assistance as scholarships, loans, and other forms of student aid.

2. Information about local and national occupational opportunities, requirements, trends, and employment conditions.
3. Special programs to inform parents and students, such as "Career Days" and "College Nights."
4. Visual aids in the form of posters, graphs, charts, photographs, pamphlets, and other materials to present information of guidance value.
5. Information concerning agencies and persons qualified to render assistance for physical, emotional, educational, vocational, or employment needs.[3]

The information may be disseminated to pupils in several ways, such as homeroom classes, orientation classes, units in core and other courses, and so on. In libraries, homerooms, and the counselor office waiting room information is frequently stored in open shelves, so that shy or embarrassed pupils may look things up without "bothering" anyone. Also, trained guidance personnel suggest references to guide the pupil to the information he desires.

THE COUNSELING SERVICE. The counseling service is the heart of the guidance program. By means of counseling, the guidance workers do most of the actual guiding. We shall discuss this aspect of the guidance program more thoroughly later in the chapter.

THE PLACEMENT SERVICE. The placement service attempts to place boys and girls in their proper niches in the curriculum, the extra-curriculum, and in post-high-school activities. This service has long been a function of the school. Nowadays, however, it is no longer simply a matter of trying to match youths and jobs or curricula. Rather, it is an attempt to develop in the young people the attitudes and understandings necessary for making their own decisions. At the present time, counselors are devoting much of their effort to selecting and preparing pupils for the right college and college curriculum. Another relatively new concern is the finding of jobs for drop-outs and for former graduates who need assistance.

THE FOLLOW-UP SERVICE. The follow-up service tells us how well our school programs have succeeded and helps us prepare to do a better job for pupils to come. By following up one can check on the success of counseling or therapy for individual pupils. From follow-up studies of the school's graduates, counselors can examine the effectiveness of the curriculum in whole or in part. A study of graduates might show whether the college-preparatory, business, or other curricula are sufficiently effective and, if not, in what ways they might be improved.

[3] Robert H. McIsaac, "Guidance Services," in Lester D. and Alice Crow (editors), *Readings in Guidance* (New York: David McKay Company, Inc., 1962), pp. 562–563.

The foregoing paragraphs should make clear that the guidance program is not fractionalized into special types of guidance. One no longer thinks of educational guidance or vocational guidance; one thinks of guidance. Educational and vocational guidance are not special types of guidance; they are different aspects of guidance. Similarly, the five pupil-personnel services should not be thought of as separate functions but as different facets of the guidance function.

❋

In what ways does guidance differ from teaching?

What contributions might you as a teacher make to each of the guidance services?

Of what value are the guidance services? If you were asked to prepare a defense for including a guidance program in your school, what would your arguments be?

❋

Guidance Service to Teachers

The guidance program helps the teacher in many ways. In the first place, it can provide the teacher with information that enables him to know the individual pupils better. The teacher, of course, can gather considerable information himself. However, by means of its specialized techniques and trained personnel, the guidance program can provide the teacher with information he otherwise could not obtain except at great cost. Furthermore, information can often be collected more effectively through the guidance program, and the teacher is left with more time to devote to other matters.

The guidance program can also help the teacher with difficult pupils and their problems. Through the use of his specialized resources, the guidance worker can often find the cause for the difficulty and help resolve the problem. Sometimes he can do this quickly. Usually, however, the problems given to guidance workers are not easy to solve; they often involve changing habits and attitudes that the pupil has taken years to develop. Therefore, teachers should not expect quick results. It is more realistic to look for long periods of slow improvement. Patience, cooperation, and understanding should be the watchwords in the teacher's relationship with the guidance worker, for they each need the other's help and support.

Teacher Contribution to the Guidance Program

Ever since the first Neanderthal shaman selected a boy to apprentice for his trade, teachers have been performing guidance functions. That today's teacher should continue to do so is not surprising. Most teachers contribute to the guidance program in a large measure. Undoubtedly, the best contribution a teacher can make is to teach well. But he can also help in other ways. Even if the school did not ask them to, most teachers would perform guidance functions anyway.

One way teachers contribute is by acting as the eyes and ears of the guidance program. Because of their strategic position in the classroom and in the extracurriculum, teachers have opportunities to gather much information not available to the guidance specialist. The teacher can often spot pupils who need counseling on specific problems long before the guidance worker would ordinarily see them. By reporting this information via the anecdotal or other reports, the teacher can greatly increase the efficiency of the guidance program.

Once the guidance person is working with the pupil, the teacher can help by cooperating with him. In fact, guidance specialists often do their best work through the classroom teachers. Guidance workers can spend only short periods with individual pupils, whereas teachers spend considerable time with them. A teacher's sympathetic understanding of the pupil and cooperation with the guidance worker may make the difference between the success or failure of the program. Lack of cooperation may undo all the good that the counselor has achieved. The competent teacher cooperates with the guidance person 100 per cent; doing so pays dividends.

THE TEACHER AS A GUIDANCE WORKER.   Teachers sometimes play a more formal role in the guidance program. Although it is difficult to conduct a satisfactory guidance program without an adequate supply of specialized guidance counselors, the trend seems to be toward pressing classroom teachers into the counseling service either as teacher-counselors or as teachers who counsel. The reason for this trend is partly economic. Not many school systems are able to provide a sufficient number of guidance specialists to do all the counseling. Certainly the poorer school systems have not been able to do so; in fact some of them have no trained guidance personnel at all. In a great many schools, then, one can expect the brunt of the counseling to fall on the classroom teacher or the teacher-counselor. Since this may be the beginning teacher's lot, let us consider some of the methods and responsibilities.

The guidance worker tries to help boys and girls make the most of their lives and their opportunities. He does not make decisions for the pupils, for the role of the guidance worker is not to play God, but rather to help boys and girls help themselves. This role is not an easy one to carry out. To live up to it the guidance worker should

1. Recognize his own abilities and limitations to counsel and guide.
2. Be familiar with the techniques appropriate for guiding individuals and groups.

3. Be able to apply appropriate principles of guidance and counseling.
4. Observe the confidential nature of the counseling and guidance process.
5. Be able to administer and interpret various types of tests.
6. Establish and maintain effective relationship with parents.
7. Recognize the ability range of the individual pupil.
8. Integrate the work of the individual pupil with the school's entire program of guidance.[4]

As the list suggests, the guidance worker needs to be master of certain professional skills. The next few paragraphs briefly discuss some techniques used by guidance workers. The first of these is the interview.

CONDUCTING GUIDANCE INTERVIEWS. The interview is perhaps the most important tool with which the guidance counselor works. It is through the interview that the counselor actually does the counseling. It is the heart of the guidance program. Some pupils require frequent interviews, while others require few. However, all pupils may need more help than one sometimes thinks. The secret is to make oneself available. The guidance worker should practice the open-door policy. No pupil problem should be too trivial for his attention, for questions trivial to the teacher may seem all-important to the pupil. A sympathetic, unhurried hearing of the pupil's story may well lead to ready identification and solution of the pupil's problems.

The interview is really a place for the pupil to talk. Merely talking out his problems is frequently good therapy. In order to create the atmosphere of permissiveness, some authorities advocate that the teacher must accept everything the pupil says. The key, they say, is to accept the pupil for what he is—a person, perhaps a troubled person. The counselor, they maintain, should never sit in judgment on the pupil, for to do so may disrupt the rapport or end the interview permanently. Some of them further maintain that the counselor should never advise the pupil what to do.

Although the necessity of accepting the client and refraining from overhasty judgments is obvious, that the counselor should suppress himself completely is doubtful. There seems little point in conducting interviews if nothing ever develops. If the interview is to amount to anything, the counselor sooner or later should give it some direction. He should probably direct the interview toward discovery of the pupil's real problem and what can be done about it. Skillful use of questions can accomplish this. The teacher, as well as the counselor, can help the pupil draw his own value judgments. Surely it is ineffective to force our

[4] Gilbert C. Kettlekamp, *Teaching Adolescents* (Boston: D. C. Heath and Company, copyright 1954), p. 364. Quoted by permission of D. C. Heath and Company.

own values and advice on a pupil; but, just as surely, it is ineffective and probably immoral not to try to help the pupil find the answers to his problems and to help him achieve higher values.

In the interview, if the counselor is really to be of help, he must have information about the pupil at his fingertips. If possible, he should study each case before the interview. He should also have available a wealth of information about the school, its curriculum and extracurriculum, and other matters to which the interview may lead. If he can supply the pupil with immediate information in answer to his questions, so much the better. If the pupil requires information that the counselor does not have, the counselor should find it, if at all possible. At times, of course, he needs only to direct the pupil to the information so that the pupil can look for it himself. The object is always to help the pupil to a better understanding of himself, his problems, and his potentialities so that he can make wise decisions and judgments of his own.

What career to follow and what educational program to pursue are among the problems that are of real concern to youth. To get at these problems, the pupil must know what his goals and potentialities are. Frequently he has no idea of what he can or wants to do. Under such circumstances the counselor may have to give the pupil information by which he can appraise his own resources and the avenues open to him, and help him form and define his goals. Nevertheless, the decisions should be the pupil's not the guidance counselor's. No guidance counselor has the right to tell the counselee in what direction he should go; his job is to show the pupil the facts so that he can understand himself and make his decisions accordingly. *The role of the guidance worker does not include playing God.*

✿

In what ways can you as a teacher contribute to the guidance program?

To what extent should a counselor advise a pupil?

How much direction should the counselor give during an interview?

✿

Group Guidance and Homeroom Guidance

Group activities can often be used to give pupils guidance information. Some schools have formed special classes in "guidance" or "group guidance." Others make group guidance a part of the core program. Some schools turn group guidance over to the homeroom teacher. Examples of group-guidance activities are career days, units on occupations, field trips, and orientation programs. Even student handbooks are instruments for group guidance and, of course, a great amount of group guidance may occur during regular classes.

Group guidance is, of course, a teacher function. Its purpose is to provide pupils with information that they need in order to understand themselves, their potentialities, and their opportunities. In effect, group guidance is instruction. It differs in no way from other instruction except that in group guidance classes pupil-centered teaching is much more needed than in classes in other subjects. In such classes techniques that emphasize pupil participation in planning, problem solving, differentiated assignments, individual work, small-group work and projects are most desirable. Role playing, discussions, and the techniques of group dynamics are particularly useful.

Homeroom guidance is likely to be a combination of group guidance and counseling. The teacher is responsible not only for teaching group guidance in homeroom periods, but also for counseling his homeroom pupils. In some schools the administration gives the teacher the same homeroom group for several years so that the teacher and pupils may learn to know each other better. In such a system the homeroom teacher becomes in effect a teacher-counselor responsible for the total guidance program of his homeroom pupils.

Group Counseling

Group guidance should not be confused with group counseling. Group counseling is a form of interview in which the counselor meets with several pupils instead of just one. Many authorities maintain that counseling should never be more than a one-to-one relationship, but E. Wayne Wright and others believe that counseling in groups yields certain benefits that individual counseling can not: (1) the lifelike setting for making decisions and choices, thus helping individuals to discover new ways of relating to others; (2) the influences of peers through group interaction and group norms; (3) the opportunity for free expression of opinion and emotions with less personal reference; and (4) the opportunity to give and receive support as a group member.[5]

Referral of Difficult Cases

The counseling of difficult cases should be left to people trained in it. For that matter, teachers should be careful to limit their counseling activities to areas in which they are competent. Teacher-counselors, homeroom teachers, and other teachers are usually not guidance experts, although many approach this status after a few years of experience and

[5] E. Wayne Wright, "Multiple Counseling: Why? When? How?" *Personnel and Guidance Journal,* 37: 551–56, April, 1959, in Lester D. and Alice Crow, *op. cit.,* pp. 216–224.

training. They cannot be expected to handle all the guidance problems that may come their way. When problems of a difficult nature come up, they should be referred to the proper person. This person is usually the guidance specialist in charge, or, in smaller schools, the principal. When in doubt about what to do in any guidance matter, a teacher should go to these persons for help.

In general, teachers should not be too hasty in referring cases to the professional guidance persons. Hasty and frequent referrals may undermine the pupils' confidence in the teacher's abilities. On the other hand, the teacher should not hesitate to refer any case in which he does not feel competent. Certainly he should refer every case in which he suspects serious difficulty or difficulties beyond his scope, such as medical or serious psychological problems. Whenever the teacher feels that the pupil needs more than ordinary help, he should refer the pupil immediately. It is far better to refer too often than not to refer often enough. As was pointed out earlier in the chapter, the teacher is in a strategic position to spot incipient troubles of all types. He should attempt to develop a sharp eye and report such cases early.

Other Professional Responsibilities

Responsibility for the School Program

By and large, in recent years teachers have been taking a greater share in developing the school program in a great number of secondary schools. Many functions formerly conducted solely by administrators are now handled by faculty committees. Typical of the type of faculty committees found in modern schools are curriculum committees, textbook committees, handbook committees, and committees on reporting to parents. You will undoubtedly find yourself on a faculty committee sooner or later. When this happens, you should welcome the opportunity. Through committee work you may be able to make real contributions to the welfare of the school, its program, and its pupils. In fact, sometimes a teacher's contribution to committee work may have an effect more far-reaching than his classwork, for it is through committee work that the individual teacher has a chance to influence the entire school program.

Young teachers have a rather anomalous position on committees. Being new and untried, they should not be too forward until they are accepted by their older colleagues. On the other hand, it is not quite a case of being seen but not heard. As a recent graduate from a teacher education program, the new teacher may have up-to-date information and ideas new to his older colleagues. The answer is to do your part willingly and eagerly in a tactful, pleasant way. Do not thrust yourself and your ideas on people, but do your best to be helpful.

What is true of committee meetings is also true of faculty meetings. Many teachers regard faculty meetings as a bore and a nuisance. Too many of them are just that, but most modern administrators attempt to make faculty meetings purposeful, interesting, and worthwhile. Many of them are work sessions devoted to solving school problems. The young teacher should pitch in and do his share.

Supervision of Pupils

A type of activity which one may not think of as administrative is the supervision of corridors, washrooms, lunchrooms, and detention halls. Frequently these duties can be handled fully as well by personnel other than teachers. In some secondary schools much of this monitoring and supervision is done by pupils. When this is the case, these activities can sometimes become learning activities. If professional teachers are to supervise corridors and lunchrooms, ideally they should take steps to see that learning takes place in these facilities as well as in the classroom. What better place is there for learning table manners and the social amenities than in the lunchroom?

RESPONSIBILITY FOR PUPIL SAFETY. Since the pupil is in the school's jurisdiction for a long part of the day, it follows that the teachers must assume the responsibility for the pupils' health, safety, and well-being during that period. Prevention is the first step in carrying out this role. Teachers should see to it that boys and girls know how to use properly the equipment they work with, and that they abide by the safety regulations when they use it. Furthermore, teachers should prevent pupils from taking unnecessary risks in the classroom. For example, in one science class the teacher wished to use the film-strip projector. As luck would have it, when she started to pull the blackout curtains to, the curtain cord jammed so that she could not move the curtains either way. A gallant boy jumped to the rescue and climbed up on the window sill to untangle the cord. This was a foolhardy thing to do, because the boy might have fallen. In the interest of safety, the teacher should have forbidden him to climb on the window sill, and sent for a stepladder instead. Teachers are responsible for seeing to it that boys and girls do not violate the rules of safety within the school or on the school grounds.

PREPARING FOR EMERGENCIES. In spite of all precautions, emergencies sometimes occur. Then the teacher must be prepared. Early in the year he should learn what the school's policies and procedures are in case of emergencies. For instance, how can one get a doctor in a hurry? How does one sound the fire alarm? Where does one go for first

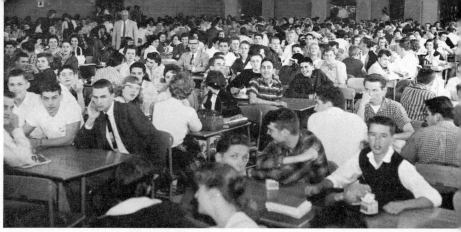

Supervision of the cafeteria is one of the teacher's extra-class responsibilities. How can he help make it a valuable educational experience for the pupils?

aid? To find out what to do when the emergency happens may be too late. The competent teacher is prepared for emergencies. If he works in a subject in which accidents are liable to happen, he should be well skilled in the emergency procedures necessary for handling accidents of this type. *All teachers should be well skilled in emergency procedures in general.* Usually the school's policies and instructions concerning emergencies can be found in the teachers' manual. The teacher should study the pertinent sections early in the year.

An important part of one's preparation for an emergency is to make it a point to learn about any unusual health or safety problem before the emergency occurs. For instance, if the teacher has an epileptic in his class, he should know it so he will be prepared in case the pupil should have a seizure. Similarly, the teacher should be aware of any pupils who are crippled or lame so that special provision can be made for them in case of fire.

Fire drill is one of the most important ways to prepare for an emergency. It is serious business and should be treated accordingly. The teacher should make a special effort to ensure that each of his pupils knows what to do in the fire drill. He should also make an effort to impress upon pupils the seriousness of fire drills and see to it that the drill is carried out meticulously with no nonsense.

✻

What precautions might you take for the safety of a pupil who is wearing a walking cast? What about such pupils during fire drills?

How might you make good learning experiences out of safety measures and corridor and lunchroom supervision?

To what extent should you, as a beginning teacher, enter into committee work?

✻

440

REPORTING THE EMERGENCY. An important aspect of the emergency procedures which teachers sometimes forget is to report the emergency immediately to the proper authorities. Although in the excitement of a genuine emergency this report may have to wait a while, the teacher should take the first possible moment to tell his superiors exactly what happened, what caused it to happen, and what was done about it. Usually the procedure for reporting emergencies can be found in the teachers' manual. Quite often all that is necessary is to notify the principal. In any case, the teacher should make his report speedily and accurately. Not to do so can lead to administrative, and even legal, complications.

Summary

Although subordinate to actual instruction, extra-class responsibilities are a necessary part of each teacher's load. High on the list of his responsibilities are extracurricular activities. Just as much as class activities, extracurricular activities are learning experiences. Like any other learning experiences, they deserve careful planning and handling. However, the pupils should have a large share in planning and conducting them.

The guidance program provides services by which the pupil can get help with his problems. This program can be a great boon for the classroom teacher. From it he can get information and help which should make his teaching more effective. In return, the teacher can make substantial contributions to the guidance program, since he is often the staff member closest to the pupil.

Other professional responsibilities, whose importance should not be minimized, include contributing to the development of the school program. Sometimes it is in this field that the teacher can make his greatest contribution to the school. Another of the teacher's major responsibilities concerns the health and safety of the pupils. This responsibility includes supervising and safeguarding the pupils to prevent accidents and taking emergency measures when necessary. In this connection, "an ounce of prevention is worth a pound of cure."

FOR FURTHER STUDY

ARBUCKLE, DUGALD S., *Counseling: An Introduction* (New York: Harper and Row, Inc., 1958).

BUSH, ROBERT N., "The Proper Place of the Extracurriculum in the High School," *California Journal of Secondary Education*, May, 1959, 34: 257–262.

CLARK, LEONARD H., RAYMOND L. KLEIN, and JOHN B. BURKS, *The American Secondary School Curriculum* (New York: The Macmillan Company, 1965), Ch. 15.

"Extracurriculum," *The Bulletin of the National Association of Secondary-School Principals*, February, 1962, 46:254–263.

FREDERICK, ROBERT W., *The Third Curriculum: Student Activities in American Education* (New York: Appleton-Century-Crofts, Inc., 1959).

————, *Student Activities in American Education* (New York: Center for Applied Research in Education, 1965).

GRINNELL, J. E., "Our Most Dangerous Neglect," *Phi Delta Kappan*, February, 1960, 41: 213–216.

JOHNSON, WALTER F., BUFORD STEFFLRE, and ROY A. EDELFELT, *Pupil Personnel and Guidance Services* (New York: McGraw-Hill Book Company, Inc., 1961).

JONES, ARTHUR J., *Principles of Guidance*, Fifth Edition (New York: McGraw-Hill Book Company, Inc., 1963).

KELZER, L. R., *et al.*, *Allied Activities in the Secondary School* (New York: Harper and Row, Inc., 1956).

MILLER, CARROLL H., *Foundations of Guidance* (New York: Harper and Row, Inc., 1961).

MILLER, FRANKLIN A., JAMES A. MOYER, and ROBERT B. PATRICK, *Planning Student Activities* (Englewood Cliffs, N.J.: Prentice-Hall, Inc., 1957).

O'NEIL, H. P., "Let's Limit Participation in School Activities," *School Activities*, September, 1960, 31: 21–22.

PETERS, HERMAN J., and GAIL F. FARWELL, *Guidance: A Developmental Approach* (Chicago: Rand McNally and Company, 1959).

RAUBINGER, FREDERICK M., and ROBERT WITTEY, *Remember the Individual in the New Jersey Secondary-School Guidance*, State Department of Education, Trenton, N.J., 1962.

TORRANCE, E. PAUL, *Guiding Creative Talent* (Englewood Cliffs, N.J.: Prentice-Hall, Inc., 1962).

PART *VIII*
The Beginning Teacher

CHAPTER *19*

The Beginning Teacher

*T*O THE beginning teacher the prospect of the first job can be both exciting and frightening. This chapter is an attempt to give to prospective teachers suggestions that will help make their first years of teaching more enjoyable.

Preparing for the New Job

In teaching, as in any other profession, the time "on the job" represents only a fraction of one's work time. Just as a lawyer does most of his work before entering the courtroom, the teacher should do much of his work before entering the classroom. This is especially true of young teachers who do not have a reservoir of experience and previous study to rely on. The beginning teacher should allow himself plenty of time to prepare for his new job. A summer's work is none too long.

As soon as you learn what your teaching assignment is to be, you should start reviewing for your courses. Much of the reviewing can be done in the textbooks the pupils are to use. This practice has several advantages. Although you will probably find the material quite elementary, it will orient you to what is expected of the pupils. Moreover, as you review for the course, you can prepare general plans for conducting it. Finally, studying a secondary-school text is a relatively easy way to review. If you are tempted to map out a more ambitious project, remember that an easy program that you finish is much better than an arduous program that you never complete.

The type of review program you plan is not so very important, but do review and study during the summer. The time for study is all too scarce once the actual hurly-burly of teaching starts. The life of a high-school or junior-high-school teacher is a full and sometimes hectic one. Long, quiet hours for study are rare indeed, particularly in the first years of teaching.

During the summer months you should not only become familiar with the subject matter you are going to teach, but you should also learn as

445

much as you can about the pupils with whom you will be working. Knowing something about the pupils when the classes start can be extremely helpful. Even if you cannot identify the individual pupils, gathering information about them from the cumulative records and any other available sources, before the opening of school, will give you a general picture of the make-up of the class which should be of assistance in your planning. Having this information on hand makes it possible for you to become acquainted with individual pupils more quickly, and should help you spot pupils with problems, special interests, or handicaps. An additional advantage of getting this information before school opens is that then you will probably have more time to go through the records carefully than you would in the fall. Thus you can eliminate one activity from the busy first weeks of school.

Preparing for the First Day

In every endeavor a good start is a distinct advantage; teaching is no exception. Therefore, you should get your classes off to a good beginning on the first day of school. On this day the pupils are often in a mood to learn. They have hopes that the new course and new teacher may have something worthwhile for them. So your first lesson should be one of your best. If you can possibly do so, use an interesting experiment, a demonstration, an exciting story, an intriguing problem, or something equally appealing. The initial activity may set the tone for the entire course.

Some teachers devote most of the first class period to administrative work; some spend the period outlining what the class is going to do for the year; others review or test during this period in order to relate the course to previous courses. All of these activities are good and necessary, but do not allow them to prevent your course from getting off to a good start. If you cannot make these activities part of an exciting initial class, you had better leave them for another day.

Usually, however, these activities can be fitted into an exciting start. Some teachers devote the first day to a lively discussion of what one might study in the course. Others introduce an interesting problem. Then, while their pupils search for the solution, the teacher records the book numbers and performs other necessary administrative duties. Another possibility is to conduct a review in the form of a game or a television quiz program. Whatever approach you use, the beginning class should include something lively, new, and worthwhile.

*

If you were going out to teach next September, what would you need to review and study? What could you do in the summer to make your work easier in the fall?

Plan a first day for a course you may teach. What introductory activities would you try? How might you work in administrative tasks? What would you do to motivate the pupils?

✸

Relationships with the Pupils

Establishing Teacher Control

The first days of school will bring you together with new pupils in a new situation. In this situation your position is much the same as that of a stage star at an opening performance. Under the circumstances, it is not at all unusual for a beginning teacher to feel nervous. You will certainly be tense; you may even suffer from stage fright. But no matter how nervous you are, you should display as much confidence as you can muster and go ahead with your work. If you act as though this were a commonplace occurrence which you are enjoying, the pupils will probably be convinced by your performance.

However, you are new and you can expect some boys and girls to try you out. In the interest of good discipline, it may be wise to be fairly strict for a few days. During this period, minimize the amount of movement around the classroom. A wise precaution is to have a written assignment ready so that you can give the class written work if the pupils become restless. In any event you should have an alternate plan of some sort to fall back on if your first plan does not work.

In order to establish good teacher-pupil relationships and teacher control, learn the names of the pupils immediately. During the first period you should probably prepare a seating plan. One way to do so is to assign some written work to the pupils and then circulate about the room to copy their names from their papers. Another method is to have the names of the pupils written on a slip of paper before the period starts, and, as you call the roll, to put these slips in the proper places in a pocket-type seating plan. No matter how you prepare the seating plan, associate the names of the pupils with their faces as quickly as possible. If a pupil realizes that you know his name, you will more readily establish good rapport with him.

Showing Respect for Each Pupil's Individuality

Teachers should learn the pupils' names not only because it helps control them, but because it is one of their rights. Pupils are people, and should be recognized as such. They should be treated courteously and tactfully. The fact that they are youthful does not give the teacher the right to be rude to them or to override their rights as persons. "Minding one's manners" is as important for teachers as it is for pupils.

Show your pupils that you have confidence in them. Secondary-school pupils are not children, although their actions will sometimes be child-like. They are approaching adulthood. Although their lack of experience necessitates giving them plenty of guidance, pupils can behave them-selves if you give them the opportunity. They can also plan, execute, and evaluate their own work. If your pupils feel that you really have faith in their good sense and judgment, they will seldom let you down.

You should also develop a real interest in your pupils. Everyone reacts well to people who are truly interested in them. To demonstrate your interest, you should learn all you can about your pupils and their prob-lems. You should also establish an "open-door" policy so that your pupils will know that you are ready to listen to their problems and help them when you can. What the pupil wishes to discuss may be trivial, but you should listen if the pupil considers it important. Problems that seem unimportant to adults frequently appear serious to adolescents.

But it is not only the pupils' problems that you should be concerned about. You should also take an interest in their activities. Their ideas, their hobbies, and their occupations are often fascinating. The teacher who participates wholeheartedly in the extracurriculum, who attends the athletic games and school dances, who knows the school traditions and cooperates in furthering them, and who shows a real interest in all of his pupils' activities is likely to be readily accepted by the pupils.

Earning the Pupils' Respect

In building good teacher-pupil relationships, mutual respect is the best foundation. This does not come naturally. Although respect for the teacher's position is something each child should have acquired by the time he reaches the secondary school, respect for the teacher as a person is something else. Each teacher must earn that respect himself.

Respect can be earned in many ways. The best way, of course, is to do an outstanding job of teaching. Another is to treat all pupils fairly and impartially. Sociological studies indicate that teachers often do not give boys and girls from "underprivileged homes" the same treatment they give to pupils from "better homes."[1] If this is true, these pupils are really underprivileged. You must treat every pupil fairly and impartially re-gardless of his color, ethnic background, or social position. Pupils will respect you if you do, and the ethics of the profession require it.

Sometimes young teachers attempt to seek popularity by becoming overfriendly with the pupils. This procedure seldom works. In dealing

[1] See for instance, August B. Hollingshead, *Elmtown's Youth* (New York: John Wiley and Sons, Inc., 1949).

with your pupils, you should be friendly, not chummy. Seek respect rather than popularity. If you are the type of person who can inculcate respect, a good teacher with a well-developed sense of humor, a wholesome personality, and a good character, popularity will take care of itself.

❉

An experienced teacher once told a new colleague that he did not care whether the pupils liked him or not, but he did want them to respect him. What do you think of this philosophy?

Think of the teacher in your high school whom you most respected. What qualities did he have which earned him this respect? Think of a teacher whom pupils did not respect. What caused him to lose their respect?

❉

Dealing with the Overaffectionate Pupil

A particularly difficult problem in teacher-pupil relations is the pupil who develops a crush on the teacher. Needless to say, the teacher should avoid emotional involvement with any pupil. Such a relationship is both foolish and dangerous. Nevertheless, pupils frequently do develop crushes on teachers. If this should happen to you, it is probably best to ignore it, at the same time keeping the relationship with the pupil on a definitely formal, although friendly, basis.

Relationships with Parents

Improving Parent-Teacher Relationships

Friendly relationships between teachers and their pupils' parents can contribute considerably to effective teaching, since parents and teachers should be seeking the same objective, the welfare of the pupils. One way to avoid friction with parents is to learn to know them as well as possible. If the teacher becomes acquainted with parents at school functions, at parent-teacher association meetings, in community activities, and in their homes, and in other social situations, teacher-parent relationships can become much more pleasant.

In meeting parents you may find your role a little difficult. Parents are often nervous about meeting their children's teachers just as teachers are often nervous about meeting parents, and for much the same reasons. After all, the teacher is in a peculiarly strategic position for judging the parent's success as a parent. The teacher sits in judgment over the activities and efforts and, to some extent, the future of the parent's child. Knowledge of this is enough to make the parent a little apprehensive when he meets the teacher. Therefore, when talking to parents, you should try to be as relaxed and friendly as possible. Above all, try to guard against the didactic tone that comes so naturally to many teachers. If parents find you a pleasant, intelligent, well-informed adult, you will probably get along with them quite well, and also dissipate any fears you may have concerning their judgments of your abilities as a teacher of their children.

Seeking Parental Cooperation

Because parents are more interested than anyone else in the welfare of their children, they almost always wish to do everything possible to help them. The teacher who so desires can often enlist the parents' aid. Many parents are glad to serve on committees and to engage in other tasks to help the school. Parents frequently have talents the teacher can put to good use in class activities. However, before soliciting the services of parents, it is wise to consult your principal. He may be able to help you avoid mistakes.

Parents can be particularly helpful by providing information about their children. Usually parents respond readily to such an approach as, "I seem to be having trouble teaching Jack to spell. I wonder if you can help me." Quite often the parent will not only cooperate in furnishing information about his child, but will also cooperate with any reasonable program for helping the youngster.

Relationships with the Community

Parent-teacher relationships lead us directly to teachers' relationships with the community in general. These relationships should be the normal ones that might be found among any adult members of the community. However, because of the teacher's peculiar position as a leader of children, the community usually expects him to adhere to a pattern of behavior that is higher than that expected of other adults. At first glance, this may seem to be a hardship, but it is merely the price of being a professional person. The community also expects a higher standard of conduct from its clergymen, physicians, and lawyers than it does from other people. Actually, all that is expected in most communities is that the teacher lead a decent, respectable life according to the mores of the community. It is the teacher's professional duty to live up to the code. If the restrictions seem unreasonable to you, you should look for a position elsewhere. In most cases, however, the mild restrictions placed upon teachers by the community should be regarded not as a burden but as a recognition of the high status that teachers hold. The community is asking you to provide leadership which it feels that others cannot give.

Under no circumstances should the reader interpret the foregoing paragraph as advocating that teachers avoid their obligations, as citizens, to espouse causes, to take stands, and to participate as their consciences direct in civil, moral, and political affairs. Professional leadership is not compatible with conformity or timidity; neither does being a teacher deprive, or relieve, anyone of his rights and responsibilities as an American and a citizen.

The members of the various professions are considered to be community leaders, and therefore should act as leaders. As a professional person, you should take part in community activities. These include civic affairs, parent-teachers' organizations, churches, service clubs, and so on. Participating in such activities will not only help to make your life fuller and more enjoyable, but will give you splendid contacts with the community. However, you should guard against becoming a "joiner." Those who join too many organizations and participate in too many activities may not have sufficient time and energy left to carry out their professional obligations properly.

✽

What advantages are there in becoming acquainted with your pupils' parents socially. Are there any disadvantages? In what ways would you attempt to become acquainted with them?

In one high school the teachers were required to visit the home of each of their homeroom pupils some time during the school year. What do you think of this practice?

To what extent should you as a teacher become involved in community affairs? What organizations would you join?

✽

Relationships with Other Staff Members

Establishing Cordial Relationships with Other Teachers

Second only in importance to your relationships with your pupils are those with your fellow teachers. You must get along with them. Some of them will undoubtedly become your good friends; others you may find not so agreeable. But you will be in close contact with them every working day. Your relationships with them can make the difference between happiness and success in your work, and unhappiness and even failure. Therefore, you should do everything you can to make these relationships cordial. Until you have been accepted by the group, you would do well to look, listen, and learn.

Not only should the new teacher look, listen, and learn, he should also pitch in to cooperate willingly. In some schools there is a tendency to give the less desirable tasks to the new teacher. This practice is also common in most business and professional establishments. It represents one of the perquisites of seniority in an organization. Most supervisors and administrators, however, try to see to it that the beginning teacher's assignment, even if not the easiest and most desirable, is a reasonable one. But whatever his assignment, the beginning teacher would do well to take it on with good grace and give it his very best effort with the sure knowledge that he will not be the junior faculty member for long. In addition, most new teachers find that they have numerous opportunities to contribute to the school program not included in their assigned tasks. Although it is not wise to volunteer for more than you can manage well, it is better to err on the side of attempting to contribute too much than too little.

As a new teacher, you will find that you have much to learn, but you will also discover that your colleagues will be pleased to teach you. They will give you much friendly advice—some good, some bad. Accept it in the spirit it is given in, but act only on that which you are convinced is good. Some of your colleagues will be outstanding teachers, while others may be lazy, incompetent, or embittered. Although you should listen courteously to the advice of all, you should heed particularly that of the more successful teachers.

Undoubtedly you will find things in your school of which you do not approve. In this case, *keep your criticisms to yourself until you are better established*. Otherwise, the older teachers may resent your criticisms and you. Members of a faculty are much like families. They find fault themselves, but bitterly resent fault-finding by outsiders. Until you have been accepted, which may take some time, you are an outsider and should refrain from criticisms. Besides, once you understand the situation better, you may change your opinion.

You should be courteous, friendly, and sociable. Join other teachers for coffee, attend the faculty parties, and accept invitations with pleasure and gratitude. Try to show your colleagues that you would like to be a member of the group, but do not let yourself become identified with any clique until you have become well acquainted with the entire faculty.

Faculty relationships are pleasant when teachers remember the common courtesies. "Please" and "Thank you" are important. So are other little things. For instance, if you share a classroom with another teacher, do not move the chairs and tables without moving them back again before you leave. Be sure to leave the blackboards clean, and do not usurp all the bulletin board space. In short, give consideration at all times to the use of the classroom by other teachers.

Relationships with Administrators and Supervisors

Administrators and supervisors can help the teacher in all sorts of ways. Although one's relationships with them may not become as intimate as those with other teachers, they are fully as important. The administrator aids the teacher by furnishing supplies, equipment, and other services and facilities, while the supervisor aids the teacher with instructional activities. Sometimes the supervisor and the administrator are the same person. In any case, make use of their services. That is why they are there.

Teachers and administrators have the same goals in mind. Both are concerned with providing the best possible education for the children of the community. Unfortunately, some teachers tend to think of themselves and their administrators as being in a labor-management situation, with the teachers being workers and the administrators the management. This may indeed be the case in some school systems, but many school administrators think of themselves not as teachers' bosses but as professional people associated with teachers in a professional responsibility. Teachers should think of the teacher-administrator relationship in the same way. On the other hand, administrators are charged with high responsibilities as agents of the board of education in directing the educational program of the school system. Classroom teachers should give them respect and loyalty as responsible members of the profession.

One of the most difficult jobs of the teacher is to learn to be a subordinate while occupying a position of influence, authority, and responsibility. Although both the teacher and the administrator are professionals, the responsibility for the efficient management of the school falls squarely on the administrator. If things go wrong, it is he who is responsible to the superintendent and the board of education. Consequently, teachers should gracefully accept decisions made by the administrator, and cooperate wholeheartedly in carrying them out.

Principals, department heads, and supervisors can be of tremendous help to beginning teachers in planning their classroom activities, in organizing classroom routine, in working with difficult pupils, and in promoting good parent-teacher relationships. They know firsthand some of the difficulties you may encounter during your first year, and will be glad to suggest ways of meeting them. Seek their advice, cooperation, and help.

Keeping Administrators and Supervisors Informed

You would be wise to consult your supervisor before you try anything that is decidedly new or unusual. He may be able to help you do it more successfully and avoid mistakes you might otherwise make. It is especially important that before you depart markedly from the practice that is usual in the school, you should get his permission. New methods and techniques may cause parental concern. If the supervisor knows what you are attempting, he will be prepared to answer parents' questions and to support you in what you want to do. Seeking his permission may also prevent you from inadvertently violating school board policy.

It is particularly wise to let the administrators know of serious incidents involving the school or the pupils especially if they may lead to adverse criticism and undesirable publicity. Administrators do not like unpleasant surprises. When a principal first learns of a fiasco in his school from a worried superintendent, or an irate parent, or worse yet, from headlines in the local press, he is greatly handicapped. If the principal has prior information of the incident, he may be able to take constructive action. Otherwise he can do little more than be embarrassed.

In dealing with supervisors and administrators, the teacher will do well to study them and try to adapt to their ways of doing things. Perhaps the methods and policies of the principal are not those you would use. If so, do not be one of those unprofessional teachers who spend their lunch hours criticizing him and the way he administers the school. Remember that he must have had good qualities to get his appointment in the first place. If you feel that you cannot give him your cooperation and loyalty, it is better to look for another position.

Relations with Nonprofessional Personnel

Secretaries, clerks, and custodians can also be helpful to the teacher. Teachers should always try to keep on good terms with these people and other nonprofessional personnel. Try to be reasonable in your demands on the secretaries and custodians. For instance, if mimeographing is to be done for you, submit the copy in ample time. One can cooperate in other ways. In some schools the heating system is designed to work with the windows closed. By noting this detail, you can make it much easier for the custodian to heat the entire building. You can also help the custodian by maintaining a neat and orderly classroom. The teacher who keeps in the good graces of the custodial and secretarial staffs may find that he can get good cooperation when it is particularly needed.

❈

Suppose that early in your teaching, one of the older teachers complains to you about what he considers the deterioration of the school's instructional program under the present principal and superintendent. What should you do?

What practical advantages may be obtained from maintaining good relationships with the custodial personnel? What would you do to keep up favorable relationships?

❈

The Ethics of the Profession

The NEA Code of Ethics

Teaching is a profession and "whoever chooses teaching as a career assumes the obligation to conduct himself in accordance with the ideals of the profession." Professions differ from other vocations in that they are primarily services. In the teaching profession the primary purpose is the education of the child; all other considerations are secondary. Because they deal so much with people, most professions have developed codes to regulate relationships between their members and those they serve, as well as among the professional workers themselves. The teaching profession has such a code in the "Code of Ethics of the National Education Association."

If teachers want the high status they deserve, the teaching profession must enforce its code. When the profession insists that all its members be professionals in deed as well as in training, it will have marched a long way toward the recognition, both in salary and status, that it can gain for its members. It begins to appear that the profession is ready to assume these responsibilities.

The Code of Ethics[2]

Preamble

We, professional educators of the United States of America, affirm our belief in the worth and dignity of man. We recognize the supreme importance of the pursuit of truth, the encouragement of scholarship, and the promotion of democratic citizenship. We regard as essential to these goals the protection of freedom to learn and to teach and the guarantee of equal educational opportunity for all. We affirm and accept our responsibility to practice our profession according to the highest ethical standards.

We acknowledge the magnitude of the profession we have chosen, and engage ourselves, individually and collectively, to judge our colleagues and to be judged by them in accordance with the applicable provisions of this code.

Principle I

COMMITMENT TO THE STUDENT

We measure success by the progress of each student toward achievement of his maximum potential. We therefore work to stimulate the spirit of inquiry, the acquisition of knowledge and understanding, and the thoughtful formula-

[2] *The Code of Ethics of the Education Profession,* adopted by the NEA Representative Assembly, Detroit, Michigan, July 1963. Reprinted by permission of the National Education Association.

In fulfilling our obligations to the student, we deal justly and considerately with each student. (*NEA Code of Ethics*)

tion of worthy goals. We recognize the importance of cooperative relationships with other community institutions, especially the home.

In fulfilling our obligations to the student, we—

1. Deal justly and considerately with each student.
2. Encourage the student to study varying points of view and respect his right to form his own judgment.
3. Withhold confidential information about a student or his home unless we deem that its release serves professional purposes, benefits the student, or is required by law.
4. Make discreet use of available information about the student.
5. Conduct conferences with or concerning students in an appropriate place and manner.
6. Refrain from commenting unprofessionally about a student or his home.
7. Avoid exploiting our professional relationship with any student.
8. Tutor only in accordance with officially approved policies.
9. Inform appropriate individuals and agencies of the student's educational needs and assist in providing an understanding of his educational experiences.
10. Seek constantly to improve learning facilities and opportunities.

Principle II

COMMITMENT TO THE COMMUNITY

We believe that patriotism in its highest form requires dedication to the principles of our democratic heritage. We share with all other citizens the responsibility for the development of sound public policy. As educators, we are particularly accountable for participating in the development of educational programs and policies and for interpreting them to the public.

In fulfilling our obligations to the community, we—

1. Share the responsibility for improving the educational opportunities for all.
2. Recognize that each educational institution may have a person authorized to interpret its official policies.
3. Acknowledge the right and responsibility of the public to participate in the formulation of educational policy.
4. Evaluate through appropriate professional procedures conditions within a district or institution of learning, make known serious deficiencies, and take any action deemed necessary and proper.
5. Use educational facilities for intended purposes consistent with applicable policy, law, and regulation.
6. Assume full political and citizenship responsibilities, but refrain from exploiting the institutional privileges of our professional positions to promote political candidates or partisan activities.
7. Protect the educational program against undesirable infringement.

Principle III

COMMITMENT TO THE PROFESSION

We believe that the quality of the services of the education profession directly influences the future of the nation and its citizens. We therefore exert every effort to raise educational standards, to improve our service, to promote a climate in which the exercise of professional judgment is encouraged, and to achieve conditions which attract persons worthy of the trust to careers in education. Aware of the value of united effort, we contribute actively to the support, planning, and programs of our professional organizations.

In fulfilling our obligation to the profession, we—

1. Recognize that a profession must accept responsibility for the conduct of its members and understand that our own conduct may be regarded as representative.
2. Participate and conduct ourselves in a responsible manner in the development and implementation of policies affecting education.
3. Cooperate in the selective recruitment of prospective teachers and in the orientation of student teachers, interns, and those colleagues new to their positions.
4. Accord just and equitable treatment to all members of the profession in the exercise of their professional rights and responsibilities, and support them when unjustly accused or mistreated.
5. Refrain from assigning professional duties to non-professional personnel when such assignment is not in the best interest of the student.
6. Provide, upon request, a statement of specific reason for administrative recommendations that lead to the denial of increments, significant changes in employment, or termination of employment.
7. Refrain from exerting undue influence based on the authority of our positions in the determination of professional decisions by colleagues.
8. Keep the trust under which confidential information is exchanged.
9. Make appropriate use of time granted for professional purposes.

10. Interpret and use the writings of others and the findings of educational research with intellectual honesty.
11. Maintain our integrity when dissenting by basing our public criticism of education on valid assumptions as established by careful evaluation of facts or hypotheses.
12. Represent honestly our professional qualifications and identify ourselves only with reputable educational institutions.
13. Respond accurately to requests for evaluations of colleagues seeking professional positions.
14. Provide applicants seeking information about a position with an honest description of the assignment, the conditions of work, and related matters.

Principle IV

COMMITMENT TO PROFESSIONAL EMPLOYMENT PRACTICES

We regard the employment agreement as a solemn pledge to be executed both in spirit and in fact in a manner consistent with the highest ideals of professional service. Sound professional personnel relationships with governing boards are built upon personal integrity, dignity, and mutual respect.

In fulfilling our obligations to professional employment practices, we—

1. Apply for or offer a position on the basis of professional and legal qualifications.
2. Apply for a specific position only when it is known to be vacant and refrain from such practices as underbidding or commenting adversely about other candidates.
3. Fill no vacancy except where the terms, conditions, policies, and practices permit the exercise of our professional judgment and skill, and where a climate conducive to professional service exists.
4. Adhere to the conditions of a contract or to the terms of an appointment until either has been terminated legally or by mutual consent.
5. Give prompt notice of any change in availability of service, in status of applications, or in change in position.
6. Conduct professional business through the recognized educational and professional channels.
7. Accept no gratuities or gifts of significance that might influence our judgment in the exercise of our professional duties.
8. Engage in no outside employment that will impair the effectiveness of our professional service and permit no commercial exploitation of our professional position.

Growth in the Profession

Cultivating One's Personal Growth

When one first starts to teach, one is only beginning to learn his trade. A retired superintendent of schools says that, judging from his more than thirty years of experience in the superintendency, it takes a beginning teacher at least two years to become "worth his salt." As one teaches, the experience should help him to become more expert. Unfortunately, some teachers do not improve with experience. As another superintendent has expressed it, "Some teachers have twenty years of experience, and others have one year of experience twenty times."

One way to keep from falling into a rut professionally is to keep growing personally. The good teacher avoids the ivory tower and gets out into the world and does things. He attempts to keep his mind sharp by interesting himself in many things and by becoming expert in some one thing. In short, the beginning teacher should try to develop an interesting, wholesome personality, and he should keep alive his intellectual curiosity.

Cultivating One's Professional Growth

Not only must one grow as a person in order to be a good teacher, one must also develop professionally. The first step in growing professionally is, of course, to do a good job of teaching. This means that you must give your heart to your work. Teaching should never be a secondary occupation. A teacher may find it necessary to combine teaching with other work—either part-time work or, for married women, homemaking—but the teacher must not let other work detract from teaching. Your first responsibility is to your pupils.

Keeping Abreast of the Field

To teach well, a teacher must keep up with his subject. Without continued study to keep up one's competence, one's teaching soon becomes dry and dusty. Therefore you will need to keep abreast of the developments in your field. Occasionally, you will need to take refresher courses at a university or college. You should take advanced work in your field and perhaps do some original research. During vacations you may be able to get work related to your subject and thus acquire additional experience. No matter how you do it, to become a competent teacher you must move forward with the growth of your field.

Keeping Abreast of the Profession

To be truly competent, you must also be an expert in the study of your profession. Particularly important are changes in methods and curriculum that affect your specialty. You should continue to study the nature of learning, the theory and practice of teaching, basic philosophical positions, and current experimentation in education. Reading professional periodicals and books, as well as course work at colleges and universities, is helpful for this purpose.

Experimenting with new techniques or materials will make your teaching more lively and meaningful. Observing your own work and that of others may help you grow considerably, particularly if you continually ask yourself: Why did this technique work? Why was this one unsuccessful? Why did this one succeed in section A and fail in section B? Attempts to find better ways to teach should never cease. They are the only sure way to professional growth.

One of the most promising ways of improving teaching is "action research." Action research is simply the application of the tools and techniques of research in a semiformal way to specific troublesome instructional or curricular problems. Although it should never be sloppy, action research does not ordinarily require as rigorous control as formal research because its purpose is limited to finding data suitable for drawing conclusions pertinent solely to a particular situation. It is not meant to serve as a basis for generalizations of any sort. The use of this technique in your classroom to study difficult problems may well prove the key to their solution.[3]

In order to find better ways of teaching you should be constantly on the alert for new ideas. Visit other teachers, talk to them, and try to get ideas from them. Try out the material and techniques other teachers have found successful. Visit the teacher conventions and other professional meetings in search of new ideas. A fine source of ideas for teaching is the book exhibit at conventions. But you should do more than make use of the work of others—you should share successful experiences of your own. One way is to write about your experiences for publication in a professional journal. Although you may not think that your work is of interest to others, editors are always anxious to obtain articles that tell what teachers are doing. Moreover, setting down your thoughts may help clarify your own professional thinking.

Membership in Professional Associations

Many teachers get inspiration and help from memberships in professional organizations. Undoubtedly you would find membership in the organization of teachers in your field rewarding. In almost every instance these organizations publish a professional journal that can help you in keeping abreast of developments in your teaching field and the methods of teaching it. For most teachers the meetings of these associations are especially valuable. Here you can meet and share experiences with others who face the same problems you do.

In addition to the professional organization of teachers in your field you should probably belong to the local teachers' organization and its state and national parent organizations. In some communities, you may have a choice between joining the local chapter of the American Federa-

[3] Hilda Taba and Elizabeth Noel, *Action Research: A Case Study*, Association for Supervision and Curriculum Development, Washington, D.C., 1957.

tion of Teachers AFL-CIO or the local affiliate of the National Education Association. Which you should join is a choice you must make for yourself; both are honorable organizations. Do not, however, let yourself be rushed into making a decision. Before deciding you should look carefully at the goals and programs of both organizations at the local and national levels. Then make your decision on the basis of what seems best for the profession and for you. You may wish to belong to both; a number of teachers do.

❈

How can you keep from becoming a person who merely repeats one year of teaching experience again and again?

What professional journals do you think you ought to read regularly? What professional organizations do you think you should join?

Map out a program of advanced study that you think would be suitable for you after you have started teaching.

❈

Becoming a Professional Teacher

Although it may be some time before you become a master teacher, you should be a thoroughly professional teacher from the day you start. A professional teacher differs from others in that he is truly competent in what he does. He is well prepared in the three things essential for teaching—he knows his pupils, his subject, and how to teach. He attempts to develop his own proficiency and to make the profession attractive to promising young people.

The truly professional teacher gives a full measure of professional service. He does a fine job at the highest possible level; he undertakes all professional responsibilities willingly. In return, he expects to be paid adequately for these services. An ethical teacher does not accept substandard salaries, neither does he undercut other teachers. He refuses to accept positions that have been vacated because of unprofessional activity. In other words, in dealing with his colleagues and employers, he does unto them as he would have them do unto him.

Above all, the professional teacher is proud of his profession, although it is arduous and exacting and in the past has not always been rewarded as well as it should have been. The professional teacher works to secure more satisfactory tangible rewards, but he will always give a little more than he is paid for. Through the schools of his community the teacher shapes the destiny of the nation. It is a profession to be proud of, and the professional teacher glories in being able to say, "I am a teacher!"

FOR FURTHER STUDY

ALCORN, MARVIN D., JAMES S. KINDER, and JIM R. SCHUNERT, *Better Teaching in Secondary Schools* (New York: Holt, Rinehart and Winston, Inc., 1964), Ch. 19.

CONANT, JAMES B., *The Education of American Teachers* (New York: McGraw-Hill Book Company, Inc., 1963).

LEE, GORDON C., "The Changing Role of the Teacher" in *The Changing American School*, Sixty-Fifth Yearbook. Part II, National Society for the Study of Education (Chicago: The University of Chicago Press, 1966), Ch. 1.

LIEBERMAN, MYRON, *Education As a Profession* (Englewood Cliffs, N.J.: Prentice-Hall Inc., 1956).

————, *The Future of Public Education* (Chicago: The University of Chicago Press, 1960).

RIVLIN, HARRY N., *Teaching Adolescents in Secondary Schools*, Second Edition (New York: Appleton-Century-Crofts, Inc., 1961), Ch. 15.

STEEVES, FRANK L., *Fundamentals of Teaching in Secondary Schools* (New York: The Odyssey Press, Inc., 1962), Ch. 18.

STINNETT, T. M., and ALBERT J. HUGGETT, *Professional Problems of Teachers*, Second Edition (New York: The Macmillan Company, 1963).

VAN TIL, WILLIAM, *The Making of a Modern Educator* (Indianapolis: The Bobbs Merrill Company, Inc., 1961).

WALTON, JOHN, and JAMES L. KUETHE, *The Discipline of Education* (Madison, Wisconsin: University of Wisconsin, 1963).

WILSON, CHARLES H., *A Teacher Is a Person* (New York: Holt, Rinehart and Winston, Inc., 1956).

Appendix

A Sample Resource Unit
and a Plan for a Teaching Unit

*T*HIS APPENDIX consists of a resource unit developed by the teachers in local school systems, a short discussion of how the resource unit may be used in drawing up a plan for a teaching unit, and an example of a plan for a teaching unit derived from the resource unit. The reader should note that a resource unit consists entirely of suggestions that the teacher might adopt for his classes. In making his plan for the teaching unit, the teacher may use many of these suggestions, but he also may delete and add to them as he sees fit.

Enjoying Animals:
(A Resource Unit for Grade Seven)[*]

Introduction

GENERAL STATEMENT

This unit provides material for the enjoyment of stories and articles about animals. It should develop a sympathetic and intelligent interest in animal life, widen the range of reading interest, and provide opportunities for the development of various language arts skills.

OBJECTIVES

1. Pupil aims in terms of knowledges, understandings, and attitudes are as follows.
   a. To understand background material about locale, environment, and habits in animal stories.
   b. To appreciate the swift-moving action and suspense given in animal stories.
   c. To understand and respect the benefits to man from wild-life conservation.

[*] *Tentative Curriculum Guide, Language Arts, Junior High School Grades 7, 8, 9* (Louisville, Ky.: Superintendent of Schools, 1958), pp. 53–79. By permission.

465

d. To recognize that the author must have a suitable background of experience and information for the kind of work produced.

e. To appreciate the varying points of view from which the story can be written.

f. To realize the need for using five senses in observing animals in their world.

g. To recognize expressions which have developed from observing the animal kingdom, such as "mad as a wet hen."

h. To develop broader interest in additional types of animal stories.

i. To understand how the environment is important in the story.

j. To recognize how animals influence the lives of man.

k. To become aware of the values of animals serving man.

l. To distinguish between stories of good quality and those of inferior quality.

2. Skills

a. Reading

(1) To understand the central idea.

(2) To enjoy the whole story.

(3) To find the background material.

(4) To identify and appreciate variety in expression.

(5) To develop vocabulary.

b. Writing

(1) To express creative ideas in good sentence form.

(2) To use capital letters correctly in sentences and proper nouns.

(3) To enlarge the vocabulary.

c. Speaking

(1) To tell stories to hold interest.

(2) To share ideas and information.

(3) To use an improved speaking vocabulary and greater variety in expression.

d. Listening

(1) To gain main ideas and important details.

(2) To follow the sequence of events.

(3) To listen critically to discussions.

OVERVIEW

By the time a child enters the seventh grade he has in one sense "been to the animal fair." Many children have their own pets or have had some experience with animals. Almost all youngsters have seen a circus, been to a zoo, or visited a natural history museum. "Enjoying Animals" will give pupils the security that comes from dealing with a relatively familiar field.

The word *animal* is used in a broad sense to include domesticated creatures, wild beasts, birds, fish, and talking beasts and other creatures.

The teacher will want to emphasize reading for enjoyment, observing for detail, writing and speaking creatively, listening for a better understanding and enjoyment, and setting up suitable standards for evaluation of books. Stress will be placed on the proper use of spelling, grammar, mechanics, and manuscript forms.

The significance of the unit lies in its relation to the pupils' interests and opportunities for developing understandings and for teaching important language arts skills.

SUGGESTED APPROACHES

1. Write on the chalkboard names of animals in fiction, motion pictures, and television with which the children are likely to be familiar. Encourage pupils to tell what they wish about animal characters. They might tell the story briefly, describe the animals, or give an incident about the animals. A class list of animal stories can be an outgrowth of the discussion.

2. Have members of the class collect pictures of animals and display them on bulletin boards. Have a class discussion aimed at stimulating interest and imagination. Choose one or more of the pictures and have the class speculate on the setting and locale. Ask the pupils to tell impromptu stories about what is happening in the picture, about what has happened prior to the picture, or what might happen as a result. This activity may be followed by the assignment of oral and written stories involving other pictures in the collection.

3. Read some entertaining poems about animals to the class. Discuss the pictures of animals that the poet presents and the way their methods have of appealing to the reader. Emphasize sense impressions gained from poetry. This discussion can lead into activities to sharpen sensory perceptions and into reading and analyzing stories for their appeal.

4. Conduct a class discussion about animals in motion pictures or television. Make a list of movies that have centered about animals. Discuss the difference between animated cartoons and full-length features.

5. Book jackets may be displayed on a bulletin board to incite interest. Invite the librarian to talk about four or five well-known authors and their books. The librarian's talk should be followed by going to the library to select books.

6. Pupils might tell about places visited during vacation and about animals they saw in national parks or other regions. This introduction could lead to a discussion and perhaps some research about the policy of the government concerning wild animals in our national parks.

7. Relate some incident experienced recently in connection with some

animals on a farm, any animals of a zoo, a circus, or of the forest. Get pupils to tell stories of their own similar experiences.

8. Have pupils give speeches about their pets and their care.

TEACHER-PUPIL PLANNING

Whatever the approach, encourage enthusiasm by being enthusiastic yourself. Encourage the pupils with such questions as "What is the finest and bravest animal you know about?" or "How would you like to have a mongoose as a pet?" or "What is the strangest animal you have ever seen?"

After the discussion has caught the interest of the students, set the stage for their positive approval with a question such as "How would you like to gain a fuller knowledge of animals?"

Ask the pupils what they would like to know and help the class organize these questions into a framework for study.

An outline of the unit follows.

1. Animals Are a Source of Enjoyment to Man.
2. Animals Work and Serve Man.
3. Animals Increase the Beauty of Man's Environment.
4. Animals Teach Man.
5. Animals Are a Source of Inspiration to Man.

Enjoying Animals:
(A Resource Unit for Grade Seven)

Developing the Unit

> *Animals Are a Source
> of Enjoyment to Man*

UNDERSTANDINGS

The enjoyment one gets from a story depends upon such factors as imagination, past experience, and reading ability.

ACTIVITIES

Name some animals from motion pictures, TV, and fiction such as

Bambi
Lassie
Smoky
Flicka

Discuss the animals listed. Describe them and give other pertinent information. Discuss familiar animal stories. List favorites; add to the list as the unit progresses.

Animals serve as pets.

Talk about pets and their care.

Read

> Ross *et al.*, *Adventures for Readers*, Book 1, (Mercury Edition)
>> Rawlings, "Old Slewfoot," pp. 109–122.
>> Thurber, "Snapshot of a Dog," pp. 123–127.
>
> Gray *et al.*, *Paths and Pathfinders*,
>> Johnson, "Polka-Dot Pets," pp. 312–320.
>
> Jewett *et al.*, *Adventure Bound*,
>> Stuart, "No Place for a Hawk," pp. 3–12.
>
> Strong *et al.*, *Teen-Age Tales*, Book 1
>> Henderson, "Brute's Christmas," pp. 142–149.
>> Terhune, "Hero," pp. 150–162.
>
> Murphy *et al.*, *Let's Read*, Book 1
>> Cottrell, "Wild Dogs," pp. 61–69.
>> Anderson, "Come Croppy," pp. 74–81.
>> Coffin, "Christmas Came in Fur," pp. 82–87.
>> Blanton, "Every Dog Has His Day," pp. 52–57.
>> Atkins, "Give Your Dog a Break," pp. 93–103.

Read such books as the following.

> Bianco, *All About Pets*
> Becktel, *Mr. Peck's Pets*
> Chrystie, *Pets, A Complete Handbook on Care, Understanding, and Appreciation of All Kinds of Pets*
> Knight, *Lassie Come Home*
> Richardson, *Finders Keepers*
> Terhune, *Lad, A Dog*
> O'Hara, *My Friend Flicka*
> Sewell, *Black Beauty*
> Willis, *Alfred the Saint*
> Faralla, *The Magnificent Barb*
> Farley, *The Black Stallion*

UNDERSTANDINGS

Farley, *The Black Stallion Returns*
Rawlings, *The Yearling*
Steinbeck, *The Red Pony*
Zitzel, *A Treasury of Cat Stories*

Discuss the central idea behind the story. Why do you suppose the author wrote the story? Why did it occur in this setting?

Vocabulary can be improved by the use of words and phrases that stimulate the imagination.

Find words in the story that describe. Read the sentences without those words. Do these words make a real difference in the meaning you get from reading?

Animals are of value to man as companions.

Discuss

How many of you ever wanted a dog very much? Try to describe how you felt about it. How many of you ever wanted something that your parents didn't want you to have? How did you feel toward your parents? Thinking back over the situation, do you feel the same way now? Why, or why not?

Owning a pet brings responsibility.

Collect pictures for a bulletin board exhibit. Write imaginative stories to go with the pictures.

Give a talk or write a composition on "Care of a Pet." Caring for a dog involves feeding him, providing shelter for him, showing affection for him, keeping him groomed, and training him properly.

Animals should be named appropriately.

Discuss the naming of animals and the appropriateness of names given to animals in fiction, such as Old Slewfoot, Bambi, Flower. Explain how pets are named.

The mood of the story is greatly enhanced if the author has a suitable background of experience and information for the kind of work produced.

Secure information about well-known authors of animal stories. The research should reveal the qualifications of the author for writing animal stories, his environment, his background, and his experiences. Consider such authors as Rudyard Kipling, Marjorie Kinnan

UNDERSTANDINGS   ACTIVITIES

Rawlings, Felix Salten, Ernest Thompson Seton, and Alfred Payson Terhune. Share findings with the class. Compile a booklet containing brief information about each author.

Compile a class list of words used with animals. Add to this list throughout the unit. Use words such as taxidermy, sanctuaries, and hibernate. The list may be in chart form.

Write a composition disclosing the type and breed of pet desired, seeking help in the library. Intelligent reasons should be given for the choice made. Draw pictures or find in a magazine pictures to illustrate compositions.

Prepare a collection of articles, pictures, poems, and clippings about unusual pets. The material may be displayed on the bulletin board for several days. Save the collection for a culminating experience.

Animals Work and Serve Man

Animals are valuable to man for work and service. Animals and man have been dependent upon each other through the ages.

Read

Murphy *et al.*, *Let's Read*, Book 1
   Gibson, "How Smart Are Dogs?" pp. 90–93.
   Lindquist, "Eskimo Husky," pp. 17–22.
   Bertino, "Diamond of the Double-K Ranch," pp. 10–17.
Jewett *et al.*, *Adventure Bound*
   McCaughey, "Dog Detective," pp. 12–17.
   Henderson and Topliner, "We Changed a Leopard's Spots," pp. 31–38.
Ross *et al.*, *Adventures for Readers*, Book 1 (Mercury Edition)
   Rawlings, "My Eyes Have a Cold Nose," pp. 104–109.

Murphy, "Champion Stock," pp. 97–102.

Frost, "The Runaway," pp. 102–103.

Gray *et al.*, *Paths and Pathfinders*
O'Brien, "A Dog Named Spike," pp. 272–282.

Bauken, "The Horse of the Sword," pp. 250–259.

Strang *et al.*, *Teen-Age Tales*, Book 1
Farley, "The Storm," pp. 250–259.

Read books such as the following.

Henry, *Album of Horses*
Caldwell, *Wolf, the Storm Leader*
Landru, *Sled Dog of Alaska*
Ollivant, *Son of Battle*
Fenner, *Horses, Horses, Horses: Palominos and Pintos, Polo Ponies and Plow Horses, Morgans and Mustangs.*
O'Brien, *Silver Chief*
James, *Smoky*
Chipperfield, *Storm of Dancerwood*
Chipperfield, *Links Tor*
Kjelgaard, *Irish Red*
        Snow Dog
Lippincott, *Wilderness Champion*
London, *The Call of the Wild*
London, *White Fang*
Balch, *Wild Horse*
Anderson, *Big Red*
        Tomorrow's Champion
        Thoroughbreds
        Deep Through the Heart
        A Touch of Greatness

View such motion pictures as:

M-690   Wheels Across India
M-1094   Eskimo Sea Hunters
M-1089   Eskimos—Winter in
                Western Alaska.

UNDERSTANDINGS	ACTIVITIES
Environment influences both people and animals.	Determine by the use of maps the locality in which the story occurred. Make brief oral reports on the setting of several selections. Compare incidents in the story to real life situations.
Exact words convey what is intended.	Locate and examine selected passages from selections because of their beauty or the unusual way in which the author has given expression to his thoughts. Read aloud.
Animals and human beings have qualities and characteristics that are similar.	Develop a wordlist in which a parallel is drawn between qualities and characteristics and human qualities and characteristics such as devotion, intelligence, and courage. Cite actual incidents in which these qualities and characteristics are shown. After several stories have been read and discussed, select from the library a book for collateral reading. Discussions may be held in groups which read books of a similar nature. Reread parts of a selection in order to understand more fully their meanings. Point out how the effect is achieved if the part is particularly descriptive.
Periodicals are an important source of information and of recreational reading.	Make a collection of true stories telling of bravery and loyalty of animals. This information can be gathered largely from newspapers and magazines.
Seeing specific details is important to a study of description.	Pick out words which best describe persons and animals. Have you seen animals or pictures of animals who look somewhat like people of your acquaintance?

> Animals Increase the Beauty
> of Man's Environment

UNDERSTANDINGS

Reading of the lives and experiences of wild animals causes boys and girls to find themselves venturing all over the world.

ACTIVITIES

Read

Ross *et al.*, *Adventures for Readers*, Book 1 (Mercury Edition)
  Scoville, "The Mahagony Fox," pp. 135–143.
  Teals, "Animals Go to School," pp. 151–156.

Jewett *et al.*, *Adventure Bound*
  Franklin, "Sooty, the Black Woodchuck," pp. 19–23.
  Johnson, "Lion Hunting with Cameras," pp. 52–59.

Gray *et al.*, *Paths and Pathfinders*
  Atkinson, "Wild Animals Come to Dine," pp. 295–303.
  Carter, "Ungor Guards the Flock," pp. 304–311.
  Scoville, "Blue Duiker," pp. 284–294.
  Ditmars, "My Strange Hobby," pp. 322–330.

Murphy *et al.*, *Let's Read*, Book 1
  Schultz, "A Death Struggle with a Giant Eel," pp. 44–48.

Read books such as the following.

Darling, *Sandy, the Red Deer*
Ditmars, *Strange Animals I Have Known*
Franklin, *Wild Animals of the Five Rivers Country*
Franklin, *Wild Animals of the Southwest*
George, *Vulpes, the Red Fox*
Hegner, *Parade of the Animal Kingdom*
Henderson, *Amik, the Life Story of a Beaver*
Kalashnikoff, *The Defender*
Kjelgaard, *Kalak of the Ice*
Lathrop, *Let Them Live*

McCracken, *The Biggest Bear on Earth*

McCracken, *The Flaming Bear*

Moe, *Animal Inn. Stories of a Wayside Museum*

Montgomery, *Amikuk*

Montgomery, *Carcajou*

Montgomery, *Kildee House*

Mukerji, *Kari, the Elephant*

Richards, *Life with Alice: Forty Years of Elephant Adventure*

Salten, *Bambi*

Sanderson, *The Silver Mink*

Scott, *Mojave Joe*

Von Hagen, *South American Zoo*

Waldeck, *Jamba the Elephant*

Waldeck, *Lions on the Hunt*

Waldeck, *The White Panther*

Buck, *Jungle Animals*

Franklin, *Tricky*

Liers, *An Otter's Story*

Rush, *Duff*

View motion pictures such as:

    2-317 Hunting with a Camera

    2-331 Animals Unlimited

    1-267 Common Animals of the Woods.

Animal stories have swift-moving action and suspense.

Make a list of specific descriptive action verbs.

Example: move, stirred, stumbled. Use the words in oral and written work.

The author sets the mood for the story.

Point out ways in which the author creates the mood for the story. Find definite descriptive phrases. Write a paragraph in which special attention is paid to description.

Distinguish between general and specific classifications.

Example: rodent, rat, mouse.

View motion pictures.

    M-689   Wheels Across Africa

    M-1014 Nomads of the Jungle (Malaya)

Discuss qualities needed by people who want to make friends with wild animals. Note the qualities and cite incidents to vivify them.

Tell experiences in taming birds or squirrels. Discuss difficulties encountered and successes accomplished.

Animals act by intelligence and not instinct alone.

List characteristics that have helped animals to become leaders. Draw a parallel between animal leaders and human leaders.

Prepare a short biography (to be presented in class) of one or several of the authors. Work in a committee or individually. The material can be taken from *Who's Who in America, The Junior Book of Authors, Who's Who Among North American Authors.*

Animals have "natural enemies."

Discuss the fact that a natural enemy is an animal that nature seems to have designed to prey on or to destroy certain other animals. Give an oral or written example of an encounter of two such animals.

Compile a class file of stories read outside the class about wild animals. Participate by writing an annotation of the stories read.

Listening is an aid to better oral work.

Plan a quiz game in which clues are given. Try to guess which animal is being considered. Stress careful listening.

The placing of modifiers is important to the meaning of the sentence.

Write a description of a setting or a background for a story. Exact words should be used for modifiers.

Show slides or pictures which families have taken of wild animals. Prepare a suitable commentary to go with pictures.

Write a short paper on the relative value of a particular wild animal to man.

UNDERSTANDINGS

Wildlife benefits to man are many.

ACTIVITIES

Discuss methods of protecting animal life. Secure information from the library for reports on such organizations as the Audubon Society or the Isaac Walton League.

Attend programs of the Beckham Bird Club and other local groups. Give short oral reports.

Write letters to several state departments of conservation to secure information on the present work being accomplished in the field of conservation.

Make book reports in class on the latest books on animal life.

Invite a resource person to speak. Compose the invitation. Write thank you notes.

View the following motion picture.

M-240 Sanctuary of the Seals

Discuss the difference between a sanctuary and a zoo. Tell which would be more interesting to visit and give the reasons why.

Participate in a panel discussion on one of the following topics.

1. How Animals Contribute to Our Way of Life
2. How We Can Learn from Animals
3. Useful Animals
4. It Takes All Kinds to Make a World.

Write compositions on "The Wild Animal I Would Like to Have for a Pet."

```
┌─────────────────────────────────────────────┐
│            Animals Teach Man                  │
└─────────────────────────────────────────────┘
```

UNDERSTANDINGS

"Talking" animals give much information about animals and man. "Talking" animals arouse the reader's imagination.

ACTIVITIES

Read

Ross *et al., Adventures for Readers,* Book 1 (Mercury Edition)
  Smith, "Raffles the Bird That Whistles and Talks," p. 127.
Strang *et al., Teen-Age Tales,* Book 1
  Carmen, "Mr. Sims and Henry," pp. 129–134.
  Tracy, "The Squirrel Who Was Scared," pp. 163–176.
Jewett *et al., Adventure Bound*
  Kipling, "Rikki-Tikki-Tavi," pp. 38–51.

Read books such as:

Coatsworth, *The Cat Who Went to Heaven*
De la Mare, *The Three Royal Monkeys*
Harris, *Uncle Remus, His Songs and Sayings*
Kipling, *The Jungle Book*
Kipling, *The Just So Stories*
Lagerlöf, *The Wonderful Adventures of Nils*
Lofting, *The Story of Doctor Dolittle*
  The Voyages of Doctor Dolittle
Lofting, *Doctor Dolittle's Post Office*
  Doctor Dolittle's Circus
  Doctor Dolittle's Zoo
  Doctor Dolittle's Caravan
  Doctor Dolittle's Garden
  Doctor Dolittle in the Moon
  Doctor Dolittle's Return
  Doctor Dolittle and the Secret Lake
  Doctor Dolittle and the Green Canary

Doctor Dolittle's Puddleby Adventures

UNDERSTANDINGS	ACTIVITIES
Reading between the lines is often necessary for the full meaning of the story.	Discuss whether the story's information is true or imaginary.
	Write humorous paragraphs as a group or individually on the effect of animals on human beings or the effect of human beings on animals.
Stories are better understood if the point of view is clear to the reader.	Tell or read an anecdote. Retell it from another point of view. The story could be told from an animal's point of view, a child's point of view, or from the point of view of some inanimate thing such as a tree or a cloud.
Stories are an aid in seeing relationship.	Discuss which is more important when both animals and people talk in stories.
	Cite incidents in the story in which animals have qualities such as perseverance or endurance. Discuss.
	Write an imaginary conversation between two animals or between a person and an animal.
	Rewrite in play form a story or a section of a story.
	Read a story in which some animal performs superhuman feats. Discuss the improbability of some animal stories. Are they written for humor?
	Discuss the use of animals in TV commercials. Do they add to the interest?
	Discuss what animal stories do for us. Develop a set of standards for judging good animal stories.

```
┌─────────────────────────────────┐
│        Animals Are a Source      │
│        of Inspiration to Man     │
└─────────────────────────────────┘
```

UNDERSTANDINGS   ACTIVITIES

Thinking and feeling are expressed by   *Read*
the poet through his work.

Ross *et al., Adventures for Readers,*
Book 1 (Mercury Edition)
Frost, "The Runaway," pp. 102–
103.
Keats, "Swarms of Minnows," p.
122.
Nash, "The Hunter," p. 143.
Gray, "On a Cat, Aging," p. 143.
Bryant, "Robert of Lincoln," p.
133.
Frost, "The Last Word of a Blue-
bird," p. 196.
Saxe, "The Blind Man and the
Elephant," pp. 198–200.
Gray *et al., Paths and Pathfinders*
Sarrett, "Four Little Foxes," p.
294.
Masefield, "Sea Fever," p. 283.
Austin, "The Sandhill Crane," p.
321.
Coatsworth, "Poem of Praise," p.
330.
Jewett *et al., Adventure Bound*
Tippett, "Sunning," p. 18.
Tennyson, "The Eagle," p. 24.
Guiterman, "Grumpy," pp. 25–
26.
Gordon *et al., A Magic World: An
Anthology of Poetry*
"God's World" (entire section),
pp. 141–163.
Pooley *et al., Action! Growth in
Reading, Book One*
"Four Poems about Pets" (entire
section), pp. 127–128.
Cross *et al., Literature—A Series
of Anthologies; Appreciating Lit-
erature*
Austin, "The Brown Bear," pp.
127–128.

UNDERSTANDINGS	ACTIVITIES

<table>
<tr><td></td><td>Miller, "Lion," p. 129.
Richards, "Eletelephony," p. 145.
Wells, "How to Tell the Wild Animals," p. 148.
Fields, "The Owl Critic," pp. 149–151.
Coatsworth, "Song of the Ship's Cat," p. 151.
Coatsworth, "Song to an Old Dog," p. 172.
McLeod, "Lone Dog," p. 173.
Garland, "Horses Chawin' Hay," p. 179.
Bailey et al., World of People
Lindsay, "The Broncho That Would Not be Broken," pp. 58–59.
Fyleman, "Bingo Has an Enemy," p. 79.
Asquith, "The Hairy Dog," p. 80.
Nash, "The Kitten," p. 80.</td></tr>
<tr><td>Vivid word pictures help set the mood and add beauty to poetry which is "music in words."</td><td>Read poetry orally to hear the sounds of the words. All words have sounds, but the words in a poem form sounds in patterns. The pattern of rhyme is the sound of the word at the end of one line rhyming with a word at the end of another line. The pattern of rhythm is like the beat of a line of music.

Discuss

Is the title of the poem appropriate? What details in the poem show the poet to be a keen observer? Do you agree with the point of view of the poet?

Advance discussion of poems with such questions as these:

How does this picture make you feel? How do you suppose the animal feels? Why do you think so?</td></tr>
<tr><td>Figurative language adds to the beauty of poetry.</td><td>Point out the use of several similes and metaphors. Watch for them.</td></tr>
</table>

UNDERSTANDINGS	ACTIVITIES
	Choose words and make lists of words that rhyme. Write a poem as a class project or individually.
	Practice choral reading with several poems such as "Robert of Lincoln" or "The Blind Man and the Elephant."
Poetry must be related to pupils' everyday experiences to be meaningful.	Collect pictures to accompany poems and arrange a bulletin board display. Write captions and explanations in rhyme for each picture.

Closing the Unit

The unit on "Enjoying Animals" presents many activities suitable for bulletin board display.

Exhibit on the hall bulletin boards such things as original poems or stories with suitable illustrations.

Have a pet show for the class.

Invite someone with an unusual pet to bring it to school and talk about it.

Conduct a jury trial in which a pupil is accused of reading a dull animal story or book. He pleads guilty or not guilty and defends himself.

Have pupils write and perform an original drama centered about animals.

Dramatize actual incidents from animal stories.

Evaluating the Unit

Continuous evaluation should be made by the teacher and by the pupils independently and as a group. Techniques that place a share of the responsibility for evaluation on the pupils are necessary if the pupils are to see the values of the unit and evaluate their own progress. The teacher and pupils need to keep their objectives in mind and should set aside periods for determining their progress toward these objectives.

The following questions will assist the teacher in evaluating the "Enjoying Animals" unit.

Did the pupils enjoy reading in class the stories about animals?

Was enough interest aroused to lead the pupil to extend his reading upon the subject?

Does the pupil have a deeper interest in animal life about him?

Does the pupil have a deeper appreciation for the life of the animal world?

Can the pupils explain in what respects animals are like human beings?

Have the pupils learned anything new about animals? Have they changed their minds about them?

Have the pupils a greater sympathy toward animals and a greater appreciation of their place in the scheme of things?

Have the pupils improved in ability to write good, meaningful sentences?

Have they improved their spelling and increased their vocabulary?

Have the pupils learned to participate in discussions with thoughtfulness for the right of others?

Teaching Aids

Teacher References

BAILEY, MATILDA, and ULLIN W. LEAVELL, *Worlds of People*. (New York: American Book Co., 1951.)

CROSS, E. A., and ELIZABETH LEHR, *Literature—A Series of Anthologies; Appreciating Literature*. (New York: Macmillan, 1943.)

GORDON, MARGERY, and MARIE B. KING, *A Magic World: An Anthology of Poetry*. (New York: Appleton, 1930.)

POOLEY, ROBERT C., and FRED G. WALCOTT, *Action! Growth in Reading: Book One*. (Chicago: Scott, 1942.)

Anthologies

GRAY, WILLIAM S., *et al.*, *Paths and Pathfinders*. (New York: Scott, Foresman, 1946.)

JEWETT, ARNO, *et al.*, *Adventure Bound*. (Boston: Houghton Mifflin Co., 1956.)

MURPHY, GEORGE, *et al.*, *Let's Read!* Book 1, The Emerald Book, Reading for Fun. (New York: Holt, 1951.)

ROSS, JACOB M., *et al.*, *Adventures for Readers*, Book 1 (Mercury Edition). (New York: Harcourt, Brace, 1953.)

STRANG, RUTH, and RALPH ROBERTS, *Teen-Age Tales*, Book 1. (New York: Heath, 1954.)

Suggested Books for Additional Reading

ANDERSON, C. W., *Big Red*. (New York: Macmillan, 1943.)
———, *Tomorrow's Champion*. (New York: Macmillan, 1946.)
———, *Thoroughbreds*. (New York: Macmillan, 1942.)
———, *Peep Through the Heart*. (New York: Macmillan, 1941.)
———, *A Touch of Greatness*. (New York: Macmillan, 1945.)
BALCH, GLENN, *Wild Horse*. (New York: Crowell, 1947.)
BECHTEL, LOUISE S., *Mr. Peck's Pets*. (New York: Macmillan, 1947.)
BIANCO, MARGERY, *All About Pets*. (New York: Macmillan, 1929.)

BUCK, FRANK, *Jungle Animals.* (New York: Random House, 1945.)

CARDWELL, FRANK, *Wolf, the Storm Leader.* (New York: Dodd, Mead, 1937.)

CHIPPERFIELD, JOSEPH, *Storm of Dancerwood.* (New York: Longmans, Green, 1949.)

————, *Windruff of Links Tor.* (New York: Longmans, Green, 1951.)

COATSWORTH, ELIZABETH, *The Cat Who Went to Heaven.* (New York: Macmillan, 1930.)

CHRYSTIE, FRANCES N., *Pets, a Complete Handbook on the Care, Understanding, and Appreciation of All Kinds of Animal Pets.* (Boston: Little, Brown, 1953.)

DARLING, F. FRASER, *Sandy, the Red Deer.* (New York: Oxford University Press, 1950.)

DE LA MARE, WALTER, *The Three Royal Monkeys.* (New York: Knopf, 1948.)

DITMARS, R. L., *The Making of a Scientist.* (New York: Macmillan, n.d.)

————, *Strange Animals I Have Known.* (New York: Harcourt, Brace, 1931.)

FARALLA, DANA, *The Magnificent Barb.* (New York: Messner, 1947.)

FARLEY, WALTER, *The Black Stallion.* (New York: Random House, 1941.)

FENNER, PHYLLIS, *Horses, Horses, Horses; Palominos and Pintos, Polo Ponies and Plow Horses, Morgans and Mustangs.* (New York: Watts, 1949.)

FRANKLIN, GEORGE C., *Tricky.* (Boston: Houghton Mifflin Co., 1949.)

————, *Wild Animals of Five Rivers Country.* (Boston: Houghton Mifflin Co., 1947.)

————, *Wild Animals of the Southwest.* (Boston: Houghton Mifflin Co., 1950.)

GEORGE, JOHN and JEAN, *Vulpes the Red Fox,* (New York: Dutton, 1948.)

HARRIS, JOEL CHANDLER, *Uncle Remus, His Songs and Sayings.* (New York: Appleton-Century-Crofts, 1935.)

HEGNER, ROBERT W., *Parade of the Animal Kingdom.* (New York: Macmillan, 1935.)

HENDERSON, LUIS M., *Amik, the Life Story of a Beaver.* (New York: Morrow, 1948 o.p.)

HENRY, MARGUERITE, *Album of Horses.* (Chicago: Rand McNally, 1951.)

KALASHNIKOFF, NICHOLAS, *The Defender.* (New York: Scribner's, 1951.)

KIPLING, RUDYARD, *The Jungle Books.* (New York: Doubleday, 1932.)

————, *Just So Stories.* (New York: Doubleday, 1912.)

KJELGAARD, JIM, *Big Red.* (New York: Holiday House, 1945.)

————, *Irish Red.* (New York: Holiday House, 1951.)

————, *Snow Dog.* (New York: Holiday House, 1948.)

————, *Chip, the Dam Builder.* (New York: Holiday House, 1950).

————, *Kalak of the Ice.* (New York: Holiday House, 1949.)

KNIGHT, ERIC, *Lassie Come Home.* (Philadelphia: Winston, 1940.)

LAGERLÖF, SELMA, *The Wonderful Adventures of Nils.* (New York: Pantheon Books, 1947.)

LANDRU, JACK, *Sled Dog of Alaska.* (New York: Dodd, Mead, 1953.)

LATHROP, DOROTHY, *Let Them Live.* (New York: Macmillan, 1951.)

LIERS, EMIL E., *An Otter's Story.* (New York: Viking Press, 1953.)

LIPPINCOTT, JOSEPH, *Wilderness Champion*. (Philadelphia: Lippincott, 1944.)

LOFTING, HUGH, *Doctor Dolittle in the Moon*. (Philadelphia: Lippincott, 1928.)

————, *D. D.'s Return*. (Philadelphia: Lippincott, 1933.)

————, *D. D. and the Secret Lake*. (Philadelphia: Lippincott, 1948.)

————, *D. D. and the Green Canary*. (Philadelphia: Lippincott, 1950.)

————, *D. D.'s Puddleby Adventures*. (Philadelphia: Lippincott, 1952.)

————, *The Story of Doctor Dolittle, Being the Story of His Peculiar Life at Home and Astonishing Adventures in Foreign Parts, Never Before Printed.* (Philadelphia: Lippincott, 1920.)

————, *The Voyages of D. D.* (Philadelphia: Lippincott, 1920.)

————, *D. D.'s Post Office*. (Philadelphia: Lippincott, 1923.)

————, *D. D.'s Circus*. (Philadelphia: Lippincott, 1924.)

————, *D. D.'s Zoo*. (Philadelphia: Lippincott, 1925.)

————, *D. D.'s Caravan*. (Philadelphia: Lippincott, 1926.)

————, *D. D.'s Garden*. (Philadelphia: Lippincott, 1927.)

LONDON, JACK, *The Call of the Wild*. (New York: Macmillan, 1929.)

————, *White Fang*. (New York: Macmillan, 1929.)

LOOMIS, J. PAUL, *Horse of the Deep Snows*. (New York: Dodd, Mead, 1954.)

McCRACKEN, HAROLD, *The Biggest Bear on Earth*. (Philadelphia: Lippincott, 1943.)

————, *The Son of the Walrus King*. (Philadelphia: Lippincott, 1944.)

————, *The Flaming Bear*. (Philadelphia: Lippincott, 1944.)

MOE, VIRGINIA, *Animal Inn, Stories of a Trailside Museum.* (Boston: Houghton Mifflin, 1946.)

MONTGOMERY, RUTHERFORD, *Amikuk*. (Cleveland: World Publishing Co., 1955.)

————, *Carcajou*. (Caldwell, Idaho: Caxton Printers, 1936.)

————, *Kildee House*. (Garden City: Doubleday, 1949.)

MIKERJI, DHEN, *Kari the Elephant*. (New York: Dutton, 1922.)

O'BRIEN, JACK, *The Return of Silver Chief*. (Chicago: Winston, 1943.)

————, *Silver Chief*. (Chicago: Winston, 1933.)

————, *Silver Chief to the Rescue*. (Chicago: Winston, 1937.)

O'HARA, MARY, *My Friend Flicka*. (Philadelphia: Lippincott, 1944.)

OLLIVANT, ALFRED, *Bob, Son of Battle*. (New York: Grosset and Dunlap, n.d.)

RAWLINGS, M. K., *The Yearling*. (New York: Scribner's, 1939.)

RICHARDS, DICK, *Life with Alice: Forty Years of Elephant*. (New York: Coward-McCann, 1944.)

RICHARDSON, MYRA, *Finder's Keepers*. (New York: Viking Press, 1951.)

RUSH, WILLIAM M., *Duff*. (New York: Longmans, Green, 1950.)

SALTEN, FELIX, *Bambi's Children*. (New York: Grosset and Dunlap, 1929.)

SANDERSON, IVAN, *The Silver Mink*. (Boston: Little, Brown, 1952.)

SCOTT, DUSTIN, *Mojave Joe*. (New York: Knopf, 1950.)

SEWELL, ANNA, *Black Beauty*. (New York: Dodd, Mead, 1941.)

STEINBECK, JOHN, *The Red Pony*. (New York: Viking Press, 1945.)

TERHUNE, ALBERT, *Lad, a Dog*. (New York: Dutton, 1926.)

Von Hagen, Victor W., *South American Zoo*. (New York: Messner, 1946, o.p.)

Waldeck, Theodore, *Jamba the Elephant*. (New York: Viking Press, 1942.)

———, *Lions on the Hunt*. (New York: Viking Press, 1942.)

———, *The White Panther*. (New York: Viking Press, 1942.)

———, *Treks Across the Veldt*. (New York: Viking Press, 1944.)

Willis, Priscilla, *Alfred the Saint*. (New York: Longmans, Green, 1952.)

Zim, Herbert, *Owls*. (New York: Morrow, 1950.)

Audio-Visual Materials

MOTION PICTURES

Louisville Public Schools

M-1094	Eskimo Sea Hunters
M-1089	Eskimos—Winter in Western Alaska
M-1014	Nomads of the Jungle (Malaya)
M-240	Sanctuary of the Seals
M-689	Wheels Across Africa
M-690	Wheels Across India

Louisville Free Public Library

2-331	Animals Unlimited
1-267	Common Animals of the Woods
2-317	Hunting with a Camera

Planning the Teaching Unit

To make a plan for a teaching unit from the resource unit "Enjoying Animals" would be quite easy. First one would decide on just what he would like the pupils to learn in a unit on the topic. Then he would describe that learning in an overview or statement of the general objective. The teacher could draw the content of the overview from the objectives set forth in the resource unit.

Next the teacher should select the specific objectives for the unit. Since the specific objectives are understandings, skills, appreciations, ideas, and attitudes that the teacher hopes the pupils will learn in order to attain the general objectives as stated in the overview, he should try to select specific objectives that will contribute to the general objectives. He can pick them from the understandings, skills, and appreciations listed in the resource unit. Note that in this resource unit the author has listed objectives and understandings separately. For our purposes these lists are both objectives. In picking the objectives for his teaching unit the teacher will want to be quite selective; he will not want to limit himself only to the objectives in the resource unit or to include all of them.

Once the goals are ready it is time to select the activities, both basic and optional. He should list them separately, being careful to choose only activities that will bring out the desired objectives. Again he may include both activities selected from the resource unit and activities of his own devising. At this point in his planning of the activities, he should consider how to launch, develop, culminate, and evaluate the unit. He may also want to prepare a study guide at this time, or he may prefer to wait until the pupils have participated in teacher-pupil planning of the unit's development. In either case, the study and activity guide should be based on basic problem-solving activities as much as possible. It should also include some mention of optional related activities suitable for the unit. Detailed directions for the various optional related activities may be kept separately in a file. Finally from the list of materials and bibliography of the resource unit the teacher selects those items he wishes to include in the list of materials and bibliography of the teaching unit. In the end his plan for the teaching unit may look something like this.

Enjoying Animals

A Plan for a Teaching Unit

OVERVIEW

Animal life and stories about animals can be fascinating. The enjoyment one gets from such stories depends upon many factors, among them one's imagination, past experience, and reading ability as well as swift-moving action, suspense, and atmosphere provided by skilful storytelling in both prose and poetry. These appreciations can be enhanced by knowledge not only of the storyteller's art, but also an understanding of the animals and their lives in the wild. If we are to continue to enjoy and understand them, it will be necessary for us to practice wildlife conservation.

SPECIFIC OBJECTIVES

Understandings

Man benefits from wildlife conservation both aesthetically and practically.

Stories can be told from various points of view. The variance in points of view can make the story's meaning quite different.

The enjoyment one gets from a story depends upon such factors as imagination, past experiences, and reading ability.

The mood of the story is greatly enhanced if the author has a suitable background of experience and information for the kind of work to be produced.

Animals are valuable to man for work and service. Animals and man have depended upon each other through the ages.

Environment influences both people and animals.

Exact words convey what is intended.

Periodicals are an important source of information and of recreational reading.

Seeing specific details is important to a study of description.

Vocabulary can be improved by the use of words and phrases that stimulate the imagination.

Figurative language adds to the beauty of poetry.

Poetry must be related to pupils' everyday experiences to be meaningful.

Vivid word pictures help set the mood and add beauty to poetry which is "music in words."

Wildlife benefits to man are many.

The author sets the mood for the story.

Thinking and feeling are expressed by the poet through his work.

Reading between the lines is often necessary for the full meaning of the story.

Stories are better understood if the point of view is clear to the reader.

Stories are an aid in seeing relationship.

Appreciations

To appreciate the swift-moving action and suspense given in animal stories.

To appreciate the varying points of view from which the story can be written.

Skills

To express creative ideas in good sentence form.

To identify and appreciate variety in expression.

To develop vocabulary.

To use an improved speaking vocabulary and greater variety in expression.

To gain main ideas and important details.

To follow the sequence of events.

To listen critically to discussions.

BASIC OR CORE ACTIVITIES

Introductory Activities

1. Read some entertaining poems about animals to the class. Discuss the pictures of animals that the poet presents and their methods of appealing to the reader. Emphasize sense impressions gained from poetry. This discussion can lead into activities to sharpen

sensory perceptions and into reading and analyzing of stories for
their appeal.

2. Write on the chalkboard names of animals in fiction, motion pictures, and television with which the children are likely to be
   familiar—for example, Bambi, Lassie, Smokey, Flicka. Ask them
   for names. Encourage pupils to tell what they wish about animal
   characters. They might tell the story briefly, describe the animals,
   or give an incident about the animal. A class list of animal stories
   can be an outgrowth of the discussion.

3. Introductory talk on the study guide.

Developmental Activities

4. Discuss what animal stories do for us. Develop standards for
   evaluating a short story. What makes a good animal story?

*5. Read "Old Slewfoot," (*Adventures for Readers,* 109–122). What
    is the central idea behind the story? Why do you suppose the
    author wrote the story? Why did it occur in this setting?

*6. Read "No Place for a Hawk," (*Adventure Bound,* pp. 3–12).
    What is the central idea behind this story? Why do you suppose
    the author wrote it? Did you find the story interesting? Why or
    why not? Is the story real or imaginary? Look up the life of
    Mr. Stuart. What experience does he have that would enable him
    to write about hawks or other animals?

*7. Read one or more of the following stories: "Snapshot of a Dog,"
    4:123–127; "Polka-Dot Pets," 1:312–320; "Brute's Christmas,"
    5:142–149; "Hero," 5:150–162; "Wild Dogs," 4:61–69; "Come
    Croppy," 4:74–81; "Christmas Came in Fur," 4:82–87; "Every
    Dog Has His Day," 4:52–57; "Give Your Dog a Break," 4:93–103;
    then, answer the following questions.

    What is the central idea of the story? Why do you think the
    author wrote the story? Is the story true or imaginary? If the story
    is imaginary, does it seem true? Why or why not?

*8. Find words in a story that describe. Read the sentence without
    those words. Do these words make a real difference in the mean-
    ing? Bring sentences to class for class discussion.

*9. (a) Discuss the naming of animals and the appropriateness of
        names given to animals in fiction. Explain how pets are
        named.
    (b) What is the importance of descriptive words? Discuss sen-
        tences pupils have found with descriptive words.

*10. Write a composition concerning a pet you would like to have, or
     how to care for a pet (including feeding him, sheltering him,

---

* Items marked with an asterisk are to be included in the study and activity
guide that will be given to each pupil.

keeping him groomed, training him properly, and showing affection for him), or describing a pet you have had or known.

*11. Read "Eskimo Husky," 3:17–22, "How Smart Are Dogs?" 3:90–93, and "My Eyes Have a Cold Nose," 4:104–109. How do animals help men?

12. View moving picture, "*Wheels Across India.*"

*13. Make a list of incidents in which animals show the same qualities as human beings do. Examples might include devotion, intelligence, courage.

14. Discussion: How animals and man depend upon each other, and the similarities of animals to men.

*15. Pick out words which best describe persons and animals. Have you seen animals or pictures of animals who look somewhat like people of your acquaintance?

*16. Read "Lion Hunting with Camera," 2:52–59; "Animals Go to School," 3:151–156; "Blue Ducker," 1:284–294. Where do these stories take place? Can you find the locale for each on a map? Are these stories interesting? Are they full of movement? How does the author make the story move quickly? Does he use suspense? Does he use action verbs? What mood does each portray? Are the moods different? How does the author set the mood for each story?
Look up the biography of the authors. What background do they have for writing these stories? (You can find this information in *Who's Who in America, The Junior Book of Authors, Who's Who Among North America's Authors.*)

17. Talk by representative of Audubon Club Chapter.

*18. Read as many of the following as you can. Pick out the one that you like the best. Why do you like it best?
"The Runaway," 4:102–103; "Swarms of Minnows," 4:122; "The Hunter," 4:143; "On a Cat Aging," 4:143; "Robert of Lincoln," 4:133; "The Lost World of Bluebird," 4:196; "The Blind Man and the Elephant," 4:198–200; "Four Little Foxes," 1:294; "The Sandhill Crane," 1:321; "Poem of Praise," 1:330; "The Eagle," 2:24; "Sunning," 2:18; "Grumpy," 2:25–26; "God's World," 6:141–163; "Four Poems about Pets," 7:127–128; "The Brown Bear," 8:127–128; "Lion," 8:129; "How to Tell the Wild Animals," 8:148; "The Owl Critic," 8:149–151; "Song of the Ship's Cat," 8:151; "Lone Dog," 8:173; "Horses Chewin' Hay," 8:179; "The Broncho That Would Not Be Broken," 9:58–59; "Bing Has an Enemy," 9:79; "The Hairy Dog," 9:80; "The Kitten," 9:80.

*19. Read the poems out loud to hear the sound of the words. All words have sounds, but the words in a poem form sounds in patterns. The pattern of rhyme is the sound of the word at the end of one line rhyming with a word at the end of another line. The pattern of rhythm is like the beat of music. Can you find one poem in the list that seems to you to have a good beat?

*20. Is there any of the poem that seems to describe a striking picture? How does this picture make you feel? Can you find any very descriptive figures of speech?

*21. Locate and examine selected passages from selections because of their beauty or the unusual way in which the author has given expression to his thoughts. Read them aloud.

22. Read chorally "The Blind Man and the Elephant."

23. Discussion of the difference between telling a story in poetry and telling a story in prose.

*24. Do one of the following.
(a) Participate in a panel discussion on one of the following topics.
(1) How Animals Contribute to Our Way of Life.
(2) How We Can Learn from Animals.
(3) Useful Animals.
(4) It Takes All Kinds to Make a World.
(b) Prepare a collection of articles, pictures, poems, and clippings about unusual pets. The material may be displayed on the bulletin board for several days. Save the collection for a culminating experience.
(c) Collect pictures for a bulletin board exhibit. Write imaginative stories to go with the pictures.
(d) Compile a class file of stories read outside the class about wild animals. Participate by writing an annotation of the stories read.

Basic Culminating Activity

25. Movie: "Hunting with a Camera."
26. Bulletin board.

OPTIONAL RELATED ACTIVITIES

1. Secure information about well-known authors of animal stories. The research should reveal the qualifications of the author for writing animal stories, his environment, his background, and his experiences. Consider such authors as Rudyard Kipling, Marjorie Kinnan Rawlings, Felix Salten, Ernest Thompson Seton, and Albert Payson Terhune. Share findings with the class. Compile a booklet containing brief information about each author.

2. Compile a list of words used with animals. Add to this list throughout the unit. Use words such as *taxidermy, sanctuaries,* and *hibernate.* The list may be in chart form.

3. Rewrite in play form a story or a section of a story.

4. Write an imaginary conversation between two animals or between a person and an animal.

5. Write humorous paragraphs as a group or individually on the effect of animals on human beings or the effect of human beings on animals.

6. Make book reports in class on the latest books on animal life.

7. Investigate methods of protecting animal life. Secure information from the library for reports on such organizations as the Audubon Society or Isaac Walton League.

8. Write letters to several state departments of conservation to secure information on the present work being accomplished in the field of conversation.

9. Tell experiences in taming birds or squirrels. Discuss difficulties encountered and successes accomplished.

TEACHING AIDS

Anthologies

GRAY, WILLIAM S., et al., Paths and Pathfinders. (New York: Scott, Foresman, 1946.)

JEWETT, ARNO, et al., Adventure Bound. (Boston: Houghton Mifflin, 1956.)

MURPHY, GEORGE, et al., Let's Read! Book 1, The Emerald Book, Reading for Fun. (New York: Holt, 1951.)

ROSS, JACOB M., et al., Adventures for Readers, Book 1 (Mercury Edition). (New York: Harcourt, Brace, 1953.)

STRANG, RUTH, and RALPH ROBERTS, Teen-Age Tales, Book 1. (New York: Heath, 1954.)

Teacher References

BAILEY, MATILDA, and ULLIN W. LEAVELL, Worlds of People. (New York: American Book Co., 1951.)

CROSS, E. A., and ELIZABETH LEHR, Literature—A Series of Anthologies; Appreciating Literature. (New York: Macmillan, 1943.)

GORDON, MARGERY, and MARIE B. KING, A Magic World: An Anthology of Poetry. (New York: Appleton, 1930.)

POOLEY, ROBERT C., and FRED G. WALCOTT, Action! Growth in Reading: Book One. (Chicago: Scott, 1942.)

Suggested Books for Additional Reading

(This part of the Unit Plan is the same as that in the Resource Unit.)

Audio-Visual Materials

(This part of the Unit Plan is also the same as that in the Resource Unit.)

INDEX

Abramowitz, Jack, 277, 278
Acceleration, 165, 170–171, 200–201
Accident, 439–441
Achievement test, 373–374
Action research, 460
Activities, *see* Learning activities, Tactics
Adams, Harold P., 423
Ad hoc teams, 210
Administrative duties
    classroom, 416–419
    first days, 446
Administrators, relationships with, 90–91, 340, 343, 453–454
Adolescence, 26–27
Agacinski, Philip J., 146
Alphabetizing, 281
American Federation of Teachers, 460–461
Amidon, Edmund J., 213
Anaheim, Calif., City School District, 315
Anecdotal report, 29–30, 354, 357
Anti-intellectualism, 153
Appreciation
    learning of, 10
    see also Objectives
Aristotle, 22
Assignment, 62–65
    and culturally deprived, 192–193
    differentiated, 166–169
    homework, 258–261
    as punishment, 89
    and study skills, 254
Association for Supervision and Curriculum Development, 225, 336
    discussion check list, 236–237
Association, teacher, 460–461
Attendance, 416–418
Attention, need for, 50
Attention span, 52
Attitudes, 17–18
    learning of, 10
    and motivation, 54–55, 59, 70
    see also Objectives
Audio-visual aids, 185–186, 212, 216, 301–325, 486
    sources of, 319–324
Authoritarianism, 189
    see also Discipline
Autobiography, pupil, 35–37

Bamman, Henry A., 285, 292–293
Basic activities, *see* Learning activities
Beggs, David W. III, 207, 209
Behavior log, 29, 354, 357
Billett, Roy O., 102, 137, 384
Billett-Starr Problem Inventory, 27
Blair, Glen Myers, 46
Bloom, Benjamin S., 350
Books, 279–282
Boston School Committee, 92
Brier, James D., 315
Brightness contrast, 413
Bulletin board, 304–306
Burks, John B., 272
Buros, O. K., 46, 374
Burton, William H., 42, 47, 260
Business management, extracurriculum, 427–429
Busy work, 207–208
Buzz session, 232

Calendar, course, 104
California State Curriculum Commission, 256
Camera
    in evaluation, 357
    in microprojection, 309
    Polaroid, 309, 323
Case study, 48
Centile, 377
Chalkboard, 233, 304–306
Charts, 306–307
Cheating, 261
Check list, 351–353, 385
    in community study, 342
    in diagnosis, 44, 46–47
    discussion, 236–237
    test items, 362
Citizenship, 125
Clarifying operations, 17, 212–213, 263
Clark, Leonard H., 272, 313, 315, 321, 331
Class register, 417–418
Classroom, 409–411, 414–415
    and discipline, 79–82
    and motivation, 69
    for television teaching, 318–319
Classroom laboratory, 411–412
    see also Laboratory class
Classroom management, 409–421
Classroom routine, 415–416
Code of Ethics, 455–458

insure efficient handling
of routine

outline day's activities

make sure nec materials are
ready for use

Indicate 2 use of time

DATE DUE
REMINDER

OCT 10 '98

Please do not remove this date due slip.